Companion Guide
To Healthy Cooking

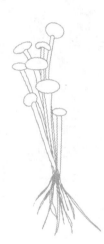

Companion Guide

TO HEALTHY COOKING

A Practical Introduction to Natural Ingredients

Natalie & Shirley Nigro

Featherstone
& Brown

Charlottesville, Virginia

All inquiries should be addressed to:
Featherstone & Brown
1301 Seminole Trail
Charlottesville, VA 22901

Printed in the United States of America

01 00 99 98 97 96   10 9 8 7 6 5 4 3 2 1

First published in 1996 by Featherstone & Brown, a division of
Featherstone, Inc.

Library of Congress Cataloging-in-Publication Data
Nigro, Natalie.
        Companion guide to healthy cooking: a practical
introduction to natural ingredients/Natalie & Shirley Nigro.
Charlottesville, Va.: Featherstone & Brown, 1996.
        Includes bibliographical references (pp.) and index.
1. Health Foods—Dictionaries. 2. Natural Foods—Dictionaries.
3. Food—Composition. 4. Food—Dictionaries. 5. Natural
Foods Industry—Directories. I. Nigro, Shirley

        TX369.N53 1996
        641.302 –DDC

ISBN 0-9641731-1-5
Library of Congress Catalog Card Number: 96-084097

TABLE OF CONTENTS

Preface   vii
Acknowledgements   ix
Introduction   1

Ingredients   9

Agar	11	Mung Beans	84
Amazake	13	Mushrooms	85
Arame	15	Navy Beans	96
Arrowroot	16	Non-Dairy Milks	97
Azuki Beans	18	Nori	102
Barley	18	Nut and Seed Butters	103
Barley Malt Syrup	21	Nutritional Yeast	105
Beans	22	Nuts & Seeds	106
Black Turtle Beans	28	Oats	118
Black-Eyed Peas	29	Oils	120
Burdock Root	30	Olive Oil	129
Carob	31	Pasta	131
Corn	33	Pinto Beans	135
Daikon	37	Quinoa	136
Dulse	39	Rice	138
Garbanzo Beans	40	Rice Syrup	147
Ginger Root	41	Salt	148
Grains	43	Sea Vegetables (Dried)	151
Great Northern Beans	60	Seitan	157
Hijiki	61	Soy Sauce	165
Honey	62	Sprouts	167
Kelp	65	Sweeteners	172
Kidney Beans	66	Tahini	182
Kombu	67	Tempeh	184
Kuzu	68	Texturized Vegetable	
Lentils	70	Protein (TVP®)	186
Lima Beans	72	Thickening Agents	189
Maple Syrup	73	Tofu	192
Millet	75	Ume & Umeboshi	196
Mirin	77	Vinegar	200
Miso	78	Wakame	205
Molasses	81	Wasabi	206
		Wheat	207

Glossary   215
References   229
Mail Order Sources   233
Index   237
Order Form   246

LIST OF CHARTS, TABLES, & DIAGRAMS

Barley Cooking Table	20
Beans Comparison Table	25
Basic Anatomy of a Corn Kernel	33
Basic Anatomy of a Grain Kernel	43
Table Illustrating Grain-to-Water Ratio as a Function of Grain Amount	51
Grain Cooking Table	54
Honey Types Based on Plant Type	63
Nutritive Value of Molasses Types	83
Mushroom Anatomy	85
Mushroom Cooking Chart	91
Mushroom Complementary Chart	93
Mushroom Buying Chart	94
Nutritional Composition of Some Nuts & Seeds	116
Oat Cooking Table	120
Oil Flavor, Smoke Points, and Uses Based on Refinement Level	125
Fatty Acid Profile and Smoke Point of Oils	128
Characteristics of Rice	138
Relationships Between Categorizations of Rice	142
Rice Comparison Table	145
Salt Measurement Equivalencies	149
Sea Vegetable Comparison Chart	152
General Uses for Sea Vegetables	154
Nutritional Composition of Sea Vegetables	156
Sources of Seitan and its Uses	158
Seitan Seasoning Ingredients	160
Flours and Their Resulting Gluten	162
Types of Gluten to Use to Make a Variety of Seitan Dishes	163
Types of Soy Sauce	166
Sprouting Table	171
Sweetness of Fresh Fruits	174
Sweeteners Comparison Chart	176
Categories of Sugars Based on Their Chemical Structure	179
Relative Sweetening Power of the Various Sugar Types	182
Reconstituted TVP® Yield	188
Thickening Agents Comparison Chart	190
Approximate Thickening Powers	191
Relationship Between Tofu Textures and Hardnesses	192
Usage Chart for Tofu	194
Approximate Tofu Volume-to-Weight Equivalent Measurements	195
Ume Plum Products Diagram	197
Wheat Cooking Table	212

PREFACE

When we got into healthy eating over ten years ago, and then decided to go vegetarian seven years ago, there really wasn't any information available to help us get started. We didn't let this deter us; we rolled up our sleeves and started the long arduous process of discovery and invention. It was hard and time consuming and it was obvious why people thought we were crazy.

Things are very different now. There is a huge number of books, magazines, columns, and articles out there that are providing mountains of information. In fact, we now have the opposite problem—there is so much material available today that it is difficult to know where to start.

Our recommendation is to buy two books—an excellent general healthy-eating cookbook (see the list provided in the Introduction) and a "companion" ingredient guide that explains what the ingredients are, their flavors and textures, their pronunciation, their general uses, issues regarding freshness and quality, how to store and cook them, where to buy them, and where to go for more information about them.

We wrote this book because there really isn't anything that fills the role of the "companion" ingredient guide and we needed one.

Enjoy the book. We sure enjoyed writing it.

ACKNOWLEDGEMENTS

We would like to thank the following individuals for their help on this book: Anne Arango, Linda and Larry Ayres, Sam Boglio, Terrel Boyack, William and Bobbi Butler, Terrance and Barbara Clark, Leona Falborn, Judy Hay, Edward Larson, Jeff Monaco, Melinda Nebeker, William Nigro, B. Eugene Parker, Jr., Ernie Pugh, Rhudy Renfro, Cynthia Rhodes, Michelle Suave, David Ward, David Wipf, and Susan Woodson.

Barbara Levisay, Martha Nigro, Lana Bowling, Chris Oakley DiMeglio, June Oakley, and Jean Ballard were very kind and helpful manuscript readers and editors. Claiborne Lange was given the unenviable task of proofing the final product.

William Shurtleff provided inspiration. Bill's valuable advice and pronunciation tips have made this book much better than it would have been otherwise.

Robane Roach at Rebecca's Natural Food and the staff at Foods of All Nations in Charlottesville, Virginia always patiently answered our questions.

The following manufacturers, producers, and distributors of natural ingredients were very helpful:

Christian Elwell at South River Miso aided us immensely with our miso research by donating some miso samples and valuable information. Debbie Athos at Natural Lifestyle Supplies was very kind to send us a sampling of their popular ingredients and an incredible amount of information. Rita Held at Nulaid Foods, Inc. provided samples of their egg-replacement products.

Steven F. Rich, Vice President of Delftree Corporation, provided invaluable information about shiitake mushrooms.

Jean Richardson at Gold Mine Natural Foods was extremely helpful in our kuzu research.

Monterey Mushrooms, Inc. was very kind to send information on their products as well as additional information about other exotic vegetables and fruits.

Martha Johnson at Eden Foods, Inc. provided quite a bit of information on the foods and ingredients that Eden carries.

Other producers, manufacturers, distributors, authors, publishers, etc. who aided us in our research were Casey Van Rysdam at American Natural Snacks, Tracy Babini at Garden Spot Distributors, Susan Stainback at Great Eastern Sun, Eleanor Lewallen at the Mendocino Sea Vegetable Company, Mary Shaughnessy at *Natural Health*, Lisa Hausman at White Wave, Nikki Riddle at Wholesome and Hearty Foods, Grainaissance, Arrowhead Mills, Spectrum Naturals, and LightLife.

This book is for everybody who wants to have more culinary choices; it is not just for vegetarians, vegans, and followers of the macrobiotic philosophy.

It is intended to be a companion volume to many of the low-fat, cholesterol-free, vegan, vegetarian, macrobiotic, allergy, wholefoods, natural, ecological, self-healing, and healthy cooking recipe books that are available on shelves today. Frequently, folks who are new to this type of cooking arm themselves with their first recipe and head for their nearest health food store. When inside, they discover a frightening thing—they don't recognize anything. It's as though they have stepped into a food market in Japan, China, Thailand, Indonesia, India, Italy, or some other foreign place. One of the goals of this book is to help newcomers become familiar and comfortable with the names and uses of many of the ingredients that have been contributed by other cultures. However, this book does not feature meat, seafood, or dairy ingredients because most people are already familiar with them.

This book is not intended to be a cookbook. There are plenty of excellent books that give delicious recipes for the ingredients that we are showcasing.

Histories and details about ingredient processing such as how they are dried, harvested, fermented, threshed, cut, etc. are omitted because they are comprehensively covered in many other books.

If you want to know what the stuff looks like, where you can buy it, and how you can use it, this book is for you.

We've put information in this book that we have accumulated or uncovered through research, experiments, experience, and common sense. We have only scratched the surface of the mountains of possibilities; but, if you are a newcomer, it will get you started, or if you are an experienced "healthy-eater," it will give you another perspective and provide some new ideas.

INTRODUCING NEW INGREDIENTS

Most of these ingredients have been around for thousands of years. Millions of people throughout the world have been marvelously creative and found personal ways in which to interact with them. Over generations, as you can probably imagine, a huge number of cooking methods have been developed and some of them flatly contradict one another. There is a great deal of diversity out there and nobody seems to agree! There is no right or wrong way to prepare these ingredients, just different ways that have different effects or consequences. Every household/person cooks differently. If you see something new that is different from what you are used to, give it a try. It might be wonderful. If you have the opportunity to explore some of these endless possibilities, you'll find things to enjoy that you never dreamed existed. Be open-minded. Experiment or try some of the many ideas and methodologies, and incorporate the ones you like into your lifestyle.

To use a food or ingredient effectively, you need to "know" it. If an ingredient is new to you, you don't know what it looks like, what it smells like, what it tastes like, what it goes well with, etc. You have no associations, good or bad, that help you to feel as if you "know" the food. If you don't know about an ingredient, how can you crave it, want it, or say, "That's going to taste so great"? When you taste a dish and ask yourself, "What would go well with this?" the list of things you think of contains only those items that are familiar to you.

There are millions of recipes that offer fantastic ideas and new taste delights. By knowing more ingredients, you can take advantage of more recipes. Often recipes are avoided when they use ingredients that are unfamiliar and strange sounding.

Because there are so many variables involved, the first time you prepare a new dish, you will be lucky if it turns out just the way you would like. The author of the recipe has different cookware, different brands of the ingredients, different ideas about what a "pinch" is, etc.—it's unlikely that you will produce exactly the same dish that the recipe author is trying to help you make. Instead, you will be using the recipe as a starting point for a dish of your own creation that will work with the equipment, ingredients, and cooking styles that you have. If the dish doesn't turn out as you hoped, you'll have lots of ideas about how you could do it "better" the next time.

You have to take the time to become familiar with new ingredients if you are to get value out of them. Give yourself some time—this familiarity doesn't happen overnight and takes a bit of interaction with the new ingredient.

EXPERIMENT & PRACTICE

Have an open mind and be willing to experiment with ingredients. Practice using ingredients in recipes and in your own creative cooking. Getting used to new ingredients and the ways of cooking them could take days, months, or even years, but once you "have it," your cooking skills will be with you a lifetime. In this fast-paced world, knowledge, experience, and intuition will enable you to prepare healthy food fast, so you won't need to rely on expensive "fast foods"—even the ones marketed as "healthy." As we enter the twenty-first century, people are just going to get busier and more stressed. It will be more and more important for folks to eat well to keep themselves going—but it will have to be quick and easy.

Experimentation in the kitchen increases knowledge and expands your horizons. Experimentation means suffering from failures, reveling in the successes, and learning from both of these experiences. Often, mistakes made in preparation of one thing will produce success for something entirely different. Look at the failures as an opportunity to discover something new. Taste and see if there isn't any useful purpose for the failed experiment. It may be good added to something else; ground into a paste, flour, or condiment; dried and used as a snack; blended to make a sauce or soup base; or cooked more with another method to produce an entirely different result. Use your imagination. For example, we were trying to make some pancakes one day. It did not turn out as we had expected, but we discovered a marvelous cracker or flat bread dough. On the next attempt to make pancakes, we made little flat, disc-like rocks. The blender threw them back at us and liquids failed to soften them. We decided to toss one to our dog and he went crazy with delight. We wrote down the recipe and saved the entire batch of twenty-four *rock cracker dog treats* to bribe the pooch. When all else fails, try grinding those disasters and giving them to the birds, who will sing for your mistakes, or to the squirrels, who will kill for your boo-boos.

To make a tasteful dish time after time takes practice. Just as musicians must practice to make music instead of noise, and heaven only knows that golfers constantly practice to improve their game, it is necessary for the cook to practice not only the preparation of a specific dish, but the skills of the kitchen. One of these skills is to understand the ingredients that are being used. Practicing with various ingredients will eventually produce excellent results, consistently!

STRUCTURE OF THE BOOK

The ingredients are listed alphabetically and the beginning of each ingredient section is easy to find because its title is placed in a gray box. Following the ingredient title, a pronunciation guide may be provided. This guide does not use any dictionary symbols; instead, it uses transliterations which are common English words or letter combinations that have an obvious pronunciation. Accented syllables are shown in all capital letters. Many of the ingredients originated from cultures that use different languages, making their pronunciation different from the spelling. It is helpful to have an idea of the way to say the ingredient if you must ask for its location in a store or ask the attendant for information about it. There may be several pronunciations for an ingredient. One may be the way it is pronounced in its native language and the other(s) may be how it is commonly pronounced in this country.

After the pronunciation, a little bit of space is devoted to introducing the ingredient. Here we try to offer some interesting pieces of information, to have some fun, to give you a feeling for the ingredient, and to describe it briefly.

In addition to the pronunciation and brief introduction for each ingredient, we have tried to provide other information that will be helpful. The headings in each ingredient section will help you find information more easily. The standard headings are shown on the following pages with a discussion of the material that is included in each subsection. It appears in the same format as the ingredient sections. Some ingredients have additional headings that explain specific topics that are important to that particular ingredient; for example, the "Beans" section has a heading on eliminating flatulence problems.

Before you act on what you see in any ingredient subsection, read through the entire section at least once. This will give you a wholistic picture of what is going on.

Nigro Tips are scattered about the book in the ingredient sections. They might give a tidbit of information that describes a trick or technique that makes preparing an ingredient easier or a neat use for it that is a personal favorite of ours. They are not absolutely essential to understand and use the ingredient; however, they do make it a little easier or more fun. By the way, Nigro is pronounced *NIGH grow* or *NYE grow* or *NI gro*.

We have placed a glossary at the end of the book. Terms that are used in the descriptions of the ingredients (names of other ingredients, cooking methods and techniques, types of culinary dishes, etc.) are briefly defined there.

An index has also been included to help you find details or information quickly and easily.

CONTACTING THE AUTHORS

We would very much like to hear from you. If you have a comment, suggestion, question, or anything else, you can contact us through e-mail or through our publisher.

e-mail: **nigro@compuserve.com**
or **104024.1770@compuserve.com**

Our publisher's address and phone number are printed on the copyright page on the back of the title page, and on the order form at the back of the book.

INGREDIENT

(pronunciation)

A brief description of the ingredient is provided here.

VARIETIES

Here we discuss the varieties, types, or forms in which the ingredient may be found. In some cases, we'll also describe how the ingredient varieties may be classified or categorized and the differences between these classes or categories.

OTHER NAMES

Sometimes an ingredient will have more than one name. The most common name is used in the ingredient title and the other names for the ingredient will be listed in this subsection.

FLAVOR/TEXTURE

This has been the most difficult subsection for us. Flavor and, to some degree, texture are relative things.

We have done our best, but until you actually taste an ingredient, you won't really know what it tastes like. (For example, how would you explain what olives, beef, or beer tastes like to someone who has never tried these things?) So put the ingredient on your tongue and see what your reaction is. Have an open mind, though; some of these ingredients are a little unusual to a palate that has never tasted them before.

Try ingredients that you didn't like in the past and plan to try ingredients in the future that you don't like today. Your taste buds evolve and change over time and things that taste bland or bitter today may taste delicately flavorful or pungent tomorrow, next month, or next year. Go slowly, allowing time for the taste buds to adjust. Some of the things that cause your sense of taste to change are the amount of salt you eat, the number of new foods you become accustomed to, the nutritional and taste balance of the foods you eat, and the age of your taste buds.

Another factor to consider when judging flavor and texture is the cooking method and other ingredients used. If you've had boiled chicken, you know that it is not representative of how chicken tastes in all recipes and all ways of cooking. For example, chicken cordon bleu is in an entirely different league. So, if you don't like how an ingredient is cooked one way, try it another way.

Even if we were to assume that everyone's taste buds are the same and that all preparation methods produce the same results, a particular ingredient may still have a large range of flavors, textures, colors, qualities, etc. depending on the manufacturer, brand, distribution method, and location and day of purchase. With the relatively unprocessed, fresh, healthy ingredients discussed in this book, it is virtually impossible to keep stamping a package of it out, day in and day out, that tastes and looks exactly the same as the package before it. Don't expect consistency!

GENERAL USES

This subsection provides some simple examples or suggestions on the uses of the ingredient. It gives an overview of how the ingredient can be used, the type of dishes it works well in, some applicable cooking methods or preparation processes, and, occasionally, some of the foods it can act as a substitute for.

We sometimes list ingredients that could be used to make specific dishes. Because this book is not intended to be a cookbook, we don't give amounts or too much in the way of cooking directions. We just want to give you an idea of what is possible with the ingredient and to give you a feel for what goes well with it. There are hundreds, if not thousands, of recipes out there in the hundreds, if not thousands, of books that are available on healthy cooking.

FRESHNESS/QUALITY

This subsection discusses freshness and/or quality issues regarding the ingredient. In some cases, both issues are not pertinent to an ingredient. For example, freshness is not an issue when it comes to soy sauce, while quality definitely is.

We have tried to present this information in a factual, unbiased way that is not judgmental or reflective of our personal views. A good product to one person may be a bad product to another. We certainly do not rate brands or ingredient varieties.

If manufacturers of an ingredient commonly put additives or preservatives in their product, we've let you know. But, even if we don't give you a "heads up," it is a very good idea to read labels so that you know exactly what you are eating. Some folks try to avoid foods with additives and preservatives. For others, the convenience and/or price of the foods outweigh the fact that they also contain these additives and preservatives.

If the ingredient can be, or commonly is, processed using chemicals, we have also tried to let you know without going into too many details about the processing methods. Again, some people care about this and some people don't.

Some of the ingredients are organically grown or made from organically grown foods. They are grown without the use of herbicides, pesticides, or synthetic fertilizers. This may be an issue to you.

Ultimately, it is up to you to decide what is important to you and we encourage you to try as many different brands as you can find that do not go against your personal views and values.

If an ingredient is not labeled (such as those found in bulk bins), ask the store attendant about the nutritional and ingredient content of the item.

STORAGE

This subsection provides some guidelines for storing the ingredient before and after preparation. Whenever times are given, they are just an average or approximation, not a hard and fast rule. Use common sense and if the condition of any food is suspicious, assume the worse and discard it. The old adage, "Better safe than sorry" certainly applies here.

PREPARATION INSTRUCTIONS

This is the area in which specifics are addressed about the general preparation of an ingredient. Of course, these instructions will vary from ingredient to ingredient. On the whole, cleaning, soaking, and cooking are topics considered and talked about. However, in those cases where they do not apply, some of these topics are omitted. In other cases, specific topics are added because they are important for that particular ingredient.

Cooking times, temperatures, and measurements are just approximations to get you started. It really depends on the freshness of the ingredients, the types of cooking containers you use, the calibration of your stove, oven, etc., the altitude at which you live (if you live at higher elevations such as in Utah or Wyoming, liquids boil at a lower temperature than at sea-level), the brands of the ingredients, and a myriad of other issues.

Roasting is a process that might be new to some people. Grains, seeds, nuts, beans, and sea vegetables can be roasted before cooking to create a different flavor. However, if you are new to roasting, you'll want to be very careful not to burn your ingredient.

HEALTH INFORMATION

General nutrition and health information about each ingredient is given for those folks who have an interest. Often, additional information is provided based on folklore, articles, studies, etc. This information is provided solely to introduce you to some interesting thoughts about the ingredient, not to state proven facts. We encourage you to learn as much as you can about the health ramifications of all the ingredients.

If you have food allergies or a diet-sensitive medical condition, be sure to consult with your doctor before trying any new food. Note that some common foods that people might be allergic to are wheat, gluten (found in wheat, barely, oats, and rye), corn, soybeans, milk and other dairy products, citrus fruits, chocolate, sugar, caffeine, yeast, and meats.

ADDITIONAL READING

Titles and authors of books that would be helpful to further understand the ingredient are listed in this subsection. Many are cookbooks that provide recipes using the ingredient and some have detailed information about making the ingredient at home, historical origins, and/or processing methods that may be of interest to individuals who want to get into it more. A reference list in the back of this book, sorted by author's last name, provides the complete bibliographic information for each book identified in the "Additional Reading" subsections.

Some general cookbooks and healthy eating handbooks that provide good information about many of the ingredients in this book are:

Abehsera, Michel. *Zen Macrobiotic Cooking.*

Aihara, Cornellia. *The Calendar Cookbook.*

Batt, Eva. *Vegan Cooking.*

Belleme, John, and Jan Belleme. *Cooking with Japanese Foods.*

Boulos-Guillaume, Nouhad. *A Lebanese Harvest: Traditional Vegetarian Recipes.*

Burke, George, Abbot. *Simply Heavenly! The Monastery Vegetarian Cookbook.*

Chelf, Vicki Rae. *Arrowhead Mills Cookbook.*

Diamond, Marilyn. *The American Vegetarian Cookbook from the Fit For Life Kitchen.*

Dinshah, Freya. *The Vegan Kitchen.*

Downer, Lesley. *Japanese Vegetarian Cooking.*

Elliot, Rose. *The Complete Vegetarian Cuisine.*

Gerras, Charles, ed. *Rodale's Basic Natural Foods Cookbook.*

Grogran, Bryanna Clark. *The (Almost) No Fat Cookbook: Everyday Vegetarian Recipes.*

Kilham, Christopher S. *The Bread & Circus Whole Food Bible.*

King, Penny. *Taste & See: Allergy Relief Cooking.*

Klapper, Michael, M.D. *Vegan Nutrition: Pure and Simple.*

Kushi, Aveline. *Complete Guide to Macrobiotic Cooking.*

Lemlin, Jeanne. *Vegetarian Pleasures: A Menu Cookbook.*

Leneman, Leah. *The Single Vegan.*

Leng, Vikki. *Earthly Delights.*

Lyman, Benjamin Smith. *Vegetarian Diet and Dishes.*

Hagler, Louise, and Dorothy R. Bates, eds. *The New Farm Vegetarian Cookbook.*

MacNeil, Karen. *The Book of Whole Foods: Nutrition & Cuisine.*

Mandoe, Bonnie. *Vegetarian Nights: Fresh from Hawaii.*

Manners, Ruth Ann, and William Manners. *The Quick & Easy Vegetarian Cookbook.*

Marshall, Anne. *The Complete Vegetarian Cookbook.*

Martin, Jeanne Marie. *The All Natural Allergy Cookbook.*

McCarty, Meredith. *American Macrobiotic Cuisine.*

Michell, Keith. *Practically Macrobiotic.*

Netzer, Corinne T. *101 Vegetarian Recipes.*

Nishimoto, Miyoko. *The Now and Zen Epicure.*

Ohsawa, Lima. *Macrobiotic Cuisine.*

People for the Ethical Treatment of Animals (PETA), and Ingrid Newkirk. *The Compassionate Cook.*

Raichlen, Steven. *High-Flavor, Low-Fat Vegetarian Cooking.*

Robertson, Laurel, Carol Flinders, and Brian Ruppenthal. *The New Laurel's Kitchen.*

Roehl, Evelyn. *Food Facts: A Compendium of Information for a Whole Foods Cuisine.*

Sass, Lorna J. *Recipes from an Ecological Kitchen.*

Stepaniak, Joanne, and Kathy Hecker. *Ecological Cooking: Recipes to Save the Planet.*

Turner, Kristina. *The Self-Healing Cookbook.*

Vegetarian Times, Editors of, and Herbert T. Leavy. *The Vegetarian Times Cookbook.*

Wakeman, Alan, and Gordon Baskerville. *The Vegan Cookbook.*

Weber, Marcea. *Whole Meals.*

Yamaoka, Masako. *A First Book of Japanese Cooking.*

BUYING SOURCES

This subsection indicates locations where the ingredient can be purchased. Types of stores that carry it and mail order sources are provided. The mail order list is provided so that you can have an opportunity to obtain any ingredient you choose, even when it is not available locally. Many of these wonderful ingredients may be hard to buy in farm or rural communities and we hope these sources will provide an opportunity for you to try cooking with them. Note that the mail order lists are not intended to be complete; if you find another source for an ingredient, by all means, give it a try.

A mail order sources list at the back of this book provides the address and/or phone number of each mail order company identified in the "Buying Sources" subsections.

BRAND NAMES

Quality producers, manufacturers, distributors, and brand names are mentioned in this subsection. However, the list does *not* include every quality provider; just because a brand is not discussed here does not mean that it is of poor quality. It is generally a safe bet that the products available at your local health and natural food stores are of good quality.

Become familiar with manufacturers and producers (not just their brands). Quality is generally maintained within a company—across the board. For example, Eden, Ohsawa, and Lundberg carry a variety of products and ingredients, all of excellent quality.

All of the brands we list may not be available at every locality or mail order source. If you are looking for a particular brand, you may have to shop around or special order it. Or try the other brands that are available. Frequently, small manufacturers supply their goods and products to just local stores. Try them, for they are often very fresh, quality products whose purchase also supports your local businesses and economy.

In fact, try all the brands that your health or natural food store carries because the brands will vary in texture, flavor, color, and character. Each brand has something to offer. You may choose to buy two or three brands of one ingredient because each one is suited for a different type of dish or creates a slightly different effect or outcome.

This book contains the opinions of the authors and is published in the interest of information exchange. Publication does not constitute approval or disapproval of the ideas and information provided herein, or endorsement or nonendorsement of this book by manufacturers and distributors mentioned within these pages.

AGAR

(AY gar) or (AH gar)

Agar is an interesting and fun addition to the kitchen. It is a jelling and thickening agent made from sea vegetables. Using agar in your cooking is like performing magic. This ingredient can help you create a wide range of dishes from light, delicate mousses to firm jelled salads or desserts. Agar is becoming well-known for its jelling qualities and as an alternative to animal gelatin which is made from bones and cartilage of animals.

OTHER NAMES

Kanten, agar-agar, vegetable Jell-O™.

VARIETIES

Agar comes in lightweight translucent bars, flakes, or powder forms.

Kanten: Kanten is agar formed into translucent bars or sticks. It is harder to find than agar flakes or powder.

Flakes: Translucent flakes are the most common agar form and many recipes use this variety. If the agar type is not specified and it's measured in tablespoons, there is a good chance the recipe is calling for the flakes.

Powder: Powder is the most concentrated form of agar. Some recipes will use this form. If the agar type is not specified, check the amount of liquid used to the amount of agar. Use the powder form if 2 to 6 cups of liquid are used and agar is measured in teaspoons.

FLAVOR/TEXTURE

Agar is colorless, odorless, and basically tasteless.

GENERAL USES

Agar is an ingredient that can be used to produce a pudding, custard, jelly, aspic, mousse, pâté, preserve, jelled cold pie, cheese cake, ice cream, and jelled salad. For example, a delectable custard-like pudding can be made with apricot juice, agar, vanilla or almond extracts, and a little almond butter. Sprinkle with toasted ground almonds for an attractive finishing touch.

Compared to animal gelatin, agar has a much wider range of uses. Agar jells at room temperature (and below) and remains firm without refrigeration, making it an ideal choice for those buffet affairs that last for many hours.

Even though agar mixes very well with sweeteners, it is a perfect ingredient when you wish to make a no-sugar-added jelly. When agar is used, sugar and pectin are not necessary. Making intriguing flavored jellies such as mint, green pepper, tomato, jalapeno, etc. can add interest and variety to the breakfast table, snacks, parties, and gifts.

Refreshing jelled molds are not for desserts alone. Gelatinous stocks made from fruit and vegetable juices, vegetable and meat stocks or broths, apple or malt vinegars, coffee, milk (dairy or non-dairy), or any other flavorful liquid can be used to suspend a variety of cold foods. Try using different vegetables, fruits, grains, and beans to create an attractive aspic or jelled salad. It's fun and easy to make a tomato aspic that suspends blanched or sautéed onions, celery, and garlic by jelling a vegetable juice flavored with a little cajun spice and a twist of lemon after the vegetables have been stirred in.

A Jell-O™-like dessert can be made with agar and your favorite fruit juice. However, the texture of the resulting gel will resemble a very firm cranberry sauce, which is slightly different from the texture of Jell-O™. Because agar sets at 98°F, you can make a Jell-O™ while camping!

And that's not all; agar is also used to thicken or add body and substance to vegetable soup stocks, sauces, and gravies.

STORAGE

Store the agar powder, flakes and kanten bars in the refrigerator. Even though dishes made with agar retain their shape at room temperature, it is a good idea to store them in the refrigerator. Compared to many animal gelatin dishes, after a period of time, agar dishes will remain more appetizing because they will release less liquid.

PREPARATION INSTRUCTIONS

MEASURING

Often, recipes do not indicate the type of agar to use. To jell 2 cups of water using agar (or to substitute for a 4 table-spoons package of animal gelatin) use:

- Two tablespoons agar flakes,
- Two teaspoons agar powder, or
- One kanten bar or strip

Of course, these measurements may vary depending on the type of sea vegetable the agar was extracted from, the manufacturing process used, and the ingredients you are mixing the agar with. It takes less agar to jell water than heavier liquids such as purées and milks. If you do not get the results you desire, increase or reduce the amount of agar the next time you prepare the recipe. When creating a dish on your own, a bit of experimentation may be required to determine the amount of agar to use.

SOAKING

Kanten: This form of agar needs to be soaked for at least five minutes and may be soaked for as long as 24 hours. The longer you soak it, the softer and less solid it becomes and the easier it will be to dissolve. Sometimes it will actually break up into small pieces. Remove the kanten from the water and squeeze out any excess water. If it is still in large pieces after soaking, it will be necessary to shred the kanten.

Flakes and Powder: These forms do not have to be soaked before cooking, but you may do so if you would like. For the soaking liquid, use the liquid you are planning to dissolve the agar in.

COOKING

Agar is easy to work with, but takes some getting used to. It must first be dissolved before being added to a recipe.

Combine agar powder or flakes with any liquid that can handle being boiled for several minutes and does not contain acetic acid, such as wines and distilled vinegars. Bring to a boil and reduce the heat to medium-high or just under boiling but still bubbling a little. Cook agar flakes for approximately 5 minutes and agar powder for 1 minute, or until completely melted, stirring continuously.

It is extremely important to completely melt the agar. However, it is difficult to determine when the agar has completely melted since it is translucent. If using agar for the first time, you may want to make a clear gel using a fruit juice, clear vegetable broth, or even water to better judge how long it takes to completely melt the agar in your kitchen. If it is not completely dissolved, the unmelted agar will collect on the bottom and become chewy and rubbery. Obviously, this will have a negative effect on the dish you are preparing.

NIGRO TIP

If you are having difficulties in completely dissolving agar, we have a couple of suggestions. Strain the undissolved agar lumps out of the hot liquid before adding it to the rest of the ingredients in the recipe! Or, soak agar flakes for 30 minutes to an hour before attempting to melt them.

If there is a problem obtaining the same firmness when repeating a recipe, a solution is to use the same brand of agar and measure and record the amount of liquid remaining *after* dissolving it. Then make sure that this measurement is the same each time you make the recipe. Adjustments can be made by boiling the liquid further or adding more hot liquid.

At this point, the agar mixture can be combined with other ingredients to make a variety of dishes. When agar is combined with foods containing oxalic acid such as rhubarb, spinach, and chocolate, the jelling effect is reduced considerably. Therefore, to get the same jelling results, more agar is needed.

Thoroughly combining the agar mixture with other ingredients is very important to create a consistent and even gel. Because agar sets at temperatures below 98°F, the mixture must be kept above that temperature while combining with other ingredients. If you add the agar mixture to cooler ingredients, the overall temperature may fall below 98°F, causing the agar to jell before it can be thoroughly mixed. This, in turn, will cause your dish to have unappetizing jelled lumps. Avoid this problem by heating the other ingredients before adding the agar mixture.

TIPS FOR SUCCESS WITH AGAR

- Completely melt agar.
- Do not dissolve agar in liquid containing acetic acid.
- Use more agar when combining with ingredients containing oxalic acid.
- Keep all ingredients above 98°F while mixing together.

If you are using a mixer or blender to combine the hot melted agar mixture to other ingredients, add it when the appliance is running. Be very careful when blending hot liquid. It is very important that the blender lid is on very tightly because the hot liquid has a tendency to expand very quickly when the blender is first turned on. If you are mixing the agar solution to other ingredients by hand, add it in a steady flow while mixing quickly and constantly to ensure an even mix.

Shredded kanten is cooked the same way as agar flakes or powder; however, it may take a little longer to completely dissolve or melt.

If you don't have an agar recipe handy, you can make a simple Jell-O™. Dissolve the agar in your favorite fruit juice (1 tablespoon agar per cup juice) and allow to cool.

HEALTH INFORMATION

Agar is high in calcium, iron, phosphorus, iodine, trace minerals, fiber, and vitamins A, B-complex, C, D and K. In addition, agar acts as a mild laxative and adds dietary bulk. Agar, like some other sea vegetables, also bonds with toxic and radioactive pollutants which assists the body in discarding them.

BUYING SOURCES

Agar can be found on shelves, with other sea vegetables, in health food stores and Japanese markets. See "Sea Vegetables" for the names of mail order companies that carry sea vegetables. Some mail order companies and stores sell agar in bulk quantities which may reduce the cost per unit.

BRAND NAMES

Ohsawa® *Agar Kanten Flakes*, Eden *Agar Agar Seaweed Gel* (flakes), and Emerald Cove *Kanten Flakes* are all excellent brands of agar.

AMAZAKE

(ah mah ZAH kee)

Amazake is a delicious, thick, and creamy shake that is as easy and convenient as opening a carton of juice. For a refreshing, thirst quenching drink, it can be chilled and poured into a tall glass and enjoyed. It is a creamy non-dairy beverage made from fermented sweet rice. Amazake has the texture of thick, malty milk. Use it in your kitchen as a pleasing snack beverage, creamy sauce, or a milk substitute in baking and desserts.

Because amazake is made by *fermenting* brown rice, it is not classified as a "non-dairy milk." Doing so is like calling wine a type of fruit juice.

VARIETIES

Commercial amazake is available "plain" or flavored with almonds, apricots, bananas, sesame seeds, cocoa, vanilla, pecans, chicory, etc. Almond amazake is very popular and widely available.

OTHER NAMES

Amasake.

FLAVOR/TEXTURE

Amazake has a sweet, rich, full, creamy, malty flavor and the texture of thick, malty, creamy milk.

GENERAL USES

Amazake can be used for making a creamy dairy-free malt-like beverage, pudding, custard, or pie filling. In addition, it is often used as a leaven-er and sweetener in baked goods such as cookies, cakes, muffins, breads, biscuits, pies, and pastries. Baking with amazake imparts a deli-cious moist texture to the items being baked.

Brands vary in flavor and thickness, so experiment to discover which work best for your cooking needs.

Note that amazake is a very mild sweetener. Thus, there are occasions when amazake can be used as an unre-fined substitute for refined white sugar. However, to obtain the sweetness of tradi-tional cakes and cookies, an additional sweetener (such as honey, Sucanat®, maple syrup, etc.) will be required. See the "Sweeteners" section in this book for more information.

When heated on a bitter cold winter day, a cup of mellow amazake warms the body and soul. Add a little carob powder to create a satisfying mug of pseudo hot chocolate. Amazake can also be used as the base of a drink that is a marvelous alternative to egg-nog.

Blend amazake with fruit (cherries, bananas, orange slices, strawberries, blue-berries, peaches, etc.), ice, and soda or sparkling water for a fantastic tasting party or summer smoothie. Add a little zing with a smidgen of grated ginger.

Chilled amazake is delicious poured over your favorite cereal or fresh fruit to make a breakfast delight. Freeze amazake in popsicle molds to make a refreshing summer pleaser.

Boiling and blending amazake with vanilla and lemon juice makes a creamy pudding or filling for éclairs and cream puffs. A creamy "chocolate" frosting can be made by dissolving kuzu (or corn-starch) in some amazake, simmering it a bit, stirring in sweetened carob chips and vanilla extract, and then allowing the frosting to cool.

FRESHNESS/QUALITY

The best quality amazake is made from 100% organic whole grain brown rice (not milled rice) and koji (a natural rice culture to initiate fermentation). It should not contain alcohol or added salt, oil, or sugars, unless they are added later by you!

STORAGE

Before opening an aseptic box of amazake, it can be stored without refriger-ation until the date printed on the box. However, the liquid will remain fresher when the unopened box is stored in mod-erate to cool temperatures. After opening, transfer the liquid to an airtight contain-er, and keep in the refrigerator. It will last from 7 to 10 days.

An unopened plastic bottle of amaza-ke should remain refrigerated to retain its freshness up to the date printed on the bottle. After opening, it should continue to be stored in the refrigerator and should also last from 7 to 10 days.

PREPARATION INSTRUCTIONS

Due to amazake's versatility, it is used as an ingredient in many dishes. It may be simmered, boiled, and stirred into sauces, gravies, soups, puddings, pie fillings, etc., but does not require any cooking when used as a beverage. Write or call Grainaissance™ (1580 62nd Street, Emeryville, CA 94608, 1-800-472-4697) to receive excellent amazake recipes.

HEALTH INFORMATION

To make amazake, koji is added to cooled whole grain brown rice, causing enzymes to break the grain carbohydrates down into complex sugars. The mixture is then fermented (i.e., incubated) to build on the natural sweetness of the grain and transform it into a nectar-like beverage. These complex sugars are unrefined and are digested more slowly than simple sug-ars such as white refined sugar, honey, or maple syrup, providing a steadier stream of energy and more consistent blood sugar level.

Amazake contains no cholesterol and is low in fat—the calories from fat range from 0% to 20%. That's not bad for a shake! Amazake is also a good source of dietary fiber and contains some calcium and iron. In addition, since amazake is a fermented food, it is easy to digest and also aids in digesting other foods.

ADDITIONAL READING

The following books contain instructions for making amazake at home:

Kushi, Aveline. *Complete Guide to Macrobiotic Cooking.*

Michell, Keith. *Practically Macrobiotic.*

Weber, Marcea. *Naturally Sweet Desserts: The Sugar-Free Dessert Cookbook.*

BUYING SOURCES

Amazake may be packaged in aseptic boxes and located on the shelf near the non-dairy milks or packaged in plastic bottles found in the refrigerated section of health food stores. It is also available through the Natural Lifestyle mail order company.

BRAND NAMES

Grainaissance™ makes excellent amazake. In addition to the *Original Flavor,* Grainaissance™ also makes many flavors: *Almond, Apricot, Mocha Java, Cocoa-Almond, Vanilla Pecan, Sesame,* and *Banana Smoothie.*

ARAME

(AIR ah may)

The wiry black threads or strands of this sea vegetable can be transformed into a unique, scrumptious, nutritional addition to any cuisine.

Once you get to know this unusual vegetable, you'll wonder how you ever lived without it. Not only does it add a sensational not-to-be-missed flavor, it also contains a huge amount of iodine as well as many other vitamins, minerals, and trace elements.

FLAVOR/TEXTURE

Arame has a sweet, delicate taste and soft texture.

GENERAL USES

Arame can be combined with vegetables, beans, fish, chicken, and grains. In addition, it may be used as a stand-alone vegetable or condiment.

It is commonly sautéed with root vegetables, tofu, or cooked soybeans. Its light taste harmonizes well with tofu, delicate flavored meats such as chicken, turkey, and fish, and land vegetables such as broccoli, mushrooms, carrots, blanched radishes or daikon, cauliflower, watercress, etc. It can be a dramatic highlight in vegetable dishes, soups, salads, casseroles, and with whole grains.

Arame is often cooked and served alone with a sprinkle of vinegar or lemon juice. It also makes an attractive dish cooked with vinegar (such as rice or umeboshi plum) and shoyu or tamari soy sauce. For a slightly sweeter flavor, add a little barley malt syrup to the cooking mixture. An arame stand-alone side dish nicely complements other vegetables or grains in your meals.

If you are a newcomer to sea vegetables, using arame as a condiment is an excellent way to introduce this fantastic food into your diet. Sprinkle a little on almost everything you make and enjoy the added nutrition along with the new flavor. See "Sea Vegetables (Dried)" for more information about using sea vegetables as condiments.

Arame can be substituted in any recipe calling for hijiki, a stronger, thicker, and longer cooking sea vegetable.

FRESHNESS/QUALITY

See "Sea Vegetables (Dried)."

STORAGE

See "Sea Vegetables (Dried)."

PREPARATION INSTRUCTIONS

WASHING & SOAKING

To clean arame, place it on a white plate and pick or shake out any loose dust. To remove sand, shell particles, and excess salt, transfer the arame to a pot, cover with plenty of cold water and rinse quickly from one to three times depending on how clean the arame is. Don't use warm water which depletes minerals. Swish completely with your hands and pour out each rinse water. The last time, scoop out the sea vegetable by hand and transfer it to a strainer. A residue of sand and grit should remain at the bottom of the rinsing pot. If you are not planning to soak the arame, the final rinse water is customarily saved for cooking. Be careful while pouring the rinse water into the cooking pot to avoid including the sand and grit settled on the bottom.

For a strong, rich taste, arame should not be soaked. A milder flavor can be achieved by soaking it for 3 to 5 minutes. The soaking water is often saved for cooking. Soaked arame doubles in volume.

COOKING

Arame goes very well with oil and is commonly sautéed by itself or with other vegetables. One ounce of dried arame will expand to about 2 cups when cooked.

We like to rinse arame, skip the soaking step, put it in a pot and add just enough water to cover. Bring it to a boil, cover, reduce the heat to low, and simmer for 20 minutes. Then, creativity takes over. You can add vegetables or tempeh and soy sauce, then boil the liquid out. For variety, mix with crisp blanched vegetables such as broccoli, carrots, radishes, watercress, etc. or roasted chopped nuts. This makes an interesting "salad" or "dry" side vegetable dish. Or, after simmering the arame, you can add vegetables and create a thick sauce by adding soy sauce and thickening the mixture with kuzu or arrowroot. This is great poured over rice or vegetables or served as a stand alone side dish.

To make a condiment, simply grind clean dried arame (by throwing it in a blender or spice/coffee grinder for few seconds) or wash, soak, and sauté some arame in a small amount of oil, allow to cool and get crispy and then grind. To keep your supply of arame condiment fresh, just grind up a small quantity and store it in an airtight container.

HEALTH INFORMATION

Arame is high in complex carbohydrates, fiber, niacin, calcium, iron, and iodine. Traditional folklore claims that arame can be used to help relieve female disorders and to bring down high blood

pressure. See "Sea Vegetables (Dried)" for a nutritional composition comparison of sea vegetables.

ADDITIONAL READING

See "Sea Vegetables (Dried)."

BRAND NAMES

Ohsawa®, Eden, Emerald Coast, Maine Coast Sea Vegetables, and Mitoku all offer an excellent quality of arame. See "See Vegetables (Dried)" for mail order sources.

ARROWROOT

(AIR owe root)

Arrowroot is a soft, fine, white powder that is used as a thickener, similar to cornstarch. It is made by a simple, natural process and thickens quickly at low temperatures.

Arrowroot is often overlooked as a thickener because, if expense is an issue, then cornstarch will be used; and if a natural thickening agent is desired, then kuzu is generally chosen. However, nothing can compare with arrowroot for thickening preparations at low temperatures.

See "Thickening Agents" for additional information and a comparison of thickening agents.

OTHER NAMES

Arrowroot powder, arrowroot flour, arrowroot starch.

FLAVOR/TEXTURE

The flavor of arrowroot is very mild and unobtrusive.

GENERAL USES

Arrowroot is used to thicken sauces and soups and to prepare thick cereals, gruels, and desserts (custards, puddings, glazes, etc.).

It can be used to produce shiny, transparent sauces that have a delicate texture. Because it thickens well at low heat, it is ideal for sauces containing egg yolks, dairy milk, or soy milk. A luscious thick white sauce can be created by adding arrowroot to a mixture of soy milk, dry white wine, and sea salt. If desired, different flavors could be added to the sauce by including blended sautéed vegetables such as onions and mushrooms. In sweet and sour sauces, try using arrowroot in recipes that call for cornstarch or flour.

Arrowroot can be put to use in glazes, cake batters, doughs, puddings, pie fillings, and other dessert mixes. It may also be used as a binder in egg-free baking. Create a basic clear cake or pastry glaze by combining hot cider (or any fruit juice), salt, and dissolved arrowroot. To jazz it up, just add coffee, spices (such as cinnamon, cloves, and/or ginger), lemon or orange rind or juice, diced fruit (such as strawberries, blueberries, apples, and pears), raisins, mint, vanilla, or roasted sesame or sunflower seeds.

This starch can also be used to prepare a tempura (or deep-fry) batter. Simply combine arrowroot with whole-wheat pastry flour, sea salt, water, and spices (try black pepper, cayenne, or basil) to generate a tasty batter.

Another benefit of arrowroot is that it does not lose its thickening power when combined with very acid fruits.

Kuzu, cornstarch, potato starch, and in some cases flour may be used in place of arrowroot. See the "Thickening Agents" section of this book to modify proportions.

STORAGE

Store arrowroot powder in a cool, dry, dark place in an airtight container. Although dishes cooked using arrowroot can be stored at room temperature, in the refrigerator, or in the freezer, they do not reheat well.

PREPARATION INSTRUCTIONS

Pre-dissolve arrowroot in cold water or other liquid to prevent it from clumping. Stir again immediately before adding the dissolved arrowroot to a mixture, as arrowroot tends to settle to the bottom

rather quickly. Add the arrowroot mixture at the end of cooking, because arrowroot-thickened sauces tend to break down if cooked too long. Use from 1/2 teaspoon to 1 tablespoon arrowroot per 1 cup liquid.

Arrowroot is only effective when used in small quantities and cooked for a short period of time. If large amounts of arrowroot are used, the dish can become a bit gelatinous, and if cooked for more than 1-2 minutes, arrowroot will lose its thickening powers.

Arrowroot will not reheat well, so items thickened with it that are to be served hot should be served immediately.

Using arrowroot with acid fruits (such as lemons, tangerines, oranges, and strawberries) may cause the mixture to set less firmly. The higher the acidity level and the larger the volume of the fruit, the more arrowroot must be used to obtain the same thickening power. If you are having trouble getting the firmness you want in a dish that contains an acid fruit, start by adding 1/2 teaspoon more arrowroot per cup of liquid and/or fruit or add another thickening agent, such as kuzu.

When using arrowroot as a binding agent in egg-free baking, sift the arrowroot in with the other dry ingredients.

HEALTH INFORMATION

Arrowroot contains no fat or cholesterol. It contains small amounts of calcium, and other minerals and vitamins. It is easily digested.

ADDITIONAL READING

Newman, Marcea. *The Sweet Life*.

BUYING SOURCES

This ingredient can be found with the spices in grocery stores and supermarkets. It is also typically available in health and natural food stores. See "Thickening Agents" for the names of mail order companies that carry thickening agents.

BRAND NAMES

A couple of good brands of arrowroot are McCormic *Arrowroot* and Esculent *Arrowroot Powder*.

AZUKI BEANS

(ah ZOO key) (beans)

What is small? What is reddish-brown? What has a nutty, almost peanut-like flavor? An azuki bean, of course! These compact little treats add a distinct red color to any dish. They are approximately 1/4 inch long, oval in shape, and have a thin white line on the ridge, or eye, of the bean.

OTHER NAMES

Aduki, adzuki, adsuki, asuki.

FLAVOR/TEXTURE

Azuki beans have a nutty, light flavor that adapts well to both sweet and savory dishes.

GENERAL USES

Although small, azuki beans are a very nourishing complement to any meal. They can be cooked with soups, pies, pizzas, vegetables, sea vegetables, squash, rice, sunflower seeds, and much, much more. When mashed or blended with your favorite spices and vegetables, they can make delicious patés and dips. Azuki beans can also be used to make an outstanding bean salad—just combine cooked azuki beans with blanched watercress, tamari, and toasted sesame oil; or toss the beans with ripe tomatoes and fresh spices such as cumin, coriander, and garlic.

Azuki beans can be used to prepare a delightful treat for friends and family. Sweetening them with sugar or honey and adding cinnamon, raisins, apples, and lemon juice can make a dessert topping for ice cream, cakes, or puddings.

Azuki beans can be used in any soup, salad, bake, loaf, or burger recipes that call for lentils.

FRESHNESS/QUALITY

See "Beans."

STORAGE

See "Beans."

PREPARATION INSTRUCTIONS

CLEANING AND SOAKING

See "Beans."

COOKING

See the "Beans" section for general instructions for cooking on the stove, baking in the oven, cooking in a pressure cooker, or simmering in a crock pot. For fresh dried beans, the typical stove-top cooking time ranges from 35 to 55 minutes and the pressure cooking time is 15 minutes. One cup of dried azuki beans will generally yield about three cups of cooked beans.

HEALTH INFORMATION

Azuki beans are high in protein, low in fat, and easier to digest than many beans. They contain calcium, iron, thiamine as well as other B vitamins and trace minerals. Many believe them to be good for the liver and kidneys.

ADDITIONAL READING

Almost all macrobiotic cookbooks will have recipes using azuki beans. For a list of books that explicitly focus on beans, see "Beans."

BUYING SOURCES

Dried azuki beans can be found in health food stores, oriental ethnic markets, and some supermarkets in bulk or prepackaged forms. For a list of mail order sources as well as brand names, see "Beans."

BARLEY

If you are ever looking for a grain that can go a long, long way, a good choice is barley. It is positively amazing how much it expands. You can feed a boy scout troop on 2 cups of barley. Better yet, this grain is up to the task of giving a full feeling to growing boys; they will feel well fed after eating a hearty barley dish.

Barley grains are around 3/16 inch long and quite plump. They have a little crease down the middle of one side. They are the fat little grains that are floating around in vegetable barley soup.

VARIETIES

Direct from the fields, barley is a short, stubby, brown grain that still has its outer hull which must be removed before the barley is fit for human consumption. The scouring of barley to remove tough outer layers is called pearling. See "Grains" to get definitions for hull and bran ("Grain Anatomy" subsection) and whole grains, flakes, and flour ("Milled & Processed Grains" subsection).

Hulled Barley: Hulled barley, also called whole barley, has had the least amount of processing; only the outer inedible layer has been removed. Although it has the highest level of nutrients, vitamins, and minerals, it is quite tough and chewy and requires a long cooking time. It is well-suited for soups and stews and other dishes that also require a lengthy cooking time. Strains of barley have been developed that have a softer hull that is easier to remove. These are often called "hull-less" barley.

Scotch or Pot Barley: This barley is the result after three pearlings. Some of the bran has been scraped away as well as all of the inedible outer hull. Although easier to chew than hulled barley, it is still quite tough. To help soften the tough kernels and shorten the cooking time, soak it overnight prior to cooking.

Pearled Barley: Pearled or pearl barley is the barley that is most commonly used in recipes. It is not nearly as tough as hulled or scotch barley but it is still pleasantly chewy. This barley is subjected to five or six pearlings and much of its protein, fiber, vitamins, and minerals are lost. These pearlings produce a pearl-like, translucent, white product that is very similar to white rice.

Rolled Barley or Barley Flakes: This type of barley has been pearled, toasted, and rolled into flakes and has a light nutty flavor. A hot bowl of "oatmeal" for breakfast is probably the most common use for this type of grain. Rolled barley or barley flakes can be used in the same manner as any of the other grains that have been rolled or flaked. It can be used in baked goods, meat loaves, and stews as well as breakfast cereal.

Barley Flour: Barley produces a starchy, soft, white flour that is low in gluten and high in maltose sugar. Barley flour is useful in making leavened breads because the maltose aids in yeast growth. Breads baked with barley and wheat flour are soft, light, and moist. Furthermore, barley flour is useful in cookies, cakes, pancakes, and other baked goods. In addition to mixing well with wheat flour, barley flour is excellent when combined with oat flour. When baking with barley flour, the final product will have a slightly grayish color unless other ingredients such as chocolate, cinnamon, or molasses cause it to have a darker color.

Barley Malt Powder: This is a cream-colored, crystal-like powder that is also called malt sugar. See "Sweeteners" for more information.

Barley Malt Syrup: Barley malt syrup is a liquid sweetener that is somewhere between molasses and honey in color and degree of sweetness. See "Sweeteners" for more information.

FLAVOR/TEXTURE

When cooked alone, barley has a mild, earthy flavor that is somewhat bland. Barley kernels are used mostly for their pleasant, chewy texture. When cooked with other grains, its texture aids in producing a lighter dish. And when cooked in soups, it generates a more hearty dish.

GENERAL USES

Barley contributes its mild flavor and chewy texture to soups, casseroles, stews, stuffings, pies, muffins, breads, vegetables, beans, pilafs, etc. For breakfast, barley kernels or flakes are perfect prepared as a hot cereal sweetened with fruit or as a porridge. Pearled barley adds substance to soup by generating an essentially fat-free, thick, creamy texture. To make a rich, creamy base for a sauce or soup, cooked barley can be puréed. Cooked whole barley is wonderful in hearty cold salads. Mix scotch barley with short grain brown rice to create a very satisfying grain mixture that can be topped with any sauce you desire or thrown into a stir fry. Since barley can be used in so many ways with so many other grains in so many dishes, cook a boat load and have it handy in the refrigerator or freezer.

Ingredients that complement barley are vegetables, beans, nuts, and other grains. Chives, as well as any member of the onion family, go great with barley. Other spices and herbs that are a good match are fennel, parsley, bay leaf, basil, caraway, rosemary, thyme, cloves, and black pepper. If barley is used with meats, use the more hearty ones like lamb, beef, and pork. Try mixing cooked barley with dill and sautéed green beans or hot buttered peas and serve with pork chops.

Cook up a stout barley and mushroom casserole by combining sautéed morel mushrooms and green bell peppers, barley, onions, vegetable stock, salt, and black pepper. Or make a cold salad for a picnic by mixing cooked barley kernels, raisins, almonds or cashews, celery, carrots, and onions with a lemon juice, almond oil, and tamari soy sauce dressing.

Make a barley pudding similar to rice pudding by combining barley, milk, raisins, rice syrup or honey, and salt and baking for 3 hours in a moderate oven. Top with whipped cream, yogurt, or blended sweetened tofu.

Whole barley can be ground into flour to make hearty breads, pastries, cakes, pancakes, and other baked goods. Barley flour is also good for thickening sauces, soups, and gravies. To make a satisfying pancake breakfast, use barley flour, baking powder, oil, milk or non-dairy milk, eggs or applesauce, and salt. Top the pancakes with butter and maple syrup, fruit spread, or fresh sweetened fruit.

Whole barley can be roasted and used to create a hot grain drink which may be used as an alternative to coffee or hot tea.

FRESHNESS/QUALITY
See "Grains."

STORAGE
See "Grains."

PREPARATION INSTRUCTIONS

CLEANING
Hulled, scotch, and pearled barley can be washed in cool water if needed or desired. See "Grains" for information on cleaning grains.

SOAKING
No soaking is required to cook barley; however, soaking hulled, scotch, or pearled barley overnight will shorten the cooking time. See "Grains" for more information about soaking grains.

COOKING
When cooked, barley will expand to almost four times its uncooked volume. If you are improvising and want to cook barley in a soup, be sure that you don't use too much uncooked barley because it will absorb all of the soup stock and create a pilaf instead. See the "Barley Cooking Table" for liquid amounts and cooking times to use to cook one cup of barley.

BARLEY COOKING TABLE ——————

	Liquid (cups)	Time (min.)
Hulled	2 1/2 - 3	80 - 100
Scotch or Pot	2 1/2 - 3	60 - 80
Pearled	2 - 2 1/2	25 - 35
Pearled (*porridge*)	3 1/2 - 4	50 - 60
Rolled or Flakes	2 1/2 - 3	15 - 20
Rolled (*porridge*)	4 - 4 1/2	20 - 30

Cooking instructions and a discussion of cooking issues can be found in the "Grains" section of this book.

REHEATING
See "Grains."

HEALTH INFORMATION
Barley is a good source of fiber, complex carbohydrates, and protein as well as potassium, iron, niacin, thiamin, magnesium, chromium, phosphorous, and some calcium. It is low in fat and contains no cholesterol. Furthermore, hulled barley contains vitamin E and insoluble fiber.

ADDITIONAL READING
See "Grains."

BUYING SOURCES

Pearled barley is available in most supermarkets and health and natural food stores in the dried goods section or with the grains and beans. Pot or scotch barley, barley grits, barley flakes, and barley flour can be found in health and natural food stores. Mail order companies are also good sources of barley and barley products. See "Grains" for a list of mail order sources and brand names.

BARLEY MALT SYRUP

Barley malt syrup is a thick, gooey grain sweetener. Sprout whole barley, roast it, and then extract it to a liquid form, and you've got barley malt syrup. This very thick syrup has a dark, opaque color that can range from a reddish light brown to a very dark brown. A rather interesting bit of trivia is that hop-flavored barley malt was sold "strictly as a sweetener" during Prohibition. Yet, if you were to add bitter-tasting hopped barley to a batch of cookies, the result would be inedible! Why would a sweetener be flavored with something bitter? Combine barley malt syrup with hops, ferment with yeast, and the result is beer. Ah ha!

VARIETIES

Liquid barley malt sweeteners are available in two forms:

Barley Extract: The extract is 100 % barley malt and usually tastes as strong as blackstrap molasses. Imported 100 % malts have a rich but less intense flavor, which gives them wider culinary applications. However, they are more costly than domestic malts.

Barley-Corn Malt: A pleasantly flavored and versatile blend of barley and corn is a more popular malt. The higher the percentage of corn, the less expensive the product and the milder the flavor. Corn cannot be malted by itself, but when corn grits are combined with barley malt, the barley enzymes reduce the cornstarch to maltose.

FLAVOR/TEXTURE

The rich, sweet, toasted flavor of barley malt can range from extremely strong to rather mild. (See the discussion in "Varieties" above.)

GENERAL USES

Barley malt syrup can be used as a topping for a cake, or in the same way as maple syrup or honey. It is useful in pies, cakes, puddings, brownies, carrot cakes, cupcakes, crumb cakes, fruitcakes, muffins, and other baked goods and desserts.

A decadent "chocolate" pudding can be whipped up by cooking carob powder, amazake, grain or instant coffee, barley malt syrup, kuzu, and agar until thickish and then cooling. To add a gourmet flair and sweeter taste, also add a little coffee liqueur or amaretto.

A simple, elegant pie filling can be made by heating fresh peaches along with barley malt syrup, kuzu, and a pinch of sea salt. A scrumptious pear crisp can be prepared by coating ripe pears with an arrowroot flour, salt, and water batter; transferring them to a baking dish, and covering with roasted walnuts, rolled oats, and barley malt syrup; and then baking in 375°F oven.

FRESHNESS/QUALITY

Some manufacturers mix commercial corn syrup with barley malt syrup to form an inferior product.

STORAGE

Store barley malt syrup in a glass or plastic container in a cool, dark place. If stored a long time (longer than twelve months) or in a warm place, the malt may ferment. A sign of fermentation is foam on top or bubbles percolating up through the malt. Should this occur, refrigerate and use quickly, or discard if it has an unpleasant aroma.

PREPARATION INSTRUCTIONS

This sweetener is much easier to work with if it is heated prior to use. For additional preparation information, see "Sweeteners."

HEALTH INFORMATION

Barley malt syrup contains gluten; thus, those who are restricted to a gluten-free diet should avoid this sweetener. It is almost 100% carbohydrates (complex sugars) and also contains potassium and other vitamins and minerals found in sprouted barley.

ADDITIONAL READING

See "Sweeteners."

BUYING SOURCES

See "Sweeteners."

BRAND NAMES

Sweet Cloud *Organic Barley Syrup*, Eden *Organic Barley Malt Syrup*, and Silver Forest *Barley Malt Syrup* are all excellent.

BEANS

Beans, beans, they're good for your heart, but the more you eat, the more you _____. In many kitchens, beans have been avoided due to the intestinal gases that can form when they are digested.  For those who are interested in eating beans and gaining the massive nutritional and taste benefits, there are cooking techniques that can be used to prevent this embarrassing gaseous problem.

Beans are extremely versatile—they can be used in many different ways and can go with just about anything.

VARIETIES

There are many different types of beans, varying in shape, size, texture, and color. They can be yellow, purple, green, red, white, black, or a combination of colors that produce interesting patterns.

There are individual entries for each of the following bean varieties: azuki, black-eyed peas, pinto, mung, lentils, black turtle, kidney, navy, Great Northern, lima, and garbanzo.

There are different methods of preserving or packaging beans and stores will have them in different sections such as canned, frozen, dry-goods, bulk, etc. The same bean type may be found in more than one of these sections. A good example is black-eyed peas since they can be found in the frozen, canned, dry-goods, and bulk sections of most supermarkets.

There are many reasons for choosing a particular packaging form. Individual priorities may vary among nutrition, ease, cooking time, freshness, convenience, texture, level of processing, etc.

Dried Beans: More varieties of beans are available dried than in any other form. They can be found in supermarkets, specialty shops, ethnic markets, and natural or health food stores as well as obtained through mail order. Dried beans are the least processed and contain no preservatives or additives. The cooking time, however, is considerably longer than the other forms. But, this gives you the ability to choose the cooking method to produce the texture that you desire for each and every recipe and eliminate the intestinal gaseous problems. It offers the power of flexibility. Typically, authors of vegetarian and healthy eating cookbooks use dried beans if they don't explicitly specify another form. However, even if another form is specified, cooked dried beans can be used in any recipe calling for canned or frozen beans.

Frozen Beans: Some varieties are frozen very quickly after harvesting. This locks in flavor and nutrition; however, they lose some textural qualities through the freezing and thawing process. These are more convenient than dried beans since they are simpler to prepare and take less total time.

Canned Beans: Due to the nature of the preserving method, canned beans are often overcooked and mushier than the other types of beans. In addition, they may contain additives, preservatives, salt, sugar, meat, and meat fat and broths. Canned beans are easy to heat and eat. But, if you are going to simmer them in a pot of soup or use them in a cold bean salad, they may not hold their form.

OTHER NAMES

Legumes.

GENERAL USES

Beans are wonderfully versatile and can be used in a variety of dishes: seafood, poultry, soups, pastas, salads, appetizers, and desserts. Try adding them to grains, noodles, vegetables, or sea vegetables, or to apples, raisins and other fruit to make a dessert. Beans are delicious when varieties are cooked together.

Once cooked, beans can be eaten and heartily enjoyed, hot or cold, mashed or whole. If you take any leftover beans and throw them in the blender with some spices—presto, you've got a great dip, sandwich spread, or gravy. Beans can be wrapped in a tortilla with cooked rice and sautéed onions and peppers, and then topped with salsa for a quick easy dish. A scrumptious cold bean salad can be created by mixing several types of cooked firm beans with fresh chopped vegetables and sprinkling the combination with rice vinegar and other seasonings. Mix a bunch of varieties of beans together in a big soup pot (say it's five types), add some veggies and spices along with a rich vegetable broth and you've got a great five-bean soup. By the way, if you're purchasing a prepackaged bean soup, be sure that the spices are packaged separately from the beans so that you can properly soak and cook the beans, as described in the following sections.

Since beans are difficult to digest and are rather high in calories, they are usually eaten in small quantities (as a side dish or combined with other ingredients to make a main dish).

FRESHNESS/QUALITY

There are many ways to determine the quality of dried beans. The color should be bright and the beans should be uniform in size. Beans should not be wrinkled, pitted, split in half, or have openings in the seams, broken skins, or chips. To determine the quality of dried beans, it is important to be able to see them before buying. Be sure to select a store that has a high turnover in beans to get the freshest dried beans possible.

Even though premium dried beans may cost 3 or 4 times the cheaper brands,

the cost is still quite inexpensive compared to the price of meat, dairy products, or prepackaged items. Just think about it: Paying a premium price of $2.99 (rather than the cheap $0.79) for a pound of dried beans (approximately 2.5 cups) will typically yield over 7.5 cups of cooked beans. That's a lot of food for three bucks. At these prices, you can afford, and deserve, the best.

STORAGE

Before cooking, dried beans should be stored in airtight containers in a cool dry place (but not in the refrigerator). They may be stored for 6 to 12 months this way, provided they were fresh when you bought them. Dried beans age over time and the longer they are stored, the longer they'll take to reconstitute through soaking and cooking. If kept too long, they may remain tough even after cooking. Beans bought at different times should not be mixed together when stored. They should be labeled with the date of purchase so that the oldest beans can be used first.

Refrigeration of leftover cooked beans is a great way to have that quick side dish on hand. The beans will store nicely for 5 days or so.

Nigro Tip

Freezing beans is one of the best kept secrets. They will keep much longer (up to one year) than refrigerated beans and when reheated they always taste better for some reason. Divide your beans into recipe-sized portions. If you freeze too many beans in a freezer bag or container they will form a solid block of beans that may be impossible to divide while still frozen.

Since freezing tends to soften beans, you may wish to undercook them slightly before freezing. To retain the shape of the beans, thaw them slowly such as overnight in the refrigerator, for several hours at room temperature, by soaking the container in a pan of warm water for approximately an hour, or by microwaving them for a few minutes.

PREPARATION INSTRUCTIONS

CLEANING

Dried beans may have inedible goodies such as weed seed, tiny twigs, pebbles, rocks, etc. in with them. You'll want to get rid of these foreign items before doing anything with the beans. Inspect the beans by placing them on a cookie sheet or something with small sides so that they won't spill over onto the counter or floor. Carefully look through the beans, a few at a time. Remove anything that doesn't look like the rest of the beans and any broken bits of beans.

Packaged beans are often quite clean, but it is best to check them anyway. Definitely check bulk beans carefully since they are more likely to have foreign items picked up with them.

After sorting the beans, rinse them with cool water to remove any dust.

SOAKING

As a general rule, all dried beans should be soaked before cooking. Most importantly, soaking helps break down and leach out the indigestible sugars that may cause intestinal gas. In addition, soaking reduces cooking time and less cooking time means that the beans will retain more of their vitamins and minerals.

During soaking, beans may rise to the surface; we call them floaters. These floaters may be older beans with little moisture, or beans that were harvested prematurely. This is the time to find, grab, and discard them. If you find too many floaters, find another bean supplier.

There are two soaking methods to choose from. There doesn't seem to be any noticeable difference in cooking times or texture and taste of the beans based on the type of soaking method.

Long Soaking Method: This method involves soaking the beans for six to nine hours in room temperature water. Aliases for the long soaking method include Overnight Soak or Go to Work and Come Back Later Soak. Use about four times the volume of water to beans for soaking and don't add

salt to the soaking water. If you have extremely hard water, avoid using baking soda in the soaking water to "soften" it; instead, consider bottled water. If, for some reason, you have to extend the soaking time for as much as a day or two, just be sure to change the water at least once a day so your beans don't spoil. If you live in a hot climate or if your kitchen is particularly hot, then change the water more frequently.

Short Soaking Method: If you are a last hour kind of person, this is ideal for you. Place the cleaned beans in a pot and add hot tap water until the beans are covered by two to four inches. Bring slowly to a boil over medium high heat. Boil for two  minutes, remove from the heat, cover, and let the beans soak for one hour.

After soaking, discard the water and rinse the beans before combining with fresh cooking water. Remember, the soaking water has the indigestible sugars that can cause those wicked intestinal gases.

COOKING

Just a reminder: Before cooking, first clean and soak your beans. Be sure to discard the soaking water and thoroughly rinse the beans.

There are many ways to cook beans. You can cook them on the stove, in a pressure cooker, in the oven, or in a crock pot. Barbecuing on a grill, however, can be very tricky and quite messy because the beans will keep falling through the holes in the grill.

Even though many cookbooks give a specific range of time for cooking beans, they are just approximations—the actual cooking time in your kitchen may be quite different. It really depends on the freshness of the bean; the type of pots or dishes you use; the calibration of your stove, oven, microwave, crockpot, or pressure cooker; the altitude at which you live (if you live in Utah or Wyoming, water boils at at a lower temperature than at sealevel); the brands of the beans; cooking method; ingredients combined with the beans during cooking; etc. For example,

Beans Comparison Table

Bean	Description	General Cooking Time*	1 Cup Dried Approx. Yields	Holds Shape Well	Common Use(s)
Azuki	Very small, reddish-brown, oval shape	Short	3 cups	No	Dessert dishes
Black Turtle	Small, shiny black, oval shape	Medium	2 1/2 cups	No	Black bean soup & black beans and rice
Black-eyed Pea	Small, cream-colored with black or dark purple "eye," oval shape	Medium	2 1/4 cups	No	Side-dish
Garbanzo	Medium-sized, roundish, tan, somewhat wrinkled	Long	2 1/2 cups	Yes	Hummus
Great Northern	Medium-sized, white, kidney shaped	Medium	2 2/3 cups	Yes	Minestrone soup
Kidney	Medium-sized, kidney shaped, deep brown-red	Medium	3 cups	Yes	Chili & salads
Lentil	Very small, lens-shape, colors vary	Short	1 2/3 – 2 1/4 cups	No	Soup
Lima	Flat, kidney shape, white or green, size varies	Short	2 – 3 cups	No	Succotash
Mung	Very small, olive green, oval shape	Short	2 cups	Yes	Sprouts
Navy	Small, white, plump, oval shape	Medium	2 2/3 cups	Yes	Boston Baked Beans
Pinto	Medium-sized, pinkish-brown swirls/speckles on cream-colored background	Medium	2 3/4 cups	Yes	Refried beans

©1996 Nigro

* General Cooking Times are broken down into the following categories:
Short = 30–60 minutes, *Medium* = 1–2 hours, and *Long* = 2–3 hours when cooked on the stove top.

although the suggested stove-top cooking time range for pinto beans is 40 to 60 minutes, we have prepared two different batches of pinto beans that took widely different amounts of time to cook (30 minutes versus 1 1/2 hours). Due to the difficulty in pinning down a narrow cooking time range, many cookbooks will provide quite different cooking times for each type of bean. Don't worry about the inconsistencies; just do a little experimentation and cook a few pots of beans in your kitchen. With a little testing, practice, flexibility, and luck, you will be able to accurately predict the cooking times for your beans.

No matter which cooking method you choose, you'll want to be sure to include the magic ingredient—sea vegetables (kombu, kelp, or wakame)—to dramatically enhance the flavor and digestibility of the beans. Per cup of dried beans, place a 2-inch wide by 6-inch long strip of kombu or wakame, or a 2-inch by 2-inch piece of kelp, on the bottom of the cooking pot or dish. If in doubt about the quantity to use, put in lots—you can always remove any unwanted sea vegetable after the beans are cooked and save it in the refrigerator for your next batch of beans or pot of soup. If you want to keep the sea vegetable as a part of the beans dish, it may be necessary to pre-soak the sea vegetable for 5 minutes in cool water if you are preparing a short-cooking-time bean (see the "Beans Comparison Table"). If you soak the sea vegetables, be sure to use the soak water in the preparation of your beans to maximize the nutritional value of the sea vegetable. For more information, see "Sea Vegetables (Dried)" or the individual sections in this book on kombu, kelp, or wakame.

Another key thing to remember to keep your beans tender and succulent is to add salt near the end of cooking when the beans are almost tender. The best way to be sure you don't add too much salt is to add just a little bit, stir, taste, and then repeat the process if more salt is needed. Add only enough soy sauce, sea salt or other refined salt substitute to make the broth taste slightly salty. The beans will not have absorbed the salt yet and may still taste somewhat flat. However, when the beans are finally done, they will taste sweet, not salty. It is better to have a little less salt, rather than too much, since additional salt can be added to the beans at serving time. Some people enjoy their beans without any salt at all!

To add flavor, vegetables (such as onions, green or hot peppers, carrots, broccoli, celery, etc.) can be cooked with beans. Seasonings such as garlic cloves, mustard, white pepper, unsalted vegetable stock, onion powder, parsley, bay leaves, or other dried herbs and spices may also be added before cooking. However, avoid adding at the beginning of cooking anything that is acidic or salty (such as tomatoes, ketchup, chili sauce, vinegar, wine, molasses, citrus juices, garlic salt, onion salt, or salted broths) since it will harden the skins of the beans and increase the cooking time. Add these items near the end of cooking, when you add the salt.

When testing to see if your beans are done, bite-taste more than one bean since some may be more tender than others. They really aren't supposed to be mushy, unless, of course, you like them that way! Test frequently to determine when they are done. If you want to reduce the risk of burning your tongue, you can test the beans' softness by mashing them with a fork or back of a spoon. Once you think they are done, it's time to taste them.

Stove-Top Cooking: Combine the soaked beans, water, and sea vegetable, along with any desired vegetables and non-acidic and non-salty spices, in a pot. Cover the beans with 2 to 3 inches of water. Bring everything to a boil and briskly boil the beans for 3 to 5 minutes, skimming off any foam that may develop. Reduce the heat to low, cover tightly, and simmer from 30 minutes to 2 hours depending of the type of bean. Be sure that the beans remain covered with water at all times while cooking. Add the salt when the beans are almost done. Uncover and cook for 15 to 30 minutes more, depending on the type of bean.

Pressure Cooking: Combine the soaked beans, water, and sea vegetable with any desired vegetables and spices in a pressure cooker, being careful not to fill the cooker more than one-third full to avoid clogging vents. Cover the beans with 2 to 3 inches of water. Bring to a boil and keep at a brisk boil for 3 to 5 minutes, skimming off any foam that may develop. Seal the lid and bring up to pressure. Cook from 10 to 60 minutes (see each individual bean type entry). Then remove the cover, add salt or tamari soy sauce to taste, and cook uncovered until the liquid evaporates or the desired texture is reached. Be sure to heed any warnings or directions and to note any tips or tricks provided by the manufacturer of your pressure cooker.

Baking Beans: First, cover soaked beans with 2 to 3 inches of water and boil for 20 minutes to loosen the skins. Discard the boiling water. Place the appropriate amount of sea vegetable on the bottom of a baking dish, add beans and water (cover beans by at least 1 inch), cover, and cook in a 350°F oven for 30 minutes to 2 hours. Additional water may be needed during baking, so keep an eye on them.

Crock Pot Cooking: Crock pot beans are delicious. Place sorted, soaked, and washed beans in the crock pot with any desired vegetables and spices along with the sea vegetable. Fill one half to two thirds of the crock pot with the beans and vegetables and add enough water to cover by 2 to 3 inches.

 Set on low or high and let the beans cook until almost tender. Add salt to taste and allow to cook for an hour or so longer. Add more water, if necessary, during cooking. Test, and record the bean and water proportions with the different bean types before leaving the crock pot unattended.

Reheating: Beans can be quickly reheated on the stove-top or in the microwave. Because beans have a tendency to absorb liquids when cooling, you may need to add liquid to the beans before reheating. Basically, if they are dry, add water until you get the consistency you want.

Nigro Tip ――――――――――――――

Beans are terrific when leftovers are reheated. They are so good, that we often cook a batch of beans with the intention of making them all leftovers! It seems the more times you reheat them, the better they are to eat them.

HEALTH INFORMATION

Beans contain many nutrients and more protein than any other vegetable product. When you eat them with grains, you get an added protein boost since grains contain amino acids that beans lack. Beans are a good source of calcium, iron, potassium, vitamin B_1, and niacin. They are brimming with soluble fiber, are low in fat, and contain no cholesterol.

Beans are difficult to digest. You can help the process by cooking with a sea vegetable, minimizing the amount of salt used, adding the salt and any acidic ingredients near the end of the cooking process, properly soaking and discarding the soaking water before cooking, minimizing the cooking time, and completely chewing each mouthful.

ELIMINATING FLATULENCE (INTESTINAL GAS)

Even though beans are one of the most healthful and delicious foods available, they are often blamed for embarrassing flatulence. However, you should be able to eat and enjoy beans to your heart's content and not have a problem with gas. There are ways to reduce or completely eliminate the sudden expulsion of intestinal gases.

First, and foremost, be sure you are not accusing the bean unjustly since there are other good foods that can cause a similar reaction: broccoli, brussels sprouts, cauliflower, peas, cabbage, oat bran, celery, raisins, raw carrots, milk, and some milk products. All of them—including beans—contain complex sugars, oligosaccharides, that the body cannot easily digest. These sugars are like candy to the bacteria waiting in the colon. The waste products of these very full bacteria are hydrogen, carbon dioxide and other odoriferous gases—and guess where those gases have to go!

If beans are truly the culprits, the solution is simple: Reduce the complex sugars or do away with them entirely. Proper soaking and cooking of beans (see prior subsections) can eliminate a great part of the problem. In addition, make beans a regular part of your diet. Then your body will adjust to the new situation and the problem of flatulence will disappear. Obviously, eating small amounts of beans more frequently is better than eating lots of beans every now and then. And lastly, don't mix your beans with any of the other gas-generating vegetables that were previously mentioned. Instead, you may want to add ginger root since it may help reduce flatulence.

Many bean recipes call for a great deal of fat, which keeps the bean's complex sugars in the digestive system much longer, allowing more gases to form. So, it might be a good idea to choose low-fat recipes for your beans and especially avoid those recipes that contain animal fat such as bacon and ham-hocks.

ADDITIONAL READING

Gregory, Patricia. *Bean Banquets: From Boston to Bombay.*

London, Sheryl, and Mel London. *The Versatile Grain and the Elegant Bean.*

Mayes, Kathleen, and Sandra Gottfried. *Boutique Bean Pot.*

Saltzman, Joanne. *Romancing the Bean.*

BUYING SOURCES

Beans are available in the dry goods, canned, frozen, and bulk foods sections of supermarkets, health and natural food stores, specialty shops, and ethnic markets. The are also available through the following mail order sources: Allergy Resources, Anzen Oriental Foods & Imports, Arrowhead Mills, Bob's Red Mill Natural Food, Clear Eye Natural Foods, Community Mill & Bean, Inc., Frankferd Farms Foods, Garden Spot, Gold Mine Natural Foods, Harvest Time Natural Foods, Jaffe Bros., Mountain Ark

Trading Company, Phipps Ranch, Sultan's Delights, Natural Lifestyle, and The Bean Bag.

BRAND NAMES

Excellent quality beans are produced by Arrowhead Mills, Bean Cuisine™, and many of the mail order sources.

BLACK TURTLE BEANS

Black turtle beans are incredibly scrumptious little treats. In fact, we'd say that these beans were created to be a perfect partner with all types of rice. Of course, being a bean, they are very versatile and go with a great many other ingredients as well. These 3/8 inch long, oval-shaped beans have a cream color interior and a shiny black or deep purple skin with a thin white line along their ridge.

OTHER NAMES

Black beans, Spanish black beans.

FLAVOR/TEXTURE

These beans have a robust, yet mellow, earthy flavor and a firm texture.

GENERAL USES

Probably the biggest reason why black beans go hand in hand with rice is that the beans retain their shape and essence while also harmonizing with the flavors of the grain. Black turtle beans can be boiled, fried, spiced, and mixed with rice and other foods.

These beans are often used in a marvelous thick soup seasoned with coriander, cumin and garlic, and topped with sour cream, chopped red onions, and fresh cilantro. They are also used for Cuban black bean soup with rum.

A dip or pâté can also be made from these fabulous beans. A hearty dip can be produced by blending drained cooked black beans with coriander, oregano, peppers (hot or sweet, yellow, red or green), cayenne, onion, garlic, and brown rice vinegar—it's wonderful with chips.

Beans can even be used to make non-traditional pancakes that can be served at any time of day. For the batter, just blend cooked black beans with water, dry sherry (or beer or rum), unbleached white flour, baking powder, vegetable oil, scallions, garlic, parsley, salt, and pepper.

Cold bean salads are delightful with black beans. Try mixing drained, cooked black beans with tomato wedges, diced onion (red, Vidalia, or scallions), corn, and avocado cubes. Then stir in the dressing; you might like to try a combination of olive oil, cilantro, hot sauce, red wine vinegar, lime juice, salt, and pepper.

FRESHNESS/QUALITY

See "Beans."

STORAGE

See "Beans."

PREPARATION INSTRUCTIONS

CLEANING AND SOAKING

See "Beans."

COOKING

See the "Beans" section for general instructions for cooking. Stove-top cooking time ranges from 50 to 70 minutes, and the pressure cooking time is 18 minutes. One cup of dried beans yields approximately 2 1/2 cups cooked. Cooked black turtle beans hold their shape well.

HEALTH INFORMATION

Black turtle beans contain protein, iron, calcium, and B vitamins.

BUYING SOURCES

See "Beans" for buying sources, a mail order source list, and brand names.

BLACK-EYED PEAS

Black-eyed peas are easy beans to spot because of the dark purplish black dot or "eye" along the ridge (or seam) of the bean. These small kidney-shaped beans are about 1/4 to 3/8 inches long and have a cream-colored skin with the exception of their "black-eye."

OTHER NAMES

Black-eyed Suzies, brown-eyed peas, black-eyed beans, field peas, cowpeas.

FLAVOR/TEXTURE

Black-eyed peas have a rich, full flavor that tastes slightly nutty or earthy like mushrooms, depending on the other ingredients they are cooked with.

GENERAL USES

Black-eyed peas are good as a stand-alone vegetable with seasonings such as onions, coriander, garlic and cumin and topped with sour cream and fresh slivered almonds. Or, combine cooked black-eyed peas with lemon zest, rosemary, white wine, water, and tamari for a little variety.

Try cooking black-eyed peas with onion, red peppers (hot and/or sweet), bay leaf, and kombu. When the beans are tender, add salt, sectioned tomatoes, cut fresh okra, fresh or frozen corn, and black pepper and then simmer for 15 minutes. They are excellent when served on a bed of cooked brown rice.

Use black-eyed peas in stews, soups, salads (to add flavor and texture), and casseroles since they go well with many seasonings. A wonderful salad can be made by combining cooked black-eyed peas with coarsely broken toasted walnuts, chopped sweet red pepper, and blanched zucchini and watercress. A complementary dressing can be made by mixing brown rice vinegar, black pepper, mustard, walnut oil, and Tabasco sauce.

FRESHNESS/QUALITY

See "Beans."

STORAGE

See "Beans."

PREPARATION INSTRUCTIONS

CLEANING AND SOAKING

See "Beans."

COOKING

See the "Beans" section for general instructions for cooking. Stove-top cooking time ranges from 40 minutes to 1 hour, and the pressure cooking time is 15 minutes. One cup of dried beans yields approximately 2 1/4 cups cooked. Over-cooked black-eyed peas disintegrate, which may be just what you want when making a thick soup or sauce for rice.

HEALTH INFORMATION

Black-eyed peas are almost a quarter protein and contain iron, calcium, phosphorous, potassium, B-complex vitamins, and a bit of vitamin A.

BUYING SOURCES

These beans are available in supermarkets and health food stores all over the country. Dried black-eyed peas can be bought loose (in bulk) and in plastic bags or boxes (pre-packaged). Cooked black-eyed peas are sold in both canned and frozen forms. See "Beans" for a list of mail order sources and brand names.

BURDOCK ROOT

(BURR dock) (root)

This hearty root supplies a "down-to-earth" quality to soups, casseroles, and other dishes that it's added to. Burdock root is a long, slender vegetable with a brown to almost black skin and white fibrous flesh. It grows up to two feet in length, yet remains as slender as a carrot.

OTHER NAMES
Gobo.

VARIETIES
Burdock root is available fresh, dried, and pickled.

FLAVOR/TEXTURE
Imagine the rich aroma of freshly dug earth—that's the aroma of burdock. Add sweetness, and you've got its flavor, which is also similar to artichoke hearts. Burdock root has a pleasant, crunchy or chewy texture along with its earthy taste.

Because burdock root has a strong fla-vor that some find unusual, it is often cooked with other familiar root vegetables, such as carrots.

The texture of burdock root is very firm and fibrous.

GENERAL USES

Burdock root can be added to stews, soups, sautéed or baked vegetables, beans, grains, or sea vegetables. Try using burdock root in any recipes where you would use other roots such as carrots, potatoes, radishes, rutabagas, etc. It is also tasty pickled, tossed into simmered and fried dishes, and used as an ingredient in nori rolls (see "Nori").

A hearty root stir fry can be made by combining julienned burdock root, carrots, rutabagas, etc. and sautéing them with sesame oil, tamari soy sauce, and lemon or ginger juice, and then sprinkling with a few roasted sesame seeds.

A creamy gravy can be prepared by sautéing carrots, burdock root, onion, and celery and seasoning with diluted dark miso at the end of cooking. This is excellent served over rice or pasta and garnished with a sprig of parsley.

FRESHNESS/QUALITY

When you buy fresh burdock root, look for firm, unbroken roots that have a taut skin. Slender roots tend to be more tender and less fibrous than thick ones. Avoid floppy roots or dry, brittle ones with wrinkled skins.

STORAGE

Store fresh burdock root in a cool, dry place. It typically lasts for months. Once it's been cut, wrap burdock root in damp paper towels and refrigerate. It will remain fresh for about a week, depending on how fresh it was when purchased.

PREPARATION INSTRUCTIONS

CLEANING

To clean fresh burdock root, scrub it thoroughly but lightly with a stiff vegetable brush, and remove any rootlets. Don't peel burdock unless you have a very tough root, since the skin contains much of the flavor and nutritional value.

After cutting up this root, immediately immerse it in cold water until it's ready to be cooked to prevent discoloration and eliminate the slightly bitter taste.

Soaking

Soak dried burdock root in warm water for 30 or more minutes to rehydrate it and make it pliable before sautéing or frying. If using it in a soup or stew that will be simmered for a while, pre-soaking may not be necessary. The soaking water contains many vitamins and minerals, so save it for use in a future soup or vegetable stock.

Cooking

Burdock root is extremely tough and difficult to cut. The best way to use it is to shave it—just like sharpening a pencil or whittling a stick.

After cutting it into slivers or chunks, cook burdock root as you would a carrot, but allow longer cooking times. Burdock root should not be eaten raw.

Since burdock combines well with oil, it is often sautéed alone or with other vegetables, or deep-fried as tempura. But, it is also satisfying simmered in a seasoned broth to make a soup or stew.

Burdock requires lengthy cooking. When combining it with other vegetables in sautéed and simmered dishes, cook it first until it becomes tender and then add the other ingredients. You'll know that sautéed burdock is tender when it changes color slightly and its strong aroma is no longer being released.

HEALTH INFORMATION

Burdock has more protein, calcium, and phosphorus than carrots and is an excellent source of potassium and B vitamins. Proponents of the macrobiotic philosophy believe it strengthens the kidneys and sexual organs and has blood-purifying qualities.

Folklore claims that burdock root hastens recovery from sickness as well as relieves arthritis and diseases of the skin.

ADDITIONAL READING

Recipes using burdock root can typically be found in macrobiotic cookbooks. Some examples are:

Kushi, Aveline. *Complete Guide to Macrobiotic Cooking.*

Abehsera, Michel. *Zen Macrobiotic Cooking.*

Ohsawa, Lima. *Macrobiotic Cuisine.*

BUYING SOURCES

Fresh burdock may sometimes be found in the producc scction of Japanese and Oriental markets, health food stores, and supermarkets. It is sometimes sold dried or canned. Dried burdock is available through the Gold Mine Natural Foods and Natural Lifestyle mail order companies.

BRAND NAMES

Mitoku *Dried Shaved Burdock Root,* Ohsawa® *Yamaki Organic Burdock Pickles,* Amber Gold *Organic Wild Burdock Concentrate* are excellent products.

CAROB

(CARE eb)

It's too good to be true! Carob is not chocolate and has no cocoa, no caffeine, and no added sugar, but tastes like chocolate. Carob is a highly nutritious pod or bean that, when ground and roasted, becomes a cocoa-like substance.

VARIETIES

***Roasted Carob Powder*:** Roasted and ground carob pods yield carob powder. The roasting is what produces the chocolate flavor.

Raw Carob Powder: If only raw carob powder is available, you may choose to roast it yourself to produce the chocolate-like flavor.

Carob Bars or Blocks: These can be used in the same way as chocolate bars or blocks. Block carob contains palm or palm kernel oil which makes it high in saturated fat and is not recommended for "everyday" cooking.

Carob Chips or Morsels: These can be used in the same way as chocolate chips. Like carob bars, carob chips contain palm or palm kernel oil and should be used in moderation. Carob chips can contain dairy products or be dairy-free.

When substituting carob for chocolate, the amount of sweetness is something to consider:

Unsweetened Carob: Unsweetened carob does not have any added sugars. Because carob is naturally sweet, it has no equivalent to unsweetened or bittersweet chocolate. In recipes that call for these types of chocolates, a solution to the problem of using a substitute is to use carob and reduce the amount of sweetener called for in the recipe.

Sweetened Carob: When buying sweetened carob, check to see what sweetener has been used. The whole-food types are those sweetened with date sugar or barley malt. Those that contain white or brown sugar, fructose, or corn syrup contain a more refined sweetener (see "Sweeteners" for more information). If desired, unsweetened carob can be sweetened by the cook—allowing a choice of the amount and type of sweeteners used.

OTHER NAMES

St. John's Bread. This is such an unusual "other name" for an ingredient, we thought we would give a simple explanation. When John the Baptist lived in the wilderness, he survived on locusts and wild honey. Locusts are actually leguminous pods of the locust tree which is called carob today. Hence, carob was Saint John's bread.

FLAVOR/TEXTURE

Carob has a flavor similar to chocolate. When carob is substituted for chocolate in recipes, many folks cannot tell the difference, unless they are chocolate connoisseurs. However, real chocolate is, after all, real chocolate and to expect another bean to have a perfect chocolate flavor is perhaps asking too much. After using carob for a period of time, its own special flavor can be appreciated for the wholesome, natural treat it is.

Carob powder can be a bit "gritty." This chalky texture is minimized, if not entirely eliminated, by adding oil or fat.

GENERAL USES

Carob powder, bars, and blocks are used as tasty additions to baked goods, snacks, drinks, and sauces. Make a cup of hot carob on a cold winter day to warm you to your toes. Just heat up a cup of milk, toss in 1 tablespoon of carob powder with a little vanilla extract and honey and enjoy it in front of a cozy fire.

Make a trail mix that the whole family will love when hiking in the mountains or woods. Combine nuts, seeds, dried fruits, pretzels, and carob chips to create a sustaining snack.

Of course, carob can be used in your favorite chocolate chip cookie, fudge, or brownie recipes.

FRESHNESS/QUALITY

Carob powder should consist only of roasted or raw ground carob pods. If you can find carob chips or bars without palm or coconut oils, you'll have discovered a healthier brand.

STORAGE

Carob powder needs no refrigeration. Carob chips and bars will react to heat just as chocolate does so store them in a cool place.

PREPARATION INSTRUCTIONS

Roast raw carob by placing the powder in a dry hot frying pan over a low  heat. Keep it in continuous motion until the carob browns and smells like chocolate. Another roasting method is to spread a thin layer of powder on a baking sheet and place it in a preheated oven (150°F) for 10 to 15 minutes. Be careful not to burn the powder because it will taste awful.

Carob power sometimes produces a grainy texture in the dishes it is added to. Should this happen, use a little vegetable oil and/or lecithin to produce a creamier texture.

Carob chips and bars should be melted in a double boiler over low heat because carob burns as easily as chocolate and it will not melt if the heat is too high.

Carob block equivalents can be made from carob powder by mixing 3 tablespoons of carob powder with 2 tablespoons of oil and 1 tablespoon of water for each 1-ounce cube of carob that is required.

NIGRO TIP

When substituting carob for chocolate in desserts, the chocolate-like flavor can be enhanced by adding instant or natural grain coffee, vanilla, and flavor extracts, spirits, or liqueurs (such as rum, amaretto, almond, mint, Irish crème, and coffee).

HEALTH INFORMATION

Carob has a high percentage of sugar—approximately 50%. It also contains protein, A and B vitamins, minerals, and less fat and calories than chocolate. Carob is caffeine-free and is an excellent source of calcium.

Candies made with carob often contain fractionated palm kernel or coconut oil which are among the highest in saturated fats.

BUYING SOURCES

Carob powder can be purchased either raw or lightly roasted. It is available in supermarkets and health food stores on the shelf or in bulk foods sections.

Carob is available through the Mountain Ark Trading Company, Clear Eye Natural Foods, Bob's Red Mill Natural Foods, Frankferd Farms Foods, Jaffe Bros., and Natural Lifestyle mail order companies.

BRAND NAMES

Chatfield's *Carob & Compliments* produces roasted carob powder and dairy-free malt-sweetened carob morsels.

CORN

Corn is not new to most kitchens. Many of the products made from corn are in pantries, refrigerators, and freezers across the country. However, thinking of it as a grain doesn't occur to many folks. In fact, if asked what type of food corn is,

they would answer that it is a vegetable.

There are many corn products on the market which provide many foods eaten in a variety of dishes, snacks, and desserts.

CORN ANATOMY

Corn kernels are attached to a corn cob and, unlike many grains, the outer hull is edible. An "ear" of corn consists of a corn cob, corn kernels attached in neat rows, and a husk, lined with corn silk, that covers the whole thing. The leafy husk is easily peeled away from the kernels. Corn can be purchased fresh on the cob with the protective husk or it can be cut from the cob and canned or frozen.

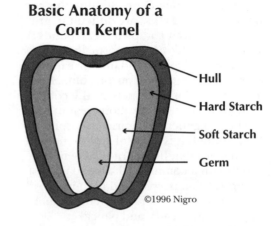

Basic Anatomy of a Corn Kernel

Hull

Hard Starch

Soft Starch

Germ

©1996 Nigro

VARIETIES

Corn comes in different varieties, with most of them ranging in color from white to yellow with multicolored in between. Multicolored corn has white and yellow kernels on the same ear of corn. White kernels are identical to yellow ones with the exception of their color and the fact that white kernels do not contain vitamin A while yellow kernels do.

Sweet Corn: This is the type of corn that people envision when they think of corn. It is what is available in supermarkets fresh on the cob or cut from the cob and canned or frozen. It has a higher sugar content than any of the other types of corn or grains. It is not a good idea to dry this variety and grind it into a meal.

Popcorn: This strain of corn is an exploding grain. The famous popcorn kernels have a small amount of moisture in them that causes the kernels to explode when heated. If your popcorn is not popping well, restore some moisture to the grain by soaking it for a few minutes in warm water and then draining it. When eaten without salt and high-fat toppings such as butter, popcorn is low in calories and high in fiber and can be eaten to your heart's content. One small drawback, however, is that little hulls can get lodged in the gums between the teeth and if they are not removed may cause some trouble and a trip to the dentist.

Flint or Indian Corn: Because this corn has hard kernels that are difficult to grind (the hard starch completely surrounds the soft starch), this corn is normally used for decorative purposes and not for eating. It comes in orange, red, purple, blue, black, and multi-colored kernels on the cob. Hang it in strategic locations around the kitchen to generate a warm atmosphere. Even though it is colorful and thought of as a decoration, flint corn is sometimes ground on a commercial basis to make a cornmeal that is sweet and high in protein. This cornmeal is excellent for making muffins, breads, and pancakes.

Dent or Field Corn: Dent corn kernels get a dent in their tops when dried because the interior soft starch extends all the way to the top of the corn and shrinks more than the surrounding hard starch. This type of corn is used as animal feed as well as in commercial products such as cornmeal, corn syrup, cornstarch, and breakfast flakes.

Flour Corn: This corn is very easy to grind into meal and flour because its starch is almost all soft. In general, flour corn is not available in whole kernel form.

The varieties of corn may be processed into different grain products. See the discussion in "Grains" under the "Milled & Processed Grains" subsection for more information.

Cornmeal: Cornmeal is much coarser than grain flours. It is normally milled from dried dent corn and can be white, yellow, or blue. Yellow and white cornmeal can be used interchangeably when the color is not an issue.

Cornmeal is famous for its corn bread, polenta, muffins, and mush. It is great for baking other goodies and as a breading for vegetables and meats. Cornmeal is used in many commercial products such as pancake and baking mixes, tortilla chips, corn chips, etc.

Cornmeal has a high oil content and can become rancid rather quickly. So purchase it in quantities that you can consume in a couple of weeks or buy it in larger quantities and freeze it.

There are a few special types of cornmeal that may be found on health food store shelves:

Blue Cornmeal: This cornmeal is slightly sweeter and nuttier and has more starch, protein, manganese, and potassium than the white or yellow. Blue cornmeal is denser than the others and can make a dish look purplish-gray. When used to make light, fluffy baked goods such as pancakes, blue cornmeal is often mixed with wheat flour to counteract the cornmeal's denseness.

High-Lysine Cornmeal: Some corn strains have been genetically engineered to produce a kernel that has more of the lysine amino acid. This corn has a sweet, nutty flavor with a crunchy texture and is ground into "high-lysine" cornmeal. This new type of cornmeal can be used in the same fashion as any other cornmeal.

Degerminated Cornmeal: This cornmeal is ground from corn that has had its oil and nutrient-rich germ removed. Although this extends the shelf life of the cornmeal, it has lost much of its character and is bland flavored. To return some of the nutritional value to degerminated cornmeal, often B-complex vitamins and iron are added to it.

Corn Flour: This is dent or flour corn that has been ground finer than cornmeal. It has a corny and sweet flavor and is typically yellow in color. Although it is not commonly used and may be difficult to find, corn flour can be used to add color to batters for muffins, cookies, pastries, and cakes. This flour produces drier and more crumbly baked goods. It may also be produced in high-lysine and degerminated forms (see the discussion in "Cornmeal").

Hominy: This corn product is the starch remaining when the hulls and germ are removed. The hominy is then dried or canned. Hominy is available more in the South, and Southwestern and Hispanic markets may sometimes carry it in cans. Hominy is also called posole. When cooked, hominy has a texture and consistency that is very similar to beans. Hominy can be used to make hearty breakfast side dishes, enchiladas, griddle cakes, soups, and stews.

Grits: Grits are dried hominy or whole corn that has been ground. They are available in fine, medium, and coarse grinds and come in white or yellow colors. They are popular for making hot cereal or a breakfast side dish topped with a pat of butter or gravy and are welcome in baked goods, breads, casseroles, burgers, loaves, and soufflés. Grits are particularly at home in Southern cuisines; however, they are enjoyable when served in any part of the country.

Corn Syrup: Corn syrup is an inexpensive mild sweetener ranging in color from very pale, almost white, to light brown. The darker varieties have had molasses or cane syrup added to increase their sweetness and flavor. See "Sweeteners" for more information.

Cornstarch: Cornstarch is a refined thickener that gives creamier, smoother results than flour. See "Thickeners" for more information.

FLAVOR/TEXTURE

Fresh sweet corn will have a mellow, sweet, and non-starchy flavor and a juicy texture. Cornmeal has a mild, corn flavor and produces a crunchy, crumbly texture in baked goods. Cooked cornmeal and corn grits can have a gritty texture and starchy, corn flavor that can be appealing in some dishes. Much of the corn flavor is absent in hominy and hominy grits.

Instead they have a very strong starchy flavor and a slight aftertaste that may not be appropriate for every dish.

GENERAL USES

First and foremost, corn is absolutely delicious when eaten just as is, as corn on the cob with butter, margarine, or umeboshi paste and a little pepper. It is great fun to crunch down the rows of sweet, juicy corn, only pausing and coming up for air when you need to.

NIGRO TIP

When eating fresh corn on the cob, have a toothpick or dental floss handy. A great deal of goodies (corn "skins" or hulls, corn silk, and/or bits of cornstarch and germ) inevitably will get stuck between your teeth.

Sweet corn goes with many vegetables, meats, poultry, other grains, and some beans. Since corn is quite starchy it needs some creativity to go well with potatoes, pasta, or rice when they are the major ingredients. For example, a heavenly, creamy corn chowder can be made by cooking corn with potatoes, onion, vegetable stock, salt, pepper, milk or non-dairy milk, and any thickening agent to obtain the desired consistency. Of course, green peppers, celery, carrot, basil, mushrooms, bay leaf, and vinegar are just a few other ingredients that can be added to the chowder.

Since cornmeal is mild in flavor it can be used with many of the other grains to make wonderful and different textured baked goods and cookies. Try adding cornmeal to your favorite pancake recipe by substituting up to half of the flour with cornmeal to produce a hearty texture.

Make a rich corn à la king to serve over toasted biscuits by sautéing corn, onions, bell peppers, and pimentos in white wine and then adding non-dairy milk, salt, black or cayenne pepper, and flour (oat, wheat, millet, etc.) for thickening. Heat until thick and serve topped with roasted sesame seeds or pecans.

Perfect for a potluck dinner, easy to make, and great tasting, a salad can be made by tossing together cooked corn (preferably cut from the cob), all colors of bell peppers, scallions, turmeric, oregano, green olives with pimento stuffings, cilantro, paprika, and black pepper with a miso, mustard, wine, and vinegar dressing. Be sure to refrigerate a few hours before serving.

Corn has unique characteristics and there are no real substitutes for it. None of the other grains looks, acts, or tastes similar to corn. Frozen corn can be substituted for fresh whenever necessary, and blue, yellow, or white corn products can be used interchangeably.

FRESHNESS/QUALITY

Purchasing fresh corn on the cob still in its husks provides all the nutrients the grain has to offer. It stores its carbohydrates as sugars, which turn to starch as the ear ages. Corn is the ultimate in fresh, and tastes the best, when you get a pot of water boiling and go out into the garden and pick slightly immature ears, then run into the kitchen, remove the husks and silk and throw the corn into the boiling water. Since, this is not an option for most of us, the ears of corn we buy should have vibrant, moist silk; bright green, compact husks; and firm, full kernels. These kernels should be plump and large, even at the tip of the cob. If the flavor is starchy and tasteless, or the kernels are withered or dry at the tip, it has lost its freshness.

STORAGE

In order to slow down the aging process that turns the sugar in corn into starch, keep the husk on the cob until just before using.

It is easy to remove the kernels from fresh ears of corn (see the "Preparation Instructions" subsection) and then bag, label, and freeze them for storage in conveniently sized packages.

PREPARATION INSTRUCTIONS

CLEANING

Fresh ears of corn will need to have their husks and silk removed before eating. This process is known as shucking an ear of corn. After shucking, a brief rinsing is perfectly okay to help remove any of the remaining silk that has stuck to the corn. A soft brush really helps to dislodge the stubborn silk.

It is not always necessary to remove the husks before cooking; sometimes the corn is cooked in its own husk. However, you may wish to peel back the husk (leaving it attached to the base of the cob) and remove the silk, cut away bad spots, and inspect the corn for worm holes, insects, and debris. When the corn has been cleaned to your liking, fold the husk back over the cob.

COOKING

Cooking corn on the cob is easy and absolutely delicious. There are several ways to prepare the corn and we will only discuss two here.

For 3 to 8 minutes, boil cleaned and shucked corn ears in enough salted water to cover (the ears will float if they can). The cooking time depends on the size and freshness of the corn. Smaller and fresher corn ears take less time to cook. Do not overcook the corn, because if you do, it will become starchy and lose some of its tastiness. The corn can be boiled in water that has also been flavored with milk, sugar, and/or spices.

Cooking corn in the microwave is another useful method for cooking a few ears of corn. It involves cooking the corn in its husk (see the "Cleaning" subsection for information on cleaning ears of corn while keeping the husk on). Note that  while you have the husk peeled back, you may wish to put seasonings, spices, or condiments on the corn such as butter, pepper, or umeboshi plum paste. Replace the husk and microwave on high for 3 minutes per ear of corn. Turn the ears over and microwave on high for another 2 minutes per ear. Test the corn for doneness and continue to microwave, if needed.

It is easy to remove kernels from fresh ears of corn. Scald the ears of corn by lowering them into boiling water, cover, and cook for 2 to 6 minutes depending on the size of the ears. Cool and cut the kernels from the cob with a sharp knife or special tool designed for this task. Fresh corn kernels should come away from the cob rather easily.

Grits are cooked in the same manner as any cracked grain. To make approximately four and a half cups of cooked hominy grits, five cups of water per cup of grits is a good starting point and the cooking time will range between 20 and 25 minutes. If cooking corn grits, less water is needed (3 1/2 to 4 cups) and more cooking time is required (40 to 50 minutes). See "Grains" for information about the stove-top method of cooking grains and various cooking issues.

HEALTH INFORMATION

Yellow corn supplies a bit of vitamin A and all corn varieties have some protein, B vitamins, iron, and calcium. Because corn is low in the essential amino acids tryptophan and lysine, it is often served with, or cooked in dishes containing, foods that have these amino acids (such as beans).

ADDITIONAL READING

See "Grains" for books that discuss grains and have grain recipes. A book that is exclusively devoted to corn is:

Woodier, Olwen. *Corn: Meals & More.*

BUYING SOURCES

Sweet corn kernels are available frozen, canned, and fresh on the cob in supermarkets. Fresh corn on the cob is tastiest when bought between June and September because these are the peak harvesting months for corn.

Yellow or white cornmeal, corn syrup, cornstarch, popcorn, and quick-cooking or regular hominy grits are available in most supermarkets. Hominy is usually available in the South and is also typically available in Hispanic markets. Corn grits, blue cornmeal, and blue popcorn are usually found in health food and natural foods stores as well as specialty markets.

Dried corn, cornmeal, flour, and grits, and popcorn are generally available through grain mail order sources, see "Grains" for a list.

BRAND NAMES

There are many producers of frozen and canned corn, as well as the prepackaged corn products. Read labels carefully to be sure that the can, bag, box, or bottle contains exactly what you want it to.

DAIKON

(DIE kon) or (DAH ee kon)

A daikon is like a bunch of radishes that are compressed into something that looks like a giant white carrot. Though a daikon's qualities are similar to a fresh radish, its flavor is milder. It can measure from 1 to 4 inches in diameter and be up to a foot long.

VARIETIES

Raw Daikon Root: The texture and flavor of raw daikon is similar to small red radishes. When daikon is cooked, it becomes very tender and juicy and its spicy flavor is transformed to sweetness.

Pickled Daikon Root: The flavor and texture of pickled daikon depends on the manufacturer and the pickling agent. These succulent pickles are often amber in color. Try a few pickles with your meals to experience a snappy "zing."

Dried Daikon Root: When daikon root is shredded and sun dried, it produces a very sweet flavor. It transmits its subtle essence when added to your favorite soups, stews, sea vegetables, beans, rice, and vegetables.

Daikon Greens: The greens of daikon roots are perfectly suited for salads and make a fabulous steamed vegetable.

OTHER NAMES

Mooli, white radish, Japanese radish, takuan (pickled daikon), kiriboshi (dried daikon).

FLAVOR/TEXTURE

The flavor and texture of fresh daikon is similar to a radish and when cooked it becomes sweet. Dried daikon is also sweet and has a mellow flavor and a chewy texture. Fresh daikon greens are slightly sharp and pungent.

GENERAL USES

Daikon can be used in a manner similar to that of radishes or carrots, in salads, sandwiches, stews, and soups. Use grated raw daikon as a garnish and to counteract the oiliness of deep-fried dishes such as tempura, fritters, and onion rings.

There are many ways to cut daikon. Slices (also called rounds) are often used in general cooking and soups, julienne strips are used in salads and stir-fries, and grated daikon is used as a topping and condiment.

Daikon can be sautéed, steamed, boiled, and fried. Cook it alone or with other vegetables, or eat it raw. Simply sauté sliced or shredded daikon with a little roasted sesame oil and sherry to make a succulent addition to spinach or any other greens. Or toss the sautéed daikon in a grain or pasta dish. Make a delicious side dish by cooking sliced daikon rounds with tamari soy sauce and tossing with toasted almonds.

Boiled daikon rounds go well with spicy, hot sauces. Try blending sesame seeds, a light miso, honey or mirin, powdered mustard, and a little water to create a tangy sauce. The contrasting hot and sweet flavors are delightful.

Dried daikon is an excellent ingredient for salads and sandwiches. It can also be sautéed with vegetables or cooked in stir-fries or rehydrated in stews and soups.

Daikon greens add flavor, color, and nutrition to soups, salads, and sandwiches. Use them anywhere you would use spinach or collard greens. Prepare a healthy stir-fry by sautéing cooked daikon greens, onions, and garlic in olive oil and then tossing with noodles and fried tofu or browned chicken.

FRESHNESS/QUALITY

Fresh daikon roots should be firm, crisp, unwrinkled, and heavy for their size. Limp roots are past their prime.

Quality dried daikon is made by a traditional method. Basically, fresh daikon root is shredded and then allowed to dry thoroughly in a winter sun. Check the label for the drying process used.

The finest pickled takuan daikon is fermented in earthen crocks with rice bran, salt, and sometimes koji. High quality tamari daikon is pickled with organic tamari soy sauce and moromi.

STORAGE

Fresh daikon should be refrigerated and will keep for 10 days. However, use grated fresh daikon immediately to prevent loss of crispness and nutrients.

Before opening, pickled daikon can be kept unrefrigerated, until the date imprinted on the package. Once opened, place it in a sealable glass jar and refrigerate. It should last for months.

PREPARATION INSTRUCTIONS

Cleaning

Quickly rinse fresh daikon. Daikon may be peeled, but this is optional.

Soaking

Dried daikon can be soaked; however, it is not always required. If you are planning to sauté or pickle dried daikon, soak it in lukewarm water for 30 to 60 minutes. After soaking it, squeeze out any excess water, chop, and add it to your dish. When using dried daikon with other preparation methods (including not cooking at all), soaking is optional.

Cooking

Use cooked fresh daikon like carrots, turnips, or potatoes. It can be eaten when slightly crunchy but it yields its sweetest flavor when completely tender.

To make a fresh raw grated daikon garnish, use a fine grater and squeeze out any excess water.

Daikon greens are slightly tough and can be softened by cooking for 15 or more minutes with a little diluted miso or tamari soy sauce.

HEALTH INFORMATION

Folk healers and scientists alike have noted the remarkable nutritional and medicinal qualities of raw and pickled daikon. Fresh raw daikon contains diuretics, decongestants, digestive enzymes, and phenolic compounds that inhibit the formation of carcinogens in the body. The digestive enzymes help transform complex carbohydrates, fats, and proteins into their readily absorbable components. In fact, daikon has been called a fat burner.

Pickled daikon made with koji is especially high in lactobacilli and niacin. It contains linoleic acid and is said to be effective in reducing blood cholesterol.

This amazing root may be considered to be calorie-free, so you can eat it to your heart's content.

ADDITIONAL READING

Kushi, Aveline. *Complete Guide to Macrobiotic Cooking.*

Downer, Lesley. *Japanese Vegetarian Cooking.*

BUYING SOURCES

Fresh daikon is available year-round. Daikon is typically found in Oriental food stores, Chinese and Indian shops, and is commonly found in the produce sections of health and natural food stores and supermarkets. Dried and pickled daikon are available through the Anzen Oriental Foods & Imports, Gold Mine Natural Foods, Mountain Ark Trading Company, Natural Lifestyle, and Harvest Time Natural Foods mail order companies.

BRAND NAMES

Mitoku *Pickled Daikon Radish* and Eden *Pickled Daikon Radish* are excellent brands of pickled daikon; and superior brands of dried daikon are Ohsawa® *Organic Sun-Dried Shredded Daikon* and Eden *Shredded Daikon Radish.*

DULSE

Present on every table and in every spice rack there is a condiment known as "salt." Ground dulse should be right alongside the salt because it's a great nutritional, healthy alternative to salt.

This purple-red sea vegetable is not only available as a condiment, but also may be purchased in large dried pieces. When rehydrated, dulse has a soft and delicate texture.

FLAVOR/TEXTURE

Though moderate in flavor compared to most other sea vegetables, dulse has a uniquely spicy flavor which adds zest to many dishes.

Dulse tastes rather salty; however, it is low in sodium. The high content of potassium, magnesium, calcium, phosphorous, iron and iodine, produces the salty taste. You may find that using additional salt is unnecessary when you are cooking with this sea vegetable.

GENERAL USES

Dulse is used as an addition to vegetable and grain dishes, as a condiment, and as a snack.

Having a unique and delicious flavor, dried dulse is a perfect ingredient in relishes, oatmeal, salad dressings, soups, and breads. It combines well with onions and complements oats and other cooked grains. Straight out of the package or soaked, dulse makes a colorful and healthy addition to a variety of salads.

NIGRO TIP

A scrumptious D.L.T. (Dulse-Lettuce-Tomato) sandwich can be created by pan-frying some dried dulse in olive oil and using it instead of bacon. We like to put fried dulse on a cucumber, onion, sprouts, and mustard sandwich, too.

Dry-roasted and crushed dulse makes a flavorful condiment that can be sprinkled on salads, soups, vegetables, pasta, or popcorn. It can also be added to breads and casseroles, or steeped to make a tea. Dulse is especially good with any potato or cheese dish.

Many dulse-lovers snack on the dried sea vegetable just as it comes from the bag. You better watch it though—you can become addicted to this marvelous, great-tasting, healthy stuff!

FRESHNESS/QUALITY

Although dulse itself is low in sodium, some producers package it with a fine dusting of salt crystals coating the dulse. See "Sea Vegetables (Dried)."

STORAGE

See "Sea Vegetables (Dried)."

PREPARATION INSTRUCTIONS

WASHING & SOAKING

Dulse does not require washing or soaking but should be inspected for tiny seashells and salt crystals. However, washing and soaking a few minutes does reduce its saltiness.

If you want to soften the dulse to the point where it will easily dissolve in a dish or melt in your mouth if you eat it directly, soak it for an hour or more.

COOKING

Dulse may be toasted by dry roasting it in a 275°F oven for 5 to 10 minutes.

To make dulse into a condiment, it is first dry roasted. Then it is crushed or ground into a powder with a blender, suribachi, or spice/coffee grinder.

Dulse may also be sautéed or deep-fried. To sauté or pan-fry dulse, place a piece of dried dulse in a well-oiled hot skillet and "straighten" the piece as it momentarily softens while it absorbs some oil. Cook for 10 to 30 seconds until it turns green-yellow and is very crisp (if it starts to turn brown or black, you're burning it; shorten the cooking time or reduce the temperature). Place the finished piece of dulse on a plate covered with paper towels and, with another paper towel, gently pat the dulse to remove excess oil. If the skillet needs more oil (there needs to be enough to almost cover the next piece of dried dulse you want to fry), add it and let it heat for a few seconds. Then fry the next piece of dried dulse. Cooked in this fashion, dulse will be rather high in fat content due to the oil it has absorbed. Fried dulse makes a great chip, topping or condiment, or a crispy alternative to bacon in sandwiches and salads (especially spinach and romaine lettuce salads).

HEALTH INFORMATION

Of all the sea vegetables, dulse is the richest in iron. It also contains an abundance of potassium, magnesium, iodine, phosphorus, protein, chlorophyll, enzymes, and vitamins A and B. After nori, dulse has the highest protein content of any common sea vegetable. See "Sea Vegetables (Dried)" for a nutritional composition comparison.

BUYING SOURCES

Dried dulse is available in health food stores and through mail order companies. See "Sea Vegetables (Dried)" for a list of mail order sources.

BRAND NAMES

Maine Coast Sea Vegetables *Dulse*.

GARBANZO BEANS

(gar BON zoh) (beans)

Frequently, our dinner guests have commented on how wonderful the upcoming chicken dinner smelled. They seemed very delighted by the prospect of chicken, which put us on the spot because we had to tell them that what they were smelling was not chicken, but chick peas (garbanzo beans).

A garbanzo bean doesn't look anything like a chicken; in fact, it is a medium to small round bean approximately 3/8 inches in diameter. It is tan or buff in color and somewhat wrinkled.

OTHER NAMES

Chick peas.

FLAVOR/TEXTURE

Garbanzos have a rich, full, nutty flavor similar to chestnuts. The taste of garbanzo beans is only slightly reminiscent of chicken; however, the smell seems to be dead on.

GENERAL USES

Blended garbanzos are used to make a famous dish known as hummus. It is a great spread for sandwiches, bagels or toast, and makes a delightful dip for fresh vegetables or crackers.

These beans are wonderful as additions to soups and casseroles. A savory soup can be made by combining cooked garbanzos with a green leafy vegetable (kale, mustard greens, chard, or spinach), tomato sauce, short pasta, other tasty vegetables (carrots, onion, corn, snow peas, etc.), other beans, salt, pepper, and garlic cloves.

Garbanzo beans are also commonly used in cold salads since they retain their shape well after cooking. Toss cooked garbanzos with a vinaigrette or with olive oil and garlic and refrigerate to make a refreshing summer dish. Or, mix the beans with unrefined sesame oil, lightly cooked vegetables, artichoke hearts, and black olives.

FRESHNESS/QUALITY

See "Beans."

STORAGE

See "Beans."

PREPARATION INSTRUCTIONS

CLEANING AND SOAKING

See "Beans."

COOKING

See "Beans" for instructions. The approximate stove-top cooking time is 1 to 1 1/2 hours, and the pressure cooking time is 20 minutes. One cup dried yields approximately 2 1/2 cups cooked.

HEALTH INFORMATION

Garbanzo beans are rich in protein, calcium, iron, and the B group vitamins.

ADDITIONAL READING

See "Beans."

BUYING SOURCES

Dried garbanzo beans can be found in health food stores and supermarkets in dried (bulk or prepackaged) or canned forms. They are also available through mail order. See "Beans" for a list of mail order sources and brand names.

GINGER ROOT

(JIN jer) (root)

Once you have discovered the wonderful and unique flavor that ginger root can add to your cooking, you will want to have this strange looking root in your refrigerator on a regular basis.

Ginger root is an irregularly shaped root that has a pale brownish or pinkish tinged skin. Beneath the skin is the pale-yellow, firm flesh that can liven up almost any dish.

VARIETIES

Ginger root is available fresh, sliced and pickled (sometimes called *sushi ginger*), and dried and ground.

FLAVOR/TEXTURE

The flavor of ginger root is refreshing and quite strong, and has a spicy, citrus taste. The smaller knobs that are attached to the main root have a more delicate flavor.

GENERAL USES

Ginger root can be grated, juiced, minced, sliced, or dried. Ginger root adds zing to beverages, salads, preserves, pickles, vegetables, sea vegetables, fruits, baked goods, and desserts. In other words, ginger root can add a delightful flavor to almost anything. However, ginger is especially good when added to sweet potatoes, winter squash, carrots, beets, pumpkin, rhubarb, peaches, apricots, and beef.

A small amount of grated ginger, approximately 1/4 teaspoon for four to six people, adds zest when it is sprinkled raw on top of a grain, noodle, or vegetable dish.

Ginger juice is very strong since it is more concentrated than grated ginger.

You probably won't find ginger juice on the shelf of your favorite supermarket or health food store. Because it is wonderful in soups, broths, beverages, and salad dressings, you might like to have some on hand. It's easy to make; just grate the ginger root and then, with your fingers, squeeze out the juice. Be careful, though, as this is strong stuff. About 1/4 teaspoon of ginger juice equals the strength of 1 teaspoon of grated ginger.

Sauté minced ginger root with onions and garlic to make a great foundation for many sauces, soups, or stir-fries. Minced ginger root also adds a new flavor dimension when added to marinades.

Sliced ginger root can be pickled itself or used as an ingredient in recipes that pickle other foods. Pickled ginger is used as a condiment or colorful garnish. The piquant flavor of pickled ginger complements fried vegetables, tempura, fish, tofu, and tempeh.

Ground dried ginger root can be used to enhance sweet puddings, quick breads, muffins, cakes, and cookies.

A cup of ginger tea is warming and invigorating. It hits the spot on a cold winter day and is a great "pick-me-up" on a crisp spring or fall afternoon. To make this ginger root tea, pour one pint of boiling water over 1 oz. of the grated root and steep for 5 to 10 minutes.

FRESHNESS/QUALITY

You can tell when ginger root is fresh by looking at it, giving it a gentle squeeze, and smelling it. Ginger root should look plump (not shriveled) and the skin should look shiny. It should also feel firm and smell like ginger. If it is soft or spongy, or doesn't have much of a smell, the ginger root is not fresh.

STORAGE

Ginger root can be stored in a cool, dry place for up to one month. Ideally, if you have a small box of sand, stick your uncut ginger root in that!

Once cut, ginger root should be stored in the refrigerator in a paper bag, or wrapped in a paper towel and placed in an airtight container. Storing it in this fashion will keep it fresh for a week or so. If you'd like to store it for up to a year, peel it, slice it, and submerge it in dry sherry in an airtight container in the refrigerator.

PREPARATION INSTRUCTIONS

COOKING

Since the skin is very fibrous, many prefer to peel the skin before grating, mincing, slicing, or drying the ginger root. However, this is not required.

If you wish to substitute fresh ginger root for dried ground ginger spice, use 1 tablespoon of grated fresh ginger root per 1/2 teaspoon of the ground ginger (i.e., multiply the called-for amount by six).

To maximize ginger root's flavor, add it at the very end of cooking and simmer it with the recipe's other ingredients for a minute or less before serving.

HEALTH INFORMATION

One quarter cup of fresh raw ginger root has only 17 calories and contains some vitamin C and potassium.

Ginger root is used as a folk remedy to improve digestion and to combat motion sickness. It is also a mild stimulant that promotes circulation and stimulates the appetite.

ADDITIONAL READING

Cost, Bruce. *Ginger East to West.*

BUYING SOURCES

Ginger root can be found in the produce section of most supermarkets, health and natural foods stores, Oriental and specialty food shops, and produce or farmer's markets.

In addition, pickled ginger root is also available through the Harvest Time Natural Foods, Natural Lifestyle, and Gold Mine Natural Food mail order companies.

BRAND NAMES

There are quite a few quality producers of pickled ginger root: Try Mitoku *Sushi Ginger*, Ohsawa® *Oindo Organic Sushi Ginger Pickle*, and Eden *Pickled Ginger*.

GRAINS

Have you ever been surprised, then pleasantly surprised, then agreeably surprised, then favorably surprised, then delightfully surprised, then fabulously surprised... each surprise better than the last and adding so much to the day that you almost can't stand it? This is what could be in store for you as you discover the potential of grains. It is amazing how such a simple food can provide such a banquet of wonders with a variety of flavors, textures, and colors.

Grains are the edible seeds of cereal grasses. They can range from the size of a poppy seed to very slender and long (up to an inch). They can be white, gray, red, brown, yellow, blue, and black in color.

GRAIN ANATOMY

First, a little biology lesson. You need to know this to understand the nutritional value and other important stuff about grains. Trust us. It'll help you make an informed choice about the types of grains that you'll want to use in your cooking. Since this book is only focusing on culinary aspects, the discussion of the structure of grain kernels also concentrates on issues that are significant to the palate and health.

Basic Anatomy of a Grain Kernel

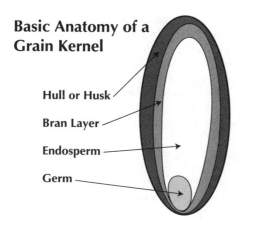

Hull or Husk

Bran Layer

Endosperm

Germ

Grain: In culinary terms, the word "grain" refers to the small, dry, edible one-seed fruit or "kernel" of cereal grasses. In general, a grain kernel is made up of four parts:

Husk or Hull: The husk or hull is the shell or outer covering that is inedible and considered worthless for human consumption. This shell provides a framework that serves to support the seed. Interestingly, there are some grains that do not have a husk or hull. Of those that do, some cling for dear life (such as barley) and must be removed by harsh methods and other grains (such as wheat) have husks or hulls that are removed simply and easily by threshing (beating the plant till the seeds loosen from their husks). Since the husks or hulls are not considered usable, the term "whole grain" refers to the grain that has had its hull removed (also called "hulled") but still has its bran, endosperm, and germ intact.

Bran: The bran is the tough, layered, protective covering of the seed just under the husk or hull. It is rich in B vitamins, minerals, and dietary fiber. The process of pearling or polishing removes the bran from a grain kernel, giving the grain a much lighter color. Many commercial flours are made from grains that have had their bran removed to make the flour look cleaner.

Endosperm: The endosperm is the nutritive, starchy mass in the center of the grain. This is the largest part of a grain kernel. Its purpose is to provide food for the baby plant once it has sprouted. Hence, if the endosperm is eaten, it will provide carbohydrates and valuable nutrition to the consumer as well.

Germ: The germ is the seed embryo. In essence, the germ is the baby plant that will sprout and grow when the seed germinates. It is rich in protein and fat, and contains some vitamins and minerals. In addition to removing the bran, the pearling or polishing removes the germ as well. Most commercial flours are ground from grains that have had their germ removed to extend the shelf-life of the flour. The fat content of the germ can cause the flour to become rancid.

MILLED & PROCESSED GRAINS

Grains with inedible husks or hulls, or very tough bran layers, require some degree of processing in order to use them. Oats, barely, rice, and wild rice must have their hard protective husks removed. Corn, wheat, and rye are processed to remove the tough bran layers; this quickens their cooking time and makes them easier to chew.

Grain milling is the process of separating the different parts of the grain. There are different types of processing techniques. Depending on how much bran and germ are removed, the processing produces an "unrefined" (also called "whole") or "refined" product. Many grain products are classified according to the milling and processing methods used to obtain them.

Whole-Grain (Hulled): These are grains that have had the inedible outer layer removed. The grain retains all of its other parts: bran, endosperm, and germ. Hulled grains can also be called whole grains, groats, or berries. This type of grain is considered to be "unrefined." It is more nutritious and digestible than many of the refined grain products.

Whole grains will keep fresher longer than the more refined grain products. They will last up to a year or so, but it is a good idea to use them within seven to nine months.

Steel Cut: This grain product is produced by cutting up whole groats with steel cutting machines. Steel cut grains contain all of the bran and germ of whole grains—making them a nutritional, chewy, and wholesome food. They are sensational when used to make a hearty, hot breakfast cereal. They can also be used as a meat extender and in baked goods to add a robust, chewy texture.

Grits or Cracked: Cracked grains, also called grits, are made by cracking or coarsely grinding whole or polished grains. If the whole grain was used, as is often the case for wheat and rye, the cracked grain product will contain bran and germ. Cracked grains cook quicker than whole grains. They will keep for several months.

Pearled or Polished: Pearled or polished grains have been scraped with an abrasive stone to remove the bran and germ from the endosperm, subsequently considerably lowering the nutritional value of the grain. In those cases where the husks or hulls cling tightly to the kernel, it may be necessary to pearl the grain to ensure that the husk is removed. In other cases, polishing is performed to transform the grain into a smooth product that has a lustrous finish resembling the color of a pearl. Polished grains cook faster and are softer than their whole grain counterparts.

Flakes (Rolled): Steamed and toasted whole grains of barley, oats, wheat, and rye can be rolled to produce thick flakes (called *grain flakes*) or thinner flakes (called *rolled grains*). In most instances, the distinction between rolled grains and grain flakes is not made and these terms are used interchangeably. Because this grain product has been squashed flat and its surface area has been increased, it cooks more quickly than whole grains.

Grain flakes can be used as a hot cereal or toasted and used as a thickening agent in soups, stews, and baked goods. For instance, barley and wheat flakes make a chewy breakfast cereal that is a nice change from oatmeal on a cold winter morning. For a delicious treat, try stirring in one-half cup of diced mixed dried fruit for the last five minutes of cooking. Then serve with fresh sunflower seed milk and accent with ground walnuts on top. Often, rolled grains are also used to make granolas and trail mixes.

Puffed: Puffed grains are cooked grains that are filled with air. They are commonly used in cold breakfast cereals, muesli, trail mixes and dessert recipes.

Meal and Flour (Ground): Meal and flour are made by grinding grains. Meal is coarsely ground and flour is finely ground. Meals and flours can be ground from whole grains or just part of the grains, such the endosperms. Whole grain flour will have a coarser texture, darker color, higher nutritional value, and shorter shelf life than flour ground from polished grains.

Grains are ground using stone mills or steel mills. Stone mill grinding is gentler and can produce a more precise grind, often leaving the oil rich germ intact. These flours are less likely to become rancid. The term "stone ground" is used to indicate that a flour was ground using a stone mill.

Normally, stone ground flours and meals are more expensive than steel ground ones. Steel mills grind the grain between steel rollers which generate heat. High heat can cause the oil in the germ and bran to go rancid more quickly and reduce the shelf life of the flour. To prevent this, the bran and germ are often removed, leaving only the endosperm to be ground. Sometimes, bran and germ are added back to the ground flour to enrich it again.

Flours are used for baking breads, cakes, crackers, biscuits, desserts, etc. When baking bread, or any other item that should be light and airy, gluten needs to be present in the dough to cause it to rise and be light. Wheat, kamut, and spelt have the most gluten; rye, barley, triticale, and oats have some gluten; and buckwheat, rice, millet, quinoa, and corn are essentially gluten-free. If you want to make a loaf of leavened bread using non- or low-glutenous grains (such as rye bread), 70% or more of the flour used should be high-gluten flour.

Try grinding your own flours. If you have a good blender, food processor, or home grain mill, grains can be ground down to produce a wonderful, hearty, nutritious, rich flour. Note that if you are grinding flakes or soft whole grains (such as oats), a nut grinder or coffee mill will work as well. Home ground flour will be much fresher and a bit coarser than commercial flour. Grinding grains will heat the flour quite a bit. If the flour is to be used in leavened breads, allow it to cool before using so the yeast will not be destroyed. Grind only the amount that is needed for the recipe; the heat generated by the grinding process will cause the oils in the germ and bran to go rancid quick-

ly. If a fine flour is desired, sift the fresh ground grain to remove any of the larger grain pieces. Of course, the large grain pieces left in the sifter can be ground and sifted again. Because bran is tough and difficult to grind down into very small pieces, sifting will reduce the amount of bran in a flour. However, the bran can be saved and put to good use in other dishes. Just collect the bits of grain remaining in the sifter after the final sifting.

Roasting flours before using them gives them a rich flavor. In half or one-cup increments, continuously stir the flour around a dry (not oiled) skillet over a medium heat. When the flour begins to smell nutty, it is finished.

Flour normally will last a few months in a cool place and can last longer if refrigerated. When a flour smells quite strong and sour, it has become rancid and should be thrown away.

Pasta: Pastas are made from a dough that is formed into shapes and dried. The dough is made from water and flour with spices, and salt, with eggs often included as well. This common food is cooked by boiling and it is the main ingredient used in many recipes. See "Pasta" for additional information.

Bran: Bran can be purchased and used to add nutrients (B vitamins and minerals) and fiber to other dishes. It is often thought of as a food supplement; however, it is actually a natural product that is eaten after being separated from its host grain. Bran can be roasted and sprinkled on top of cereal or baked into muffins and breads. It provides a nutty, almost sweet flavor with a crunchy texture. See the "Grain Anatomy" subsection for more information about bran.

Germ: Wheat germ is another product that is considered by many to be a food supplement. It is beneficial in diets that use mainly white flour products to satisfy the body's requirement for grains. Germ is the embryo of the grain and contains many nutrients, protein, iron, and, excluding B_{12}, all of the other B-complex vitamins. Because germ contains oil, it can become rancid easily. It is best to keep it refrigerated. Grain germ can be roasted to enhance its flavor. The aroma of roasting germ is heady and permeates the whole house. See the "Grain Anatomy" subsection for more information.

VARIETIES

Grains may be broken down into two main categories: bread and dish grains.

Bread Grains: Bread grains are mainly ground into meal or flour and are used to make doughs for bread, pastries, crackers, pasta, dumplings, chips, cakes, cereals, etc. However, they may also be cooked whole for inclusion in many dishes. They are tougher, chewier, and take a longer time to cook than dish grains. Often, bread grains are used whole in soups, stews, casseroles, and other dishes that have long cooking times. Combining bread grains with dish grains can make a memorable, robust, and hearty dish with a chewy texture. The grains that fall squarely into the bread grain category are wheat, rye, and barley. These are discussed briefly later in this subsection.

Dish Grains: These grains make wonderful "single-grain" dishes when whole, cracked, or rolled forms of the grain are cooked. Of course, they are also delightful when combined with other grains or used as an accent in other types of dishes (such as soups, salads, casseroles, and burritos). Furthermore, these grains can be ground into flour or meal and added to flour mixes that consist primarily of bread grains. The grains that belong to the dish grain category are millet, buckwheat, quinoa, oats, rice, and wild rice. These are discussed briefly later in this section.

Corn is a special case because it can be used as both a bread and dish grain.

There is a whole host of grain varieties. The most common ones are:

Amaranth: This tiny grain is beige in color and has a mild, nutty, woodsy, almost peppery flavor. Toasted, amaranth is ideal for granolas, trail mixes, muesli, and as a condiment. Of course, it can also be cooked in water to make excellent breakfast cereals, pilafs, and a salad ingredient. Use 3 cups of liquid to 1 cup of grain and give it around 25 to 30 minutes to cook. The grain will remain firm and chewy after cooking. To make a tasty Armenian salad, mix cooked amaranth, green pepper, mushrooms, red onion, tomato, cucumber, black olives, feta cheese, garlic, parsley, mint, black pepper, sesame oil, red wine vinegar, and lemon juice. Amaranth is also ground to make a flour that, when mixed with a high-gluten flour, can be used to make baked goods (breads, pancakes, etc.) with a new twist. This flour is also used to make amaranth pastas. Amaranth is extremely high in calcium (one cup cooked amaranth gives over a quarter of the recommended daily allowance), and vitamins A and E. It is also a good source of dietary fiber and protein.

Barley: Barley has chewy texture and mild flavor which brings body to any soup, harmonizes with other grains, and contributes handsome appeal to salads. See "Barley" for more information.

Buckwheat: Buckwheat can be either unroasted or roasted. The unroasted buckwheat is white and is called buckwheat or white buckwheat. It has a delicate, almost bland flavor that goes well with other delicate flavored foods like veal, fish, and tofu. It will soak up the flavors and seasonings of the foods it is cooked with. It can be used in soufflés, soups, casseroles, desserts, and as a stuffing for vegetables or mild flavored meats. Whole buckwheat groats are perfect for stuffings and pilafs and can be cooked with other grains. Furthermore, they can be used instead of rice in many recipes. A light buckwheat flour is available and is terrific in baked goods and cakes, and can be used as a thickening agent. This flour has also become famous for its delicious buckwheat pancakes.

Buckwheat groats that have been roasted are called kasha and they have a dark color and a strong, earthy, nutty flavor. Kasha is delicious when prepared with beef, duck, pork, chicken, liver, veal, lamb, mushrooms, onions, dairy products, and other grains. If kasha is not available at your local stores, you can make it at home. White buckwheat can be roasted and, optionally, coarsely ground, in your kitchen to make kasha.

Buckwheat comes in the form of whole groats, grits, and flour. Kasha comes in a variety of grinds—fine, medium, and coarse—as well as whole groats. See the "Grains Cooking Table" for liquid-to-grain ratios, their cooking times, and approximate yields.

Despite its name and the fact that it has a small amount of gluten, buckwheat is not a type of wheat.

Corn: Although it is a grain, corn is often thought of as a vegetable. It is the sweetest grain and comes in a variety of colors. It is processed to create many foods that are very useful in a multitude of dishes, snacks, and desserts. See "Corn" for more information.

Kamut: Kamut has a soft, chewy texture and a buttery flavor. This large, golden grain looks sort of like a cross between a wheat and rice kernel with a bump. Kamut is pronounced *KA moot*. It contains gluten and is higher in protein than regular wheat. It also contains a great deal of folacin, thiamin, niacin, potassium, and magnesium. Kamut grains are very hard and will cook faster if soaked before cooking. They retain all of their bran, making them a healthy addition to pilafs, stuffings, stews, and soups. A different vegetarian chili can be created by mixing cooked kamut, tomatoes, onion, celery, cooked pinto and azuki beans, garlic, chili powder, cumin, and black pepper and simmering for an hour or more. Try using kamut in place of wheat in any of your recipes. See the "Grains Cooking Table" for liquid-to-grain ratios, cooking times, and yields.

Millet: Millet is a dainty grain that produces big results. It is delightful when used in cereals, stews, stuffings, spreads, burritos, loaves, and casseroles. See "Millet" for more information.

Oats: Oats are most commonly known for the wholesome, warming, and filling hot oatmeal cereal made from them. They are also prized for their considerable contributions in producing delectable baked goods. See "Oats" for more information.

Quinoa: This grain is an ancient food that is relatively new to the marketplace. It is worth a try because its mild, nutty flavor and fluffy texture is perfect for casseroles, burgers, stuffings, and salads. To get a quick start, substitute quinoa for rice, millet, or bulgur in any of your favorite recipes. See "Quinoa" for more information.

Rice: This dish grain is a staple in many kitchens. Its large variety of types are suited for an array of uses to meet any cooking need. It can be used for breakfast, lunch, dinner, dessert, and snacks. See "Rice" for more information.

Rye: This grain isn't just for making bread, although that is its most common use. It is terrific when added to other grains such as rice and millet. Whole grain rye berries or groats are sweeter than wheat and much chewier than rice and can be used in soups, salads, casseroles, and stuffings. To shorten the cooking time, presoaking is recommended. Whole rye can also be sprouted and used in any of the dishes already mentioned. Rye flakes make a tasty and even more hearty breakfast than oatmeal. Other rye products are cracked rye and rye grits, meal, and flour. See the "Grains Cooking Table" for liquid-to-grain ratios, cooking times, and yields. When used to make bread, low-gluten rye flour is combined with high-gluten flour such as wheat, kamut, and spelt. Rye is a good source of insoluble fiber, protein, vitamin E, thiamin, niacin, magnesium, zinc, copper, iron, and selenium.

Spelt: Spelt is bigger, redder, and softer and has a higher gluten content than wheat. This makes spelt flour an ideal alternative to wheat for making bread. The spelt berries have their bran and germ intact and have a sweet, nutty flavor. They can be soaked overnight to quicken their cooking time. If presoaked, use between 2 1/2 and 3 cups of liquid per cup of spelt and expect a cooking time around 1 1/2 hours. If spelt has not been presoaked, use 4 cups of liquid and anticipate a cooking time that exceeds 2 hours. Spelt can be used in a similar fashion as many of the other grains. Use them in soups, casseroles, pilafs, puddings, etc. A very tasty spelt grain salad can be created by combining spelt that was cooked in chicken or vegetable broth, snow peas, red pepper, mushrooms, and water chestnuts with a dressing made of lemon juice, dill, red wine vinegar, olive oil, salt, and black pepper. A wonderful, rich pudding can be made by combining cooked spelt, milk or non-dairy milk, a sweetener, vanilla or almond extract, fresh fruit, and spices (such as nutmeg, cinnamon, ginger, allspice), and grated lemon or orange zest. Spelt can also be found in the form of flakes that may be used in baking, or to make a great bowl of hot breakfast cereal. This grain is a good source of protein, thiamin, riboflavin, magnesium, zinc, copper, and iron.

Teff: This tiny grain is available in three colors: red, white, and brown. The white teff is mild and the red and brown have a stronger, nutty flavor. The brown colored teff is the most common of the three and is available in health food stores. It comes in whole grain and flour forms and is used to make pasta. Cooked whole grain teff has a very thick, sticky texture. In fact, it can make a wonderful, tasty breakfast cereal which should be cooked until the grains burst open. Or teff can be cooked with beans (lentils and garbanzo are popular) to make a delicious dish that has a complete amino acid balance. It takes around 15 minutes and 3 cups of liquid to cook 1 cup of grain. If teff flour cannot be found in health food stores, you can grind your own if you have a grain mill. In the case of teff, a coffee or spice grinder or a blender will not produce very good results because the grains are too small to be ground properly in

these devices. Teff is a good source of fiber, protein, thiamin, calcium, and iron.

Triticale: This grain is pronounced *trit ih KAY lee.* It is a sort of cross between wheat and rye that has a bit more flavor than wheat, but is not as strong-flavored as rye. Triticale whole grain can be used to make tabbouleh and other grain salads,  pilafs, and casseroles as well as in soups, and grain and bean dishes. Use 2 3/4 to 3 1/4 cups liquid to 1 cup soaked triticale berries and expect to cook it for around an hour and 15 minutes. The flour or meal made from this grain can be used to create breads, waffles, dumplings, cakes, cookies, tortes, and gingerbread. Cracked triticale may be used as a meat extender in burgers and meat loaves as well as to make vegetable and meat stuffings. Rolled triticale can be used to make a filling, hot breakfast cereal and can be substituted for oat, wheat, or rye flakes in any recipe. Triticale is an excellent source of insoluble fiber, protein, thiamin, riboflavin, niacin, folate, pyridoxine, vitamin E, magnesium, iron, copper, zinc, and selenium.

Wheat: This is by far the most common bread grain. In fact, the word flour is almost synonymous with wheat flour. For example, unbleached white flour is understood to be a wheat flour. Wheat lets its presence be known in any dish it is cooked in. Its chewy texture does not go unnoticed when used whole in soups, casseroles, and salads. See "Wheat" for more information. Wheat is also used to make seitan, a chewy, protein-rich meat substitute (see "Seitan").

OTHER NAMES
Cereals.

FLAVOR/TEXTURE
Grains can be very mild flavored or very strong and distinctive. They may also be very soft, creamy, and sticky or dry, firm, and chewy. See the individual grain

sections in this book for flavor and texture information on wheat, oats, barley, rice, millet, quinoa, and corn. For the other grains, see the discussion in "Varieties" in this section.

GENERAL USES

Grains are an important part of our daily diet; they are an excellent source of complex carbohydrates that provide steady energy. According to the food pyramid and the macrobiotic philosophy, approximately 40 to 50% of our entire diet should consist of grains and grain products. In order to eat this much of one type of food, a great deal of variety had to be invented and, indeed, it has. There are a large number of grain types, products made from each grain, and grain cooking methods. The uses for grains are almost endless and certainly too numerous for all of them to be mentioned. However, we can discuss a small sampling of them. They can be used to create main dishes, breakfasts, appetizers, side dishes, condiments, drinks, snacks, desserts, casseroles, and baked goods.

They can be used in the morning as a breakfast cereal, hot or cold. And they can be used for making toast, French toast, muffins, doughnuts, pancakes, jelly rolls, waffles, granola, grits, etc. And they can be used to make fried patties that, depending on the grain and spices used, can be similar to hash browns, sausage, or hamburger. And they can be used to make a non-dairy milk that can be added to your coffee or tea.

There are plenty of opportunities to use grains in lunches and dinners. They

are excellent in casseroles, burgers, stroganoffs, burritos, dumplings, cacciatore, chili, chop suey, croquettes, fritters, fried rice, goulash, vegetable and meat pies, salads, stuffed vegetables and meats, spanish rice, tacos, sushi, stuffed cabbage and other leaves, soups, stews, meat or vegetable loaves, curries, pâtés, etc.

Wonderful desserts can be made from many of the grains such as Danishes, éclairs, pies, cakes, cream puffs, crumpets, turnovers, scones, strudels, sweet rolls, cookies, biscuits, brownies, fig bars, rice pudding, shortcakes, tortes, cobbler, and muffins.

Grains can be used as a thickener, meat extender, binder, meat substitute, sweetener, and milk. They also go well with sausage, poultry, game, fish, shellfish, dairy products, vegetables, legumes, mushrooms, fruits, nuts, seeds, and herbs.

Some uses for each of the grain types are listed in each individual section. Try them, learn about them, and enjoy them. There are many books that have tasty recipes using many types of grains to help you get started or expand your knowledge about cooking grains. See the "Additional Reading" subsection.

NIGRO TIP

To get a wonderfully rich, full, and sweet flavor from grain dishes, chew them so much that they turn to liquid. By doing this you are breaking the complex carbohydrates down into some of their simple sugars while the grain is still in your mouth.

FRESHNESS/QUALITY

It is a good idea to get to know the producers of the grains you use often. Many mills produce many of the different types of grains and the quality among them is similar. Many producers change the brand names they use for each grain type, so note the manufacturer's or distributor's name that is typically located somewhere on the package in small letters. If the grains are sold in bulk, ask the store the name of the supplier.

A good guide to follow in considering the quality of a grain is its nutritional value. The more nutritious grains are the ones that have been processed the least— whole grains. Good quality grains are whole, contain minimal broken pieces, and look clean. Because whole grains can not meet all the needs of the kitchen, processed grains (such as flakes, flours, and pastas) will also appear on shopping lists even though they may have less nutritional value.

Bulk purchasing is a great way to get many of your grain products. Health food and natural food stores have a vast variety to offer and you can also purchase any amount you wish, whether large or small. These bulk sales bins allow you an opportunity to try different types of grains and grain products because you can purchase just enough to check them out without a major investment. With any bulk item, and grains are not any different, select a store that has a good product turnover rate so that the grains will be fresh. The store should not be damp and the air should be dry in general. Ask the attendants how they store bulk grains and flours. If the answer is in the refrigerator, then you are in the right place.

It is easy to tell if a grain has become bad or rancid, because it will smell pretty awful. Feed anything that you are finding questionable to the garbage disposal, trash bin, or compost pile.

STORAGE

All types of grains should be stored in an airtight container in a cool, dry location—a root cellar is good, a refrigerator is excellent, and a freezer is ideal. If the storage area is damp, the grains will absorb moisture and grow molds. Never wash grains before storing them.

Generally speaking, without preservatives, whole grains will keep fresher longer than grains that have been processed.

Label your grains with the date of their purchase, never add fresh grains to older ones, and use the oldest grains first.

If a grain sits for a long time, it may become infested with bugs, worms, or moths. If the grains stick together in little clumps that look like they have static cling, moth eggs are the cause. Vigorously and thoroughly washing the grain before cooking will solve the problem of insect eggs. In cases where there is a large quantity of grain infested, wash it, dry-roast it, and then store it again. Use it as quickly as possible because dry-roasting shortens the life of a grain. If you see any moths or

other bugs, discard the grain. To help deter insects, you can place a bay leaf in the grain containers in addition to keeping the grain in a sealed, cool, dry place.

After the grains are cooked, they can be refrigerated. Be sure to cover them tightly so they will not pick up any lurking refrigerator "flavors." Grains prepared using only water and salt can sit out on the counter for one to three days depending on the temperature of the kitchen. If the grain is left out too long, it may sour and produce molds. It can be used if soured, but should be discarded if moldy. Once grains have been cooked with vegetables, beans, broths, or meats they should definitely be refrigerated.

Freezing cooked grains is purely a matter of taste. Some people think that defrosted grains are soggy and have lost their al dente texture. However, we freeze grains often and use them frequently in all types of recipes and find it convenient and the flavor and texture quite suitable.

Although grains are "hard," handle them with care and gentleness because most of them can be bruised easily.

PREPARATION INSTRUCTIONS

MEASURING

There is something about the dynamics between cooking pot size, heating surface area, and depth of the grains cooked that makes it a bad idea to cook less than one cup of a whole grain at a time.

Measuring grains and their cooking liquids accurately is a good first step to ensuring that the same results will be achieved time after time. Measure the dry ingredients, including grains, in a dry measuring cup and the liquids in a liquid measuring cup. Shortly before the time of preparation, measure the amount of grain needed in the recipe when it is dry. It is more difficult to accurately measure grains when they are wet. Then rinse the grains, if desired, and mix them with the other ingredients.

Increasing the quantities in grain dish recipes can be a bit tricky. Grains do not maintain the same ratio with liquid when the amount is increased. As the volume of grain increases, the amount of liquid needed per cup of grain is less. See the "Table Illustrating Grain-to-Water Ratio as a Function of Grain Amount" to see the general trend. For example, a recipe may call for 2 1/4 cups of liquid to 1 cup of grain to produce 3 cups of cooked grains. However, if you tripled the amount of grain, the liquid amount should not be tripled as well and the yield will not be three times the original. In our example, when cooking 3 cups of grain (1 cup x 3), 5 1/2 cups of liquid, not 6 3/4 cups (2 1/4 cups x 3), might be needed to produce the same quality of cooked grain. Furthermore, the amount of finished cooked grains will be around 7 cups, not 9 cups (3 cups x 3). See the subsection "Amount of Liquid" for tips on the amount of liquid to use.

TABLE ILLUSTRATING GRAIN-TO-WATER RATIO AS A FUNCTION OF GRAIN AMOUNT

Grain (cups)	Liquid (cups)	Approximate Yield (cups)
1	1 3/4 - 2	2 1/4
1 1/2	2 1/2 - 2 3/4	3 1/2
2	3 1/4 - 4	5
3	5 - 5 1/2	7

CLEANING

Never wash grains and then store them. A washing process should only occur right before preparation, if performed at all.

Packaged grains (i.e., non-bulk) are usually quite clean and may not need rinsing before using. The first time you cook a washable grain from a given producer, wash it and see how dirty it is. Use this information to determine whether you will wash it in the future—dirty grains should be washed before cooking. Of the grains, basmati and brown rice are more likely to need a washing. Quinoa, even if quite clean, must be washed prior to cooking to remove a naturally occurring bitter outer coating. See "Quinoa" for additional information.

Precooked grains such as instant rice, rolled oats, bulgur, or couscous should not be washed prior to preparation for this will result in their absorbing too

much water and generating a mushy texture after they are cooked.

Natural whole grains obtained from the bulk sections may contain small bits, weeds, pebbles, or seeds in with them. Place the grains on a flat baking sheet or plate and sort through them to remove any unwanted matter and then rinse them. Rinsing many of the natural whole grains will not hurt them, and will ensure that they are clean and free of dust and fine debris. Grains with softer outer skins, such as millet, quinoa, and buckwheat, should be washed very quickly to prevent them from absorbing too much water.

To wash grains, place them in a container along with fresh, clean, cold water (use two to three times water to grain). Stir the grains with your fingers to loosen any dust and dirt, then pour off the water. If the water was quite dirty, repeat the process until the water remains clean. This may take several washings. Drain the grains for a few minutes before cooking them. The longer damp grains sit, the more water they will absorb and the more the grains will soften. This may affect the cooking time and the final resulting texture of the dish.

SOAKING

Soaking softens grains, increases their moisture content, and reduces their cooking time. The cooking time of long-cooking grains can be reduced by as much as half if the grains are first soaked overnight. The length of soaking time depends on the grains being soaked and can range from two to fourteen hours. Grains soaked longer than fourteen hours may ferment if not kept in a cool place. Fermentation may be desirable or undesirable, depending on the effect you are trying to achieve.

If you are following a recipe, it will generally state if soaking is required and for how long. If there isn't a reference to soaking, chances are that it is not really necessary.

Soaking grains before cooking will make grains swell more and cause them to be stickier and heavier than those grains that were not soaked.

PRE-TREATMENTS TO COOKING

Pre-treatments are carried out before grains are cooked. They are used to change the cooking time and final resulting grain texture.

Dry-Roasting: Roasting grains creates a wonderful nutty aroma that fills the whole house, making everyone hungry. Roasting intensifies and enhances the flavor of grains—so much so that, in some cases, the flavor is transformed into something "different." Roasting also increases the ability of the grain to absorb the liquids they are cooked with. Thus, if the cooking liquid is flavored, roasting the grains may be a good idea. When preparing long-cooking grains, roasting shortens the cooking time slightly and makes them lighter and less sticky in texture.

Before roasting, wash the grains, if necessary, according to the "Cleaning" subsection. Allow the grains to drain.

For small amounts (two cups or less), dry roast grains in a heavy, medium-hot skillet until golden. While roasting, keep the grains moving either by stirring them or moving the skillet. As the grains begin to emit a delicious nutty aroma, turn the heat down to medium-low. The grains are done when they are very dry and, if they are small, begin to pop or jump around a bit. This process can take up to 15 minutes, but it is worth the time.

To roast more than two cups, the oven is the optimum place to do it. Get a baking sheet with sides and spread a thin layer of grains onto it. Bake in a 300 to 375°F oven. Stir the grains every 10 minutes until the nutty aroma begins. Then stir them every 3 to 5 minutes and keep your eye on them. They are done when the aroma is magnified and the color is darker. If you are in doubt about their state of doneness, remove them from the oven. A grain that is a little under roasted is still delicious, but a grain that is burned is not worth eating in any dish.

Sautéing: When sautéing grains in oil or butter, the idea is to coat each of the kernels with a thin layer of hot fat. When these coated grains are cooked, the result will be individual, separable grains that are al dente, moist, and non-sticky. Sauté grains quickly in a small amount of oil or butter along with any desired herbs, spices, and vegetables until the grain is hot and coated. Continuously stir the grains during the cooking period. Sautéing is often a pre-treatment for grains used to prepare pilafs and risottos.

STOVE-TOP, BASIC COOKING METHOD

Cooking grains is the process of getting grains to absorb water. This sounds so simple and it really is. Yet, grains seem to be one of the most difficult things for people to cook. Hopefully, armed with a little more knowledge, cooking grains will become easy and fun for those folks who were initially having difficulties with it.

Grains have been around for thousands of years, and millions of people  have perfected their process for preparing them. Therefore, there are millions of ways to cook grains to perfection. The perfect cooked grain dish is the dish that you enjoy! Try cooking grains in any way you think sounds good. If you are in doubt, try it and see if you like it.

It is easy to cook grains and the process can be adjusted to produce a grain to your liking. Our discussion will provide some general guidelines to help you get started. Remember, as with any new food, when starting to cook with grains, a little experimenting and testing may be needed before you consistently get the results you desire in *your* kitchen, using *your* utensils with the grains purchased in *your* local area.

Because this book is an introduction to many ingredients, we cannot dedicate the entirety of its contents to grains, which we would have to do if we were to attempt to discuss even a small portion of the grain cooking possibilities. Instead, we will discuss in some detail one method and then briefly touch on a few others. This shouldn't be too limiting though because, strangely enough, with just the one basic method, a huge variety of grain dishes can be prepared.

When starting to get to know grains, it is a good idea to cook all the varieties using the same "basic method." This way you will become familiar with the similarities and differences among the grain's cooking times and water volumes, resulting textures and flavors, and aromas and characters. A basic cooking method that may be used for all grains involves cooking the grains on the top of the stove. We call it the "basic method" and the basic concept behind it is to add the grain to water, bring it to a boil, reduce the heat, cover and simmer or cook over a low heat until the grain has absorbed the desired amount of liquid.

Do not stir whole grains while cooking them because they will stick and burn. However, after the grain has finished cooking, it can be fluffed up with a fork after it has rested for 5 to 10 minutes.

It is easy to tell when your grain is done. A minute or two before the grain is supposed to be done, remove the cooking container's lid just long enough to grab a couple of the grains and bite them to determine if the center is to your liking. If the grain is done and there is still liquid in the pot, poor off the excess liquid and return to the heat with the lid slightly ajar. This will allow the remaining moisture to evaporate and dry out the cooked grain. If the grain is not quite done, it will still be hard in the middle and have a crunchy, unpleasant texture. Boiling liquid should be added and additional simmering will need to be performed if undercooked grains have absorbed all of the initial cooking liquid. After the grains are no longer hard in the center, continued cooking causes the grains to absorb more water and become softer and more mushy. It is up to you to decide if you have overcooked the grain. If the grain has become too mushy for the dish you wanted, save the grain and use it in another recipe for which it will be more appropriate (such as a grain pudding, porridge, breakfast cereal, etc.).

When mixing types of grains (such as long grain rice and wild rice or short grain rice and wheat berries), cook the two grains separately and mix them before serving. Or start the longer cooking grain first and add the shorter cooking grain (and water) later and cook them together until both are tender.

Some things to consider when cooking grains are the amount of liquid, the temperature of the liquid and grain when combined together, the amount of heat, and the cooking time. Changes to any one or more of these conditions will change the results of the cooked grain. This provides ample opportunities for you to control and change the effects obtained to satisfy very different recipe requirements. For example, if all you have is long grain brown rice, you can cook it under different conditions to make it perfect for a rice pudding or a fluffy pilaf. You are not locked into the same old rice, barley, etc. texture for every recipe. Creativity and imagination can produce wonderful, exciting dishes.

Amount of Liquid: The amount of liquid used to cook a grain affects the texture of the final dish. The texture can range from a soft and starchy gruel, porridge, or cereal to a chewy and separate grain often used in pilafs. The more liquid that is used in cooking the grains, the more water will be absorbed and the softer and mushier the grain will become. Note, however, that to make a grain soft, the amount of water is not the only factor to consider—the grain cooking time must also be increased.

See the "Grain Cooking Table" for suggested grain and liquid ratios for each grain type. This table should only be used as a starting place, and not be taken as hard-and-fast rules. The grain-to-liquid ratios and yields will vary depending on the grain type, freshness, desired final consistency, cooking liquid used, the cooking method used, etc. For example, if you want a drier grain, use a little less liquid. If you want a moist grain and you are cooking it in a pot or cooker that does not have a heavy lid, use a little more liquid. If you have a very fresh grain, less water is needed. Grains that have been stored for a while may need extra water in cooking because they have dried out and

Grain Cooking Table

Grain (1 cup)	Variety	Liquid (cups)	Cooking Time (minutes)	Yield (cups)	Rinsing	Salt*
Amaranth	Whole	2 1/2 to 3	25 to 30	2 1/2	No	No
Barley	Hulled Whole	2 1/2 to 3	80 to 100	3 1/2	Optional	Optional
	Scotch or Pot	2 1/2 to 3	60 to 80	3 1/2	Optional	Optional
	Pearled	2 to 2 1/2	25 to 35	3 1/2	Optional	Optional
	Pearled (porridge)	3 1/2 to 4	50 to 60	4	Optional	Optional
	Rolled or Flakes	2 1/2 to 3	15 to 20	3	No	Optional
	Rolled (porridge)	4 to 4 1/2	20 to 30	3 1/2	No	Optional
Buckwheat	Groats	2 to 2 1/2	15 to 25	2 1/2	No	Optional
	Kasha Groats	2 to 2 1/2	20 to 30	2 1/2	No	Optional
	Grits	2 to 2 1/2	10 to 15	2	No	Optional
Corn	Sweet Corn (on cob)	Cover	3 to 8	–	Yes	Optional
	Hominy Grits	5	20 to 25	4 1/2	No	Optional
	Corn Grits	3 1/2 to 4	40 to 50	4 1/2	No	Optional
Kamut	Groats	2 to 2 1/2	70 to 90	3	Optional	Optional
Millet	Whole	2 to 2 1/2	25 to 35	3 1/2	Optional	Optional
Oats	Groats	2 to 2 1/2	60 to 120	2 1/2	Optional	Optional
	Steel Cut	2 3/4 to 3	50 to 70	2 1/2	Optional	Optional
	Irish	2 3/4 to 3	50 to 70	2 1/2	Optional	Optional
	Rolled or Flakes	2 to 2 1/2	7 to 15	2 1/2	No	Optional
	Rolled (porridge)	3 to 4	20 to 30	3 1/2	No	Optional
Quinoa	Whole	2 to 2 1/2	10 to 15	3 1/3	Recommended	Optional

Grain	Variety	Liquid	Cooking Time	Yield	Rinsing	Salt*
Rice	Brown	2 to 2 1/2	30 to 45	3	Optional	Optional
	White	2 to 2 1/2	15 to 20	3	Optional	Optional
	Sweet, Brown	2 to 2 1/2	50 to 70	3	Optional	Optional
	Sweet, White	2 to 2 1/2	30 to 50	3	Optional	Optional
	Black	2 to 2 1/2	25 to 35	2 1/2	Optional	Optional
	Red	2 to 2 1/2	45 to 55	3	Optional	Optional
	Basmati, Brown	2 to 2 1/2	40 to 60	3 1/4	Recommended	Optional
	Basmati, White	2 to 2 1/2	15 to 20	3 1/4	Recommended	Optional
	Wehani	2 to 2 1/2	40 to 60	2 3/4	Optional	No
	Wild	3 to 4	50 to 70	3	Optional	Optional
Rye	Berries	2 to 2 1/2	90 to 120	2 1/2	Optional	Optional
	Cracked or Grits	2 1/2 to 3	20 to 35	2 1/2	Optional	Optional
	Rolled or Flakes	2 1/2 to 3	15 to 25	2 1/2	No	Optional
	Rolled (porridge)	4 to 4 1/2	20 to 30	3 1/2	No	Optional
Spelt	Berries (pre-soaked)	2 1/2 to 3	90 to 100	3	Optional	Optional
	Berries	3 1/2 to 4	120 +	3	Optional	Optional
Teff	Whole	2 3/4 to 3	15 to 20	3	No	Optional
Triticale	Whole	2 3/4 to 3	70 to 90	2 1/2	Optional	No
Wheat	Berries	3 to 3 1/2	60 to 90	3	Optional	No
	Cracked	2 to 2 1/2	25 to 35	2 1/2	Optional	Optional
	Farina	2 to 2 1/2	5 to 15	2 1/2	No	Optional
	Rolled or Flakes	3 to 3 1/2	30 to 40	3	No	Optional
	Couscous	2 to 2 1/2	15 to 25	2	No	Optional
	Bulgur	1 1/2 to 2	10 to 20	2 1/2	No	Optional

* Salt may be added at the beginning of cooking.

will absorb much more liquid. See the prior discussion in "Measuring" for tips on how to modify the ratio when cooking more or less grain, and the following "Cooking Container and Lid" discussion for information on adjusting liquid amounts based on the cooking container. Once you become familiar with the grain you are using, adjusting recipes will be much easier.

Cooking Container and Lid: The container that the grains are cooked in does not really matter. What matters is that the amount of liquid used is adjusted to account for the type of container used. If the container is heavy with a tight fitting lid, steam can't escape and less liquid will be needed.  If, on the other hand, the container is thinner and the lid is not tight fitting, then more liquid will be needed because some will be lost when steam escapes. If you wish to prevent steam from escaping when you have a light or non-tight fitting lid, try covering the container with aluminum foil or a tea towel and then placing the lid on top.

Initial Temperature of Grain and Liquid: The next consideration is the temperature of the liquid and the temperature of the grain when combining them for cooking. The liquid can be made hot by pre-boiling it (don't let it boil too long before adding the grains and starting the cooking process or some of your liquid will escape as steam) and grains can be made hot by dry roasting or sautéing them. A cold liquid is anything from cold to room temperature and cold grains are uncooked or raw grains.

To produce the most individually separable, light, and fluffy grain possible, combine hot grain with hot liquid. Carefully and slowly add the hot grain to the hot liquid to prevent a bubbling over situation. On the other hand, if a sticky, heavy, and chewy texture is desired, combine cold grain with cold liquid. When the temperatures of the grain and liquid are opposites, one hot and the other cold,

the texture produced is the "normal" one typically thought of for that grain (e.g., somewhat chewy and fluffy). These general rules hold in a relative way for each grain type. For example, a grain that is by nature very sticky (such as oats) will still be sticky when the grain and liquid are both hot, the resulting dish will just be less sticky than those cooked with cold-cold, and hot-cold initial temperatures for that grain and liquid.

Note that when adding flour, meal, or other ground grains to a liquid, be sure the liquid is cool or cold. If the liquid is warm, the grain will lump together.

Cooking Time: The next thing to think about is the length of grain cooking time. Grains that must absorb more liquid (grains that are to be soft and mushy or old grains) must also be cooked for a longer time. In addition, grains take longer to cook in an oily broth than they do in water.

In general, higher temperatures mean shorter cooking times, as long as the grain is not being scorched or burned. Temperature is dependent on your kitchen equipment and interpretation of the word "simmer." You can tell when a pot is simmering when the liquid surface is calm with just a few bubbles.

On electric stoves, the reduction in heat from high to low (the action to take to bring boiling grains to a simmer) takes longer than on a gas stove. If an electric stove is used, more water can be used to compensate or pre-heat another burner to the simmer temperature and when the grain comes to a boil, just transfer the pot to the burner set on simmer.

On some gas stoves, the flame cannot go low enough to simmer the grain and may, in some cases, scorch or burn the bottom of the pan. A simmering pad or a flame tamer or diffuser can solve this problem. They are inexpensive and can be found at your local kitchen shop and department or discount stores.

Ovens, in general, are not kitchen equipment that have precision temperature control. When the temperature knob is set to 350°F, the oven might actually be 325°F or 375°F. Or there may be a large temperature difference between various locations in the oven.

Adding Salt: Most of the grains cook very well in salted water or other salty liquid. However, some grains, such as amaranth, wheat berries, triticale, and Wehani rice turn out rather unpleasant when cooked in a salty liquid. They will not absorb the cooking liquid, producing undercooked grains and an excess amount of water. You may still wish to add salt to these—simply do it at the end of cooking or at the table.

Grains do not need to be cooked in a salted liquid to cook properly. If you are on a sodium restricted diet, you can easily incorporate grains into it. However, even if you are not on a sodium restricted diet, you don't want to use too much salt because it will mask the wonderful flavor of the grains. Start with little or no salt and add more if it is needed after the grain is cooked or add it in the sauce or recipe the grain is being used with.

Cooking Liquids: Grains are delicious when cooked in flavored liquids. Try replacing all or some of the water with a vegetable or meat stock, nut or seed milk, fruit or vegetable juice, beer or wine, unrefined oil, and/or vinegar or soy sauce. Seasonings can be added to the liquid to add even more flavors to the grain dish. Try fresh ginger root, garlic, basil, oregano, thyme, sage, whole peppercorns, cinnamon stick, cloves, saffron, cardamom, or any of your favorites. Or if you want to add a little color, try using turmeric, paprika, or beet juice. With all of these choices, it is good to note that just plain water used in cooking grains will produce a versatile, ready-to-use ingredient for many other dishes.

Delicious vegetable stocks made from any vegetable or combination of them are great in preparing grains. Boil a carrot, stick of celery, leek or onion, a couple of garlic cloves, black pepper, and ground ginger root in some water for an hour or so. Strain the vegetables out and you have a stock ready to use to create a flavorful grain dish.

Using fruit juice as a cooking liquid for grains will reduce the final volume of the cooked grains, produce a heaver texture, and create a sweeter flavor. In fact, if the grain cooking liquid is mainly fruit juice, the dish is going to be sweet and will be best suited for desserts. However, if only a portion of the cooking liquid is fruit juice, a very delicious dish suitable for a main course can be created. Fruit juices that are good to try are orange, pineapple, apple, and lemon juice. Of course, feel free to try any juice that you have a fancy for.

Make a deliciously heavy and creamy grain dish by using a nut milk as the cooking liquid. Increase the amount of milk by one fourth when cooking the grains and serve them immediately after cooking. The texture will change once the dish cools down and may not be quite what you had in mind for the dish.

When cooking grains with wine, sherry, beer, and sake, they are usually diluted with other liquids such as meat and vegetable stocks, water, fruit juices, and nut or seed milks.

Of course, any flavored liquid can be used to make a delectable sauce that is served over grains.

OTHER COOKING METHODS

The grain preparation issues of cooking temperature and time, liquid amount and flavor, adding salt, initial temperatures of the grain and liquid, and judging doneness also apply when baking, slow cooking, boiling, rice cooker cooking, and microwaving grains. See prior discussions in "Stove-Top, Basic Cooking Method" for details on these issues.

Baking: Baking grains can be as easy as combining water, grain, and salt in a baking dish and then covering and baking at a medium oven (about 350°F) until the grains are tender. The grain is done when it is open, soft, and golden in color. Baked grains can stay warm in the oven once it is turned off and can be served hot as an entrée or they can be allowed to cool and be served cold in a salad.

Slow Cooking: Grains can be cooked in a slow cooker or crock pot. Try using the usual grain-to-liquid ratios. Combine the grain, liquid, and any desired spices and vegetables in the ceramic pot and cook on low all day. If there is still liquid in the pot when the grain is done, just pour it off and continue to cook until the remaining liquid has evaporated.

Steaming: Steaming grains produces a fluffy texture as every grain separates. This method involves cooking the grain in a large amount of boiling water for 10 to 15 minutes. Maintain a rapid boil during this whole time. Drain the grain and rinse with cold water to remove any excess starch. Transfer the grain to a steaming basket placed in a large pot. Cover and steam over boiling water for 15 minutes or until the desired consistency is achieved.

Boiling: Cooking grains in this manner is similar to the procedure used to cook pastas. Add the grain to a large amount of boiling water and simmer uncovered until the grain is tender. Be sure you have at least four times the amount of water as you have grain. If the grain absorbs so much water that it no longer covers the grain, add more hot water to the pot. Drain the cooked grain in a strainer and, optionally, rinse it with hot water to remove any starch. If a dryer grain is desired, return the grains to the now dry pot and cook over a low heat, stirring occasionally to prevent sticking, until the desired moisture level is reached.

Microwaving: Some packaged supermarket grains have microwave instructions printed on them, and you may, of course, follow these. If instructions are not available, put one cup grain with the usual quantity of water into a non-metallic container big enough to hold twice as much as you put in (if the container is too small the whole thing will boil over and create a big mess in your microwave). Cover the bowl with clingfilm/ plastic wrap or a plate (not a metal lid), and cook on full power for 5 minutes. Leave the grain undisturbed and cook on half power for another 15 to 35 minutes depending on the type of grain being cooked. Then fluff with a fork and serve.

Rice Cooker Cooking: In addition to rice, this little machine can also cook most of the other grains because it works on an absorption principle. It simply continues to cook the grain until it has absorbed all the liquid. Many of the manufacturers provide some instructions and measurements of water and grain for their cooker. If not, then try experimenting a little. It will definitely be worth your time in the long run. Try making a batch of any grain you like. As a starting place, try using the liquid-to-grain ratio provided in the "Grains Cooking Table." Hit the rice cooker button and let it rip. Once it is done, check the contents and if the grain is still hard, add a little hot water and start it up again. If the grain is done, but it still has water in it, pour off the excess water and let the cooker crank on the warming mode for a while to dry the grain out. Then the next time, adjust your liquid-to-grain ratio.

SPECIAL GRAIN DISHES

Porridges & Gruels: To make a creamy breakfast cereal from grains, combine 1 cup of grain with 4 cups water, fruit juice, or milk. Bring to a boil and reduce to a simmer and cook until the grain is as soft as you like. Frequent stirring of the porridge or gruel may be required.

These types of dishes are often thought to be useful only for the sick, the elderly, children, or perhaps those folks with a bit of a hangover the morning after. But everybody can enjoy them. Discover the delicious flavor of the hot cereals that grains can make when served with fruit, nuts or seeds, sweeteners, and milk. To cause whole grains to cook faster  and be a bit creamier, soak them overnight before cooking them. Other than modifying the liquid-to-grain ratio, these dishes are prepared the same "basic" way. See the "Stove-Top, Basic Cooking Method" subsection and the "Grains Cooking Table" for more information.

Puddings: Making puddings is another treat that grains can offer. The most well known kind of grain pudding is the famous rice pudding. If you like it, you'll love what the other grains can do.

To make a grain pudding, combine 1 1/2 cups cooked grain (dish grains make creamier puddings), 2 cups milk or non-dairy milk, and 1/4 to 1/2 cup liquid sweetener. Add other goodies as well, like spices: nutmeg or ginger, ground lemon or orange rinds, or cinnamon; fruit: blueberries, cranberries, strawberries, blackberries, apricots, peaches, raisins, dates, or prunes; nuts: almonds, pecans, Brazil nuts, or pine nuts; and flavorings or extracts: vanilla, almond, rum, or coffee. For a more custard-like texture, add 3 beaten eggs. Bake the mixture in a pre-heated 325°F oven for 15 minutes and stir. Continue to bake for another 30 minutes or until the pudding has set. Remove it from the oven and let it rest for another 15 minutes to allow it to firm a little more. Serve it hot or cold with hot coffee, tea, or grain beverage.

Pie Crust: Making a pie crust is a wonderful way to use leftover grains to make a nutritious shell for your favorite sweet or savory filling. Start by using a dish grain that is well-cooked and has a little stickier texture. Combine cooked whole grains (one type or a combination of several), eggs or flour, and non-dairy milk with the seasonings of your choice. For sweet pies, use a sweetener such as honey, date sugar, etc. and complementary spices such as nutmeg, cinnamon, allspice, etc. If using the crust for a savory pie such as a casserole or vegetable pie, try adding garlic or onion powder, chives, basil, shoyu soy sauce, etc. to the grain. Cheeses may also be added to this crust to change its flavor and texture. For example, grated parmesan cheese or nutritional yeast is a wonderful addition to a broccoli pie crust. After mixing the pie crust "dough," coat a pie pan with a little oil and simply press the mixture into it. Bake it a little, 10 minutes in a 350°F oven, before adding a filling and baking more.

Milks: A non-dairy substitute for milk can be made from many of the grains. Oats and rice make wonderful milks that can be used in many of the ways traditional for dairy milks. See "Non-Dairy Milks" for more information on how to make and use them.

Molds: Making a grain in a mold is a fantastic way to show off the grain when it

is served. The shape or size of the mold can be anything that can hold a mixture of grains, spices, and sautéed vegetables. The possibilities are numerous; for example, Bundt or sponge cake pans, bowls, and loaf pans will do nicely. Coat the mold pan generously with butter or oil and pack the cooked grain into it. It is optional to bake it in the oven for a few minutes. Unmold the grain by placing a hot serving plate over the top of the mold pan, inverting the mold pan and plate, and lifting the mold pan to leave the shaped grain sitting on the plate. The grain can be garnished on top with roasted nuts, parsley, or dried fruit. Furthermore, the center of the grain mold can be filled with complementary thick sauces and vegetable, fruit, bean, nut, or meat creations.

REHEATING

Many of the grains will become somewhat dense and dry when placed in the refrigerator. To reheat them and return them to their moist, tender state, water often needs to be added back to the grains. It is best to steam them in a steaming basket, place them in a microwave oven with a small amount of water, or cook them for 5 to 10 minutes on a low heat stove-top along with 3 tablespoons to 1/4 cup of hot water per cup of grain. Occasionally stir the reheating grain with a fork to prevent sticking.

HEALTH INFORMATION

Whole grains contain complex carbohydrates, fats, protein, vitamins (especially B and E), minerals (potassium, calcium, phosphorus, iron, copper, zinc, magnesium, manganese, and molybdenum), and fiber.

The small amount of fat in grains is mostly found in the germ. Thus, whole grains have a slightly higher fat content than polished or pearled grains. Of all the grains, whole oats have the highest fat content although they are not considered to be a high fat food.

Many grains contain gluten: wheat, rye, barley, oats, triticale, kamut, and spelt. The other grains only contain trace amounts of gluten and may be considered gluten-free.

ADDITIONAL READING

Almost any healthy cooking, natural foods, low-fat, or whole foods cookbook will have a whole host of grain recipes and tips. A few books that focus expressly on grains are:

Bumgarner, Marlene Anne. *The Book of Whole Grains.*

Cole, Candia Lea. *Gourmet Grains: Maindishes Made of Nature.*

Fletcher, Janet. *Grain Gastronomy: A Cook's Guide to Great Grains from Couscous to Polenta.*

Gelles, Carol. *The Complete Whole Grain Cookbook.*

Keane, Maureen B., and Daniella Chace. *Grains for Better Health.*

London, Sheryl, and Mel London. *The Versatile Grain and the Elegant Bean.*

Saltzman, Joanne. *Amazing Grains.*

BUYING SOURCES

Some grains are available at your local supermarket (such as white rice and oat flakes). However, health food and natural foods stores typically carry a whole range of grain varieties, both prepackaged and in bulk, many of which are organic.

Grains are also available through mail order companies such as Allergy Resources, Anzen Oriental Foods & Imports, Arrowhead Mills, Black Duck Company, Bob's Red Mill Natural Foods, Clear Eye Natural Foods, Community Mill & Bean, Inc., Dean & Deluca, Frankferd Farms Foods, Garden Spot, Gold Mine Natural Foods, Jaffe Bros., King Arthur Flour Baker's Catalogue, Lundberg Family Farms, Mountain Ark Trading Company, Natural Lifestyle, The Bean Bag, White Mountain Farm, Natural Way Mills Inc., Harvest Time Natural Foods, and Walnut Acres Organic Farm.

BRANDS

Arrowhead Mills, Lundberg, Southern Brown Rice, Ohsawa, Eden, Quinoa Corporation, as well as many of the mail order companies produce excellent quality grains.

GREAT NORTHERN BEANS

"Great Northern" is not just another name for a white bean. There is some confusion about whether white beans are all the same or whether they are different. Although they share similar characteristics (such as having mild flavors and thin skins), the different varieties of white beans are harvested from different varieties of mature green beans. Indeed, this very fact makes them different.

Great Northerns are bright white, medium-sized, slightly kidney-shaped beans that are about 1/2 inch long.

OTHER NAMES

Some packagers do not differentiate between navy beans, Great Northern beans, and other white beans. Thus, there may be several varieties in one package.

FLAVOR/TEXTURE

Great Northern beans do not have a dominant flavor and are very compatible with the flavors of other beans, vegetables, meats, and sea vegetables. They hold their shape after cooking surprisingly well, considering their thin skins.

GENERAL USES

White beans, such as Great Northern beans, are useful all-purpose beans that absorb other flavors well.

For light, refreshing salads, Great Northerns are a perfect choice. A delectable white bean salad can be made by coating firm cooked Great Northern beans and dry-roasted peanuts with a well mixed combination of red wine vinegar, mustard, chopped scallions, unrefined sea salt, black pepper, and olive oil.

This bean, when combined with other beans and/or vegetables makes a very good soup or casserole. Combining fresh garden vegetables and pasta or grains with cooked Great Northern beans in a mild tomato broth will produce a fabulous Minestrone soup.

Puréed (i.e., blended) Great Northern beans make a thick, rich, white cream-style base for soups and sauces. A "hot" white sauce can be made by blending sautéed onions and garlic with cumin, cayenne pepper, parsley, salt, a rich vegetable broth, and mushy Great Northerns. Or, to make a mild white dip, cook the beans with onions, turnips, garlic, carrots, bay leaf, and celery, and then blend the result with parsley, sage, lemon juice, and olive oil. If you want to add a little texture, fold a little finely chopped red onion into the dip.

Any of the white beans (such as Navy, Great Northern, Steuben yellow- eyed, Jacob's Cattle, Anasazi, Cannellini, Soldier, and Calypso beans) may be substituted for one another in most recipes.

FRESHNESS/QUALITY
See "Beans."

STORAGE
See "Beans."

PREPARATION INSTRUCTIONS

CLEANING AND SOAKING
See "Beans."

COOKING
See the "Beans" section for general instructions for cooking. Stove-top cooking time ranges from 40 minutes to 1 hour, and the pressure cooking time is 20 minutes. One cup of dried beans yields approximately 2 2/3 cups cooked.

HEALTH INFORMATION
Great Northern beans are high in protein and have a great deal of carbohydrates, as well as iron, calcium, and B-complex vitamins.

ADDITIONAL READING
See "Beans."

BUYING SOURCES
These beans are available in supermarkets and health food stores all over the country. Dried Great Northern beans can be bought loose (in bulk) and in plastic bags or boxes (prepackaged). See "Beans" for a list of mail order sources and brand names.

HIJIKI

(hee JHEE kee)

Hijiki is not just another pretty sea vegetable with wavy thick tresses. The large coarse black strands of hijiki become very tender when properly cooked, and its unique texture improves any meal.

Hijiki's black tresses are especially beautiful and flavorful nestled in an array of colorful vegetables, beans, and grains.

OTHER NAMES
Hiziki, hijicki.

FLAVOR/TEXTURE
Hijiki has the strongest ocean flavor of all the sea vegetables, but compared to fish, shrimp, crab, and lobster, it is very mild. Hijiki has a strong, robust flavor and seafood aroma.

GENERAL USES
Hijiki is used as a vegetable in main course and side dishes, as a condiment, and in soups, stews, casseroles, stuffings, burgers, loaves, burritos, etc.

It is sweetened considerably when cooked with onions and/or squash and it also combines well with nuts and root vegetables such as carrots, turnips, parsnips, and beets.

If you've never had the pleasure of using sea vegetables before, use hijiki as a condiment to become familiar with this invaluable food. Spread a little on everything you cook and welcome the added nutrition as well as the new flavor.

Hijiki can be substituted in any recipe calling for the milder, thinner, and shorter cooking sea vegetable called arame. Just be sure to take into account hijiki's longer cooking time.

FRESHNESS/QUALITY

See "Sea Vegetables (Dried)."

STORAGE

Hijiki can be prepared in a large batch since it keeps well under refrigeration (up to 7 days) and freezes well.

PREPARATION INSTRUCTIONS

WASHING & SOAKING

The best method of washing hijiki to remove sand, shell particles, and excess salt is to cover the hijiki with water and stir. Then move it to a second bowl (with a slotted spoon or your fingers) and repeat with fresh water. Repeat one last time. Then soak for 20 minutes. Hijiki will expand considerably on soaking, yielding up to five times its dry volume. As with other sea vegetables, the water from soaking can be used in cooking, but if it is too salty, dilute by adding some fresh water. Be sure not to use the sandy sediment at the bottom of the soaking bowl.

The sodium content of hijiki can be reduced by more than 85% by rinsing and soaking it since nearly all of the sodium is located in a powdery surface residue.

COOKING

Hijiki goes very well with oil and is commonly sautéed. In fact, the "ocean" flavor of hijiki can be reduced by sautéing it lightly in sesame oil after soaking it.

Another common method for cooking hijiki is to place it in a small pan and add water until it is just covered. Then boil, reduce heat, cover, and simmer for 15-20 minutes. Add tamari soy sauce and cook for 10 more minutes.

In general, hijiki requires longer cooking than most other sea vegetables.

HEALTH INFORMATION

High in minerals, dried hijiki contains ten times more calcium than a comparable volume of milk, cheese, or other dairy food. It is also high in iron, protein, vitamins A, B_1, B_2, and B_{12}. See "Sea Vegetables (Dried)" for a nutritional comparison table. Hijiki has an abundance of trace elements and their overall effect is to tone up the system, purify the blood, regulate the blood sugar level, and revitalize skin and hair. See "Sea Vegetables (Dried)" for a nutritional composition comparison of sea vegetables.

ADDITIONAL READING

See "Sea Vegetables (Dried)."

BUYING SOURCES

Hijiki is found in health food stores, Japanese markets, and is also available through mail order. See "Sea Vegetables (Dried)" for a list of mail order sources.

BRAND NAMES

Emerald Cove, Eden, Ohsawa, and Mitoku are all excellent hijiki producers.

HONEY

(HUN ee)

To be, or not to be, a bee? That's an easy question to answer. Would you choose to be a bee that works a lifetime to produce a single teaspoon of honey? No wonder, historically, honey was considered the nectar of the gods. You too can share in such wealth by a simple trip to the grocery store. Fortunately, for bees' sakes, less honey is needed than sugar to give the same sweetening effect. For a comparison of sweeteners, see the section "Sweeteners" in this book.

Plant nectar is processed through enzymatic action in the stomachs of bees to form a highly concentrated and refined sweet product. Without a doubt, this unique manufacturing process is entirely natural and organic.

VARIETIES OR TYPES

Honey can be classified in two ways: as coming from a certain type of plant pollen the bees process, or the geographical region the bees travel. Honey can come in a variety of colors, depending on the plant source: golden-yellow, black, white, and green.

See the "Honey Types Based on Plant Type" table for information about the various honey types. The standard golden yellow honey that immediately jumps to mind when you hear the word "honey" is made from clover pollen. Wildflower honey, the next most common type, is produced from free ranging bees that visit a variety of flowers and plants in their regional area. Typically, darker honey is more mineral rich and stronger tasting.

Single source honeys are obtained when bees are allowed access to only a single type of plant. Whenever this is not the case, a *blended* honey is created. Blended honey can also be produced by mixing two or more single source honeys. This is often done to modify the flavor, or change the moisture content, of the resulting honey to be more appropriate for particular uses.

FLAVOR/TEXTURE

Honey has a definite flavor that is very dependent upon the time of year, the type of plant pollen the bees processed, and when the honey was removed from the bee hive. It can range from light and delicate to dark and strong. The aromatic plants such as thyme, orange and lime blossom, rosemary, lavender, and eucalyptus impart a distinctive flavor to the honey created from them. Conifers (pine, sycamore, alder, etc.) as well as buckwheat and heather create a strong flavored honey. Neutral, mild-flavored honey is created from leguminous plants (such as acacia and plants in the pea family), clover, alfalfa, and wildflowers.

GENERAL USES

Used in baked goods, honey promotes even browning of the crust, helps to produce a "soft crumble" product, tends to prolong freshness, and helps baked goods retain moisture. For general use, choose a light flavored honey such as clover or wildflower.

Honey is frequently used in pastries, gingerbread, croquettes, and a variety of confectioneries as well as in drinks such as eggnog, grog, shakes, and liqueurs. Honey is also suited for use in meat dishes

Honey Types Based on Plant Type

©1996 Nigro

Plant	Color	Consistency	Typical Uses
Acacia	very pale yellow	fine	at the table, sweeten drinks
Alfalfa	yellow	very crystalline & thick	cooking
Buckwheat	dark reddish-brown	coarsely crystalline	gingerbread
Black Alder	greenish-brown	thick	cooking and baking
Clover	very pale yellow	almost oily	at the table
Eucalyptus	dark brown	thick	specialty
Gooseberry	green	thick	at the table
Heather	reddish-brown	fairly thick	baking
Lavender	amber	thick	at the table
Lime Blossom	greenish-yellow	thick	at the table and cooking
Orange Blossom	very pale golden yellow	oily and smooth	at the table
Pine	greenish to black	thick	at the table
Rape	white to yellow	thick	at the table and cooking
Rosemary	white or golden	soft	at the table
Sycamore	green	thick	cooking and baking
Thyme	golden yellow	oily	spreads

including lamb, poultry, chicken, mutton, wild game, fowl, pork, and ham.

Mouth-watering honey pecan cookies can be made with honey, soy butter, vanilla, whole-wheat pastry flour, broken pecan pieces, and a little salt. A tasty treat can be whipped up by melting semisweet chocolate (or carob) pieces with honey and vanilla, adding chopped pecans and salt, pouring into a shallow pan and then allowing to cool. These chocolate nut squares are a real crowd pleaser.

A delightful fruit dressing can be easily created by mixing nut oil (walnut, almond, or hazelnut), orange juice, paprika, and salt with honey. Then pour it over apples, strawberries, or blueberries. A warming grog can be created by mixing hot water, rum, honey, and lemon.

A sweet glaze that can be used in meat dishes uses honey, orange juice, mustard, butter, cloves, soy sauce, and ground ginger. Try spicing up some of your honey by simply placing cinnamon sticks in it, sealing, and letting it sit for a couple months.

FRESHNESS/QUALITY

During any stage of processing, the highest quality honey has not experienced temperatures in excess of 105°F. Too high a temperature discolors the honey and negatively affects its flavor. Typically, the best selection is unpasteurized honey from a reputable local apiary.

Some producers add high-fructose corn syrup or other sugars to their honeys; thereby, creating an inferior product. Fortunately, this mix cannot be legally sold as honey because it is not 100% pure. The addition of sucrose, high fructose corn syrup, or even water to honey will prevent it from being labeled "honey." Thus, all brands of honey, regardless of their quality, are natural and undiluted.

Before filtering, honey contains contaminants such as bee parts, pollen, wax, and dirt. The USDA grades honey according to its degree of filtration, not any other measure of quality such as processing temperatures or methods, liability to crystallize, flavor, or consistency. The highest grades are "US Grade A" and "Fancy" and refer to the finest filtering;

this honey will be clear and shiny. "Substandard" is the lowest rating and involves the least amount of filtering. An apiary that does not filter its honey at all removes the larger contaminants by letting the honey sit for a while to allow the larger particles to settle to the bottom. Unfiltered honey will be cloudy.

It is very difficult to be sure that a single source honey is "pure." As long as more than 50% of a blend of honeys is a particular type, the honey can be called that type of honey—implying that it's single source.

STORAGE

Crystallization will develop in honey with either long or cool storage. See "Sweeteners" for information on how to reliquefy it as well as on basic storage information.

PREPARATION INSTRUCTIONS

The acidity of honey can be neutralized by adding a pinch of baking soda per 1/2 cup honey used. For additional preparation instructions, see "Sweeteners."

HEALTH INFORMATION

The total sugar content of honey is higher than that of any other natural sweetener. Seventy-five percent of honey is glucose and fructose. Like white sugar, honey is absorbed quickly into the bloodstream and upsets the blood sugar level. Honey should be used in moderation. For information about the types of sugars, see the glossary.

Even though honey has proteins, amino acids, vitamins, and minerals, they exist in such small quantities that they have virtually no effect.

A form of botulism (*C. botulinum*) is associated with honey consumption and causes some infant botulism deaths. To be safe, avoid giving honey to babies under two years old.

ADDITIONAL READING
See "Sweeteners."

BUYING SOURCES
See "Sweeteners."

BRAND NAMES

Draper Honey, Deer Creek Honey Farms, and Rainforest Honey are manufacturers that provide excellent quality honeys. Try the brands of local apiaries; they are generally of very high quality.

KELP

The kelps make up a large family of brown algae (a type of sea vegetable). Usually sold in powder form, kelp is a flavorful, nutritious salt substitute that is particularly rich in calcium and iodine.

FLAVOR/TEXTURE

Kelp has a delicate, sweet flavor that embodies the spirit of the ocean.

GENERAL USES

Kelp is used as a vegetable in other dishes, stand-alone vegetable side dish, condiment, stock generator, or softening or tenderizing agent. It is sold in whole, granulated, or powdered forms.

Granulated and powdered kelps are used as condiments or flavorings. They can improve the food value of soups, sauces, and spreads, as well as thicken and flavor these mixtures. Kelp powder is often used as an alternative to table salt. Just use about one-half as much kelp as you would table salt.

One of the most important aspects of kelp is that it enhances the natural sweetness of the ingredients it is cooked with. It contains glutamic acid, a natural flavor-enhancer and tenderizer. Glutamic acid is the original natural version of the powerful flavoring agent monosodium glutamate (MSG), which nowadays is chemically synthesized from molasses. Kelp also adds body to any long cooking dish.

Whole dried kelp can be used as an alternative to using the kombu sea vegetable in beans to tenderize, improve their taste, and increase their digestibility. See the "Beans" section for more information. Kelp cooks slightly faster and tastes slightly sweeter than most kombu.

Pickled, steamed, or boiled whole kelp can be added to salads for a flavor and nutrition boost. Chop it coarsely and marinate it in lemon juice or vinegar for a refreshing summer salad. Soak, sliver, and sauté kelp with some fresh greens to bring out the natural sweetness and flavor of the greens.

Kelp is especially good with root vegetables. Bake kelp on the bottom of a root casserole (containing a mixture of chopped onions, carrots, potatoes, turnips, rutabagas, etc.) with just enough vegetable broth (or a beer-tamari soy sauce mixture) to cover.

Add a small amount of kelp to make a thick, rich broth for soups and stews.

FRESHNESS/QUALITY

See "Sea Vegetables (Dried)."

STORAGE

See "Sea Vegetables (Dried)."

PREPARATION INSTRUCTIONS

WASHING & SOAKING

In some cases, dried whole kelp may be partially covered with a white powder of natural salts and sugars that are discharged from the kelp during storage. To maximize its tenderizing and flavor enhancing properties, be careful not to remove this powder during cleaning. However, you may choose to quickly rinse kelp to minimize its intensity.

Dried whole kelp is quickly restored to its original tenderness and dark green color by a brief wiping down and then soaking for 3 to 5 minutes. However, kelp does not need to be soaked.

COOKING

Kelp may be fried or sautéed as well as eaten raw, boiled, or dry roasted.

Soaked briefly, kelp may be eaten without cooking. This is useful for salads. Kelp may also be blanched briefly in boiling water before being added to salads. It also makes an excellent soup stock when brought to a boil and then simmered for just 3 to 5 minutes.

To make a condiment, roast the kelp in a 300°F oven for a few minutes and grind it into a fine powder (in a blender, suribachi, or spice/coffee grinder). To add variety to the "seasoning," add dry roasted pumpkin or sesame seeds to the kelp before grinding it.

HEALTH INFORMATION

Kelp is a rich source of vitamins, minerals, and many trace elements, especially calcium, iodine, and the B-complex vitamins. See "Sea Vegetables (Dried)" for a nutrition comparison table. Soluble fibers give kelp more total dietary fiber than oat bran. Its high sodium content, however, warrants its use in moderation. See "Sea Vegetables (Dried)" for a nutritional composition comparison of sea vegetables.

Kelp contains alginic acid, which has been shown to combine with certain toxins (such as radioactive elements and heavy metals), allowing them to be eliminated from the body.

ADDITIONAL READING

See "Sea Vegetables (Dried)."

BUYING SOURCES

Kelp is available in health food stores as well as through mail order. See "Sea Vegetables (Dried)" for a list of mail order sources.

BRAND NAMES

Maine Coast Sea Vegetables *Kelp* (also called *Wild Atlantic Kombu*) and Mitoku *Kelp* are excellent.

KIDNEY BEANS

(KID nee) (beans)

Kidney beans are probably one of the most popular beans. They are often credited for adding fantastic flavor and texture to many chili recipes. These 1/2 inch long beans typically have a deep brown-red or liver color and, oddly enough, they are kidney-shaped.

OTHER NAMES

Mexican bean, chili bean.

FLAVOR/QUALITY

These beans have a robust, full-bodied flavor and a rich, creamy texture.

GENERAL USES

Kidney beans are a common ingredient in many Mexican dishes such as chili, enchiladas, tacos, tostadas, and green chili stuffing. Kidney, as well as pinto or pink, beans can be used in refried beans. To make these, cooked beans are mashed and combined with spices and then fried. Try using onions, tomato, and garlic; or garlic, oil, and cumin; or any other spices.

These beans can be cooked with vegetables and seasonings such as garlic, bay leaf, onions, carrots, sweet red pepper, thyme, and celery. A little post-simmering with tomatoes, salt, black pepper, and beer is worth the effort. They are wonderful when baked alone or with other cooked beans, onion, and peppers and combined with barbecue sauce, mustard, soy sauce, and maple syrup.

Kidney beans are great in cold bean salads. The dark red kidney adds a filling texture and rich color accent.

Dips for vegetables and chips can be made from kidney beans. Blend garlic, bean juice (from cooked kidney beans), umeboshi plum vinegar, olive oil, and a little miso with well cooked beans. And, interestingly, the kidney bean can be used to make a dessert mousse or sweet pie filling. To produce these, place drained cooked kidney beans in a powerful blender and purée them. Sweeteners, raisins, cinnamon, nutmeg, ginger root, etc. may be added to provide the dessert-like qualities.

FRESHNESS/QUALITY

See "Beans."

STORAGE

See "Beans."

PREPARATION INSTRUCTIONS

CLEANING AND SOAKING

See "Beans."

COOKING

See the "Beans" section for general instructions for cooking. Kidney beans foam easily when they are boiled. Stove-top cooking time ranges from 1 to 1 1/2 hours, and the pressure cooking time is 30 minutes. One cup of dried beans yields approximately 3 cups cooked.

HEALTH INFORMATION

Kidney beans are a good source of protein, iron, and the B-group vitamins.

ADDITIONAL READING

See "Beans."

BUYING SOURCES

See "Beans" for a list of mail order sources and brand names.

KOMBU

(KOM boo)

Absolutely, positively, no kitchen should be without this essential, highly nutritious, very versatile, sea vegetable. Kombu is usually sold in dried strips 2 inches wide and 3 to 18 inches long. It looks very dark green, brown, or black when in dried form.

FLAVOR/TEXTURE

Kombu has a divine, distinctive flavor that captures the essence of the ocean.

GENERAL USES

Kombu is used as a vegetable in other dishes, wrapper, stock generator, condiment, or softening or tenderizing agent. It is also made into teas, pickles, snacks, and candy.

Kombu contains glutamic acid, a natural flavor-enhancer and tenderizer that enhances the natural sweetness of all the ingredients it is cooked with. As such, it is enjoyed as an accompaniment to grains, beans, and root vegetables. Kombu is especially delicious with root vegetables such as carrots and parsnips.

It may also be used as a wrapping for other foods such as rice, other grains, tofu, tempeh, and vegetables.

You can make a handy vegetable stock for soups, sauces, noodles, or any other recipes calling for chicken or a vegetable broth. When used for this purpose, kombu's nutrients are leached into the stock very quickly. So you'll not want to cook it for more than 30 minutes to avoid cooking away nutrients and flavor.

A multipurpose kombu condiment can be sprinkled on just about anything—grain, vegetable, bean, bread, meat, and fish dishes.

Although it has a great many other uses, we would not think of cooking beans without this "magic" tenderizing, anti-flatulence ingredient. Added to a pot of beans, kombu helps them to cook faster and renders them more digestible and flavorful. See the "Beans" section for more information.

Wakame and kelp, which are thinner and cook more quickly, may be substituted in any recipe that calls for kombu.

FRESHNESS/QUALITY

The Japanese kombu available in health food stores may be called dashi-kombu and is considered to be high quality. See "Sea Vegetables (Dried)" for more information.

STORAGE

See "Sea Vegetables (Dried)."

PREPARATION INSTRUCTIONS

WASHING

To clean, wipe off any dust with a dry or moist towel. Do not, however, scrub the tiny white flecks off the outer surface of the kombu. These are mineral salts and complex sugars that contribute to kombu's delicious taste and energy. Kombu's flavor enhancers reside mostly on its surface so you don't want to remove them by washing it.

SOAKING

Soak kombu only long enough for the kombu to soften, typically 7 to 10 minutes. If soaked too long, it becomes slippery and hard to cut. Save the soaking water for use in the recipe or for use as a base for soups or stews or to cook beans, grains, and noodles in.

CUTTING

There are many shapes that kombu can be cut into, including very fine, small cubes or squares, large slices, and long strips used to tie around other vegetables. The best way to cut dried kombu is with a pair of scissors. And soaked kombu is most easily cut on a cutting board with a sharp knife.

COOKING

To make a vegetable stock, boil kombu for 10 to 15 minutes, remove it, and add any vegetables that you like (such as carrots, turnips, radishes, onion, mushrooms, and watercress). Boil for a few minutes more until the vegetables are at the desired tenderness, then season with a little tamari soy sauce. After using the kombu in making stock, remove it from the pot and save it for use in another dish. Re-dry it by placing it on a paper towel or bamboo mat.

Because kombu is thick, it requires a minimum of about 30 minutes to cook to become tender, and it can stand to be cooked even longer. It is normally boiled or toasted, not fried or cooked in oil, because it is naturally oily.

A strip of kombu may be placed at the bottom of a pot of rice or vegetables to prevent sticking. When cooking kombu with root vegetables, it should be soaked first for fifteen minutes, then cooked beneath the vegetables until tender.

To make a kombu condiment, roast it in a 375°F oven for 7 to 10 minutes and then grind it into a fine powder with a suribachi, blender, or spice/coffee grinder. To add zest to your condiment, add roasted and ground sesame, pumpkin, or sunflower seeds.

For a high-powered, rich-flavored snack, clean and chop the kombu into small squares, marinate it in tamari soy sauce for 1 to 2 days, and cook on the stove-top for 3 to 5 hours on very low heat until the tamari has evaporated. Due to its high salt content, this treat is usually eaten in very small amounts.

HEALTH INFORMATION

The proportion of nutrients varies with the type of kombu and the time at which it is harvested, but all kombus are highly endowed with vitamins, minerals, and protein. Kombu is rich in iodine and also contains vitamins A, B_2, C, and calcium. See "Sea Vegetables (Dried)" for a nutritional composition comparison of sea vegetables.

Kombu is high in alginic acid. This acid, because of its indigestible nature and binding quality, acts as a natural cleanser for the intestines by gathering together the toxins within the colon wall and allowing for their natural elimination. This process also strengthens the intestines.

ADDITIONAL READING

See "Sea Vegetables (Dried)."

BUYING SOURCES

Kombu is found in health food stores, Japanese markets, and mail order catalogs. See "Sea Vegetables (Dried)" for a list of mail order sources.

BRAND NAMES

Ohsawa, Ocean Harvest, Eden, and Emerald Cove provide excellent quality kombu.

KUZU

(KOO zoo)

Kuzu is a high quality thickening agent which adds a sparkling, translucent, and shiny gloss to the foods it's cooked with without interfering with their flavor. It is made from the root of the kuzu plant, which is native to the mountains of Japan and now grows wild in the southern United States, where it is called kudzu. It comes in a white powder and chalky or irregular lumps.

See "Thickening Agents" for additional information.

OTHER NAMES

Kudzu (pronounced *KUD zoo*, in the deep South, or *KOOD zoo*, everywhere else).

FLAVOR/TEXTURE

Refined kuzu is odorless and flavorless. In some very unrefined brands of kuzu, the high concentration of minerals can be tasted.

GENERAL USES

Kuzu is an excellent thickening agent for sauces, gravies, stews, soups, vegetable and noodle broths, puddings, icings, shortcake toppings, pie fillings, and beverages. Kuzu adds a translucent gloss to the foods it's cooked with—without affecting their flavor. It does not add a starchy taste or make the foods feel heavy.

Prepare a savory brown sauce by using miso or soy sauce with kuzu and puréed sautéed onions and mushrooms.

The kuzu root starch does not cloud clear soups while adding body and substance to them. This is extremely useful in soups that use a vegetable broth for a base liquid because vegetable broths are typically lacking in the fats and natural thickening gelatinous substances that are normally found in beef and chicken stocks.

Furthermore, kuzu is often used with agar to produce jelled salads and aspics. The agar provides the basic firmness and keeps the salad jelled at room temperature while the kuzu adds an iridescent or satiny quality and gives the salads a softer and more delicate texture. See "Agar" for more information.

Creamy-smooth drinks can be created with the use of a little kuzu. A marvelous lemon basil tea can be made by boiling some fresh lemon basil in water and letting it steep for 10 to 15 minutes. Body and substance can be added to the tea by cooking it with a small amount of kuzu along with a touch of sweetener (such as Sucanat®). Slightly sweetened non-dairy milks can also be thickened with kuzu to create an alternative to dairy cream. See the section "Non-Dairy Milks."

A kuzu batter can be used to coat deep-fried foods. You can deep-fry onions, green peppers, pumpkin, mushrooms, potatoes, sweet potatoes, green beans, squash, tofu, and anything else you can think of.

FRESHNESS/QUALITY

There are two issues to be considered when evaluating the quality of a particular brand of kuzu. The first is that the kuzu starch should consist of 100% wildly grown organic kuzu root. Lower quality products (often found in Oriental markets) are frequently a combination of kuzu and potato or sweet potato starch. Furthermore, low quality kuzu may be processed with chemicals. Be sure to read labels carefully.

The second issue involves the level of refinement. The less the kuzu starch is washed and filtered, the more mineral content it retains. However, too much mineral content can cause the kuzu to have too strong of a "clay-like" flavor that is almost impossible to mask. The color of the kuzu starch will give you a good indication of its refinement level; the grayer the starch, the less refined it is. Bright white kuzu is very refined and has almost no mineral value left. Kuzu that is slightly gray (i.e., experienced 50 or so washings) is a good compromise; there is some mineral value remaining, but not enough to cause the kuzu to have a bad flavor.

STORAGE

Store kuzu powder in a cool, dry, dark place in an airtight container. Dishes cooked using kuzu can be refrigerated or frozen and will retain their thickness when reheated.

PREPARATION INSTRUCTIONS

Kuzu tends to form clumps or crystals in storage, so it may be necessary to pound it to a more powdery state before measuring. The clumps can be crushed with the back of a spoon.

You must dissolve kuzu in *cold* liquid (water, soy sauce, fruit juice, wine, vinegar, etc.) prior to cooking. Use 1/3 to 3 tablespoons per cup of liquid, depending on the thickness desired. For example, use around 1 1/2 tablespoons of kuzu per cup of liquid for sauces and gravies; and to thicken a beverage, use 3/4 to 1 teaspoon of kuzu per cup of liquid.

Immediately after giving the kuzu mixture its last stir, gradually add it to hot liquids at the very end of the cooking time. These liquids should be continuously stirred until they become clear or transparent and shiny. This is the indicator that the kuzu is as thick as it is going to get. It cooks quickly, usually in one to two minutes.

When using kuzu with acid fruits (such as lemons, tangerines, oranges, and strawberries) the resulting mixture may set less firmly. The higher the acidity level and the larger the volume of the fruit, the more kuzu must be used to obtain the same thickening power. If you are having trouble getting the thickness you want in a dish that contains an acid fruit, start by adding 1/2 teaspoon more kuzu per cup of liquid and/or fruit.

A distinct advantage of kuzu is that it can be cooked for a long period of time, and at high temperatures, and still retain its thickening power.

A kuzu batter, for coating deep-fried vegetables or tofu, can be made by dissolving a minimum of 2 tablespoons of kuzu powder in 3 tablespoons of cold water. The more kuzu that can be dissolved in a given amount of water, the better the batter will coat the foods. Vegetables covered with a kuzu batter are crispier and less fat-saturated than those vegetables that are deep-fried without a batter. More information and recipes can be found in William Shurtleff's *The Book of Kudzu*.

Arrowroot flour or cornstarch may be substituted for kuzu. See the "Thickening Agents" section of this book to modify proportions.

HEALTH INFORMATION

Over 83% of kuzu starch consists of carbohydrates. Less refined varieties may contain small amounts of ash, calcium, phosphorous, iron, sodium, and potassium. However, kuzu does not contain any vitamins.

Kuzu is known to be a powerful folk remedy. Since ancient times, it has been popular in the Orient as an aid to digestion and as a treatment for colds, headaches, intestinal ailments, general fatigue, and circulatory system problems. Studies have shown that kuzu is effective in reduc-

ing high blood pressure; relieving chronic migraine headaches; and easing aches in the shoulders, neck, and head. Followers of the macrobiotic philosophy, believe that kuzu can be taken for the relief of flu, fever, and hangovers. They also believe that kuzu aids the body in creating alkaline blood which is necessary for restoring and maintaining good health.

It is also interesting to note that research has been conducted that indicates kuzu may be effective in reducing the desire for alcohol.

ADDITIONAL READING
Shurtleff, William, and Akiko Aoyagi. *The Book of Kudzu*.

BUYING SOURCES
The kuzu starch is available on shelves or hanging racks in health food stores and oriental markets. See "Thickening Agents" for the names of mail order companies that carry thickening agents.

BRAND NAMES
The following brands are excellent: Eden *Kuzu Root Starch*, Ohsawa *Kuzu Root Starch*, Emperor's Kitchen *Authentic Kuzu Japanese Arrowroot*, Mitoku *Kuzu*, and Morino *Wild Organic Kuzu*.

LENTILS

(LEN tills)

It's not often that such small things offer so much value for such a small price. These tiny lens-shaped legumes are little treasures, since they are probably the most versatile and easiest to cook of all the beans. Lentils come in an assortment of colors and can be green, red, orange, yellow, grey, brown, black, or even mottled.

VARIETIES
There are a variety of lentils, with a variety of colors to choose from. The most available types are:

Green Lentils: This type of lentil has a flat, disk shape, about 1/4 inch in diameter. It has a dull olive green color that almost looks brown. These lentils are easy to distinguish from green split peas; the peas have a much brighter green color and are halved or split. It is interesting, however, that it is much more difficult to distinguish green lentils from brown lentils—their coloring is not that different. If in doubt about the identity of the lentil you are buying, ask your friendly market attendant. The main concern is that the two lentils will cook somewhat differently. The cooking times and resulting textures differ. Green lentils take longer to cook, and hold their shape better than brown lentils.

Brown Lentils: These lentils are smaller than green lentils and are slightly more plump. They are quicker to cook than green lentils and may disintegrate during cooking. As the name implies, brown lentils are russet or grey brown.

Red Lentils: This type of lentil is a 1/4 inch, flat bean, and may have a range of colors: pink, red, salmon, and orange. They turn yellow once they are cooked. Red lentils are actually brown lentils with their skins removed. This makes them very fast to cook and much more susceptible to disintegration during cooking.

French Green Lentils: This type of lentil is also 1/4 inch in diameter, but is more plump than flat. French green lentils are mottled with colors ranging from owl-grey to green-black with hues of greenish-bluish-black. They take slightly longer to cook than green lentils.

OTHER NAMES

Red Lentils: Split red lentils, orange lentils.

French Green Lentils: French lentils, Puy or Le Puy lentils, ponotes.

FLAVOR/TEXTURE

Lentils have a delicate, earthy, nutty to pungent flavor. When puréed they have a creamy texture.

GENERAL USES

Lentils are often used as a side dish, spread for sandwiches, vegetable or chip dip, and sauce for pastas and grains. These little legumes can be combined with grains and vegetables to make hearty and satisfying dishes. They are especially good with winter squash, such as acorn and butternut, and root vegetables like burdock, carrots, and onions. And that's not all! They are also a good addition to soups, stews, and casseroles.

It seems that lentils were created to make a wonderful thick creamy soup. Place some spices, carrots, onions, and water along with your lentils in a crock pot and in just few hours, out comes soup.

Blend cooked lentils, along with your choice of spices and seasonings, and you have a delicious dip. Red lentils are the best variety to use to make a perfect dip for your chips and spread for your breads. Lentils are perfect for making pâtés and purées for hors d'oeuvres and parties.

And believe it or not, you can even make lentil "dogs" and "burgers." A lentil "loaf" is also a possibility; just mix cooked lentils with bread crumbs, your favorite spices, and a smidgen of oil in a loaf pan, top with a tomato or barbeque sauce, and bake it in a medium high oven (350°F). Lentils are excellent as a replacement for minced meat in a Shepherd's Pie recipe.

And lastly, green lentils are wonderful when mixed with your favorite herbed vinaigrette dressing and served cold.

FRESHNESS/QUALITY

See "Beans."

STORAGE

Cooked lentils will keep in the refrigerator, tightly covered, for five days. You can store extra lentils in the freezer for up to nine months. See "Beans" for more storage information.

PREPARATION INSTRUCTIONS

CLEANING

See "Beans."

SOAKING

Lentils may not require soaking before cooking; however, doing so aids in the digestion process. See the "Beans" section for additional soaking information.

COOKING

See the "Beans" section for general instructions for cooking beans. Lentils are a short-cooking legume. They usually will take 30 to 45 minutes to cook on the stove-top and 8 to 12 minutes in the pressure cooker.

Green Lentils: Green lentils retain their shape. One cup dried yields approximately 2 cups cooked.

Brown Lentils: One cup dried yields approximately 2 1/4 cups cooked.

Red Lentils: Red lentils turn golden when cooked. They do not hold their shape well; we like to use them for soups and purées. They are quite foamy at first, so skim the surface before simmering. One cup dried yields approximately 1 2/3 cups cooked.

French Green Lentils: One cup dried yields approximately 2 1/4 cups cooked.

HEALTH INFORMATION

Lentils are rich in protein. They are also high in other nutrients, including the B vitamins and iron.

ADDITIONAL READING

See "Beans."

BUYING SOURCES

Dried lentils can be found in health food stores, oriental ethnic markets, and some supermarkets in bulk or prepackaged forms. See "Beans" for a list of mail order sources and brand names.

LIMA BEANS

(LYE muh) (beans)

Lima beans offer a smooth, buttery texture that complements other flavors well, making them an enhancer to almost any meal.
Small or large, white or green, they are always flat and kidney shaped.

VARIETIES

Large Lima Beans: These beans are large, 3/4 inch to 1 inch long, and have a creamy white color if dried, and light green color if fresh or frozen.

Small Lima Beans: These beans are about 1/2 inch in length and are thinner-skinned than the large lima beans. After cooking, they are very tender and smooth.

Christmas Lima Beans: These beans are a large heirloom variety about 1 inch to 1 1/4 inches long. They are plumper than the large lima and have maroon splashes on a creamy background. This coloring is preserved when the bean is properly cooked.

OTHER NAMES

Large Lima Beans: butterbeans, curry beans, Madagascar beans.

Small Lima Beans: baby limas, sieva beans, butterbeans.

Christmas Lima Beans: large speckled beans, speckled butterbeans.

FLAVOR/TEXTURE

Large lima beans have a flavor that is smooth, creamy, delicious, and slightly starchy with a distinctive sweet taste. Compared to large lima beans, the small limas have a more firm texture and are sweeter in flavor. Christmas lima beans have a buttery texture and subtle chestnut-like flavor.

GENERAL USES

Limas can be used as a stand-alone vegetable or can be added to casseroles, soups, vegetables, and grain dishes. Limas are marvelous when cooked with sweet, fresh corn to make succotash. They are a nice ingredient in a "mixed" vegetable dish; combine them with corn, carrots, peas and onions.

On the elegant side, you can create a gourmet stand-alone lima dish by combining sautéed button or shiitake mushrooms with cooked lima beans, a thick almond milk (see the "Nut Milks" section), a splash of lemon juice, salt, and white pepper. Top with parsley and paprika.

We like to add large lima beans to a hearty vegetable barley stew. They thicken the broth wonderfully. To make a fantastic lima bean soup, cook some of the beans until they have disintegrated to create a thick soup stock, then add firm cooked limas along with spices, vegetables, and grains.

Since they retain their distinctive markings, Christmas lima beans make an excellent addition to soups, fresh vegetables, salads, or pastas.

A scrumptious luncheon salad can be created by adding fresh crisp carrots to tender warm, lima beans and mixing with a honey-mustard vinegarette. Garnish with thinly sliced scallion greens.

FRESHNESS/QUALITY

Although the "Beans" section on Freshness/Quality indicates that beans that are "beat-up" are "bad" or inferior in quality, large lima beans are more susceptible to being chipped, broken, nicked, or having skins broken due to their large size and tender skins. This condition does not necessarily affect their flavor and nutritive quality. However, if the bean's appearance is of primary importance, as in a salad, you may want to pay the price for a very premium bean that does not have these visual defects.

STORAGE

See "Beans."

PREPARATION INSTRUCTIONS

CLEANING AND SOAKING
See "Beans."

COOKING
See "Beans" for general instructions on cooking dried lima beans. They are very foamy during cooking. During cooking, a creamy liquid forms as some of these beans disintegrate. The remaining beans are very tender.

Large Lima Beans: Some skins slip off after soaking. They may either be kept with the beans or skimmed off and discarded, depending on personal preferences and the type of dish being made. Stove-top cooking time ranges from 45 minutes to 1 hour, and a suggested pressure cooking time is 20 minutes. One cup dried beans yields approximately two cups cooked beans.

Small Lima Beans: The cooking time ranges from 60 to 90 minutes on the stove-top and 15 minutes in the pressure cooker. One cup dried beans yields approximately three cups cooked beans.

Christmas Lima Beans: These beans can retain their markings when cooked; however, if cooked too long, the markings fade and the beans take on a rosy hue. Similar to large limas, some of their skins may slip off. Stove-top cooking time ranges from 45 minutes to 1 hour, and the pressure cooking time is 20 minutes. One cup dried beans yields approximately two cups cooked beans.

HEALTH INFORMATION

Lima bean are higher in fat and oil than other beans. They are high in protein, and are a source of B vitamins, iron, calcium, potassium, phosphorous, and trace minerals.

ADDITIONAL READING
See "Beans."

BUYING SOURCES

Lima beans can be found in health food stores and supermarkets in dried (bulk or prepackaged), canned, or frozen forms. See "Beans" for a list of mail order sources and brand names.

MAPLE SYRUP

(MAY pul) (SIR up)

Maple syrup is often linked to fond memories of hearty flap-jack breakfasts in a warm, cozy kitchen. Those stacks of pancakes, smothered with butter and soaked with hot, sweet maple syrup were and still are the greatest!

A highly concentrated sweetener that is rich in minerals, maple syrup is a nice natural, healthful alternative to refined white sugar. It is less sweet than honey and white sugar. For a comparison of sweeteners, see the section "Sweeteners" in this book.

VARIETIES

There are four grades of maple syrup. The highest quality grade is Fancy, which is produced from the first sap of the season. This syrup has the lightest color and highest sugar content. Grades A, B, and C come from subsequent tappings. Grade A is the lightest of this bunch; Grade C is the darkest syrup and has the highest mineral content.

FLAVOR/TEXTURE

Maple syrup has a unique, distinctive, sweet taste that blends well with and complements many foods.

GENERAL USES

Maple syrup can be used for a great many purposes in addition to sweetening breakfast waffles and pancakes. It adds moisture and denseness to baked goods.

This sweetener is also useful in making desserts and candies. A fun thing to make in the winter is maple candy. A sweet, waxy, caramel-like treat is instantly created by pouring boiling maple syrup on clean ice or snow.

Bean, grain, and vegetable dishes can also be sweetened with maple syrup. Many Boston Baked Beans recipes use maple syrup as the sweetener to add flavor and a dark color to white beans. A delectable grain dish can be made by simmering cooked rice and raisins in milk (dairy or non-dairy) and maple syrup, then adding vanilla, sprinkling with nutmeg, and making a brown, crispy top by baking it in an a moderate oven.

FRESHNESS/QUALITY

Maple syrup is extracted by drilling holes into the sides of maple trees and inserting wooden taps to let the sap flow out into the buckets. After the buckets have been filled, the sap is boiled down until it becomes highly concentrated. Because maple tree sap is only about 3% sucrose, it takes forty gallons (the sap of about nine maple trees) to make one gallon of syrup.

Beware of manufacturers that place a paraformaldehyde pellet in the tree's taphole to prolong sap flow. The Canadian government prohibits use of these pellets and Vermont producers reportedly also refrain from using the pellets. However, some producers get around this restriction by directly injecting trees with formaldehyde. Formaldehyde not only contaminates the sap and the resulting syrup, but shortens the lifetime of the tree by many years.

Maple syrup may be contaminated with very high levels of lead. The FDA regulates the lead content of imported maple syrups; thus, imported Canadian brands do not have this problem. However, there is no sure-fire way to determine if a domestic syrup has toxic quantities of lead without visiting the producer. Since, in most cases, this is not practical, check with your local health food store to find brands that have a good reputation for quality, and read labels carefully. To avoid the problem of lead contamination, manufacturers must process their syrup in stainless steel buckets, evaporating pans, and storage tanks, and package their syrup in glass or plastic containers. However, stainless steel equipment is expensive and forces manufacturers that use it to charge more for their products.

"Maple-flavored" syrup may contain as little as 3% actual maple syrup and contains many additives and preservatives.

STORAGE

Store maple syrup in a cool, dark place. During cool months, this may mean just placing it in the cupboard, and then refrigerating it during warm months.

Heavy syrups have a tendency to crystallize, and light syrups tend to ferment. This does not ruin your syrup. See "Sweeteners" for information on how to get the syrup back into a usable form.

PREPARATION INSTRUCTIONS

When heated, maple syrup thins down considerably and tastes sweeter. So don't count on using maple syrup as a thickener as well as a sweetener in hot dishes. For additional preparation instructions, see "Sweeteners."

HEALTH INFORMATION

The sucrose content of maple syrup is 65%, which means that it is best used and enjoyed in moderation. Though not as intense as the reactions caused by refined white sugar, maple syrup causes insulin and adrenaline surges that upset the blood sugar level. For additional information about sucrose and white sugar, see "Sweeteners."

ADDITIONAL READING
See "Sweeteners."

BUYING SOURCES
See "Sweeteners."

BRAND NAMES
A couple of good brands of maple syrup are produced by Firth's and Shady Maple Farms.

MILLET

(MILL it)

Millet is often believed to be food for the birds but, when hulled, is actually a wonderful, very tiny, delicate grain that can be used as a new material in any kitchen to create masterpieces. Millet is sometimes mistaken for mustard seeds because the size and color are similar—dry, small, bead-like yellow balls.

VARIETIES
Millet can be purchased whole or it can be processed to make flakes, meal, and flour. However, these processed products may be difficult to find. See the discussion in "Grains" under the "Milled & Processed Grains" subsection for more information.

Whole Millet: Whole millet is a tiny, yellow grain that has had its inedible hull removed. It can be used to make tasty burgers, pilafs, spreads, loaves, grain and vegetable molds as well as act as a substitute for rice in many dishes.

Millet Flakes: Millet flakes are whole millet kernels that have been squashed flat by heavy rollers. They can be used to make a creamy porridge—there is nothing quite like hot millet cereal on any morning of the year. Millet flakes can also be added to soups, stews, casseroles, and baked goods.

Millet Meal: Millet meal is coarsely ground whole millet that is terrific when used in breads, cakes, cereals, muffins, and pancakes.

Millet Flour: Millet flour has a delicious, sweet flavor and gives a delicate, dry, cake-like crumb to baked goods. It can be used to thicken sauces and to make flat breads. It also adds a golden color to cakes and breads. If you are expecting a dough made from gluten-free millet flour to rise, it won't; therefore, it must be mixed with wheat flour or some other high-gluten flour. For breads that require yeast, it is best not to exceed 20% of millet flour to 80% of wheat. However, in other baked goods that are not expected to rise so much, such as cookies, pancakes, and muffins, a mixture of 50% millet and 50% high-gluten flour may be used. Millet flour has a sweet flavor when it is fresh and becomes bitter when old. It can be revitalized, if not too bitter, by toasting it in a heavy frying pan until it darkens slightly and begins to smell nutty. This will reduce the bitterness.

OTHER NAMES
Poor Man's Cereal.

FLAVOR/TEXTURE
Millet has a mild, sweet, nutty flavor. Some people think that millet has a bit of a bitter flavor as well. This seem to be dependent on individual taste. If it is bitter tasting to you, be sure you are using fresh millet or try using millet with sauces or other ingredients that have strong flavors that will overwhelm the bitter taste.

Millet can be cooked in different ways to create different consistencies: light and fluffy (good for stuffings, enchiladas, and for covering with sauce), slightly chewy and individual (appropriate for pilafs), dense and sticky (used for molds and as a binding agent), and creamy and runny (ideal for porridge or cereal). When cooked light and fluffy, millet has a texture that is very similar to the less well-known grains couscous and quinoa.

GENERAL USES

Millet can stand alone at breakfast, lunch, or dinner, or it can be complemented by other grains. It is ideal for stuffing vegetables, meats, fish, and poultry. It is a fun addition to stews and soups, and can make a satisfying foundation for casseroles. Millet may be added to custards, puddings, and other desserts, and is superb when cooked as a porridge or breakfast cereal. Raw millet makes a crunchy statement when sprinkled on salads, vegetables, beans, deserts, and other cooked grains.

NIGRO TIP

Raw millet can be used as an alternative to nuts when it is used as a topping. It has a nut-like flavor, especially when roasted, a crunchy texture, and does not have the high fat content that nuts do.

Try making a creative pilaf using millet, onions, mushrooms, sweet peppers, and a savory stock of vegetable broth and white wine. Another neat use for millet is as a stuffing for tomatoes, peppers, mushrooms, or meats. Make a mixture of millet, roasted pecan pieces, onion, olives, and pimento to stuff a fresh, garden-ripe beefsteak tomato.

Millet can become sticky when prepared with a sufficient quantity of liquid. This sticky millet is perfect in dishes where a binding property is needed such as in croquettes, grain burgers, and loaves. Furthermore, this sticky millet, when cooled has the perfect texture for use in molds and creating self-binding shapes that can be re-fried, deep-fried, and broiled.

Build a bunch of millet croquettes and store some in the freezer for quick and easy dishes. To make tasty  croquettes, combine cooked millet with vegetable broth, salt, onion, garlic, basil,

oregano, tahini, parsley, etc. Shape into patties and cook by frying in a small amount of oil or broil until brown. Top with a sauce of your choice such as tomato, mushroom, or bean sauce or a salsa.

Make a refreshing, chewy, millet pudding by cooking millet in 4 to 5 times its volume of milk or non-dairy milk until tender. Chill in the refrigerator and then mix in a sweetener, nuts, and fruit. Keep the pudding refrigerated until ready to serve and enjoy.

Millet does not do well with dishes that are supporting subtle flavorings and delicate herbs. However, millet does go well with most meats, beans, fruits, and vegetables.

Millet can be used as an alternative to rice in many recipes. Have some fun by using a sticky millet in a nori sushi roll instead of sweet rice.

FRESHNESS/QUALITY

Old or improperly milled millet is dingy, dull, or dark in color and fresh millet is bright gold. Millet should have very little smell; if it smells musty, pass it by.

STORAGE

See "Grains."

PREPARATION INSTRUCTIONS

CLEANING

Millet does not require cleaning before cooking; however, it may be washed. If you choose to wash millet, rinse it very quickly to prevent an excess absorption of water. See "Grains" for information on cleaning grains.

SOAKING

Millet should not be soaked prior to cooking.

COOKING

Millet can be dry roasted in a heavy skillet to help reduce any bitter flavor that it might possibly have. The roasting has the added benefits of causing the aroma of roasted nuts or popcorn to travel throughout the house and causing the millet to cook a bit more evenly (which is important if you want a dry, light, and fluffy result).

Because millet can actually be eaten raw, if some millet is undercooked and a bit crunchy, you may be achieving the effect that you are aiming for. If, on the other hand, you don't want any crunchies, just be sure to cook the millet long enough and in enough liquid. To cook one cup of millet requires 2 to 2 1/2 cups of liquid and 25 to 35 minutes of cooking.

Cooking instructions and a discussion of cooking issues can be found in the "Grain" section of this book.

REHEATING

Millet that has been refrigerated will become hard, dry, and clumpy. Steaming or microwaving will restore and reheat the millet. See "Grains" for additional information.

HEALTH INFORMATION

Of the grains, millet has the most protein and iron; and it has the second highest fat content (approximately 5%), with oats having the most. It is also quite high in the B vitamins, potassium, calcium, magnesium, zinc, copper, and phosphorous.

Millet does not contain gluten and, therefore, can be used if you are on a gluten-free diet. In fact, whatever your diet, millet is very easy to digest.

ADDITIONAL READING

See "Grains."

BUYING SOURCES

Hulled millet can be found in some supermarkets and in most natural and health food stores, either in bulk bins or prepackaged in boxes. Should you find millet in a feed supply store, it is very possible that this millet is intended for bird feed and has not been dehulled. See "Grains" for a list of mail order sources and brand names.

MIRIN

(MEER in)

Mirin is an enchanting, sweet, golden rice wine, with a very low alcohol content, that is used only for cooking. It is a condiment that adds a sweetness, roundness, and mellowness to a dish.

OTHER NAMES

Chinese Cooking Wine, sweet rice wine.

FLAVOR/TEXTURE

This condiment imparts a distinctive mild sweetness to the dishes it's added to.

GENERAL USES

Add mirin to glazes for meats and desserts, simmering stocks, dipping sauces, salad dressings, and marinades to introduce a harmonious sweet flavor. It is also used to flavor gravies, noodle broths, sautéed vegetables, dips for tempura and sushi, seafood dishes, and teriyaki.  On some occasion when you are tempted to cook with a sweet wine, consider using mirin instead, to make a delightfully different dish.

Due to its sweetness, mirin may also be used as an alternative to refined white sugar in glazes, frostings, and other dessert toppings. See "Sweeteners."

FRESHNESS/QUALITY

Quality mirin is naturally brewed and fermented from sweet brown rice, rice koji (an enzyme used to start fermentation), and water.

Most of the mirin available in Oriental markets has not been naturally brewed and contains sugar or corn syrup, distilled alcohol, dextrose, and other starches. On the other hand, mirin found in natural food stores is generally a natural and high-quality product. Read labels to select naturally fermented mirin. The alcoholic content can be an indication of how natural the product is; generally, the higher the content (10%-14%), the higher the quality. Mirin that contains sugar and other ingredients typically has a low alcohol content (2%-3%).

The sweet flavor of quality mirin is obtained by the natural fermentation process rather than by added sweeteners such as barley malt, glucose, refined sugar, or corn syrup.

STORAGE

A bottle of mirin that has not been opened will last indefinitely. After opening, it can be stored at room temperature for over a year.

PREPARATION INSTRUCTIONS

The alcohol content in mirin evaporates quickly when heated.

Mirin does not require cooking. It can be used right out of the bottle in salad dressings, dipping sauces, marinades, etc.

NIGRO TIP

To reduce the alcohol content in mirin without cooking it, pour it into an uncovered bowl and allow it to sit for an hour or so. Some of the alcohol will evaporate.

If mirin is unobtainable, simply omit it the from the recipe or use sake or dry sherry, along with a small amount of sugar or honey (1/2 teaspoon per 1 tablespoon mirin) as a substitute.

BUYING SOURCES

Natural, health, Oriental, and Japanese food stores and even some supermarkets stock mirin. Mirin is also available through the Gold Mine Natural Foods, Anzen Oriental Foods & Imports, Granum Organic Specialties, and Natural Lifestyle mail order companies.

BRAND NAMES

Mitoku *Macrobiotic Mikawa Authentic Mirin* and Eden *Mirin* are excellent brands.

MISO

(MEE so)

Miso may look somewhat like peanut butter but that is where any resemblance ends. Miso is to soybeans what wine is to grapes. The soybeans are fermented slowly and leisurely in wooden tubs to produce a delicately sweet to robust savory paste. Like fine wines, misos have their own distinct flavor, color, and aroma.

This paste is truly versatile and should become a familiar household item. Miso is not just an ingredient, it is a staple that adds flavor, texture, and a gourmet touch to the most commonplace dishes.

VARIETIES

Commonly, miso is made from soybeans, salt, grain, and sometimes vegetables. Depending on the types, quantities, and treatment of these ingredients, different types of miso are produced. Furthermore, these types of miso vary when made by different manufactures or miso makers.

Although there are a great many types of miso, there is no universally recognized system to name or classify them. Manufacturers may use attributes, raw ingredients, traditional or Japanese names, or a combination of these systems to name their misos. The following information is provided to give you a framework for grouping and organizing misos.

The important attributes to consider when determining the type of miso to use in your cooking are its flavor and color. Factors such as raw ingredients, time for aging, method of production, and where it was made affect the attributes of a miso.

Flavor: Even though all misos are salty, they do not contain the same amount of salt. A loose labeling system that some manufacturers use to indicate the amount of salt in their misos classifies them as *sweet, mellow,* or *salty.* The *sweet* contains the least amount of salt and is mildly sweet. The *salty* has the highest salt content and the *mellow* falls somewhere in between.

Color: Like wines, misos are divided into *reds* (darks) which are more like a russet and warm chestnut brown and *whites* (lights) which range from soft light-yellows to creamy beiges. Two things have an effect on the color of a miso: the length of the aging process and the raw ingredients it is made from. The *reds* get their color from the lengthy aging process and the *whites* must rely on their raw ingredients for color because their aging process is relatively short.

Even though the sweetness or saltiness of a miso has no direct relationship to its color, the darker misos are generally more salty and the lighter ones are sweeter. Using this as a basis, we can define three basic or generic types of miso:

Light or White and Sweet: Light miso is often made using rice which contains a large proportion of carbohydrates and not much salt. The short fermentation process of this miso, combined with the natural sweetness of rice, produces a light and delicately sweet product. Although light rice misos are sweet, not all light misos are. Sweet misos are wonderful when used in dressings, spreads, sauces, toppings, light gravies, and vegetable side dishes. They may also be used as a dairy substitute. Because sweet miso is still quite salty, be sure to reduce or eliminate the amount of added salt that is called for in recipes.

Dark or Red and Salty: These misos are robust and savory with a prominent flavor which adds a rich, meat-like taste to dishes. They are usually made from barley or soybeans and aged for years. These misos are best suited for soups, stews, hearty gravies, and marinades. They are also used as a pickling agent for vegetables and a tenderizing medium for meats, poultry, fish, and tough vegetables (such as burdock root and daikon greens). These misos usually will replace the salt in the recipes they are used in.

Light to Dark and Mellow: These misos are the middle-of-the-road misos. Their flavors and salt content are midline. They are sometimes referred to as brown misos. They can be used in cooking when the light miso won't do the trick and the dark miso would dominate the dish.

Many miso manufacturers do not use the attributes to name their misos. Instead, they sometimes use a traditional Japanese name or a name that includes the raw ingredients. These misos do possess the attributes of all misos; they are just not obvious by their names.

Barley (Mugi) Miso: Mugi, pronounced *MOO ghee*, miso is a rich, full-bodied miso with a sweet flavor. It is a good all-purpose miso. It is deep chocolate brown in color, often has a chunky texture, and has a prominent fragrance. Barley misos are perfect for making soups and hearty vegetable broths.

Chickpea Miso: This miso has a mild flavor and is light in color because it is made from chickpeas or garbanzo beans. It can be used whenever a light miso is called for and makes ambrosial creamy soups and sauce bases.

Hatcho Miso: Hatcho, pronounced *HOT cho*, miso has a uniquely astringent flavor with an underlying mellow sweetness. This combination of bitter and sweet flavors is reminiscent of chocolate. Hatcho miso is dark cocoa brown, may have a slightly chunky texture, and is often so firm that it can be cut with a knife. It contains less salt than many of the dark misos. Frequently, instant miso soups contain hatcho miso.

Soybean Miso: This miso might be thought of as a milder Hatcho. Its flavor is less rich, its color is redder, and its texture is softer.

Natto Miso: Natto, pronounced *NAT toe*, is a sweet miso containing whole soybeans, barley, kombu, and ginger and in some cases natural rice, millet, or barley sweeteners. This combination of ingredients produces a rich sweetness.

Rice (Kome) Miso: Most of the sweet misos are made from rice. In general a kome (pronounced *COMB ay*) miso is another term for sweet miso.

Because miso is becoming more popular, new types are being created. For instance, millet, azuki, and dandelion-leek misos are now available. For interesting new flavors, keep an eye out for other new varieties.

OTHER NAMES
Soya Bean Paste.

FLAVOR/TEXTURE
Depending on its type and manufacturer, miso can have a wide variety of flavors. Once you have tasted one miso, you have definitely not tasted them all. Even the same types vary considerably among

producers. In general, misos are salty and have a fermented flavor. Of course, fermented flavors can be quite different and distinct. For example, the flavors of wine, and beer are not very similar at all. The best way to determine the flavor of misos is to taste them.

Using a peanut butter analogy, miso is available in chunky or smooth. Pieces of grains, beans, or vegetables in the paste make up the chunks in miso. Be warned, however, that "chunky miso" is not a term in common use. Whether a particular miso is smooth or chunky depends on the type of miso and the manufacturer's chosen processing method. If a smooth texture is desired when only a chunky is available, simply blend the miso in a suribachi (or mortar and pestle) until smooth.

GENERAL USES

Miso is often used in making soups, sauces, gravies, casseroles, dressings, marinades, and dips.
Experiment with all the different misos to find the brands and flavors best suited for your different needs. In general, misos go well with vinegar, onion, tofu, lemon, peanut butter, honey, grain syrups, ginger root, mirin, sake, tomato, beans, vegetables, and grains.

All the many different types of miso can be diluted with water or other liquids to compose an enormous variety of extraordinary bouillons or broths. Barley miso makes an excellent hearty vegetable stock which can be used instead of a meat stock. You can make an awesome French onion soup by boiling onions in water until tender and adding barley miso and simmering a minute or two. Serve garnished with your favorite croutons and cheese.

Try adding a little sweet miso to mashed potatoes or cream soups instead of milk. Combine some sweet miso, tofu, and lemon or vinegar to make a substitute for sour cream in dips and spreads. Add miso to your guacamole or avocado dips for a refreshing change. Natto miso makes

a delicious dip for fresh, crisp vegetables.

Tenderize meats and seafood while adding to their flavor by marinating them in a miso solution.

Miso can be used to create a savory topping for hot rice, fried tofu, crackers, baked potatoes, etc., as well as exquisite cold sauces and dressings. Along with the miso, use sesame tahini and other seasonings such as orange juice, shoyu soy sauce, vinegar, mirin, garlic, onions, ginger root, and honey or rice syrup to create a harmonious blend.

Pickle cucumbers by simply covering them in a container of miso for a few days. Make a tofu cheese by spreading miso on all sides like you were icing a cake. Place it in the refrigerator and let it sit there for at least 4 days. Do not worry if you forget about it, for the cheese just gets stronger and better the longer you leave it. We sometimes find a block of tofu cheese tucked in the back of the refrigerator weeks or months later and it's almost like Christmas! It's not often that you are rewarded with a treat for being forgetful.

For a quick dessert, mix miso and peanut butter and use it as a topping over fresh banana slices. Miso has so many uses and with a little imagination the possibilities are endless.

FRESHNESS/QUALITY

The quality of miso varies greatly depending on the method of manufacturing and its raw ingredients. The best misos are made from natural, organic ingredients and are unpasteurized so that the healthy enzymes contained in the miso are not destroyed. The manufacturing process should be free from chemicals, preservatives, and additives. Many of the misos sold in natural food stores are good quality. However, miso sold in Oriental markets, and some supermarkets, may be of a lower quality. Read the labels on the miso packages. Good quality misos will often state that they are organic, unpasteurized, and traditionally made.

STORAGE

Miso should be kept refrigerated in airtight containers. If it is exposed to the air for too long, it may lose some of its moisture and dry out. Should this happen, just mix in a little water and return it to an airtight container. If it is stored in a warm area, a harmless layer of mold may form on the surface. This is not a problem; scrape off the mold before using or refrigerating. Sweet misos may develop an alcoholic fragrance which can be removed by light cooking. Light misos tend to darken during storage which has no effect on their flavor or quality.

When using miso for pickling, its salt is drawn out. For example, this happens when making tofu cheese. The original flavor can be returned to the miso by mixing in sea salt.

We like to use miso that has lost some of its salt content as a sandwich spread.

PREPARATION INSTRUCTIONS

It is not necessary to cook miso. In fact, simmering unpasteurized miso for a long period of time or cooking it at high temperatures will destroy its enzymes and the friendly bacteria that aid in digestion. So, when using miso in your cooking, remove the pot from the heat, stir in the miso, and serve.

Before adding miso to any hot or cold dish, thoroughly mix it with a little water or other liquid ingredient from the dish. This will prevent someone from unexpectedly getting a huge mouthful of concentrated miso flavor. This can be a little traumatic; it's equivalent to taking a huge swig of soy sauce!

The amount of miso used is up to the personal preference of the cook. However, a good rule of thumb is not to overpower the dish with a strong, miso taste, but to integrate the flavor and color to enhance the dish and provide a balance with the other ingredients. If unsure how much to use, start by using one teaspoon miso per cup of liquid.

At times, miso may be the perfect ingredient for dishes that require long cooking times and/or high heats. When this is the case, the flavor will certainly add to the dish, however the nutritional value of any enzymes and some vitamins will be lost.

HEALTH INFORMATION

In general, miso is a source of the essential amino acids, vitamin B_{12}, and minerals. It is low in calories and fat. Furthermore, miso neutralizes ingested environmental pollutants. Unpasteurized miso, like yogurt, contains lactic acid bacteria and enzymes, which assist in digestion and food assimilation.

Light, sweet miso is high in simple sugars and contains about twice the niacin and ten times the lactic acid bacteria of dark miso. On the other hand, dark miso is higher in protein and, because it is made using more soybeans, contains more fatty acids, which are believed to be effective anticarcinogenic agents.

ADDITIONAL READING

Shurtleff, William, and Akiko Aoyagi. *The Book of Miso.*

BUYING SOURCE

Asian shops and many health food stores sell several types of misos in the refrigerated section in small tubs or in plastic bags with a one-way valve. Miso is available through the Clear Eye Natural Foods, Gold Mine Natural Foods, Frankferd Farms Foods, Anzen Oriental Foods & Imports, and South River Miso mail order companies.

BRAND NAMES

South River Miso, Mitoku, and Miso Master produce excellent misos.

MOLASSES

(muh LASS iz)

This humble sweetener can provide an elegant and sweet glaze or topping for meats, beans, desserts, and breads. It has a distinct essence that adds a fullness and richness of texture and flavor to dishes. A nice feature is that it can hold its own flavor when combined

with other very powerfully flavored foods.

A black, thick, sweet, sticky liquid, molasses is an extract of sugar cane. Although it can have a high sugar content, it is used sparingly due to the strength of its unique flavor.

For a comparison of sweeteners, see the section "Sweeteners" in this book.

VARIETIES

When just the term "molasses" is used, it is normally referring to syrups made from sugar cane. There are four types of molasses:

Light Molasses: This is the residue from the first extraction of sugar from sugar cane and is quite sweet.

Dark, or Blackstrap, Molasses: This is slightly sweet and strongly aromatic. It is the last residue of the cane syrup, after the sugar crystals have been extracted the third and last time. Because almost all of the sucrose has been removed from it, blackstrap molasses is not very sweet and is used for its intense molasses flavor.

Medium Molasses: This molasses is from the second extraction and is in between the light and dark molasses in color and flavor.

Barbados Molasses: This is the starting material for making rum, and is occasionally sold as a sweetener. This kind of molasses is also made from sugar cane, but it differs from blackstrap in that it is not a by-product of the sugar industry. Instead, it is made by crushing sugar cane stalks in roller mills to extract the juice, which is then filtered and slowly boiled down to a syrup. Barbados molasses has a very low mineral content when compared to blackstrap.

There is another sweetener that is often confused with sugar cane molasses:

Sorghum Molasses: This sweetener is not made from sugar cane; instead, it is made from sweet sorghum. It is called a "molasses" because its texture and color is very similar to blackstrap or Barbados molasses. Sorghum molasses generally has a high iron content and a tart, fruity taste compared to blackstrap. It is made in much the same way as Barbados molasses. In most recipes, sorghum molasses can be used as a substitute for any sugar cane molasses, and vice versa.

FLAVOR/TEXTURE

Molasses, a thick liquid, ranges in sweetness and has a strong unique flavor that may be called smoky and bittersweet.

GENERAL USES

Molasses adds moisture and denseness, as well as its dramatic flavor to baked goods. In making bread, use molasses instead of honey to produce a rich, sweet whole-wheat loaf. In addition, molasses is used in a great many historical, traditional American dishes such  as shoofly pie, baked beans, apple pandowdy, and Indian pudding.

Tasty ginger glazed carrots can be made in minutes by combining and heating cooked carrots, soy butter, molasses, lemon juice, and ground ginger root and then garnishing with parsley. Stuffed sweet potatoes are a wonderful dish when stuffed with a mixture of the mashed sweet potato flesh, molasses, soy butter, nutmeg, milk (dairy or non-dairy), and a dash of salt, and then allowed to brown and gain a crusty top.

For a delicious holiday ham, a glaze made of molasses, pineapple juice, and cloves can be poured over the ham and baked. Garnish with fresh or canned pineapple slices and cherries.

Prepare a downright delicious cinnamon toast by drizzling molasses on top of a butter-soaked slice of hot raisin toast and sprinkling with ground cinnamon. Warming a bit of molasses and liberally pouring it over a butternut-flavored fine ice cream makes an absolutely heavenly quick gourmet dessert.

FRESHNESS/QUALITY

Sulfur may be used in the process of converting sugar cane into sugar. This process causes the molasses to have a bitter, unpleasant, overpowering flavor; it is "de-bittered" to make it palatable.

Higher quality molasses, where no sulphur is used during the sugar extraction process, is often called "unsulfured molasses" and does not require any chemical processing to eliminate the bitter sulfur taste.

STORAGE

See "Sweeteners."

PREPARATION INSTRUCTIONS

To neutralize acidic properties of molasses, add 1/2 teaspoon baking soda for every 3/4 cup molasses used. For additional information, see "Sweeteners."

HEALTH INFORMATION

Molasses contains all the minerals that have been refined out of white sugar. Its calcium, iron, potassium, silicon, and manganese content are significant. Molasses also contains small amounts of copper, chromium, and vitamin E. See the "Nutritive Value of Molasses Types" table for the amounts of other vitamins and minerals.

Molasses has plenty of vitamins and minerals, but much of its bulk and fiber has been stripped away, causing it to have an adverse effect on the blood-sugar level.

Nutritive Value of Molasses Types
Per 1 Tablespoon

| | RDA* | | Molasses Type | | |
	Male, 154 lbs. 5'-10", 23-50	Female, 128 lbs. 5'-4", 23-50 yrs.	Light Molasses	Medium Molasses	Blackstrap Molasses
Calories	2700	2000	43	46	50
Carbohydrate (gm.)			11	12	13
Fat (gm.)			0	0	0
Protein (gm.)	56	44	0	0	0
Sodium (mg.)			3	6	20
Calcium (mg.)	800	800	33	60	137
Phosphorous (mg.)	800	800	9	14	17
Potassium (mg.)	1000	1000	200	213	600
Iron (mg.)	10	18	1.0	1.4	4.4
Thiamin (mcg.)	1400	1000	14	–	56
Riboflavin (mcg.)	1600	1200	12	–	50
Magnesium (mg.)	350	300	9.2	–	51.6

©1996 Nigro

* Recommended Daily Allowances

Source: Composition of Foods, Agricultural Handbook No. 8, United States Dept. of Agriculture, and Food and Nutrition Board, National Research Council (Revised 1980).

Note: a "–" indicates that data was not available.

ADDITIONAL READING
See "Sweeteners."

BUYING SOURCES
See "Sweeteners."

BRAND NAMES
Sucanat Organic Molasses (blackstrap), Silver Forest Molasses (Barbados, blackstrap, and sorghum), Plantation Molasses (Barbados and blackstrap), Deer Valley Molasses, and Arrowhead Mills Molasses (sorghum) are all excellent quality products.

MUNG BEANS

The claim to fame for mung beans is their sprouts. They are the plump white bean sprouts (sometimes called Chinese stir-fry bean sprouts) that are found in supermarkets everywhere. Mung beans that are not used for sprouting can be eaten in the same manner as any other bean. They are 1/4 inch and round in shape. Their skins are usually olive green and the inside is a yellow color.

VARIETIES
Fresh mung beans are extremely rare; whereas, dried ones are readily available. This being the case, we will target our discussion to the dried variety.

Whole Beans: These beans are left whole in their hulls and are green in color. They are good for sprouting as well as cooking.

Hulled or Split Beans: These beans are a pale yellow and will cook more quickly than the whole bean. Split beans cannot be sprouted.

Bean Sprouts: Dried whole mung beans that have been sprouted provide a crunchy, nutritional addition to many dishes. See "Sprouts."

OTHER NAMES
Whole Beans: Green gram, mung pea, moong dal.

Sprouted Beans: Chinese bean sprouts.

FLAVOR/TEXTURE
Mung beans have a strong, hearty, and somewhat sweet flavor and a soft texture. Mung bean sprouts are crisp and refreshing.

GENERAL USES
Whole mung beans are delicious in salads, soups, stews, burritos, dips, spreads, Shepherd's pies, Sloppy Joes, rice dishes, etc. Try using them in salads with other vegetables such as onion, celery, and carrots, and then finishing them off with a tangy lemon vinaigrette. They are perfect when cooked in soups or slow-cooked dishes, but they require some hearty spices to accommodate their powerful flavor. Mung beans can go Mexican, Indian, Thai, or Indonesian. For a spicy hot dip, use cooked mung beans blended with your favorite hot peppers or a pepper sauce, onions, tomatoes, and twist of lemon. In addition, mung beans can add their robust flavor to create a filling vegetarian loaf or burger (or extend a meat dish). To pump up the heartiness of other beans, adding mung beans to the dish will do the trick.

Bean sprouts can be served in salads, hors d'oeuvres, sandwiches, or by themselves to make a crispy, refreshing vegetable side-dish. They can be used instead of lettuce on any sandwich or in tacos or other Mexican dishes. Furthermore, they add a pleasant color and texture to grain and vegetable dishes, soups, and stir-fries when added a few seconds before the dishes are done.

FRESHNESS/QUALITY
For information about whole and split dried mung beans, see "Beans." Sprouts should be white, plump, firm, and break with a snap when bent. Their "heads" should be green, not brown or black.

STORAGE
For information about whole and split dried mung beans, see "Beans." Mung bean sprouts should be placed in a plastic bag and stored in the refrigerator. Depending on how fresh they were when you bought them, they may last from one to five days.

PREPARATION INSTRUCTIONS

CLEANING AND SOAKING

For dried mung beans, see "Beans." In general, mung bean sprouts do not need any cleaning, but they may be rinsed with cool water right before using if they look like they need it.

COOKING

See "Beans" for general instructions on cooking dried mung beans. Stove-top cooking time ranges from 50 to 70 minutes and the pressure cooking time is approximately 15 minutes. One cup of dried beans yields approximately 2 cups.

For instruction on how to grow mung bean sprouts in your own kitchen, see "Sprouts." Don't make more than can be eaten in a four-day period because they will start to lose crispness after that time. Homemade or store-bought, these sprouts can be eaten raw or blanched. When using sprouts in hot dishes, add them at the end of the cooking time.

HEALTH INFORMATION

Whole mung beans are quite rich in vitamins A and B. However, they have five times more food value after they are sprouted and are easier to digest because the starches in mung beans are reduced to simple sugars during the germination process. Sprouts contain vitamins C and B_{12}, as well as small amounts of protein and iron.

ADDITIONAL READING

See "Beans" and "Sprouts."

BUYING SOURCES

Mung beans can be purchased dried and the sprouts can be bought either fresh or canned from supermarkets, health food stores, and Oriental markets. See "Beans" for mail order sources of dried beans and brand names.

MUSHROOMS

(MUSH rooms)

What a delight to eat the "fruit of the fungus" which has a sponge-like property and soaks up whatever precious juice or liquid it is cooked with and adds a meat-like flavor to boot. What a delight to eat delicious sautéed mushrooms cooked in butter, sherry, and a little garlic. And what is even more delightful is that the word "mushroom" no longer means a single type of fungus; it now encompasses a grand variety of mouth-watering fungi that are easily purchased.

VARIETIES

Because there is an incredible number of varieties of mushroom and they are becoming far more popular than ever before, interesting uncommon ones will be coming to markets. The varieties that are generally available are listed and described next. The foods and dishes that complement each mushroom are listed in the "Mushroom Complementary Chart." If you should see a type of mushroom in the store that is not listed and you are not familiar with it, definitely give it a try!

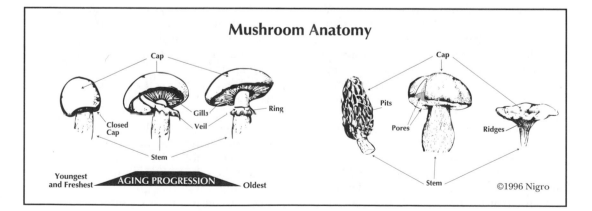

Mushroom Anatomy

Cap — Closed Cap — Gills — Veil — Ring — Stem

Youngest and Freshest — AGING PROGRESSION — Oldest

Cap — Pits — Pores — Ridges — Stem

©1996 Nigro

Button Mushrooms: These mushrooms are white to light brown and range in size from small to large. They can be found in most supermarkets in the produce department. The freshest button mushrooms have a closed cap that prevents the gills from being seen. The mushrooms which  have exposed gills are softer, more mature, and will have a stronger taste that drifts towards "musty" once they've aged too long.

When most people think "mushroom," they visualize these little guys. Button mushrooms are the stereotype that is used as the basis for judging other mushroom types.

Button mushrooms have a mild flavor which intensifies when cooked. They release a considerable amount of liquid when prepared, causing them to shrink dramatically. Therefore, plan on a large amount of raw mushrooms producing a small amount of cooked mushrooms!

The stems of button mushrooms are also edible, both raw and cooked, and are just as tasty as the caps while having a slightly more fibrous texture. However, only the tender caps are used in more delicate dishes.

Sliced or whole, small button mushrooms are welcome in creamy sauces, salads, marinades, and sautées. Mid-sized mushrooms are very nice deep fried and nifty added to stews, soups, and casseroles. Large button mushrooms are perfect for stuffing, broiling, frying, and using as an impressive garnish.

Bolete Mushrooms: This large mushroom ranges from whitish to dark red in color and has a texture which is reminiscent of filet mignon. It has a memorable piney, pungent, and earthy flavor. Although it should not be eaten raw, you can use it in any recipe that calls for cooked mushrooms.

Fresh bolete (pronounced *bow LEET*) mushrooms are hard to come by. They are not grown commercially but may be obtained from independent collectors. If you are lucky enough to see fresh boletes, check to see that they are firm. Plan to cook them on the very day you purchase them, because they will not last very long.

These mushrooms consist of two main parts: the cap, which looks like a hamburger bun, and a bulbous stem. The cap, in turn, also has two parts: the fleshy part and the pores (see the figure "Mushroom Anatomy"). The fleshy parts of the caps are prized for their meat. The spongy mass of pores is enjoyed when firm, young, and fresh. If the bolete pores become too soft, soggy, or green, simply cut them away before using. When the pores reach this state, they cook badly, are not very appetizing, and are impossible to dry. The stems are particularly appropriate for duxelles (see "Preparation of Other Mushroom Ingredients").

A simple but tasty dish of sautéed boletes can be made by using a quality olive oil, garlic, and parsley.

Bolete mushrooms are far more often available dried than fresh. Treat them as you would any dried mushroom. An absolutely ambrosial extract can be made from dried boletes. Reconstituted, they are very leathery and tough and should be sliced thinly before use.

Chanterelle Mushrooms: This golden to red-orange trumpet-shaped mushroom is pronounced *shan teh RELL* and plays to the tune of a wonderful nutty, peppery flavor with a fragrance similar to that of apricots or peaches. The smooth caps and slightly more fibrous stems have a chewy texture and will keep this texture regardless of how long they are cooked. Their flavor blends with anything that would taste good with a fruit. They are especially delicious with butter, onion, and chopped dried apricots.

A fragrant aroma is a sign of a fresh chanterelle. Of course, it should not be slimy or slippery, or have any decaying areas. The ridges should be intact and firmly attached to the mushroom. If the mushrooms look a little brown and dry around the edges, they might be revived by running them very quickly under cool or cold water just before using.

Crimini Mushrooms: The crimini (pronounced *crih MEAN ee*) looks like a brown button mushroom. Often they can be mistaken for button mushrooms that have aged just a little too long. You know you have a crimini if the brown mushroom is dry and firm. If the brown mushroom is slimy, slippery, or overly soft, it is either a too-far-decayed button or an almost-spoiled crimini.

Other than their color and taste, which is a more intense button "mushroom" flavor, the crimini is equivalent to a white button mushroom.

Enoki Mushrooms: These light, mild flavored mushrooms are long, thin, and white with a tiny button on the end. They look somewhat like bean sprouts with little mushroom caps and are even used in a similar manner. They are eaten raw in salads and on sandwiches, and they are added to soups, stews, sauces, and stir-fries during the last few minutes of cooking or just before serving. These mushrooms make a terrific eye-catching side dish when steamed for about 30 seconds. Enoki mushrooms (pronounced *ee KNOW key*) are fun to use and often add an interesting and unique appearance to a dish.

Enoki mushrooms have a very mild, fruity, or radish-like flavor and a crisp texture. Similar to fresh radish, they add a hint of pepper flavor or a mild hot flair to dishes.

These mushrooms are often packaged with their roots still intact. Before using, cut off the roots and the lower tough and fibrous portion of the mushrooms. Fresh enoki 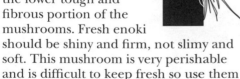 should be shiny and firm, not slimy and soft. This mushroom is very perishable and is difficult to keep fresh so use them within a day or two of purchase.

Matsutake Mushrooms: This heavy, meaty mushroom with a short, broad stem is white or brown in color and has a smooth and dry surface. "Matsutake" (pronounced *mot su TAH key*) is a Japanese word that means pine mushroom. Their strong odor and distinctive flavor take on a resin-scented character from the pine trees they grow below. When buying matsutake mushrooms, select a firm whole mushroom that has a minimum number of rust-colored stains (they indicate the mushroom has been bruised) and has a strong, spicy odor.

These mushrooms are impressive when marinated in soy sauce, dry sherry, sugar, and a good quality oil and then roasted on a grill until golden brown. Or toss chopped matsutake in a pot of rice to add a secret ingredient which will produce a slightly spicy, but not peppery flavor. These mushrooms are often cut into julienne strips, matchsticks, or thin slices before sautéing. An herb called savory blends harmoniously with these mushrooms. An extract made from matsutake mushrooms (see the "Preparation of Other Mushroom Ingredients" subsection) will be faintly green and will have the flavor of a pine forest.

Although the unique matsutake flavor suffers somewhat when dried, it still has a great deal to offer.

Morel Mushrooms: These mushrooms don't really look much like most mushrooms. Instead they look like a loofah (natural sea sponge) on a stick! In fact, another name for this choice mushroom is "the sponge mushroom." It may be light yellow or black. Because of its porous honeycombed-like cap there may be some concern as to what little critters and dirt may be hiding in its crevices. Normally the morel (pronounced *meh RELL*) is naturally quite clean and tidy; but, if you are worried, cut it up to see what's there. Avoid washing them because the water will reduce their flavor. If you feel it is necessary to clean them, run water over them very quickly and cook immediately.

The caps and stems of morel mushrooms are hollow. Fresh morels, if you can find them, should smell either mildly nutty or have no smell at all. Furthermore, they should not contain any moisture and are acceptable if even a little dry.

The morel is a favorite choice to add to cream or white sauces made with sherry. An appetizer of large stuffed morels

adds interest to any table. Fry the smaller or young morels whole for a special treat. Morels should not be eaten raw. Mushroom extract made from dried morels (see the "Preparation of
Other Mushroom Ingredients" subsection) is excellent, rivaled only by the extract made from bolete mushrooms. Rehydrated, cooked, dried morel mushrooms have just as much special flavor and strong aroma as the fresh morels.

When sautéing morels, use a low heat and keep the amount of liquid to a minimum. This will maximize the mushroom's sweet pepper flavor and earthy character. Caraway seeds, garlic, Madeira wine, and cream sherry blend especially well with morels and enhance their flavor.

Oyster Mushrooms: These mushrooms have a soft meaty texture and delicate, sweet, nutty, almost oyster- or zinfandel-like, flavor when cooked. They add a pleasant character, contrast, and flavor to chowders, stir-fries, gravies, etc. Preparing them with butter and onions heightens the heavenly flavor of oyster mushrooms. They have fluted caps that resemble a fan or oyster shell and are typically beige, cream, or gray in color. Sometimes, though, blue, yellow, pink, and white ones can be found. The caps of the oyster mushroom are thin and quick cooking. If you are preparing a dish that requires a long cooking time, add the mushroom at the end. The stems of these mushrooms taste slightly different from the caps and are a bit tough. These stems are also delicious despite their slightly more bitter or sharp character.

Portabella Mushrooms: These huge tan to dark brown mushrooms can range from three to six inches in diameter. They look a bit like giant crimini mushrooms on steroids. A portabella mushroom has a rich, warm, woodsy, almost meat-like flavor and its texture and size make it the steak of the mushroom world. Grilling, baking, or broiling a whole portabella mushroom that has been lightly brushed with oil makes a tip-top meat substitute in

sandwiches and main courses. Sliced or chopped, portabellas can substitute for meat in sauces, stir-fries, and casseroles. Due to their size, these mushrooms are excellent stuffed. When purchasing fresh portabellas, look for smooth caps and intact gills.

Shiitake Mushrooms: Shiitake (pronounced *she TAH key*) mushrooms have a pleasant, distinctive, rich, hearty, smoky, woodsy, almost garlic-like flavor and a firm, chewy, meaty texture. Shiitake growers and enthusiasts will tell you this mushroom is the best flavored cultivated mushroom available and may be used in any recipe that calls for mushrooms. Unlike most mushrooms, the shiitake's flavor is not overwhelmed and is even enhanced by strong spices such as chili powder, coriander, and black pepper. They also have a strong affinity for garlic, soy sauce, and ginger root.

In general, the stems are very tough and are removed. The exception is the delightful crunchy stems on very young, small shiitakes. However, all shiitake stems make a delicious duxelles, soup stock, broth, or mushroom extract (see the "Preparation of Other Mushroom Ingredients" subsection).

Fresh shiitakes are out of this world. Select mushrooms with thick, medium-to-dark brown, smooth, unbroken caps. These caps can range from one to five inches across. Check the underside of the mushroom as well; if it is fresh, it will have a creamy-white rather than brown color.

 Dark, thin, limp mushrooms with upturned caps should be avoided. Fresh shiitakes are very clean and only require a light brushing of the caps before using. Although some people eat them raw, they are usually cooked before eating.

Dried shiitakes are probably the easiest to find. Use caution when buying them, for all dried shiitake mushrooms are not created equal. There are many different grades and prices. The more expensive ones are usually better quality.

A good quality shiitake is known as *donko*, which has a very thick, cracked-top. They are meaty and have a superb flavor. The cheaper, thinner mushrooms, with upturned caps, are less flavorful and have a leathery texture. Reconstituted dried shiitake mushrooms are a bit tougher than fresh ones; however, the rehydrating liquid gains an incredibly rich flavor that is perfect for soups, sauces, etc.

Shiitake mushrooms are scrumptious when used in stews, grain dishes, sauces, stir-fries, etc. Simmering them in a seasoned broth or sauce before tossing them in soups can add another dimension to their flavor.

Wild Mushrooms: Wild mushrooms are free for the picking, but there is a hitch—many wild mushrooms are highly poisonous. Proper training in the identification of mushrooms is a must if you are going to pick your own. If you buy wild mushrooms from a collector, be sure that the harvester is qualified. Or, if you pick them up at a grocery or health food store, satisfy yourself that the store obtained the mushrooms from a specialist or other very reliable source.

FLAVOR/TEXTURE

The flavor of mushrooms ranges from very mild to incredibly strong and from delicate to distinct. They can be fruity, piney, smoky, earthy, buttery, nutty, etc. See the discussion in the "Varieties" subsection and the "Mushroom Cooking Chart" for the flavors of specific mushroom types.

If you have not tried a specific type of mushroom, you may want to perform a little "taste test" before deciding how you want to use it in your kitchen. First slice one mushroom and sauté it in a small amount of butter, broth, or just water. Once it is brown or tender, eat it plain or with a cracker or toast and evaluate the texture and the intensity of its flavor. This test will help you to determine which mushrooms will be best suited for your favorite recipes.

GENERAL USES

Mushrooms are incredibly useful, adding flavor and texture to a huge variety of dishes: meats (beef, poultry, pork, ham, bacon, lamb, veal, shellfish, fish, game); breads, pastries, and tarts; pâtés; eggs (omelettes, quiches, etc.); cheese (pizzas, fondues, al fromage dishes); soups, stews, and chowders; chutneys and relishes; desserts, strudels, and sweetbreads; grains (rice, pasta, wheat, barley, etc.); salads; sauces and gravies; tofu; tempura; and vegetables. However, they are perhaps most delicious when simply simmered and served whole.

To add variety and a gourmet flair to your cooking, mushroom extracts, broths, pastes (called duxelles), powder, purées, and butters can be easily made. For details, see the "Preparation Instructions" subsection.

Mushrooms can be baked, boiled, deep-fried, fried, sautéed, stewed, broiled, grilled, steamed, stuffed, marinated, braised and may be eaten raw.

Try marinating whole, sliced, or halved mushrooms in a favorite oil and vinegar combination (such as unrefined almond oil and brown rice vinegar). These are sublime eaten by themselves or when added to salads, vegetable side dishes, and sandwiches.

A tasty, elegant dish can be created by sautéing portabellas in a little olive oil, along with shallots and garlic. When browned, the mushrooms can then be deglazed with port and topped with bread crumbs and fresh chopped parsley and broiled for a few minutes.

FRESHNESS/QUALITY

Shop for fresh mushrooms that are firm, dry, shiny, fragrant, and fresh-looking. They should not be slimy or slippery, show evidence of insects or worms, or have color spots or bruises. The morel mushroom is an exception to the firmness rule because it is hollow!

When purchasing dried mushrooms, check to see if the bag contains solid, clean, thickly sliced or whole mushrooms. Often there are broken pieces of mushroom which may not rehydrate well.

Whether considering fresh or dried mushrooms, their size is not an indication of quality, but is a matter of preference.

Nigro Tip

If the stems are tough, purchase the mushrooms with the shortest stems because you are paying for them by the pound.

STORAGE

Since fresh mushrooms deteriorate rapidly, you can extend the length of time they remain fresh by removing any dirt or other materials with a soft brush or your fingers before storing. Do not use water to clean the mushrooms unless you are ready to use them.

As a general rule, mushrooms and plastic bags do not go well together. The plastic traps in moisture, which keeps the mushrooms damp and hastens their decay. If you buy the mushrooms in a plastic bag, transfer them to a clean paper bag and store in the refrigerator on a regular shelf—not in the crisper. When stored in this manner, most mushrooms will last about a week; however, button, crimini, portabella, and shiitake mushrooms stored in the refrigerator will never go bad; they will just dry out. If they do dry out, they can be rehydrated and plumped up by soaking them in warm water or stock for 10 minutes to an hour.

If dried mushrooms are kept in a cool, dry place in a tightly sealed container, they can last for months and, if frozen, they will last indefinitely.

PREPARATION INSTRUCTIONS

Cleaning

Just before cooking, fresh mushrooms should be cleaned with your fingers or a very soft brush. Wipe them clean of soil, log stuff, or forest debris. If they are still dirty, use a damp cloth. In those cases when water is needed to clean the mushrooms, use as little as possible and allow the mushrooms to drain and dry before cooking. Mushrooms are like sponges and they can't absorb juices and flavors if they are already filled with water. Remove any tough stems or trim ends as needed.

Soaking

Dried mushrooms need to be soaked. To rehydrate, place them in hot water, or soup stock, for at least 15 to 30 minutes. They are ready to use when soft and pliable. The more hearty mushrooms can be soaked for hours or overnight.

Nigro Tip

If the mushrooms float on top of the soaking water, weigh them down by placing a saucer on top of them in the soaking container.

Once the mushrooms have softened, lift them out carefully and gently squeeze out excess water. Strain the soaking water using a cheesecloth or coffee filter and save it for use in soups, stews, etc. To make a stronger stock, place the dried mushrooms into boiling water and simmer for 5 to 10 minutes, then strain. If you have the time, simmer longer to produce an extract (see "Mushroom Extract" in this subsection for more information).

After soaking, trim away any of the tough stems or ends and hard portions of the mushrooms that refused to rehydrate. If the recipe calls for sliced, diced, or halved mushrooms, do the cutting after the dried mushrooms have soaked.

Cooking

Of the mushrooms listed, only the button and enoki can be enjoyed raw. The others should be cooked before eating.

They may be cooked whole, with or without the stems, thinly sliced, or finely chopped. Slicing mushrooms shortens the  cooking time and promotes more water loss than cooking them whole. Sliced mushrooms will also absorb more of the flavor of the other ingredients. Thus, mushrooms that are mild in flavor should be cut into large pieces so that they maintain their own unique flavor.

Mushrooms can be prepared in many ways: baked, boiled, deep-fried, fried, sautéed, stewed, broiled, grilled, steamed, stuffed, marinated, and braised.

Mushroom Cooking Chart

Common Name	Cooking Method(s)*	Cooking Time	Flavor	Texture	Stem Usage	Culinary Quality
Button	All	Long	Basic "mushroom"	Firm to soft, limp	in dish	Excellent
Bolete	All except steaming & stir-frying	Medium	Buttery & nutty	Firm	in dish	Superior
Chanterelle	Sautéing, baking, marinating, stir-frying	Medium	Earthy, apricot-like	Chewy	in dish	Superior
Crimini	All	Long	Richer basic "mushroom"	Firm to soft, limp	in dish	Excellent
Enoki	Stir-frying	Short	Mild	Raw: crisp, Cooked: limp	in dish	Average
Matsutake	Sautéing, braising, grilling	Long	Peppery & pine-like	Firm	in dish	Very Good
Morel	Stuffing, braising, deep-frying, grilling, sautéing, steaming, stewing	Short	Sweet pepper, earthy	Firm	save for duxelles	Superior
Portabella	All	Long	Richer basic "mushroom," earthy	Firm & meaty	in dish	Excellent
Oyster	Sautéing, braising, deep-frying, baking, stir-frying, grilling	Short	Delicate, oyster-like	Silky, soft, meaty	in dish	Very Good
Shiitake	All	Medium	Rich & smoky	Firm	save for duxelles	Excellent

©1996 Nigro

* Cooking Methods include: baking, braising, broiling, deep-frying, grilling, marinating, sautéing, steaming, stewing, stir-frying, and stuffing.

Butter complements and enhances the flavor of all mushrooms. Unfortunately, vegetable oil does not do the same thing; instead, it has a rather neutral effect. Onions, garlic, sweet peppers, nuts, and soy sauce can be used to enhance the overall flavor of a mushroom dish. Spices that go particularly well with mushrooms are savory, marjoram, thyme, and sage. Highly acidic foods such as lemon and wine can suppress the natural flavors of mushrooms. However, if you would like to make a wine-mushroom sauce, try using sherry, port, or Madeira—they have pleasing flavors and lower acid contents. Salt and sugar (mirin, refined white or brown sugar, date sugar, etc.) are also beneficial to a mushroom dish. Note, however, that after adding these ingredients, you don't want the dish to taste at all salty or sweet! Add just enough, at the end of the cooking process, to bring out the flavors of the mushroom and create a roundness and fullness. Although many foods go well with mushrooms, don't use too many at once, or the mushroom flavor will be drowned out.

PREPARATION OF OTHER MUSHROOM INGREDIENTS

Mushrooms can be made into magnificent primary ingredients that add a divine quality to your entrées, hors d'oeuvres, appetizers, side dishes, and desserts.

Duxelles: A duxelles is a basic mixture of finely chopped mushrooms, onions and/or shallots sautéed in butter, making a paste-like ingredient. It is used as stuffing or garnish, as a complementary ingredient in sauces, and in the preparation of various dishes called à la duxelles. Naturally, the preparation of duxelles has broken from strict tradition, and creative variations have come about. It is best to remember a fundamental point when making any duxelles—keep any additional enriching and embellishing ingredients to a minimum. The onion and butter are, after all, perfect for mushrooms, bringing out their exquisite flavors.

To create a duxelles, sauté 1 1/3 cups of finely chopped onions in 4 tablespoons of butter until they are just transparent. Add 4 cups finely chopped mushrooms

and 1/2 teaspoon salt, 1/2 teaspoon sugar, dash of black pepper, and 1 teaspoon soy sauce. The sugar and pepper are optional. Cook over a brisk heat, stirring occasionally, until the liquid from the mushrooms has evaporated and a paste-like mixture is formed. The amount of cooking time varies because the amount of liquid released by different mushrooms also varies. Let it cool and then refrigerate. It will keep for several days.

Make large batches whenever possible. Once you get accustomed to using this ingredient in your sauces, on sandwiches, and in dips, you will never have enough on hand. Fortunately, it freezes beautifully. Package it in a half or one cup sizes for convenience.

Mushroom Purée: A mushroom purée is different from a duxelles. The same ingredients are used, but the purée ingredients are blended to produce a smooth thin paste. The most common purées are made from button mushrooms. To make your own purée, sauté an onion in 1/2 cup of butter. Add 1 pound of fresh, clean, sliced mushrooms and continue cooking over a low heat for 5 minutes. Add 1 teaspoon salt, 1 teaspoon sugar, 1/4 teaspoon black pepper, and 1 tablespoon water and cook for an additional minute. Remove the mixture from the stove and while it is still hot, blend until smooth. You may need to add extra water to achieve a smooth texture. Allow to cool and refrigerate or freeze.

Mushroom Butter: A freshly made mushroom purée is the basic ingredient for mushroom butters. Blend the purée with softened butter and minced garlic and/or onions. The amount of butter added is up to you. It is not unreasonable to use equal parts butter and purée. While blending, be sure to prevent the butter from getting too hot or it will separate. Allow the mushroom butter to cool and then refrigerate or freeze it.

These butters are excellent for a last minute topping for meat and fish entrées.

Mushroom Complementary Chart

©1996 Nigro

Common Name	Complementary Ingredients*	Complementary Dishes
Button	All-purpose, goes with just about anything.	All-purpose. Basic mushroom for duxelles, mushroom powders, and excellent for stuffing. Delicious in soups and stews.
Bolete	Rice, grains, pasta, vegetables, cheese, eggs, onions, butter, garlic, beef, veal, pork, lamb, fowl, sword fish, tuna, shark. Don't use with fruit or mild fish.	The best mushroom for duxelles. Used for extracts, mushroom powder, soups, stews, casseroles, meat stocks, and breads.
Chanterelle	Fowl, game, nuts, bread, cheese, and vegetables. Avoid using with beef, fish, and potatoes.	Chowder, desserts, grains, pasta, rice, soups, salads, and relishes.
Crimini	All-purpose, goes with just about anything.	All-purpose. Ideal for duxelles and stir-fries. Can be used in same manner as the button when a stronger flavor is desired.
Enoki	Tofu, vegetables, and shellfish.	Salads, soups, and stir-fries (added at end).
Matsutake	Beef, fish, game, poultry, shellfish, grains, and vegetables.	Stews, casseroles, soups, stir-fries, and stuffings.
Morel	Caraway, sweet peppers, veal, fowl, beef, shellfish, cheese, eggs, grains, pasta, and vegetables.	Soups, sauces, duxelles, stuffings, casseroles, chowders, mushroom purées and butters, crêpes, pastries, soufflés, and strudels.
Portabella	All-purpose, goes well with just about anything.	All-purpose. May act as a meat substitute. Perfect for stuffing.
Oyster	Veal, poultry, eggs, tofu, and vegetables.	Mushroom extracts, duxelles, relishes, sauces, and soups.
Shiitake	Beef, poultry, pork, shellfish, fish, grains, breads, pasta, eggs, tofu, and vegetables.	Duxelles, chowders, salads, sauces, soups, stuffings, mushroom butter and powder.

* Ingredients that complement all mushrooms are discussed in the Cooking section of the "Preparation Instructions." They include butter, onion, garlic, sweet peppers, nuts, soy sauce, savory spice, marjoram, thyme, sage, sherry, port, Madeira, salt, and sugar.

Mushroom Buying Guide

Common Name	Other Names	Forms Available	Preserving Method(s)
Button	domestic, common, market, cream, meadow, *Agaricus brunnescens*	Fresh, Canned, Dried	Canning, Drying, Freezing, Pickling
Bolete	cepe, Steinpilz, porcini, stensopp, borowik, byelii-greeb, *Boetus edulis*	Dried, Fresh	Drying, Canning, Pickling
Chanterelle	girolle, pfifferling, kurka, liszka, *Chantharellus, cibarius, Chantharellus cantharellus*	Fresh, Dried	Canning, Pickling
Crimini	California, Italian brown, Roman brown	Fresh	Canning, Drying, Freezing, Pickling
Enoki	enokitake, enokidake, golden, velvet stem, winter, golden needle, velvet foot	Fresh	Canning
Matsutake	*Armillaria pondersa, Tricholoma magnivelare*	Dried	Pickling, Freezing
Morel	sponge, spongy, *Morchella esculenta*	Dried, Fresh	Drying, Freezing, Pickling
Portabella	portabellini, portobello	Fresh	Canning, Drying, Freezing, Pickling
Oyster	shimeji, Phoenix sovereign, pleurotte, *Pleurotus ostreatus*	Fresh, Dried	Freezing, Canning
Shiitake	black forest, golden oak, *Lentinus edodes*	Dried, Fresh	Drying, Freezing

©1996 Nigro

Use them as a sautéing medium or to grease a pan before preparing dishes such as an omelette. Mushroom butters are superb in baked goods or as a spread. Think what it can do to garlic bread or corn on the cob! A pasta tossed with an exotic mushroom butter and lightly toasted almonds makes for a quick and irresistible dish.

Mushroom Powder: Mushroom powder is simply made by grinding dried mushrooms of any kind. Use a spice or coffee grinder, or a blender. If you want a stronger flavor, you can roast the dried mushrooms in a warm oven for several minutes before grinding. This powder is very handy when combining dry ingredients. Use it in flour when making pastas, breads, and even cakes. Of course, the mushroom powder can be used as a spice in soups, sauces, grain dishes, etc.

Mushroom Extract: Think of the mouth-watering possibilities of having liquid mushrooms. Creating mushroom extracts is easy and produces a rich brew. First select a dried mushroom that has a flavor that you want to intensify. A couple of good ones to start with are Bolete (cepes) and morels. If they are not available, then the shiitake will do nicely. Combine 1 to 1 1/2 ounces of dried mushrooms with 3 cups water. Bring to a rapid boil and then reduce the heat to a light simmer for 20 to 30 minutes. Remove the mushrooms and bottle the extract. Then refrigerate or freeze it. The intensity of the extract is dependent on the amount of water you started with. Feel free to experiment and start with more or less water. Of course, the mushrooms that were boiled to make the extract can be saved for use in other dishes.

PRESERVING MUSHROOMS

If you are lucky enough to get your hands on a large quantity of mushrooms, drying or freezing them is not very difficult and will preserve them nicely. See the "Mushroom Buying Guide" table for the appropriate preserving method(s) for each mushroom type.

Drying: Although there are many methods for drying, you only need to learn one. The object of this preserving method is to get the mushrooms bone dry. Dehydrators make drying mushrooms a snap. If you are not sure if they are completely dry, place them in paper bags where they can hang in a warm dry place. You may want to add bay leaves or whole pepper corns to keep the insects out during this final drying period.

Freezing: Blanched or precooked mushrooms can be frozen. Small ones can be frozen whole but the larger ones should be sliced. Freezing mushrooms in plastic bags is the easiest way to go. Be sure that your precooked mushrooms are completely immersed in liquid to prevent freezer burn.

"Prepared mushroom ingredients" such as duxelles, extracts, purées, and butters will freeze nicely. All of your frozen mushrooms, mushroom dishes, and mushroom products will keep for 6 months. Powdered and dried mushrooms will keep in the freezer for years.

HEALTH INFORMATION

Mushrooms contain no cholesterol and negligible amounts of fat and sodium. They are very low in calories and have a bit of potassium and dietary fiber.

The only mushroom that has had any extensive study is the shiitake. It has an extraordinary nutritional profile. Compared to the common white button mushroom, shiitakes have more than twice the protein and fiber, and almost three times the minerals. They are a good source of calcium, phosphorus, iron, and B vitamins. Shiitakes contain all nine essential amino acids in proportions similar to those required by the human body. This means that shiitakes are rich in the amino acids leucine and lysine, which are often deficient in grains. U.S. and Japanese studies show that the chemical compounds in shiitake mushrooms lower cholesterol, act as an anti-viral, have anti-cancer properties, and stimulate the immune system.

ADDITIONAL READING

Books that cover culinary aspects of edible mushrooms are:

Freedman, Louise. *Wild About Mushrooms.*

Czarnecki, Jack. *Joe's Book of Mushroom Cookery*.

Snyder, Jennifer. *The Shiitake Way*.

A book that discusses the health and medicinal qualities of mushrooms is:

Mori, Kisaku. *Mushrooms As Health Foods*.

Books that list mushrooms (edible and poisonous) in an encyclopedic style and provide full color pictures are:

Miller, Orson K., Jr. *Mushrooms of North America*.

Rinaldi, A., and V. Tyndalo. *The Complete Book of Mushrooms*.

BUYING SOURCES

A large variety of fresh, dried, and canned mushrooms can be found in Japanese, specialty, and natural food stores as well as many supermarkets. Mushrooms are available through the Delftree Farm, Mountain Ark Trading Company, Hardscrabble Enterprises, Inc., Gold Mine Natural Foods, Anzen Oriental Foods & Imports, Granum Incorporated, and Jaffe Bros. mail order companies.

BRAND NAMES

With the popularity of the different varieties of mushrooms, new producers of wonderful mushrooms are entering the marketplace every day. Try the different types and brands to see which ones you prefer. Some good ones are: Delftree Mushrooms (*fresh and dried shiitake mushrooms and dried other mushrooms*), Campbells Mushrooms (*fresh portabella, crimini, and button mushrooms*), Woodland Pantry (*dried oyster, shiitake, morel, and porcini (bolete) mushrooms*), Epicurean Specialties (*dried morel, cepe and porcini (types of boletes), chanterelle, and oyster mushrooms*), Mitoku (*sun-dried shiitake mushrooms*), and Monterey Mushrooms (*fresh shiitake, enoki, oyster, and button mushrooms*).

NAVY BEANS

Did you know that these little white beans are used to make the incredibly rich, dark, famous Boston baked beans? They really are! Navy beans are plumpish, oval-shaped, and approximately 1/4 inch long.

OTHER NAMES

Small white beans. Some packagers do not differentiate between navy beans, Great Northern beans, and other white beans. Thus, there may be several varieties in one package.

FLAVOR/TEXTURE

Navy beans have a mild flavor and are very compatible with other foods.

GENERAL USES

Navy beans are a "white bean," a useful all-purpose bean that absorbs other flavors very well. They are good additions to salads, soups, stews, and casseroles, and make a good purée, dip, gravy, or sauce.

As previously mentioned, these beans are used to make the traditional dish, Boston baked beans. A great many cookbooks give good recipes for this favorite. A delicious version involves combining cooked navy beans with mustard, molasses or maple syrup, minced fresh ginger root, cider vinegar, black pepper, strong coffee, and onions. Bake covered in a 275°F oven for 6 to 7 hours, stir in some bourbon, recover, and bake an hour more. Then uncover and bake an additional 30 minutes to make the top of the beans crusty.

An extremely satisfying, warming, filling stew can be made by cooking navy beans with more water than usual along with kombu and diced onions. When the beans are just becoming tender, add salt, black pepper, chopped kale, sliced scallions, diced turnips, cubed potatoes, and cooked long-grain or basmati brown rice. Simmer, covered, for an hour more.

Any of the white beans may be substituted for one another in most recipes.

FRESHNESS/QUALITY
See "Beans."

STORAGE
See "Beans."

PREPARATION INSTRUCTIONS

CLEANING AND SOAKING
See "Beans."

COOKING

See the "Beans" section for general instructions for cooking. Stove-top cooking time ranges from 45 minutes to 1 hour, and the pressure cooking time is 15 minutes. One cup of dried beans yields approximately 2 2/3 cups cooked.

HEALTH INFORMATION

Navy beans are high in protein and have a great deal of carbohydrates, as well as iron, calcium, and B-complex vitamins.

ADDITIONAL READING

See "Beans."

BUYING SOURCES

These beans are available in supermarkets and health food stores. Dried navy beans can be bought loose (in bulk) and in plastic bags or boxes (prepackaged). See "Beans" for a list of mail order sources and brand names.

NON-DAIRY MILKS

If you haven't discovered the wonder of non-dairy milks yet, you have a treat in store for you. They are easy to make and add variety to your cooking and an unique appeal to your gourmet dishes. Almond, soy, and rice milks are available in health food stores, but many nut and seed milks have not yet come to the marketplace. When making your own milks, the possibilities are endless. The simple process of creating your own fresh milk is inexpensive and can be made to match your own special tastes and needs.

For some reason, manufacturers of non-dairy milks choose to call them non dairy beverages even though they have a milky consistency and may often be used as an alternative to cow's milk. However, we could categorize orange juice as a non dairy beverage, too, but we would not call it a non-dairy milk! So, we choose to use the term non-dairy "milk" to refer to beverages that are milky in nature.

VARIETIES

There really are a surprising number of non-dairy milks. They fall into five main categories:

Nut Milks: This category includes milks made from almonds, cashews, pecans, pine nuts, Brazil nuts, and walnuts. Commercial almond milk is available in regular and vanilla flavors.

Seed Milks: This category includes homemade milks created from pumpkin, sesame, and sunflower seeds.

Soymilk: This category includes milks made from soybeans. Commercial soymilks are available in plain (has a unique nutty flavor), chocolate, vanilla, carob, and almond flavors. Generally, these flavors are available in regular, low-fat "lite," and vitamin and mineral fortified varieties. In addition, powdered soymilk is also commercially available.

Rice Milk: This category includes milks made from brown rice. Commercial rice milks are available in regular as well as vitamin and mineral fortified varieties.

Grain Milks: These milks are used mainly for creating creamy, milk-like bases for soups and sauces. They are made from various grain flours such as wheat, oat, barley, and millet. See "Grains" for more information about grain flours.

FLAVOR/TEXTURE

Non-dairy milks have a satisfying, refreshing, full-bodied taste. Depending on the type and amount of nuts, seeds, beans, or rice, as well as sweeteners and spices used, a wide range of flavors and thicknesses can be generated.

Individual commercial brands and types within each brand have their own unique flavor, thickness, and color. Try as many as you can find to determine which ones are your favorites.

Powdered soymilks typically have a little more bean flavor. Some brands attempt to mask this stronger flavor with sweeteners. Check labels.

GENERAL USES

Whether non-dairy milks are bought in stores or made at home, they are exciting alternatives to using dairy milk. Furthermore, you can use non-dairy milks in place of evaporated milk when preparing cobblers, custards, and pumpkin pies. They can be thickened to produce a creamy-smooth, thick liquid that can be used as an alternative to dairy cream.

They can lend a cholesterol-free richness and depth to many dishes, sauces, and soups, and can also add their unique flavors to creams, puddings, shakes, smoothies, pancakes, waffles, etc. A delicious shake can be created by blending non-dairy milk with ice, silken tofu, fruit or carob powder, and a little sweetener. A delightful dark cream-style soup can be prepared by combining a non-dairy milk with tamari soy sauce, onions, mushrooms, and broccoli (or any other combination of vegetables). If a pale colored, creamy soup is desired, use a light miso instead of the soy sauce.

When chilled or warmed, non-dairy milks can be used as a quick energy drink. A rich and warming coffee cappuccino (also called a white coffee—coffee with milk) can be made by whizzing hot Irish Creme coffee, heated non-dairy milk, and a touch of sweetener in a blender. In addition, non-dairy milks can be poured on hot or cold cereals and used in all your cooking and baking needs.

FRESHNESS/QUALITY

When buying a commercially produced non-dairy milk, use it before the date imprinted on the carton. There is a large range of ingredients that may be added to non-dairy milks. Check labels to determine which of the milks sound good or have only the ingredients you want.

When making your own non-dairy milks, use the freshest ingredients possible. See the individual sections "Beans," "Nuts and Seeds," and "Grains" for information regarding freshness and quality.

STORAGE

If buying a commercial non-dairy milk, the unopened, aseptically packaged box of milk can be stored on a shelf at room temperature until the expiration date (usually a matter of months). Once opened, the milk should be transferred to a sealable container and stored in the refrigerator. Most packages indicate how many days their contents will remain fresh after opening. However, if this information is missing, an assumption of five days is rather safe.

Powdered soymilk should be stored in the refrigerator or freezer after exposing the powder to air, and stays fresh for about 5 days after mixing with water.

Homemade non-dairy milks can last in the refrigerator for 4 to 10 days. This is a big range, but much depends on the type of nuts, seeds, soybeans, or brown rices used and their freshness.

Many of the milks will separate during storage so be sure to shake them well before use.

PREPARATION INSTRUCTIONS

We like to make our milks thick. This way we can use them directly as a cream or add water or any other liquid (such as vegetable broth, fruit juice, sugar water, etc.) to create thinner milks. If you make your milks the consistency of a low-fat or non-fat milk, it is almost impossible to use them as a cream.

COOKING

Nut, seed, rice, and grain milks may be boiled if stirred frequently. Soymilks (including those made from powder mixes), on the other hand, are very easily burned. If you must cook soymilk at high temperatures, watch it very carefully, constantly stir it, and lift it from the heat whenever the milk looks like it is in danger of scalding.

A cream substitute can be created by thickening non-dairy milks with kuzu. Dissolve 1 1/2 tablespoons of kuzu in 3 tablespoons of cold milk to create a kuzu mixture. Heat one cup of milk until it is just about to boil and then add the kuzu mixture a little at a time, stirring constantly to prevent the kuzu from lumping. While still stirring, add 1/4 teaspoon of salt and cook for four minutes or until the milk is no longer thickening. One to two teaspoons of honey can be stirred in to create a sweeter cream-like substance. Whether hot or cold, this non-dairy cream will retain its thick, creamy consistency. See "Kuzu" for more information.

HOMEMADE NUT AND SEED MILKS

Many nut and seed milks can be made in only 5 minutes. Use 1/3 to 1/2 cup of nuts or seeds with 1/2 to 3 cups of water, a pinch of salt, and any desired sweeteners. The amount of water you use will depend on the nuts or seeds chosen and determine how thick or creamy the milk will be. Place the ingredients in a blender for 2 to 3 minutes, until absolutely smooth. This makes a great basic milk and no straining is necessary if you don't mind small nut or seed particles in your milk. We enjoy the additional texture and flavor, not to mention fiber, of unstrained nut and seed milks over our cereal and fruit in the morning.

Although milks can be made using just nuts or seeds, salt, sweeteners, and water, you can enhance the milk with high-protein flaxseed and low-calorie lecithin granules. Flaxseed adds body and nutritional bulk to the milk and lecithin granules bind the ingredients, making the resulting milk creamier. If desired, per 1/3 to 1/2 cup nuts or seeds used, add 1 tablespoon of fortified flaxseeds and 1 teaspoon of lecithin granules before blending. The addition of the flaxseeds will require that you strain the milk.

NIGRO TIP

A nice cold nut or seed milk can be made in minutes—when blending, just replace some of the water with ice cubes. Freshly made cold milk is particularly delicious first thing in the morning with your breakfast.

HOMEMADE RICE MILKS

Making a rice milk is a little bit more involved than making a nut or seed milk, because the rice must be cooked first. Combine 2 cups of raw rice with 5 cups of cold water, bring to a boil, lower the heat to a simmer, cover, and cook for 45 minutes to an hour. Don't worry if the rice is a little soupy as long as it is soft. Let the rice cool to a pleasantly warm temperature. For a creamy texture, blend the rice in batches—1 cup cooked rice with 1 cup warm water—until all the rice is blended. Use a sterilized cheesecloth to strain the milk (see the later subsection "Straining or Filtering Prepared Non-dairy Milks"). Place the strained milk in a sealable container and refrigerate.

HOMEMADE GRAIN MILKS

These milks can be created in a manner similar to rice milk using other grains such as oats and barley. Or, they can be created by mixing a grain flour with cold water and then heating until the flour is thoroughly cooked. The flour-to-water ratio is dependent on the final consistency that you desire. These milks, if made thick, can be effectively used as a thickener in soups and sauces.

HOMEMADE SOYMILK

There are as many methods for making soymilk as there are books that describe the process. Some are simpler than others. Our philosophy is to start simple, because it always seems to get complicated later. So the simplest way to make soymilk that we know of is described next. Unlike cow's milk and commercially made soymilk, this homemade soymilk has a beany taste and distinctive odor that we like.

Measure out the desired amount of dried soybeans and sort them (see the "Beans" section). For your first batch, try using 1 cup to get a feel for the process. Soak the dried soybeans from 8 hours to 2 days until they are fully saturated with water; in other words, until they are soft and are no longer expanding. Test for saturation by splitting a bean into its two halves: if the faces of the halves have a consistent color across the whole surface, the beans are ready; If the faces are slightly concave and appear more yellow at the center than the edges, the beans need to soak more. If in doubt about whether they are ready, change the water and let them soak longer. Because the beans will approximately double in size, be sure to use a large enough soaking container. It is important that the beans remain covered with water at all times. If soaking for more than 8 hours, change the soaking water twice a day. When the beans are fully saturated, discard the soaking water and rinse the beans with fresh water and drain.

Separate the soybeans into 1-cup portions and combine each portion with 1 cup water and grind in a blender to make a bean mash. Place all the mash in a rather heavy large pot and add kombu (1-inch dried piece per 3 cups dried soybeans used, see "Sea Vegetables" and "Kombu") and enough water to obtain the final desired consistency (between 2 and 5 cups water per 1 cup dried soybeans used). Less water will produce a cream-like texture, whereas more water will create a thin milk.

The soybean mash is very foamy after blending and will remain foamy throughout its cooking. Bring the mash to a boil, reduce heat to low and simmer for 5 minutes, stirring continuously to prevent the milk from scalding. Whenever the mixture starts to bubble, sprinkle cold water on the mash to suppress it. Don't cover the mash or it will bubble over the pot and make a terrible mess. Once the mash has cooked, let it cool. Use a sterilized cheese cloth to strain the milk (see the subsection "Straining or Filtering Prepared Non-dairy Milks"). Place the strained milk in a sealable container and refrigerate.

For those who wish a bland soymilk, the enzyme that causes the distinctive odor and taste (called lipoxygenase or lipoxidase) needs to be neutralized while keeping the soy protein soluble. We told you that things can get complicated! The process for doing this is based on the method developed by scientists at Cornell University and involves blending the beans with boiling water. If you are klutzy like us, this can be highly dangerous. If you don't like the strong taste and smell of the simple homemade soymilk, we suggest buying the mild commercial products that are available. However, if you want to

give it a try, William Shurtleff, Laurel Robertson, and Tokuji Watanabe provide step-by-step instructions in their books listed in "Additional Reading."

STRAINING OR FILTERING HOMEMADE NON-DAIRY MILKS

Straining or filtering any of the milks may be preferred when you don't want small particles in the liquid. These particles may be undesirable in dishes that should have a creamy, smooth consistency such as puddings, mousses, soups, etc. Pulp removed from non-dairy milks contains valuable nutrients as well as fiber, flavors, and texture. Nut and seed pulps are scrumptious when added to cereals, pastries, breads, pie crusts, etc.

Soybean pulp, called okara (*oh CAR ah*), has a crumbly, fine-grained texture and may be used as a ground meat extender or an alternative to ricotta cheese in burritos, lasagna, etc. This beige-to-white high fiber food absorbs flavors well and gives body to vegetable and grain dishes, soups, casseroles, breads, and salads. It can also be used to create croquettes, fritters, pancakes, chapaties, granola, and doughnuts. However, if you choose not to cook with okara, still save it because it also is an excellent organic mulch and fertilizer. For recipes and more information about okara, refer to William Shurtleff's *The Book of Tofu*.

To strain or filter non-dairy milk, pour it through a small tea strainer, cheesecloth, or other filtering media, to separate pulp from the liquid. The tea strainer is easiest and fastest to use, because it allows some of the pulp to get through. Use a spoon to stir the pulp so that the milk will strain through more quickly. To remove the very fine particles and create a smoother milk, line a sieve or strainer with one or more layers of cheesecloth, place it over a large container, and pour the milk mixture into the cloth. Collect the corners of the cheese cloth to prevent the pulp from escaping and squeeze out as much liquid as possible.

When it is difficult to force the milk through the strainer, it is much easier to strain the milk in stages. You have a couple of options; change the mesh size or the amount strained at a time. To use the varying mesh size method, strain several times, each time decreasing the strainer mesh size. If you don't have a series of strainers with different meshes, you can still solve the problem by straining a small amount at a time and thoroughly rinsing the strainer between batches.

If your milk still has unwanted particles in it, you'll need to strain it again using a finer strainer. This might mean adding another layer or two to your cheesecloth filter.

If you would like your milk to remain fresh for more than a couple of days, sterilization of the straining material before use is highly recommended. This is accomplished by holding the straining device over a sink and pouring a goodly amount of boiling water through it.

NATURAL ADDITIONS TO HOMEMADE NON-DAIRY MILKS

Feel free to add sweeteners: barley malt syrup, honey, maple syrup, brown rice syrup, molasses, or Sucanat®; spices: cinnamon, coriander, cardamom, allspice, nutmeg, mint, anise, or grated ginger root; food flavoring extracts: orange, banana, lemon, almond, vanilla, cinnamon, coconut, butterscotch, cherry, pineapple, or rum; fruit: raisins, pitted dates, peaches, strawberries, blueberries, or bananas; juices: orange, grapefruit, or pineapple; carob or cocoa powder; coffee; or anything else you can think of. In case you are one of those people who wish to add fat to their diet, oil or nut butters can be combined with any of your non-dairy milks to increase body, fullness, and smoothness. The addition of some ingredients may add unwanted particles that should be strained out.

HEALTH INFORMATION

Plain, unfortified soymilk is a good source of protein, B-vitamins, and iron. Fortified soymilks typically have calcium, vitamin D, and vitamin B_{12} added. Soymilk has the same amount of protein as cow's milk. And it has less fat than whole milk, almost all of which is unsaturated.

Nut milks are high in fiber and fat, but cholesterol-free, and they are also high in magnesium, calcium and other valuable minerals.

Non-dairy milks are easy to digest and make a good choice for people with lactose-intolerance.

ADDITIONAL READING

Good sources for additional information about, and alternative preparation instructions for, a variety of non-dairy milks are the following books:

Cole, Candia Lea. *Not Milk...Nut Milks!*

Elliot, Rose. *The Complete Vegetarian Cuisine.*

Hagler, Louise, and Dorothy R. Bates, eds. *The New Farm Vegetarian Cookbook.*

Nishimoto, Miyoko. *The Now and Zen Epicure.*

Robertson, Laurel, Carol Flinders, and Brian Ruppenthal. *Laurel's Kitchen Recipes.*

Shurtleff, William, and Akiko Aoyagi. *The Book of Tofu.*

Watanabe, Tokuji, D. Agr., and Asako Kishi. *Nature's Miracle Protein: The Book of Soybeans.*

Williams-Heller, Annie, and Josephine McCarthy. *Soybeans from Soup to Nuts.*

BUYING SOURCES

Soy, almond, and rice milks are sold in health food stores, specialty food  shops, and some supermarkets. They are typically labeled as a non dairy beverage or drink and packaged in aseptic (non-refrigerated) quart and 8-ounce "drink" boxes. Less commonly, refrigerated soymilk is sold in plastic quart or half gallon jugs. Powdered soymilk can be found in some health food stores. Non-dairy milks are available through the Clear Eye Natural Foods, Frankferd Farms Foods, Allergy Resources, The Mail Order Catalog, and Natural Lifestyle mail order companies.

BRAND NAMES

There is a huge variety of non-dairy milk brands offered commercially. Some good ones are: Wholesome and Hearty *AlmondMylk*™ (regular and vanilla), Pacific *Non Dairy Beverage* (*Lite Vanilla* and *Ultra Plus Vanilla*), West Soy® *Non Dairy Soy Beverages* (*Original, Non Fat, Plus, Lite,* and

100% Organic, some flavored with vanilla and cocoa), *Rice Dream®* and *Rice Dream® Enriched, Eden Rice®, EdenBlend®, Edensoy®, Edensoy Extra®* (some Eden varieties offer different flavors such as vanilla and carob), Solait™ *"Milk of the Sun"* Instant Soy Beverage (soy powder).

NORI

(NOR ee)

Nori is distinct from all the other sea vegetables because it usually comes packaged in useful 7-inch square sheets that are perfect for wrapping around delectable combinations of ingredients. The dark hue of nori adds a nice contrast to the lighter colored foods it's typically wrapped around.

Nori is the wrapping typically used for sushi. This dish, from Japanese cuisine, consists of flavored rice and vegetables and/or cooked or raw fish wrapped in a sea vegetable. Because sushi is growing in popularity, nori is becoming better known. The upshot of all of this is that nori is being used as an ingredient in many more cookbooks.

VARIETIES/TYPES

There are two basic forms that nori comes in:

Sheet Nori: Sheet nori is made by drying cultivated nori and pressing it into 7-inch square sheets. Sheet nori is also available ready-toasted, known as *sushi nori*, or toasted and shredded into fine strips for garnishing, known as *kizami nori*. Toasted sheet nori has a deep green hue while the untoasted nori has a purple hue.

Wild Nori (or Laver): Wild nori is not pressed into sheets. It contains more minerals, is stronger tasting, and is slightly tougher than cultivated nori.

In this book, we will only discuss the sheet nori, because the laver (pronounced *LAY ver*) is rather uncommon and difficult to find.

FLAVOR

Nori has a pleasing, mild flavor that is reminiscent of the ocean.

GENERAL USES

Sheet nori is used as a wrapper or as a condiment.

After being roasted, sheet nori is ideal wrapped around delicious combinations of grains, vegetables, beans, tempeh, and tofu. Traditionally, roasted sheet nori is wrapped around rice balls, used for sushi, or cut into strips for a garnish.

In the Japanese culture, nori is like the tortilla of the Mexican culture. It can quickly and easily be wrapped around almost anything. In just five to ten minutes, you can make delicious "nori rolls." (See "Preparation Instructions" in this section.) They can be filled with rice, millet, or any sticky grain and any combination of ingredients that sound good together, such as: asparagus and hollandaise sauce; avocado, cucumber, and garlic; and kidney beans, scallions, chili powder, and green peppers. Top the nori roll with a slice of pickled ginger, dab of wasabi or horseradish, slice of scallion or hot pepper, sprig of watercress, piece of cherry tomato, etc. Then dip the roll in a sweetened tamari sauce, mustard sauce, hot sauce, tomato sauce or salsa, etc. right before popping the roll into your mouth. Nori rolls are a very fast way to make something delicious and nutritious. Just as quick as a sandwich, you may wish to have a nori roll for lunch for a change of pace. Nori rolls make great hors d'oeuvres, snacks, and side dishes.

Nori condiment prepared from sheet nori has a light and delicate flavor. This condiment can be used as a garnish or seasoning and may be used as the secret ingredient in many salad and grain dishes.

FRESHNESS/QUALITY

High quality nori possesses a deep color and brilliant luster, while lesser-quality nori is dull and flat.

Nori can vary considerably both in price and quality with the higher price generally reflecting a higher quality, but not necessarily better nutrition. A good grade of sheet nori will be somewhat brittle and shiny and when held up to the light should have an overall green (for sushi nori) or purple translucency with an even texture. Beware of cheap grades, which can be limp and uneven. They may also be artificially dyed green and chemically lacquered.

STORAGE

Sheet nori needs to be kept very dry to preserve its delicate flavor. So don't leave open packets lying around. Should it become damp, re-dry it. See the section "Sea Vegetables (Dried)" for more storage information.

NIGRO TIP

If you buy sheet nori that is folded in half, you'll want to unfold and flatten them out and then put them in a large airtight baggie. Later, this will make roasting the sheets much easier because they will not keep trying to refold.

PREPARATION INSTRUCTIONS

WASHING & SOAKING

Sheet nori is not washed or soaked at any time.

TOASTING

Sheet nori is most commonly toasted briefly before use by carefully waving over a flame until the color changes to a bright green. If you have an electric range (i.e., you can't easily generate a controllable flame), you can toast the nori by placing it in a 350°F oven for 2 to 3 minutes. Sheet nori toasts up quickly and does not need any further cooking.

COOKING

Toasted nori can be ground or sliced into strips to make a nutrition-packed condiment or may be used as a wrapper. Our favorite nori "wrapper" recipes always seem to involve some form of the versatile nori roll.

Nori rolls, also called nori maki sushi, are easy to make. All you need is some precooked sticky grain, such as sweet brown rice. (Purposely make some leftovers to have on-hand in the refrigerator.) Just toast the nori, lay it flat and spread a thin layer of warmed sticky grain all over it except for 1/2 inch along the top and bottom of the nori. Along the bottom edge of the grain put your filling ingredients. Tightly roll and slightly wet the edge of the top of the nori sheet to seal the rolled up nori roll—you'll know when you have it tight enough when the filling is in the center of the roll. However, even if your nori roll filling is off to one side, it will still taste just as good. Cut the nori roll into 1/2 to 1-inch rounds (make them small enough that you can pop a whole round into your mouth and easily chew it). Place them on the serving dish, rice and vegetable side up. Top the rolls with something that complements the ingredients you put inside such as pickled ginger root, peanut butter-miso sauce, nuts or seeds, etc.

HEALTH INFORMATION

Nori is one of the richest sea vegetable sources of protein and also contains large amounts of vitamin C and B_1. It is especially rich in vitamin A, containing as much as some carrots. Because it can decrease cholesterol in the body by helping to break down and eliminate fat deposits, nori is especially beneficial to people with a background of heavy dairy food consumption. It is also an aid to digestion and is often served in combination with fried foods. See "Sea Vegetables (Dried)" for a nutritional composition comparison of sea vegetables.

BUYING SOURCES

This sea vegetable is commonly found in health food stores and Japanese markets. See "Sea Vegetables (Dried)" for a list of mail order sources.

BRAND NAMES

A few good quality brands of nori are Emerald Cove *Nori* and *Sushi Nori*, Eden *Nori Sheets*, and Ohsawa *Sushi Nori*.

NUT & SEED BUTTERS

Nut and seed butters are delightfully creamy and rich. They add an element of elegance and sensuality to your cooking.

VARIETIES

Almost any nut or seed can be made into a butter. The common ones that can be purchased pre-made in health food and natural foods stores are:

Almond Butter: This wonderfully sweet nut butter provides the same richness and versatility as peanut butter while providing a bit of variety as well as being more digestible. Doesn't an almond butter cookie sound good?

Cashew Butter: This light colored, incredibly rich butter blends well with other ingredients. Doesn't a creamy, cashew butter sauce over succulent, juicy, fresh fruit sound delectable?

Peanut Butter: This is the most common nut and seed butter. The best peanut butters are those that consist of only ground peanuts, and perhaps a little peanut oil. Doesn't a peanut butter and jelly sandwich on lightly toasted whole wheat raisin cinnamon bread sound absolutely appealing?

Sesame Butter: This butter is made from whole unhulled sesame seeds. Doesn't melted sesame butter over hot steamed broccoli sound marvelous? For more information about sesame butter, see the section "Tahini."

Sunflower Butter: This butter has a distinctive flavor that is ideally suited for Indian and Middle Eastern dishes. Doesn't sunflower butter mixed with curry, raisins, and olives sound like a superb dip for pita bread slices, crackers, and fresh vegetables?

Tahini: This butter is made from hulled sesame seeds and is lighter than sesame butter. Doesn't a mock herb mayonnaise dressing of tahini, chives, mustard, black pepper, white wine vinegar, lemon juice, and a dash of salt sound fabulous for a potato or pasta salad? For additional information about tahini, see the section "Tahini."

FLAVOR/TEXTURE

Nut and seed butters taste like the nuts or seeds from which they were made.

They are very thick, rich, creamy, hearty, and satisfying.

GENERAL USES

Nut and seed butters make excellent substitutes for the more common peanut butter as well as thickening and flavoring agents in soups, sauces, dressings, and dips. Furthermore, they make marvelous additions to batters for muffins, pancakes, cakes, and cookies, not to mention icings and candies. Nut and seed butters, mixed with a little water, are also useful as a partial or full substitute for milk or cream in sauces, puddings, and baked goods. And that's not all—Because they are about 50% oil, they are also suited to replace oil and other fats (such as butter, shortening, or margarine) in baked goods, desserts, and candies.

They can be spread on a piece of freshly baked bread with a little salt sprinkled on top, fresh banana slices, or your favorite jam, jelly, or fruit spread.

Make a butter out of your favorite nut and blend it with lemon juice, soft tofu or yogurt, and herbs for a delightful dressing for vegetable and fruit salads. A marvelous peanut dip can be created by blending peanut butter, tofu, garlic cloves, scallions, and plain yogurt along with some soy sauce, a few drops of hot sauce, and a dash of black pepper.

A delectable cashew sauce can be whipped up by blending sautéed onions with soft tofu, cashew butter, tarragon, salt, lemon juice, and black pepper. An exquisite lemon-walnut pesto can be created by mashing basil and garlic with walnut butter and then blending in grated Parmesan cheese, silken tofu, lemon juice, and olive oil. A mouth-watering sauce made of sunflower seed butter, curry powder, minced garlic, soymilk, lemon juice, and wine vinegar is fabulous over basmati rice or baked potatoes.

FRESHNESS AND QUALITY

Some manufacturers create butters by hydrogenating unsaturated liquid oil to make it a saturated solid, spreadable fat. Look at the labels carefully. If they contain the words "partially hardened oil" or "hydrogenation," you'll know this has been done. Manufacturers do this is to prevent the butter from separating.

STORAGE

Nut and seed butters contain a great deal of oil and can quickly turn rancid if stored in a warm place. They should be refrigerated or frozen. However, the lower temperatures will cause the butters to stiffen. To improve their spreadability, simply let them sit at room temperature for 5 to 10 minutes before use. Once opened, they will last in the refrigerator for approximately 3 months.

Often, because the oil is lighter than the nut or seed purée, the oil in nut and seed butters will separate from the purée and appear as a distinct layer at the top. Butters that do this are perfectly acceptable. Simply stir them a couple of times before using them.

PREPARATION INSTRUCTIONS

COOKING

Before using, stir the nut or seed butter thoroughly to mix any oil that may have separated from the butter back into the nut or seed purée. Nut and seed butters may be eaten raw or cooked. These butters are easily made at home in your kitchen. See the following sections.

HOMEMADE NUT AND SEED BUTTERS

Many nut and seed butters are available at your local health food store. However, they are very easy to make at home to get the perfect flavor and consistency that appeals to you. Simply grind and blend roasted or unroasted nuts and seeds along with a little unrefined oil until the mixture is smooth and creamy. Cheap blenders are not usually up to the task of creating a nut or seed butter; so use a good quality, powerful butter machine, grain grinder, blender, or meat grinder (with its finest attachment). To start with, try using 2 cups nuts or seeds to 2 or 3 tablespoons unrefined oil to make about a cup of butter. Variations in flavor and texture can be achieved by changing the type of oil used or adding a little salt, herbs, lemon juice, garlic cloves, or vanilla extract. Because nuts and seeds have a bit of sodium in them already, it is easy to over-salt the butters made from them. So, when adding salt, do it just a little at a time and taste the butter between each addition of salt.

Butters made out of almonds, cashews, sunflowers, sesame seeds, and peanuts are very popular. But don't stop there; try making butters out of any of the nuts and seeds (see "Nuts & Seeds") and discover additional delights.

HEALTH INFORMATION

See the nutritional profile listed on the purchased container or see "Nuts & Seeds" and "Oils" if making your own nut or seed butter.

BUYING SOURCES

Health food stores typically carry a variety of nut and seed butters. They are usually found next to the "healthy" peanut butter. Nut and seed butters are also available from the Mountain Ark Trading Company and Jaffe Bros. mail order companies.

BRAND NAMES

Some excellent brands of nut and seed butters are Maranatha Natural Foods *Nut Butters* (*Roasted Pistachio Butter, Roasted Macadamia Butter, Organic Raw Almond Butter,* and *Roasted Cashew Butter*), Spanky's *Chunky Almond Butter,* Woodstock *Old Fashioned Nut Butters* (*Cashew Butter (unsalted) and Almond Butter (crunchy/unsalted)*), East Wind *Cashew Butter,* and Summer Corn *Almond Butter.*

NUTRITIONAL YEAST

Nutritional yeast is not the same as the yeasts used in baking or brewing. It is an inactive yeast and can't ferment anything, and definitely will not rise to the occasion of making breads. It is renowned for its appealing, cheese-like flavor and nutritional content.

VARIETIES

This yeast comes in golden or bright yellow flakes and powder. In a recipe calling for flakes, you can substitute half as much powder.

OTHER NAMES

Saccharomyces cerevisiae.

FLAVOR/TEXTURE

It tastes cheesy and, at times, has a nutty flavor.

GENERAL USES

Use nutritional yeast in spreads, soups, gravies, sauces, salad dressings, fondues, breading meal, and on crackers, toast, vegetables, popcorn, salads, and pasta. It is often added to dry mixes for baked goods such as croissants, pastries, pie crusts, breads, biscuits, etc. Furthermore, it can deepen the fullness and richness of savory dishes.

Sprinkle nutritional yeast on a fresh tossed salad and enjoy the cheese-like flavor without the fat and cholesterol. Combine this yeast with almonds and salt and you have a "parmesan" blend for spaghetti, pizza, and garlic bread.

Use nutritional yeast to make a chowder by combining the yeast with milk, flour, lemon juice, potatoes, and your favorite spices and vegetables.

A phenomenal stuffed potato can be fashioned by scooping the meat from a baked potato and mashing it with nutritional yeast, ground black pepper, scallions, salt, and shoyu soy sauce. Gently brush the potato skins with olive oil and bake for several minutes until the skins are crisp. Then stuff the potato skins and top with ground sundried tomatoes or bacon bits.

Do not use brewer's yeast or torula yeast in any recipes calling for nutritional yeast. Use only *Saccharomyces cerevisiae*. If you use any other kind of yeast in your recipes you may have some pretty interesting, undesirable results and flavors.

FRESHNESS/QUALITY

This yeast is a "food yeast" that should be manufactured by growing it in a molasses solution.

STORAGE

Store nutritional yeast in a cool, dark, dry place.

PREPARATION INSTRUCTIONS

Nutritional yeast can be mixed with liquids such as water, milk, or vegetable stock and heated to make a basic sauce. Nutritional yeast does not need to be cooked to use.

HEALTH INFORMATION

Nutritional yeast is a fat-free ingredient that is a good source of quality protein and B vitamins, including B_{12}.

ADDITIONAL READING

Stepaniak, Joanne. *The Uncheese Cookbook*.

BUYING SOURCE

Nutritional yeast is often available in health food stores on the shelf or in the bulk food section. It is available through The Mail Order Catalog and Bob's Red Mill Natural Foods mail order companies.

BRAND NAMES

Red Star *Nutritional Yeast* is an excellent brand.

NUTS & SEEDS

Nuts and seeds have traditionally played a role in many holiday feasts. What Pilgrim would have Thanksgiving dinner without a pecan pie? Nuts and seeds can also play an important role in everyday cooking.  They are very rich in protein and have important unsaturated fats (required to metabolize fat-soluble vitamins). However, because they are high in fats, they are commonly eaten in small quantities and used as condiments or complements to other ingredients to make savory and sweet dishes.

Nuts and seeds are really both seeds. In the strict sense, seeds are embryonic plants that contain the food needed to sustain themselves through their first stage of life. Nuts are the seeds of trees and have a hard, removable outer shell and a softer, edible, inner kernel often called a nutmeat. The foods called seeds are produced by smaller plants (such as flowers, legumes, and vegetables) and have softer, sometimes edible hulls.

VARIETIES

Nuts and seeds are sold in a variety of forms: shelled or in the shell; raw, roasted, or dry-roasted; salted, spiced, or unseasoned; and prepackaged or in bulk.

Shelled: The hard outer shell of these nuts and seeds is removed. They are far more convenient than nuts and seeds that are purchased still in their shell. However, they are a bit more expensive and have lost some of their nutritive value. They are typically exposed to light, which promotes degradation, and are not protected from rough handling.

In the Shell: Nuts and seeds in the shell cost less than shelled ones. They are often more nutritious too because the hard shell protects the kernels from chemicals and light. The natural shell locks in the nutrients far better than any man-made process or packaging. The major drawback, however, is that they must be shelled before use and this can be a time-consuming process. In many cases, it is extremely difficult to get the nut out in a whole form.

Raw: These nuts and seeds are not cooked in any way (with the exception of pistachios and cashews which are treated with heat to open the shells or remove them). Although they will last longer, raw nuts and seeds are not as flavorful as those that are cooked. On the other hand, many roasted nuts are rancid by the time you purchase them. To avoid this problem, nuts and seeds can be purchased raw and roasted at home just before using them in a recipe.

Roasted: Shelled nuts that are fried in oil are roasted nuts. These nuts look and taste oily and are not very crunchy. Because the frying oil used by many producers is frequently rancid, these nuts are often heavily salted to divert the taste

buds. Roasted and salted nuts are often called "cocktail nuts."

Dry-roasted: These shelled nuts and seeds are cooked without adding any oil. Be aware that many manufacturers add sugar, salt, starch, monosodium glutamate, vegetable gums, spices, and/or preservatives to these nuts and seeds. Read labels carefully.

Salted: Roasted or dry-roasted nuts and seeds are often salted. The problem with buying them this way is that the amount of salt is not controllable.

Unseasoned: Nuts and seeds that have not had any salt, spices, or other seasonings added have just the pure original nut or seed flavor. If flavorings are desired, it is easy to add your own, in the proportions you desire.

Prepackaged: Prepackaged nuts and seeds have a tendency to be fresher than those sold in bulk. Glass jars, cellophane bags, and vacuum packed cans keep the air from the nuts and seeds and protect them during shipping. Packages that let in light are convenient for judging the quality of the nuts or seeds, but these packages also speed the ultimate breakdown of the foods they contain.

Bulk: Bulk nuts and seeds are typically older, exposed to light and air, and are not protected from rough handling.

There is a large number of edible nuts and seeds. A brief description of each of the common ones follows:

NUTS

All nuts can pretty much be substituted for one another if their different flavors and fat contents are kept in mind. The "General Uses" subsection gives a description of how all these nuts can be used and the "Nutritional Composition of Some Nuts and Seeds" table provides the fat content information. When a nut has a specialty or is particularly suited for something, it is described in the following discussions for each nut type.

Almonds: These nuts are oval shaped and have a reddish brown skin and smooth, white meat. There are two types of almonds: sweet and bitter.

The bitter almonds are not used in household cooking; instead, they are used in cosmetics and liqueurs. The sweet almonds are the type seen in food stores. They are available shelled (with or without their skins) and in the shell. Common preparations made from almonds are macaroons, pralines, and marzipan (almond paste).

Try tossing toasted slivered almonds with cooked hijiki, soy sauce, mushrooms, and blanched broccoli to create an unforgettable side dish that has the added benefit of being packed with mega-nutrition.

Brazil Nuts: These large nuts have a very hard, dark, brown shell and smooth, creamy, beige meat that has a delicate and delightful flavor.

Because the super-hard shells are snug against the nutmeats, shelling Brazil nuts can be rather diffi-

cult. See the "Preparation Instructions, Shelling Nuts" subsection for tips on how to free the nutmeats in one piece. It certainly is more convenient to buy them already shelled. In addition to the uses listed in the "General Uses" subsection, Brazil nuts can be chopped or shredded and used in a manner similar to coconut in baked desserts.

A tempting nut burger can be made by combining sautéed onions, mushrooms, and garlic along with ground Brazil nuts, bread crumbs, coriander, salt, black pepper, and a strong vegetable stock. Form the mixture into patties and bake in an oven until crispy and brown. You can serve them in a traditional burger way: on a burger bun with ketchup, mustard, relish, and slice of tomato.

Cashews: These creamy-beige kidney or crescent-shaped nuts are crisp and solid and have a sweet, mild flavor. They are the only nuts that are not available in the shell. Cashews are commonly used in Indian and Chinese dishes and a popular American dish is "cashew chicken."

A divine stuffed loaf can be created by first making a batch of sweet or savory stuffing and then mixing sautéed onions and tomatoes with ground roasted cashews, vegetable stock, bread crumbs, basil, salt, black pepper, nutmeg, and free-range eggs. Place half of the mixture into an oiled, sesame seed-lined, loaf dish. Then spoon the stuffing into the loaf pan and cover with the remaining loaf mixture. Bake in a 375°F oven until this exquisite loaf is brown and firm.

Chestnuts: These nuts have heavy, hard, glossy brown shells and white interiors. When roasted, they are a traditional favorite during winter holidays. Chestnuts have an unusually low amount of fat, compared to other nuts, and can be ground to make a flour that is excellent in soups, stews, porridges, fritters, etc. Instead, chestnuts have a high starch content, making them a suitable alternative to potatoes or pasta.

Chestnuts must be peeled before they can be eaten. This involves roasting them (see the "Preparation Instructions, Roasting Nuts and Seeds" subsection for more information). After peeling, chestnuts can be deep-fried, boiled, or placed in a fireplace beneath very hot coals.

Pre-peeled, canned chestnuts can be purchased in supermarkets and specialty food shops on the shelves where the oriental foods are stocked.

Although they are sweeter, dried chestnuts can be used in place of fresh ones. First measure out the amount needed. Use a 1:3 ratio—if 3 cups of fresh chestnuts are called for, measure out 1 cup dried chestnuts. Then soak the dried chestnuts until they are fully rehydrated and use them in the recipe as though they were fresh.

A voluptuous pudding-like dessert can be made by boiling peeled chestnuts until they are soft, mashing them into a purée along with sugar or a sweetener and a pinch of salt. Top the purée with whipped cream that has been spiked with vanilla or brandy and a sweetener.

Or a flavorsome savory pie can be made by combining peeled chestnuts, chopped fresh apples, sage, thyme, black pepper, sautéed onions, and free-range eggs and then pouring the mixture into a pastry pie shell. Top the pie with more pastry and glaze with an egg and almond milk mixture and bake it in a 375°F oven until the top is a golden, crunchy brown.

Cobnuts: See "Hazelnuts" in this subsection.

Filberts: See "Hazelnuts" in this subsection.

Hazelnuts: Hazelnuts, filberts, and cobnuts are so closely related that their names are used interchangeably. They have a reddish-brown shell that is easily cracked and a creamy-beige nutmeat with a thin, brown skin. They are typically flattish on one end and taper to a rounded point at the other. These nuts have a very pleasant, mildly sweet flavor and smell. If needed, they can replace walnuts and almonds in most recipes.

Hazelnuts are sometimes used as a garnish for alcoholic beverages such as martinis. A delectable dessert can be prepared quickly by combining hazelnuts and ripe cherries, letting them chill, and topping with a chilled mixture of sunflower oil, red wine vinegar, orange juice, plain yogurt (or silken tofu), ground cinnamon, salt, and black pepper.

Macadamia Nuts: These nuts are sometimes referred to as Queensland nuts. Their hard shell protects a light, buff-colored nutmeat that has a deliciously mild, sweet and buttery flavor and soft texture. Unfortunately, unlike most nuts, the large amount of fat in macadamia nuts is mostly saturated. They are particularly well-suited for desserts as well as salads, curries, and stews. Shelled macadamia nuts spoil very rapidly; they typically last only a month or so in the refrigerator.

These nuts make a splendid dessert snack when dipped in honey or chocolate. Or a delectably sweet, white cream sauce can be made by blending roasted macadamia nuts with water, vanilla, port, and white wine vinegar and then folding in sautéed onions and oyster mushrooms. This sauce is perfect when served over a bed of white or brown rice, baked potatoes, or biscuits.

Pecans: These native American nuts have two sweet nutmeat halves with a rough texture. They are flat on one side and ridged and lumpy on the other. The shells are a smooth and dull, irregular brown or tan color. Pecans are particular-

ly tasty in rich dishes, such as pecan pie, other pies and cakes, cream desserts, and stuffings for meats. If desired, they may be used as an alternative to walnuts. Because pecans have a very high oil content, they should be removed from any applied heat before they appear done because the nuts will continue to cook from the internal hot oil. Mark Blazek has written a book, called *Pecan Lover's Cook Book,* that consists of nothing more than a huge number of pecan recipes.

A yummy, frozen yogurt can be concocted by stirring together crushed pineapple, roasted chopped pecans, brown rice syrup or honey, and silken tofu or plain yogurt and folding the mixture into agar or gelatin that has been dissolved in fruit juice or water. Freeze the yogurt in popsicle molds or ice trays.

Pine Nuts: These light brown, miniature candy-corn-shaped nuts are known by a great many names: pignoli, pinoli, pinocchio, pinons, pinyon, pine kernel, and Indian nuts. Although some pine nuts are almost almond flavored, most have the flavor of a pine forest—strong, spicy, even resinous—a taste that some liken to turpentine. To eliminate or reduce this "bite," pine nuts can be roasted. Pine nuts are especially delicious in spicy Italian, Indian, and Thai dishes.

Mature pine nuts have dark-colored shells; the light-colored ones house underdeveloped kernels. The shells encasing the nutmeats are very thin and easily removed. Shelled pine nuts should be creamy white or beige and plump.

Traditionally, pine nuts are an essential ingredient for pesto sauce, an aromatic basil and garlic sauce for pasta. To make this sauce, blend toasted pine nuts, garlic cloves, basil leaves, salt, Parmesan cheese, and olive oil to create a sauce that is thick, creamy, and smooth.

Pistachio Nuts: These nuts are a contrast of colors with green kernels in their reddish-pink skins covered in smooth tan shells. If the shells are red, then they have been dyed. Although they are from the same family as cashews, pistachios are sometimes called green almonds. These mild flavored nuts are used extensively in rich Middle Eastern desserts and pastries such as baklava and pistachio ice cream.

If using pistachios as a substitute for other nuts in recipes, be aware that the pistachios' green color may not blend with every food they may be added to.

An appetizing grain salad can be made by combining shelled pistachios with currants and a cooled long grain brown and wild rice mixture and then tossing with a dressing consisting of unrefined oil (safflower, olive, peanut, or almond), vinegar (brown rice, wine, or apple cider), ground cinnamon, salt, and black pepper.

Queensland Nuts: See "Macadamia Nuts" in this subsection.

Walnuts: These nuts contain kernels that are shaped like two halves of a brain. Their powerful flavor ensures that a few walnuts go a long way. When chopped, ground, or only available in "pieces," walnuts are commonly used in cakes and pastries. When the precious halves are obtained whole, they are typically used as a decorative garnish.

Many walnuts are kiln-dried in their shells to extend their shelf life. This process has a tendency to make the walnuts taste bitter. If you are dealing with whole nuts, the bitterness can be reduced by blanching shelled walnuts and removing the brown outer skin (see the "Preparation Instructions, Removing the Skins from Nuts" subsection).

Walnuts are labeled with a variety of terms: English, Persian, Carpathian, American, and black. The English, Persian, and Carpathian all refer to the same type of very common walnut. The kernel is white and covered with a thin, light to dark yellow skin. If the kernel looks greyish, the walnut is getting old. American (or black) walnuts have a rich, distinct flavor that is a bit bitter, but addictive once you've acquired a taste for them.

Honey and walnuts add variety and excitement to tried and true pancakes

and waffles. An enticing pâté can be made by blending sautéed mushrooms, onion, and garlic with silken tofu, walnuts, salt, and black pepper. Use the pâté to top toasted French bread or to stuff celery or small tomatoes.

SEEDS

Some seeds can be used just as nuts are and some have more limited culinary applications.

Alfalfa Seeds: These tiny brown seeds add flavor and nutrition when mixed into doughs before baking breads, muffins, cakes, etc. However, these seeds are more commonly used to produce the famous little green alfalfa sprouts used in sandwiches and salads.

Flaxseeds: These little brown glossy seeds, also called linseeds, add a new flavor and nutritional dimension when ground and added to cereals, whole grain dishes, breads, sauces, salads, sandwiches, casseroles, etc. They can also be used as a thickening agent for sauces, gravies, and dressings and as a nutritional fortifier in nut and seed milks. Ground flaxseeds will last only around 10 days when stored in the refrigerator.

Linseeds: See "Flaxseeds" in this subsection.

Poppy Seeds: These tiny round black seeds are excellent in cookies, candies, cakes, muffins, pastries, fruit salads, dressings, and breads, as well as savory dishes containing grains, beans, and vegetables. They also make a lively topping when sprinkled over salads, pasta, grains, potatoes, and breads.

A sweet poppy seed dressing can be created by mixing silken tofu, honey, Dijon mustard, pressed garlic cloves, safflower oil, poppy seeds, salt, and freshly ground black pepper. Use this dressing for spinach salads and gourmet mixed lettuce salads.

Pumpkin Seeds: These large, green, flat seeds are more suited to savory dishes—unlike the pumpkin flesh which is suited for sweet dishes. They are good in stuffings, loaves, burgers, sauces, trail mixes, granolas, stews, casseroles, and grain, bean, and vegetable dishes. When ground into a meal, they can be easily added to flours for pancakes, waffles, muffins, biscuits, etc. They are typically available unsalted and salted and are crunchy little marvels when roasted.

In Autumn and around Halloween time, it is rewarding fun to harvest pumpkin seeds from fresh pumpkins. The seeds obtained this way are far fresher than any purchased in a store and you can taste the difference. To harvest these seeds, scoop out the interior of a pumpkin and separate the seeds from the pulp. Cook the seeds in a low temperature oven (250°F) for an hour or so. Or put the seeds in a dry, room-temperature or warmish place, for a couple of days so the seeds can dry out before you store them. If damp when you store them, they will grow interesting molds in a relatively short time making them only good for the trash can or a Science Fair project.

A nice cold stuffing for fresh tomatoes, that would be perfect for lunch, can be created by mixing pumpkin seeds, cooked green lentils, chopped celery, a mild mustard, lemon juice, chives, and parsley.

Sesame Seeds: These little seeds that most people recognize on the top of hamburger buns can be used in a great many other ways. Sesame seeds can be used in all the same ways that nuts can be used (see the "General Uses" subsection). More than any other nut or seed, they are splendid when toasted, because the roasting process brings out their tempting, heavenly aroma as well as their rich, nutty flavor. Sesame seeds come in a variety of colors: white, black, and red. These seeds are not typically sprouted.

Try making a delicious breakfast or dessert drink by blending bananas or peaches, ground sesame seeds, and cold water. Or make a special garlic bread by toasting whole wheat bread that has been liberally topped with butter, granulated garlic, sesame seeds, paprika, and a dash of black pepper.

Sesame seeds are often used to make an incredible condiment called gomashio, or sesame salt. This condiment is a staple for those who eat according to the macrobiotic philosophy. It can be sprinkled on almost any savory dish: rice and other grains, beans, vegetables, fruits, casseroles, salads, meats, fish, pasta, etc. It may also be used as a sprinkle for desserts such as chocolate nut ice cream. For directions on how to make it, see "Preparation Instructions, Making Condiments from Seeds."

Sesame seeds make a fine butter when ground into a paste. See "Tahini" for more information.

Squash Seeds: The seeds from all squashes are edible. Some taste better than others. The most common squash seeds are pumpkin seeds. Other squash seeds can be used in the same manner as pumpkin seeds. See "Pumpkin Seeds" in this section for more information.

Sunflower Seeds: These medium sized seeds have a unique, almost nutty flavor that complements many sweet and savory  preparations. They can be used just as nuts are in a huge variety of recipes (see the "General Uses" subsection). For example, they are good in hot and cold breakfast cereals, cakes, cookies, breads, trail mixes, loaves, burgers, casseroles, salads, etc. And they can be ground down into a meal and mixed into flours for pancakes, waffles, breads, muffins, etc. Of course, they are excellent when used as a condiment.

The shells of sunflower seeds can be black with white stripes or just white, brown, or black. These seeds can be purchased hulled, or in the shell, and may be salted or unsalted.

For a refreshing salad, try mixing fresh spinach leaves, sunflower seeds, and any other vegetables you like (such as carrots, onions, tomatoes, fried dulse, etc.) and covering with a dressing made of almond oil, shoyu soy sauce, and honey or rice syrup.

NUT AND SEED PRODUCTS

Nuts and seeds are so versatile, they can be made into milks, butters, and extracts:

Nut and Seed Milks: Nut and seed milks are created by adding a little water (and, optionally, flavorings) to nuts or seeds and then simply blending. These make excellent alternatives to dairy milks. See "Non-Dairy Milks" for additional information.

Nut and Seed Butters: Nut and seed butters are wonderfully rich and creamy. They can be used in place of peanut butter, added to soups and sauces as a thickener, or mixed with other ingredients to make marinades, dressings, and batters. Because they are almost 50% oil, they can also be used as a substitute for oils and fats in baked goods. See "Nut & Seed Butters" for more information.

Nut and Seed Extracts: These are thick liquids that have a concentrated flavor of the nut or seed from which they were made. They are perfectly suited for flavoring baked goods, drinks, desserts, and sauces. Check the label to be sure that the extract is pure or a true extract of the nuts or seeds. If it is made of some kind of "flavor," it is highly probable that the extract is artificial in nature and does not contain any nut or seed products.

FLAVOR/TEXTURE

Nuts and seeds have a wide range of flavors, from mild and sweet to sharp and distinct. However, no nut or seed is sweet enough to be used as a sweetener by itself. When used in sweet dishes, the sweetness must come from other ingredients (see "Sweeteners"). In all cases, roasting nuts and seeds transforms their flavors into something richer and more mellow.

The textures of nuts and seeds are similar: crunchy and firm when raw and meat-like and firm when cooked.

GENERAL USES

Nuts can be used whole, chopped, ground, or puréed in sweet and savory dishes. They can be eaten raw or cooked with other ingredients to make cakes, biscuits, sweets, stuffings, puddings, milks, and butters. Furthermore, nuts and seeds can be added to flour when making pastries, breads, pie crusts, and other baked goods.

Examples of sweet dishes are: puréed nut pastry fillings and confections; whole nuts covered with chocolate, carob, or caramel; ground nuts sprinkled over or mixed into ice cream; and whole or chopped nuts in fruit cakes, muffins, cookies, and breads.

The ability of nuts and seeds to add to savory preparations should not be discounted. Add whole or chopped nuts and seeds to stuffings for poultry, lamb, peppers, mushrooms, tomatoes, cabbage leaves, and other large vegetables. Chopped or ground nuts and seeds are excellent mixed into casseroles or sauces, incorporated in curry dishes and sweet and sour sauces, folded into loaves and burgers, tossed into salads or stews, cast into stir-fries and pot-pies, added to fresh or cooked vegetables and fruits, cooked with sea or land vegetables, or used to top or garnish grain, pasta, bean, meat, fish, egg, and fruit dishes.

To clear out your nut and seed cupboard, you can make a wonderful, rich, one-of-a-kind bulgar-nut loaf. Combine cooked bulgar that has been seasoned with soy sauce, a variety of nuts and seeds (you can't choose to use too many types), onion, parsley, thyme, and free-range eggs to make a loaf. Bake the loaf and top with a sweet sauce. To make the sauce, try combining your favorite fruits (apples, cranberries, raspberries, pears, etc.) with your favorite fruit juice (apple, grape, or orange juice) and your favorite liquor or liqueur (such as brandy, rum, peach schnapps, and amaretto).

Nuts and seeds make wholesome and satisfying snacks or additions to cereals and muesli. When mixed with grains and fruits, they make an excellent trail mix for camping, backpacking, or plain snacking.

They can be ground or blended into a meal or paste and added to baked goods (such as pancakes, muffins, and breads) or used to thicken sauces. The nuts and seeds that contain a lower concentration of fat will produce a meal while those higher in fat will generate a paste when blended. To find the fat content of each nut and seed, see the "Nutritional Composition of Some Nuts and Seeds" table. Adding a bit of oil to the meal or paste and blending will create a nut or seed butter (see "Nut & Seed Butters").

Although most seeds can be sprouted and used in sandwiches, stir-fries, and salads, alfalfa seeds (along with various beans and grains) are the only ones commonly used in this manner. See the "Sprouts" section for more information.

Some nuts, such as walnuts, can be pickled in vinegar; other nuts, such as chestnuts, may be canned in a sweet syrup or sugar water.

FRESHNESS/QUALITY

Limp, dark, shriveled, or rubbery shelled nuts and seeds are old and have lost much of their nutrients and flavor, and may even be rancid. Fresh ones are firm and uniform in size and color.

Whenever possible, buy shelled nuts in their "skins." The skins should completely engulf the nut without any scratches, nicks, or flaky parts. If you want to use a recipe that calls for nuts without their skins, the skins can be removed. See the "Preparation Instructions, Removing the Skins from Nuts" subsection.

A nut can be tested for rancidity by cutting or breaking it in half. Fresh nuts have a firm and light colored, meaty interior. If, on the other hand, the inside has a honeycomb-like texture and/or a yellowish color, the nut is rancid.

For maximum freshness, choose unshelled nuts and seeds. Select those that are heavy, whole, and clean and free from cracks, splits, holes, pinholes, and stains. Avoid nuts that have dried out in their shells; these may rattle or be very light in weight. Nuts and seeds are freshest and most plentiful in autumn and early winter. When stored properly, they will last till the next year's harvest.

Shelled, or in the shell, nuts and seeds should not look very dull or darker than usual which is an indication of age. Never eat any nuts and seeds that look moldy because some of them are very dangerous.

Many nuts and seeds are treated with chemicals to extend their lifetimes. While this may prevent the nuts and seeds from becoming rancid too quickly, it does mean that you are ingesting the chemicals and artificial preservatives.

STORAGE

Because nuts and seeds contain a high percentage of oil that can go rancid, a bit of care must be taken to prevent them from spoiling. Keep nuts and seeds in an airtight container in a cool (preferably the refrigerator or a very cool root cellar), dark, dry place. Whole nuts and seeds in their shells will remain freshest the longest (about a year). Shelled nuts and seeds typically last from 2 to 4 months in a cool place and can be refrigerated and even frozen to extend their lifetimes. Crushed, chopped, sliced, and ground nuts and seeds have the shortest lifetime.

PREPARATION INSTRUCTIONS

WASHING

Most seeds are very clean with today's manufacturing processes. Be that as it may, seeds should be washed if they look dusty or dirty. They can also be washed to remove any empty hulls that are mixed in with the seeds. Wash the seeds by swishing them around in a bowl of cool water. Pour off the top water to remove the hulls, and then pour the rest of the seeds and water through a strainer, except for the last bit that may contain sand particles. Nuts do not require washing.

COOKING

Crushing, grinding, or chopping roasted nuts and seeds enhances their flavor.

When adding nuts and seeds to flour for making pastries, breads, and pie crusts, be careful not to over work the mixture. This will cause the nuts or seeds to release oil and make the baking result quite a bit heavier than you may have intended.

ROASTING NUTS AND SEEDS

The rich flavor of nuts and seeds is enhanced considerably when they are toasted in an oven or on top of the stove.

When only a small amount of nuts and seeds is to be cooked (a cup or less), stove-top roasting is easier; however, when a large volume is desired, oven roasting is simpler. Because roasted nuts and seeds have a tendency to become stale and then rancid rather quickly, they should be prepared just before you are planning to use them in a recipe.

To stove-top roast nuts or seeds, place them in a cast iron pan and cook, stirring frequently, on the stove over a low heat for 10 to 15 minutes or until they are done. Indicators that nuts are done are that they are lightly browned and aromatic. Seeds have a couple of additional indicators: popping or jumping about the pan and loss of about 50% of their weight. However, if the seeds pop too much, the heat is too high.

To oven roast nuts or seeds, spread them on a baking sheet and bake them in a 300°F oven, shifting them once or twice, until fragrant and lightly browned. This takes between 5 and 15 minutes for most nuts and seeds.

There is a fine line between the moment when the nuts and seeds are perfectly toasted and when they are burned. It is easy to tell when they are burned because they will taste horribly bitter. The trick is to catch them before they reach this point, but still cook them as long as possible to maximize the roasting flavor enhancement. In addition to the outside browness and smell tests, nuts can be tested for doneness by cutting one of them in half and viewing its center—it should be brown, not white or cream colored. Because of the high content of oil in nuts and seeds, the hot oil has a tendency to continue cooking them after they have been removed from the stove-top or oven.

When it comes to roasting, chestnuts are a special case. They must be roasted to peel and they must be peeled before they can be used. The stove-top, oven, and over-an-open-fire roasting processes for chestnuts are unique. For all methods, first cut an "x" through the shell on the flat sides of the nut to prevent their exploding when heated. The stove-top method involves placing the slit nuts in a pan of cold water and bringing it to a boil. Once the water is boiling briskly, remove the pan from the stove and peel off the shells and inner skins while the nuts are still hot. If they are allowed to boil for more than a few minutes, the nuts will become floury and become almost impossible to peel. The oven roasting method involves placing the slit nuts, cut-side up, on a baking sheet and baking in a 400°F oven for 6 to 8 minutes or until they are tender. The chestnuts should be peeled while still hot. If you want to roast your chestnuts over an open fire, put the slit chestnuts in a pan and cook over a fire's hot embers, often giving the nuts a shake. When they are tender, peel them while they are still hot.

As with nuts and seeds that are purchased already roasted, home-roasted nuts and seeds should also be stored in an airtight container in the refrigerator or other cool place.

TAMARI SOY SAUCE ROASTING

Roasting nuts and seeds with tamari soy sauce adds a rich and distinctive salty and savory flavor. Sunflower and pumpkin seeds, as well as almonds, cashews, and walnuts are all excellent when roasted with tamari.

For full-flavored decadent tamari nuts and seeds, soak the raw ones in a solution of half tamari and half water for a few minutes. Drain and place them on a baking sheet and proceed with the oven roasting process as described in the previous subsection ("Roasting Nuts and Seeds").

For milder flavored tamari nuts and seeds, first oven roast them until they are light brown or golden. Then, using a spray bottle, lightly cover them with the tamari solution, stir them around, and spray them again. Return them to the oven and roast two or three minutes more. Allow the soy sauce to dry before storing the roasted nuts or seeds.

SHELLING NUTS

It takes a bit of practice to get the shell off most nuts while keeping the nutmeats whole. To make shelling a little bit easier, first soak the nuts in hot water for 30 minutes or more. The tougher a nut's shell, the longer it can be soaked. In fact, if a nut's shell is super tough, like a Brazil nut, it can be frozen for 8 to 10 hours and slightly defrosted or boiled for 5 to 8 minutes to make shelling easier. Once the shell has been softened, the nutmeats can be freed with a nut cracker by gently cracking the shell just a little bit in lots of places. If you try to get the shell off with one big crack, there's a high probability of crushing the nutmeat as well as the shell into lots of itty-bitty pieces.

REMOVING THE SKINS FROM NUTS

Unless you are preparing a recipe that explicitly needs skinless nuts, keep the skins on them. The skin contains nutrients that are lost when the skin is removed and discarded. There are two methods for removing the skins from nuts: blanching and squeezing, and roasting and rubbing.

The blanching and squeezing method is effective for almonds and walnuts and involves placing the nuts into a strainer or metal colander and plunging them into boiling water for 2 minutes. The skins should puff up or get wrinkly. Remove the strainer from the boiling water and run a little cold water over the nuts so that they cool enough to handle easily. Squeeze or rub each nut with your fingers to remove the skin. Pass the skinless nuts through a bowl of cold water to prevent them from cooking more and place them on towels. When finished with the nuts, dry them first by patting them with a towel and then dry roasting them.

The roasting and rubbing method involves oven-roasting the nut (per the instructions given in a previous subsection) and then briskly rubbing them together until the skins flake off. This method works well with hazelnuts and Brazil nuts.

MAKING CONDIMENTS FROM SEEDS

A popular macrobiotic condiment called gomashio is really sesame salt. To make it, roast a cup of sesame seeds (see "Roasting Nuts and Seeds" in this subsection), combine with one tablespoon sea salt, and pulverize the mixture in a suribachi, mortar and pestle, or blender. Grind

the seeds until they are crushed but not so much that they turn to butter or start to release oils. This doesn't happen instantaneously when using a suribachi or mortar and pestle; in fact, your arm's going to get tired before you make a true butter. But if using a blender, you can make butter in the amount of time it takes to blink thrice. To reduce the risk, blend on a slow speed for very short bursts of time. The idea is to make a condiment that does not clump together and is easily sprinkled. However, the worst thing that can happen is that you make a delicious salted sesame butter! If you really want the condiment, just try again. The ratio of salt to sesame seeds is something that you can modify to suit your tastes or it can be continuously modified according to a program to reduce salt consumption.

HEALTH INFORMATION

Most nuts and seeds contain protein, fat, fiber, vitamin A and E, some B vitamins, and minerals. See the "Nutritional Composition of Some Nuts and Seeds" table. To get all nine essential amino acids, nuts and seeds should be eaten with grains, legumes, or dairy products. With the exception of macadamia nuts, most of the fat in nuts and seeds is unsaturated. Furthermore, nuts and seeds contain absolutely no cholesterol.

ADDITIONAL READING

Radecka, Helena. *The Fruit & Nut Book.*
Blazek, Mark. *Pecan Lover's Cook Book.*

BUYING SOURCES

Shelled and in-the-shell nuts and seeds are available in supermarkets, convenience stores, health food and natural foods stores, and specialty markets. Although they should be refrigerated, they typically are not in the refrigerated section of the store. Instead, they are found in the baking goods or in the bulk foods section.

Nutritional Composition of Some Nuts & Seeds—Vitamins*

©1996 Nigro

Nut or Seed	Quantity	Vitamin E (mg)	Folacin (micro grams)	Niacin (mg)	Pantothenic (mg)	Vitamin A (iu)	Vitamin C (mg)	Riboflavin (mg)	Vitamin B6 (mg)	Thiamin (mg)
Almonds	10 nuts	3.400	14.167	0.521	0.082	0.000	0.000	0.136	0.014	0.037
Brazil Nuts	10 nuts	2.600	1.840	0.710	0.090	4.285	0.010	0.045	0.055	0.400
Cashews	10 nuts	1.745	10.727	0.286	0.184	15.909	0.001	0.039	0.045	0.682
Chestnuts	10 nuts	5.400	49.000	0.146	0.342	0.000	2.000	0.160	0.226	0.160
Hazelnuts	10 nuts	3.045	9.818	0.122	0.156	13.636	0.000	0.075	0.076	0.063
Macadamia Nuts	10 nuts	4.250	17.000	0.325	0.225	0.000	0.000	0.027	0.070	0.085
Pecans	10 halves	2.433	3.458	0.113	0.209	15.583	0.229	0.016	0.023	0.105
Pine Nuts	1 oz.	1.700	19.200	0.950	0.256	4.000	0.000	0.167	0.080	0.250
Pistachio Nuts	10 nuts	0.304	3.367	0.082	0.042	1.533	0.000	0.023	0.012	0.040
Walnuts	10 halves	2.930	11.100	0.142	0.141	5.000	0.287	0.020	0.127	0.050
Alfalfa Seeds**	1 cup	—	12.000	0.200	0.190	51.000	3.000	0.040	0.010	0.030
Poppy Seeds	1 Tbsp.	—	—	0.000	—	—	—	0.030	0.030	0.060
Pumpkin Seeds	1 Tbsp.	0.935	8.000	0.219	0.179	6.250	0.000	0.017	0.008	0.022
Sesame Seeds	1 Tbsp.	2.125	12.500	0.505	0.281	2.810	0.000	0.023	0.008	0.092
Sunflower Seeds	1 Tbsp.	4.730	18.750	0.497	0.125	4.375	0.000	0.021	0.113	0.178

Nutritional Composition of Some Nuts & Seeds—Minerals*

©1996 Nigro

Nut or Seed	Quantity	Calories (kcal)	Fiber (g)	Fat (g)	Protein (g)	Carbohydrate (g)	Calcium (mg)	Iron (mg)	Sodium (mg)	Magnesium (mg)	Zinc (mg)	Potassium (mg)
Almonds	10 nuts	88	2.108	7.967	2.708	2.875	34.583	0.665	0.521	64.833	0.454	114.167
Brazil Nuts	10 nuts	264	3.600	27.100	5.850	4.425	75.500	1.140	0.000	127.000	1.910	290.000
Cashews	10 nuts	89	0.964	7.245	2.727	4.655	6.018	1.018	2.382	42.455	0.755	73.818
Chestnuts	10 nuts	141	4.900	2.000	3.000	30.600	26.000	1.000	5.000	28.000	1.000	332.000
Hazelnuts	10 nuts	86	0.831	8.818	1.718	2.273	31.182	1.100	0.236	22.727	0.320	90.000
Macadamia Nuts	10 nuts	173	1.525	18.833	1.950	3.967	0.200	0.500	—	30.167	0.665	66.000
Pecans	10 halves	84	0.747	8.750	1.133	1.792	8.917	0.319	0.104	17.500	0.496	74.167
Pine Nuts	1 oz.	170	0.252	13.400	8.800	3.300	38.000	1.500	—	75.000	1.200	208.000
Pistachio Nuts	10 nuts	35	0.292	3.143	1.143	1.123	7.700	0.390	0.208	9.167	0.138	57.667
Walnuts	10 halves	98	0.780	9.600	0.222	0.237	14.800	0.525	0.250	19.700	0.371	67.500
Alfalfa Seeds**	1 cup	10	0.700	0.200	1.300	1.300	10.000	0.320	2.000	9.000	0.300	26.000
Poppy Seeds	1 Tbsp.	45	—	3.900	1.500	2.100	123.000	0.780	3.000	27.000	0.870	60.000
Pumpkin Seeds	1 Tbsp.	48	0.166	4.085	2.535	1.310	4.435	0.875	2.625	3.375	4.625	86.500
Sesame Seeds	1 Tbsp.	53	0.590	4.605	1.740	2.025	109.000	0.980	5.600	16.900	0.825	68.000
Sunflower Seeds	1 Tbsp.	51	0.344	4.285	2.185	1.810	10.850	0.525	2.685	3.435	0.434	83.500

* Sources: Pennington, Jean A.T., Ph.D., R.D, Bowes and Church's Food Values of Portions Commonly Used (15th Ed.) and Robertson, Laurel, Carol
Flinders, and Brian Ruppenthal, The New Laurel's Kitchen.

** Sprouted

Nuts and seeds are available through the Deer Valley Farm, Allergy Resources, Anzen Oriental Foods & Imports, Arrowhead Mills, Bob's Red Mill Natural Foods, Chestnut Hill Orchards, Clear Eye Natural Foods, Harvest Time Natural Foods, Community Mill & Bean, Dean & Deluca, Diamond Organics, Frankferd Farms Foods, Garden Spot, Jaffe Bros., King Arthur Flour Baker's Catalogue, Mountain Ark Trading Company, Natural Lifestyle, Sultan's Delights, Gold Mine Natural Foods, and Walnut Acres Organic Farms mail order companies.

BRAND NAMES

No specific brands are listed here because there is such a large variety of brands on the market, many of which are provided to the public in bulk, and many that are regional or local. When you visit your supermarket or health food store, read the labels carefully to be sure that the nuts and seeds contain only the substances you want.

OATS

Don't say neigh to oats. They are more than a special treat for horses. Oats are enjoyed by people, too.

VARIETIES

Oats are available whole and milled to make many oat products. See "Grains" for a discussion of the anatomy of a grain kernel and more information about grain milling methods and their resulting products.

Oat Groats: Whole oat kernels, minus only their hulls, are called oat groats. Groats are quite nutritious because they still contain their germ and bran. Often hulls cling to oat groats and may be found with the grains when purchased. This 1/4 inch long, light brown, pale yellow, or beige grain is similar in shape, size, and flavor to long-grain rice. Oat groats are chewy, starchy, and slightly sweet in flavor. They add a satisfying heartiness to soups, stews, salads, and baked goods.

Steel-Cut or Cracked Oats: These oats are produced by cutting the whole groats into small pieces with steel cutting machines; the bran and germ remain with the oats. Steel-cut oats make a very tasty, hearty, and chewy porridge or hot cereal. They are also great for making scones, griddle cakes, and oatcakes.

Irish or Scotch-Cut Oats: These oats are made by grinding whole groats with stones. The grind is coarser than for oat flour. Irish oats are ideal for making a warming, creamy, thick porridge with a hearty flavor. They can be used interchangeably with steel-cut oats.

Rolled Oats or Oat Flakes: These are whole groats that have been rolled and flattened to make the familiar looking gray-white flakes made famous by Quaker Oats. Also called "old-fashioned" oats, rolled oats are available in medium and thick flakes. The traditional use for rolled oats and oat flakes is oatmeal or porridge which has a starchy, soft consistency with a mild, nutty flavor. A bowl of piping hot oatmeal for breakfast provides enough energy for us to shovel two feet of snow off the drive-way and walk the dog on a cold, winter day.

Rolled oats are also used in making cakes, cookies, biscuits, fillings, pancakes, toppings, and pie crusts. In addition, they can be used as a meat extender when added to loaves and burgers.

Old-Fashioned Oats: See "Rolled Oats or Oat Flakes" in this subsection.

Quick Oats or Instant Oats: These oats are very thin rolled oats or rolled oat pieces that have been partially cooked. They are the most processed form of oats. Often salt, wheat germ, sugar, and in flavored oatmeals, a number of flavoring agents are added to these oats. Although they have little texture and are the least nutritious, they do cook far quicker than the other types of oats.

Oat Bran: This is the fiber-rich outer layer of whole groats. Studies have been conducted that show that the soluble fiber in oat bran can be useful in lowering cholesterol levels (if large quantities are eaten). Oat bran has a sweet flavor that can enhance breads, muffins, cereals, cakes, pies, doughnuts, crusts, crackers, etc. It can also be mixed with other grains to make baked goods. Oat bran is not as "sticky" as other oat products.

Oat Flour: Oat flour is made by grinding the endosperm of oat grain kernels. It is sweet and contains very little gluten. Because oats have a natural antioxidant (to counter the relatively high fat content in oats), it is a first-rate ingredient to use in baked goods to help them maintain their freshness longer. Oat flour is excellent  for use in baking breads, cookies, pie crusts, crackers, muffins, etc. To make a leavened bread, oat flour must be combined with a flour which has a high gluten content (wheat, kamut, or spelt). Oat flour can also be used as a thickener that creates a creamy, milk-like consistency in soups and sauces, a breading for meats and vegetables, and a binder in meat and vegetable burgers and loaves.

FLAVOR/TEXTURE

Oats have a mild, light, nutty flavor and a chewy texture. Oat flakes, steel-cut oats, and Irish oats have a soft, creamy, and moist consistency.

GENERAL USES

Oats have a tendency to absorb and dissipate the flavors of other ingredients that they are cooked with. So large amounts of strong spices or powerfully flavored ingredients should be mixed with the oats if you want their flavor to come through.

Oats go with almost any strong seasonings, herbs, and spices such as garlic, oregano, mustard, bay leaf, rosemary, thyme, sage, tarragon, and pepper. They work very well when combined with meats, fruits, vegetables, nuts, dairy products, and other grains (especially rice).

Whole oat groats are a hearty but mild flavored grain that is delicious in pilafs, casseroles, stuffings, soups, and grain salads.

Rolled oats are a wonderful addition to breads, cookies, granola, trail mixes, muesli, casseroles, and croquettes. Oats are the foundation of muesli mixes, which are used for cereals, snacks, and granolas. Try combining toasted oat flakes with raisins, almonds, pecans, dried apples and apricots, and a little unrefined almond oil and baking for 10 to 15 minutes in a 325°F oven to make a crunchy granola.

Oat bran is used as a nutrition enhancer when added to grain dishes, bread and other baked goods, and cereal.

In addition to being useful in breads, cookies, and other baked goods, oat flour can be used to make a creamy, thick base for sauces and soups. And the natural antioxidant in oat flour makes it ideal for dusting baked goods such as rolls and pastries to help them maintain their freshness longer.

FRESHNESS/QUALITY

See "Grains."

STORAGE

Oats have a high level of fat but they also have a built in anti-rancidity agent (i.e., antioxidant), which causes them to have the relatively lengthy storage time of a year if they are stored in a cool, dark, dry place. See "Grains" for more information on storing grains.

PREPARATION INSTRUCTIONS

CLEANING

Whole oat groats can be washed if desired. If washing steel-cut or Irish oats, do so very quickly to prevent them from absorbing too much water. Oat flakes and oat bran should not be washed. See "Grains" for additional information.

SOAKING

Whole oat groats and steel-cut oats can be soaked overnight. This will reduce the time required to cook them.

COOKING

The cooking time for oats depends on the type being cooked. Oat groats take the longest to prepare. Steel-cut and Irish oats are the next longest and rolled oats or oat flakes are fairly quick cooking. Of course, instant and quick cooking oats are the fastest to make. Roasting all of the oat types brings out their nutty flavor. See "Grains" for more information about cooking and dry roasting grains. See the "Oat Cooking Table" for liquid amounts and cooking times for one cup of oats.

OAT COOKING TABLE

	Liquid (cups)	Time (min.)
Whole Groats	2 - 2 1/2	60 - 120
Steel-Cut	2 3/4 - 3	50 - 70
Irish	2 3/4 - 3	50 - 70
Rolled (*drier*)	2 - 2 1/2	7 - 15
Rolled (*porridge*)	3 - 4	20 - 30

Due to the high fat content of oats, you may wish to pick a cooking method for them that does not use a lot of oil or fat. If you are looking for a grain to deep-fry, try using any of the others in place of oats.

Oat groats are suitable for salads when the starch is reduced by rinsing the grains after cooking and before mixing with other salad ingredients.

Whole oat groats can be simmered overnight so that they will be soft, warm, and ready in the morning. Use a very low heat, a flame diffuser, and lots of water (6 to 7 cups per cup of oats).

Oat flour is easy to make. See the "Grains" section.

REHEATING

Oats can be used cold in grain salads. If you need to reheat them, oats can be warmed by steaming or microwaving. See "Grains" for additional information.

HEALTH INFORMATION

Oats are rich in soluble fiber, protein, linoleic acid, vitamin E, thiamin, folate, pantothenic acid, iron, calcium, phosphorous, magnesium, copper, and zinc. The bran and germ are the primary source of the B vitamins (thiamin, folate, and pantothenic acid) and minerals.

Oats have a natural antioxidant that extends its shelf-life as well as that of the products it is used in. Oats and oat products are essentially gluten-free but do contain a bit of sodium, when compared with other grains.

ADDITIONAL INFORMATION

See "Grains."

BUYING SOURCES

Oats can be found in prepackaged bags or boxes as well as in bulk bins. The bulk bins are convenient because you can buy just the amount that you want. However, they can cause problems if you are allergic to any of the other grains that are also sold in bulk nearby because the grain scoops are often shared or unintentionally swapped around.

Rolled oats and instant oats are generally found in supermarkets in the breakfast cereal aisle. Sometimes oat bran can be found in supermarkets as well. Whole oat groats, steel-cut oats, Irish oats, oat flakes, oat bran, and oat flour are generally available in health and natural food stores as well as through mail order sources. See "Grains" for a list of mail order sources and brand names.

OILS

To many people, oil is just a utilitarian substance only good for frying food and greasing pans. In fact, many of the oils available are so highly refined that they are not capable of doing much more. However, oils can be far more than just a lubricant; unrefined oils have an incredible variety of flavors and colors.  The oil you choose for a dish can be the key ingredient that makes the dish sensational.

Cooking oils are commonplace in American homes. Although the nutritional value of this highly used ingredient is a controversial issue, there does seem to be some agreement among the scientists, doctors, and nutritionists that oils are a concentrated food consisting of 100% fat, which should be used in moderation.

VARIETIES

The term "vegetable oil" generally refers to a liquid fat that is not derived from animal products. Because quality oils impart the flavor of the food they came from and have different sensitivities to heat, there are limits in how they are used. If you want to buy a minimal set of oils to meet all of your kitchen needs, buy olive (for salad dressings), safflower (for high temperature cooking), and sesame (for sautéing) oils.

Oils can be categorized in many different ways: type of plant it was extracted from, the level of refinement, the method of extraction, and the temperatures at which it can be cooked. The following subsection, "Methods of Oil Extraction," discusses the issues involved in the level of refinement and methods of extraction.

Most plant foods (fruits, grains, legumes, nuts, and seeds) contain varying proportions of oil that can be extracted for culinary uses:

FRUIT OILS

Avocado Oil: This rather unusual light, slightly nutty tasting oil is considered primarily to be a novelty. To add a different twist to salad dressings, try using avocado oil in place of the oil you would normally use. This oil is often made from damaged and cosmetically inferior avocados. It is low in saturated fatty acids and high in polyunsaturates.

Olive Oil: Olive oils are available in a wide range of qualities: extra virgin, virgin, pure, and blended. They range in flavor from rather bland to very distinct and fruity. See the "Olive Oil" section in this book for more information about this ingredient.

GRAIN OILS

Corn Oil: This oil is one of the most popular and is manufactured in large quantities. The majority of corn oils are extracted from corn germ, which is a by-product of corn breakfast cereals, cornstarch, and corn syrup manufacturing processes. Oils made from corn germ are light yellow and mild in flavor. Darker corn oil is obtained when the oil is extracted from whole kernels of corn.

These darker oils have a strong aroma that is rather popcorn-like.

Expeller-pressed unrefined corn oil has a rich, almost buttery, corn taste and hearty aroma that may be too strong for delicately flavored dishes. However, it is good for sautéing and baking, and in sauces and dressings. In short, it is a versatile, general purpose oil for light cooking. It should not be used for deep-frying because it easily foams and boils over.

Refined corn oil is very pale in color and very bland in flavor. It is suitable for general purposes and for cakes, pastries, and baking. Furthermore, highly refined corn oil may be used for deep-frying.

Corn oil is 87% unsaturated and is exceptionally high in the essential linoleic acid (60%). It also contains a significant amount of vitamin E, which helps to retard oxidation.

LEGUME OILS

Peanut Oil: Because peanuts are about 50% fat, they are an excellent source of oil.

Cold-pressed and expeller-pressed peanut oils have a full rich peanut flavor and delightful nutty fragrance. While the strong flavor of unrefined peanut oil limits its culinary uses, in those cases where it is called for, its distinct flavor produces a heavenly effect. Try heating a teaspoon or two of unrefined peanut oil with a touch of unrefined sesame oil and pouring it over steamed or stir-fried spinach, lettuce, or other leafy green. Or mix unrefined peanut oil with grated ginger, thinly sliced scallions, and coarse sea salt to make a fantastic dipping sauce for steamed or boiled chicken. A dipping sauce for shrimp, crab, or sushi can be quickly prepared by combining unrefined peanut oil, shoyu soy sauce, minced garlic, grated ginger, and scallions. A distinctive vinaigrette can be created by using unrefined peanut oil, sesame oil, grapefruit juice, wine vinegar, and watercress.

Refined peanut oil is very bland and has almost no peanut flavor. Keeping this in mind, it does make an excellent cooking oil. It has a high smoke point and is stable when heated; thus, it can be used to fry tempura, chicken, fish filets, vegetables, or anything else you desire.

Nineteen percent of peanut oil is saturated, which is higher than most other natural oils. It is low in linoleic acid and vitamin E and high in mono-unsaturated fats. Furthermore, its trace mineral content is low.

Soy Oil: Soybeans contain oil that is inefficient to extract in a "natural" manner; therefore, unrefined expeller-pressed soy oil is rather expensive. Unrefined soy oil has a strong, distinctive flavor and aroma—some like it, some don't. It has a dark yellow color with a faint green tint. It is good in baked goods because it contains lecithin (approximately 3%) which acts as an emulsifier. In addition, it is high in polyunsaturates and linoleic acid. Unrefined soy oil is more susceptible to oxidation and rancidity than sesame, olive, or corn oil.

Highly refined soy oil is reasonably priced, very mild and versatile, accounting for over 80% of all oil used in commercial food production in the U.S. Almost any product that lists vegetable oil as an ingredient probably contains refined soy oil. This is a good all-purpose oil that is also good for cakes and pastries.

Nut Oils

Nut oils are a bit more expensive than other oils, but a little bit of their rich, nutty flavor goes a long way.

Almond Oil: Unrefined almond oil has a delicate, fresh almond flavor, with a hint of sweetness, and a beautiful amber color. It is delicious in vinaigrettes accompanied by slivered almonds. Try heating a few teaspoons of almond oil instead of butter, and pouring it over freshly steamed green beans or broccoli. Almond oil is particularly good with artichokes; melt a tablespoon of butter, add a tablespoon of almond oil, and use as a dip for hot or cold artichokes.

Filet of sole is marvelous when lightly covered with a mixture of flour, salt, and black pepper, and then sautéed with unrefined almond oil. For added flavor, sauté

some slivered almonds in the almond oil that was used to cook the fish and cover the sole with the golden-brown almonds. Garnish with lemon wedges.

Furthermore, unrefined almond oil may be used in desserts when its flavor enhances the dish.

Refined almond oils are made by crushing almonds and then heating them until they turn to a thick golden-brown paste. The paste is then subjected to hydraulic pressure to squeeze out every possible ounce of oil.

Hazelnut Oil: Hazelnut oil (also called filbert oil) is fairly new in the United States but has long been popular in France, where it is made.

Unrefined hazelnut oil is extremely difficult to make and is quite expensive. It has a deep, rich aroma and substance. Use hazelnut oil in vinaigrettes, sauces, homemade mayonnaise, marinades, salad dressings, meat coatings, and hot sauces. Unrefined hazelnut oil is wonderful in sautéed, braised, and refried grain dishes. Try lining a cookie or cake tin with hazelnut oil; it will give a wonderful hazelnut flavor to whatever you are baking.

A simple, elegant dish can be created by broiling your favorite fish filets, tempeh cutlets, or tofu slices with unrefined hazelnut oil, lemon juice, and ground black pepper and then garnishing with a lemon or lime wedge.

Refined hazelnut oils are made in the same manner as almond and walnut oils: by crushing, heating, and squeezing out the oil.

Walnut Oil: This expensive, delicate, light-colored, unrefined, specialty oil is generally made in the Perigord and Burgundy regions of France. Unlike other nut oils, unrefined walnut oil is made from nuts that are dried and then cold-pressed. Walnut oil is high in polyunsaturated fats. It has a rich, nutty flavor that is perfect for salad dressings, to flavor fish and steaks, to toss with pasta, and to jazz up desserts. Walnut oil is best used uncooked or in cold sauces because when it is heated, it can become slightly bitter. This flavor, however, can be a pleasant taste when experienced in moderation.

Unrefined walnut oil is terrific on salads, particularly when you combine it with bits of walnuts. Add walnut oil to a chicken or turkey salad along with some grapes and chopped walnuts. Brush a thin coat of walnut oil on grilled fish and steaks just before serving. Toss freshly cooked pasta in a mixture of walnut oil and spices. Try using walnut oil in dessert recipes that will be enhanced by the nutty flavor.

If needed, hazelnut oil may be used instead of walnut oil.

Refined walnut oils are made in the same manner that refined almond and hazelnut oils are made: crushing the nuts and heating them until they turn into a thick paste and then pressing out the oil.

SEED OILS

Canola Oil: This oil is made from rapeseed (a plant in the mustard family). It has a mild flavor and aroma. It is most commonly available in a refined form. Its mild flavor and relatively high smoke point make refined canola oil a good all-purpose oil. Of all the oils, it has the least amount of saturated fat and is one of the least expensive.

Safflower Oil: Safflower oil is the most versatile of the unrefined oils. This excellent all-purpose oil is relatively light in weight and color. Its mild flavor allows it to go anywhere, and its ability to accept a high temperature without bubbling over, makes it the perfect choice for deep-frying. The flavor of expeller-pressed or natural safflower oil is almost corny but with a nutty overtone. It makes a nice ingredient in dressings, sauces, and desserts.

Safflower and sunflower oils are often regarded as interchangeable but are, in fact, quite different, even though both plants are members of the same family. Safflower oil is richer in linoleic acid (up to 80%) than any other oil. Of the quality oils, it is the least expensive and most mild.

The extraction of safflower oil is difficult. The very hard husk resists the extraction process. Quality safflower oil is obtained via a mechanical process by pressing with hydraulic machines. Low quality oil is produced when chemical solvents are used. It is not always possible to know which method has ben used, because the law does not require that the extraction method be shown on the label.

Safflower oil is high in vitamin E and is the second highest of all oils in unsaturated fats (canola being first). It is rich in polyunsaturates. Cold-pressed safflower oil can be mixed with olive oil to further increase the polyunsaturates.

Sunflower Oil: Sunflower oil is light in color and substance and has a distinctive mild taste. Sunflower oil is an excellent all-purpose oil; however, some people find its flavor too strong for baked goods and salads. And some find the flavor of this oil to be a bit odd when it is heated. To determine when sunflower oil will work best for you, try it in both a cold and warm dish and evaluate it. If you prefer not to heat it, try it in cold sauces.

When compared with all the oils, sunflower oil is the second richest in linoleic acid (safflower oil is the richest) and is high in polyunsaturated fats. It stores well and may be used instead of sesame or corn oil. This oil has a high resistance to rancidity.

Sesame Oil: There are two types of sesame oil. The oil that is made from roasted sesame seeds has a strong, distinctive flavor. It is called *dark sesame* or *toasted sesame* oil and has a intensely rich, smoky,

sesame aroma; nutty taste; dark, brown color; thick consistency; and cloudy appearance. It is used a great deal in Chinese and Indian cooking. Just a few drops of this oil can add an outrageously delicious flavor that enhances many foods. Dark sesame oil is ideal for stir-fries, baking, sauces, and spreads. Snow peas and water chestnuts are delicious sautéed in a little toasted sesame oil with ginger. Or sauté green beans, artichoke hearts, or thinly sliced cucumbers in sesame oil and garnish with chopped sweet red or green bell pepper.

For a simply amazing dish, sauté garlic, ginger, scallions, and shrimp in a mixture of unrefined dark sesame and virgin olive oil. Then stir in some Dijon mustard, orange juice, and tamari soy sauce. This is great served over brown basmati rice.

The oil made from raw sesame seeds is much lighter (pale with a strong yellow tint) and far less aromatic. It is called *light sesame* or just *sesame* oil and has a mild but clear sesame flavor. It is a quality oil suited for general cooking and for baking, sautéing, and dressings. Use light sesame oil for large quantities of food or for delicate dishes where the strong flavor of the dark oil might be too much.

A few drops of sesame oil are delicious with scrambled eggs; aside from adding flavor, sesame oil can be used instead of butter to keep the eggs from sticking to the pan.

Sesame oil adds flavor to mild soups and stews. A boring vegetable broth can be jazzed up into a delightful soup by cooking the broth with slices of fresh peeled ginger, scallions, and watercress and just before serving, adding a few drops of hot sesame oil. The oil adds a wonderful nutty flavor without making the soup the least bit greasy or oily.

This oil mixed with a few tablespoons of peanut oil, shoyu soy sauce, grated ginger, and sliced hot chili peppers makes a great dipping sauce for seafood and chicken or tofu and tempeh.

Sesame oil is highly stable and resistant to spoiling and oxidation. An advantage of sesame oil is that in hot and tropical climates it is not turned rancid.

High in polyunsaturates, sesame oil is considered by many to be the most healthful of all oils. Sesame oil contains 87% unsaturated fats, 41% of which is linoleic acid.

FLAVORED OILS

These oils can be bought or made. Oils from various plants, flavored with fresh herbs, chili peppers, garlic, and spices are hot items in specialty food shops these days. While a number of these products are terrific, many are overpriced. You can make your own flavored oils at home for a lot less. See the "Preparation Instructions" subsection.

METHODS OF OIL EXTRACTION

Because the method of extraction is such an integral part of an oil's quality, nutritional value, flavor, and color, its processing method is addressed. Be aware though that although the method of extraction is extremely important, manufacturers are not obliged to state which methods they use.

There are two things to keep in mind when considering the methods by which an oil is extracted from a plant—the refinement level and the physical process used to extract the oil.

REFINEMENT LEVEL

Oils are generally grouped into two camps—unrefined and refined.

Unrefined Oils: These oils are used as salad oils (warm salad dressings, marinades, and pasta sauces) or light cooking oils (light sautés and low heat baking). As a general rule, they should not be cooked at high temperatures. However, safflower oil is the one unrefined oil that can become hot enough to reach the temperature necessary for deep-frying.

Unrefined oils are processed by cold-pressed and expeller-pressed methods (see the "Extraction Processes" subsection). Unrefined oils carry with them the true bouquet of olives, corn, sesame seeds, peanuts, soybeans, safflower, or whatever plant was the oil's original home. The strong flavors of unrefined oils can dominate whatever dish or baked good is made with them. Of course, strong flavor is not always a drawback; in some cases unrefined oils are used as flavoring agents. And, typically, where there is strong natural flavor and aroma, there is a higher amount of nutritional value.

Refined Oils: These oils are used as medium cooking oils (225°F - 350°F), high cooking oils (350°F - 450°F), and deep-frying oils (greater than 450°F).

If the oil you buy is bland and pale, you can be certain that it has been fully refined, bleached, and deodorized. In essence, refined oils have negligible flavor and aroma which can be useful in delicately flavored dishes.

See the "Oil Flavor, Smoke Points, & Uses Based on Refinement Level" chart.

Oil Flavor, Smoke Points, & Uses Based on Refinement Level

Refinement Level	Flavor	Smoke Points	Uses, Best for
Very Unrefined*	Full Nut, Seed, & Fruit Flavor	< 225°F	Low Heat Oil: Soups & Salads
Unrefined		225 – 350°F	Medium Heat Cooking Oil: Light Sautéing & Sauces
Conditioned** (Semi-Refined)	Mild Flavor	350 – 400°F	Medium-High Heat Cooking Oil: Baking & Sautéing
Refined	Bland Flavor	400 – 450°F (high in polyunsaturates	
		> 450°F (high in monounsaturates)	High Heat Cooking Oil: Deep-Frying

©1996 Nigro

* Fresh, organic, biologically active oils that have been processed via purely mechanical means involving refrigeration, opaque containers, bottling with inert gas to prevent unnecessary exposure to oxygen, etc.

** Lightly refined oils that are *not* exposed to caustic or toxic chemicals or agents.

EXTRACTION PROCESSES

All oil extraction processes involve heating the oil in some way. However, temperatures over 300°F destroy the proteins and natural vitamin E in oils. Lower temperatures (in the 120°F to 160°F range) do not damage the oil significantly, but do reduce the yield, making good oils a little more expensive. It is essential to retain vitamin E in an oil because it prevents the oil from oxidizing. Oils with little vitamin E tend to go rancid quickly unless treated with antioxidant chemicals.

Expeller-Pressed: These oils are obtained by squeezing the seed, grain, or fruit at pressures up to 15 tons per square inch. The higher the pressure, the more heat is generated. At extremely high pressures, the temperature can exceed 300°F.

Cold-Pressed: The term "cold pressed" theoretically means that an oil is expeller-pressed at low temperatures. However the term has no legal definition and is absolutely meaningless when used as an indication of quality. Olive oil, sesame oil, and peanut oil are really the only kinds that can be truly cold-pressed on any sort of large commercial scale. They are the only substances that will easily yield their oil by simple, low-intensity pressure, which does not generate a great deal of heat. True cold-pressed oils are prized.

Extracted: Extracted oils are invariably subjected to some sort of applied heat during processing.

Chemical or Solvent Extraction: The cheaper brands of oil (most regular commercial brands) generally use chemical solvents to extract the oil. A description of how the majority of oils are processed, or refined, is sobering. The oil is separated from its food source with hexane or other petroleum solvents and then boiled to drive off the toxic solvents. The oil is next refined, bleached, and deodorized, which involves heating it to over 400°F. The oil extracted this way still contains some undesirable solvent residues, while the amounts of many key nutrients (especially vitamin E) are significantly reduced. Antioxidants or preservatives such as BHA (butylated hydroxyanisole) or BHT (buty-lated hydroxytoluene) are then frequently added. The resulting product lacks flavor, aroma, pigments, and nutrients. All that can be said for such an oil is that it has an extended shelf life, a clear, uniform color, and an oily texture.

FLAVOR/TEXTURE

Unrefined oils taste more like the substances they are made from, while refined oils are more bland. Consider the rich aroma and nutty flavor of hazelnuts, almonds and walnuts; the luscious, fruity taste of the olive; the light, pure, nutty essence of peanuts; and the flavor of lightly toasted sesame seeds. These are characteristics of pure, unrefined oils that complement and enhance food.

Most unrefined oils may be used in cooking, but they must be experimented with in recipes because they have a strong flavor and some of them can overpower the other ingredients in a dish! At first, the rich aromas and flavors of unrefined oils can be a bit overwhelming. However, the new enhancing flavors and the nutrients imparted by these unrefined oils are easy to become accustomed to.

GENERAL USES

Oils are used to flavor dressings, dips, spreads, sauces, soups, and marinades; to brown, coat, sear, or sauté vegetables and meats; to braise and coat grains; and to deep-fry vegetables, meats, fish, and tofu.

Everyone has heard of the "oil and vinegar" or vinaigrette salad dressing. This boring sounding dressing can really be jazzed up by using a flavorful high quality unrefined oil. For a real treat, try sprinkling a mix of walnut oil and red wine vinegar on a salad of gourmet lettuce, cucumbers, tomatoes, and olives. Or use flavored oils in vinaigrettes along with fresh herbs.

Unrefined oils complement fish and meats. Try making a marinade for beef or chicken using a flavored oil, vinegar, red wine, and fresh herbs. Brush an unrefined

oil onto fish, chicken, steaks, tofu, grain burgers, and shish kebabs before broiling or barbecuing.

Toss cold or hot pasta with a flavored oil, herbs, nuts, and olives. Add a few tablespoons of herb-flavored oils to a homemade mayonnaise. Use a basil- or mixed-herb-flavored oil as the base of a pesto sauce.

Great recipes for homemade flavored oils can be found in Kathy Gunst's book called *Condiments*.

FRESHNESS/QUALITY

Three vegetable oils not recommended are cottonseed oil, because it may be chemically contaminated, and highly saturated palm kernel and coconut oils. Note that these oils are not discussed in the "Varieties" subsection because they are typically used in only commercial foods. Also it is best to avoid oils that contain the preservatives BHA, BHT, or EDTA.

An oil's label does not have to say how it was extracted or whether it is refined, bleached, or deodorized. Thus, it may be a good idea to purchase your oils from a store you trust or to stick with quality brands that you know.

The highest quality unrefined oils are pressed at relatively low temperatures, filtered, and bottled. They appear cloudy and maintain a good, strong aroma, color, and flavor. Beware, just because an oil is labeled "cold-pressed" does not mean that the oil is of high quality. Producers of chemically-extracted, alkali-washed, bleached, deodorized, and degummed oils can claim their products are "cold-pressed." Your nose and taste buds can immediately recognize a quality 100% true cold-pressed (i.e., low-temperature expeller-pressed) oil, for such an oil will smell and taste like the food from which it was made. The higher the grade, the better the flavor and aroma.

RANCIDITY

Rancid oils can cause a loss of vitamins in the body. A rancid oil tastes acrid and burns the tongue and throat.

However extensively it is processed, oil can become rancid quickly if exposed to heat, light, or air. To prevent this, many companies add preservatives and show this on their labels.

Just a warning—if your refined oil is adding quite a bit of flavor to your dish, you are probably tasting the rancidity of the oil. Strangely enough, this is what some people actually like about the dish. Think of some fast food restaurants that sell french fries—most folks wouldn't think they tasted right if they weren't cooked in rancid oil!

STORAGE

After opening, oils should be kept tightly sealed in their bottles or other containers and stored in the refrigerator or a cool, dark place. If the oil goes a bit cloudy or solid while in the refrigerator, don't worry; it will return to normal if you take it out 15 to 30 minutes before you need it and leave it at room temperature.

Oil should not be stored in metal containers, or it may become rancid; when oils are sold in soldered steel containers, as olive oil often is, the container has been lined with a plastic polymer to prevent reaction with the oil.

Oil will become rancid if exposed to extreme heat, or light or air for prolonged periods of time. Don't let the oil sit out of the refrigerator too long, especially on a hot day. Rancidity is a serious problem with oils, because even a hint of a rancid flavor can ruin an entire batch of dressing. A thin film of oil, such as might be left on containers through careless washing, becomes rancid very quickly. Clean all dressing containers thoroughly, and never pour a fresh batch into a jar containing older dressing. Rancidity is not the only process that damages fats

and results in degradation. Long exposure to light or heat can lead to reactions which result in brown colors in the oil and the formation of chunky bits.

Discard oils after the date on the label or 4 months after opening. It is a good idea to purchase your oils in small enough quantities that can be consumed within four months.

Once oil is poured out of its bottle, never pour it back, as it may easily collect bacteria or dust once poured.

High quality unrefined oils tend to become rancid faster (i.e., have a shorter shelf life) than oils that have had preservatives added to them.

PREPARATION INSTRUCTIONS

NON-COOKING

Many unrefined oils make excellent condiments and are best appreciated at room temperature, straight from the bottle—sprinkled over salads, vegetables, fish, and meat. In salad dressings, the oil's flavor is of paramount importance, so use high quality unrefined oils.

COOKING

You can also cook with unrefined oils but, in many cases, their distinctive flavor is lost when heated. A high quality unrefined oil is analogous to a fine wine, while a lower quality highly refined oil is like a cheap bottle of cooking wine. You would not want to cook with your fine wine, or unrefined oil, in high temperatures or in heavily herbed sauces.

The continuous reuse and reheating of an oil is not advisable because it can lead to the formation of unusual and possibly harmful by-products.

Fats undergo destructive chemical changes when overheated. When you are heating oil to sauté vegetables, watch it closely: once oil begins to smoke, it has overheated and should be discarded. Just before the smoke point has been reached, the surface of heating oil will take on a rippled look. That's your signal to quickly add whatever vegetables you're about to sauté—their moisture will cool the oil sufficiently to prevent the smoke point from being immediately exceeded.

See the "Fatty Acid Profile and Smoke Point of Oils" table for more information. Note that the smoke points of oils can vary depending on the natural ingredients in the oil.

As previously mentioned in the "Methods of Oil Extraction, Refinement Levels," unrefined oils are used as low and medium-heat cooking oils. They are best suited for light sautéing, sauces, and low-heat baking. For high-heat and all-purpose cooking, choose a refined oil.

FLAVORED OILS

It makes a lot of sense to make your own flavored oils. For one thing, it's generally much less expensive than buying commercially produced oils. But the real fun of making them at home is that you can create your own combinations and flavors. Making herb-flavored oil is a great way to use up an abundance of herbs from a summer garden. To start, try using olive, sesame, and/or peanut oil as the base oil and then adding one of the following combinations: garlic, peppercorns, and bay leaf; chopped dried red chili peppers and cayenne pepper; chopped fresh fennel and fennel seeds; ginger, garlic, and shallots; chile peppers; fresh rosemary, thyme, and oregano; fresh coriander, parsley and crushed coriander seeds; red and green chili peppers; or lemon wedges and cloves. Let the herbs steep in the oil until the desired flavor is reached.

HEALTH INFORMATION

Generally, it is better to sauté vegetables in water, because frying food increases the fat content of your meal, and at extreme temperatures fat decomposes to produce irritants such as acrolein, which can affect skin and mucous membranes.

Cold-pressed vegetable oil contains

Fatty Acid Profile and Smoke Point of Oils[1]

Oil	Smoke Point (°F)[2]	Saturated	Monounsaturated	Polyunsaturated[3]	Superunsaturated[4]
Almond, refined	495	9%	65%	26%	0%
Avocado, refined	520	20%	70%	10%	0%
Canola, refined	400	6%	60%	24%	10%
Corn	225-350, 450	13%	27%	60%	0%
Olive	280	10%	82%	8%	0%
Peanut	225-350, 450	19%	51%	30%	0%
Safflower	225, 450	8%	13%	79%	0%
Sesame	250, 410	13%	46%	41%	0%
Sunflower	225, 450	12%	19%	69%	0%
Soy	250, 350	14%	28%	50%	8%
Walnut	275, 400	16%	28%	51%	5%

[1] Source: Spectrum Naturals *Kitchen Guide*
[2] If two values are given, the first is for an unrefined oil and the second is for a refined oil.
[3] Vitamin F_1 (also called linoleic acid or omega-6 fatty acid)
[4] Vitamin F_2 (also called linolenic acid or omega-3 fatty acid)

©1996 Nigro

minerals, phosphatides, and vitamin E and is high in trace nutrients. Unrefined oils contain varying amounts of omega-3 (also called linoleic acid or Vitamin F_1) and omega-6 (also called linolenic acid or Vitamin F_2) fatty acids. See the "Fatty Acid Profile and Smoke Point of Oils."

Vegetable oils contain mono- and polyunsaturated fats that reduce the "bad" LDL cholesterol level and increase the "good" HDL cholesterol level. Exceptions to this rule are coconut oil and palm oil, which, though both liquid fats, are mostly saturated.

Hydrogenated oils have been chemically altered to transform liquid oil into a solid margarine-like substance. The hydrogenation process changes polyunsaturated fats into saturated fats. Butter and lard are natural saturated fats and margarine and shortening are hydrogenated vegetable oils.

ADDITIONAL READING

For additional information about oils, fatty acids, and nutrition, write Spectrum Naturals at 133 Copeland Street, Petaluma, CA 94952. A book that discusses oils in detail is:

Gunst, Kathy. *Condiments.*

BUYING SOURCES

Oils can be purchased at supermarkets, health and natural foods stores, and ethnic and specialty food markets.

Oils are also available through the Deer Valley Farm, Allergy Resources, Arrowhead Mills, Clear Eye Natural Foods, Dean & Deluca, Frankferd Farms Foods, Gold Mine Natural Foods, Granum Incorporated, Harvest Time Natural Foods, Jaffe Bros., Mountain Ark Trading Company, Loriva Supreme Foods, and Walnut Acres Organic Farms mail order companies.

BRAND NAMES

Some recommended manufacturers or distributors of unrefined oils are Flora, Arrowhead Mills, Omega, Spectrum, Lifestream, Walnut Acres, Eden, and Hain.

OLIVE OIL

The delicate, fruity essence of olives can be captured in quality olive oils. These oils add a Mediterranean brightness and cheeriness to the foods they are added to.

See "Oils" for a comparison of oil types and a discussion of general oil concepts and issues.

VARIETIES

Olive oils are graded depending on the number of pressings of the olives and the processing method used.

The highest grades are called extra virgin. The next grades are called virgin and then pure. The lowest quality grade is blended.

Extra Virgin Olive Oil: This is the highest grade of olive oil. It is made from the choicest olives. The fruit is hand-picked and the oil is extracted mechanically by cold stone presses. No heat is used when making extra virgin olive oil; although a hot press can extract additional oil from the olive, this oil is of poorer quality. The sediment is then filtered out of most oils; some producers, however, believe that the sediment contains a rich, olive flavor that should be left in. If you notice that your oil is cloudy with bits of sediment floating around the bottom of the bottle, there's no cause for alarm. It's further evidence that you've got the real thing. Extra virgin olive oil is full-flavored and fruity because it is produced from the first pressing of the olives. This oil is the purest oil and the most expensive.

Extra virgin olive oil is prized for its low acidity. To be labeled "extra virgin," it should be less than 1% acid.

Virgin Olive Oil, Supreme Olive Oil, and Fine Olive Oil: All these names refer to the same grade of oil. They are produced from the second pressing of the olives that is done with high pressure and with the addition of heat. These oils have a higher degree of acidity, ranging from 1.5 to 5%.

Pure Olive Oil: This is the least expensive grade of olive oil you can buy. Sometimes it is mixed with a higher grade olive oil to give it a better flavor. Pure olive oil is produced either from a second pressing of inferior olives or the third pressing of higher quality olives used to make extra virgin and virgin oils. These pressings generally require the use of high temperatures, and sometimes chemical solvents are also used to extract the oil. The word "Pure" on the label simply refers to the fact that no other types of oil have been added.

Blended Olive Oil: Very much less expensive are blends of some cheap refined oil with a very small amount of good olive oil for flavor.

The flavors of olive oils are, of course, different per manufacturer, but they are also different depending on the country where the olives grow. The four major olive oil-producing countries are Italy, France, Greece, and Spain.

Italian Olive Oil: This oil is considered by many people to be the finest in the world—particularly those oils produced in the Tuscany, Liguria, and Umbria regions. These oils are rich and heavy with a full olive flavor and a deep, almost emerald-green color.

French Olive Oil: This oil is more delicate. It is known for its sweet, fruity flavor and light, golden-yellow color. Many people feel that the olives grown in Provence, in southeastern France, make the most delicate and fruity olive oil in the world. This oil is usually more expensive.

Spanish Olive Oil: This oil has a strong, assertive olive flavor and a thick consistency.

Greek Olive Oil: This oil, compared to Spanish oils, is also thick but has a lighter olive flavor.

The Spanish and Greek oils are generally less expensive than the Italian and French.

American Olive Oil: In the past few years, there have been a growing number of American olive oils, produced primarily in California. In general, these oils are excellent. They range from rich, olivey, Italian-style oils to more delicate French-style oils. Since most of these oils are produced on a small scale, the prices tend to be high.

FLAVOR/TEXTURE

The higher the grade, the better the flavor and aroma, the lower the acidity. Olive oil has a very distinctive, rich, fruity flavor and aroma as well as a yellow-greenish color.

GENERAL USES

Each type of olive oil has its own set of uses. Just because extra virgin oil is considered the best doesn't mean it's appropriate for every dish. You are wasting your money if you use extra virgin oil in complex sauces and recipes that call for dozens of ingredients. They are best served at room temperature because high heat can destroy their delicate flavor.

Because of the intense flavor in an extra virgin olive oil, it is not an all-purpose oil. It is perfectly suited for flavoring sauces and specialty salads, such as a Caesar salad. Sprinkle a combination of this excellent oil and wine vinegar over a lettuce, cold seafood, chicken, steamed vegetable, or meat salad. Use extra virgin olive oil for making pesto sauce. Make a rich vegetable dipping sauce with extra virgin olive oil, coarse sea salt, and coarsely ground black pepper.

For a wonderful hors d'oeuvres or snack, spread a tablespoon of extra virgin olive oil onto a thick chunk of Italian bread and top with paper-thin slices of prosciutto (or for vegetarians, seasoned sun-dried tomatoes) and a few grindings of black pepper.

If you like sun-dried tomatoes that are packed in oil (available in stores, but usually imported and very expensive), you can make your own. Simply rehydrate a few sun-dried tomatoes in water, pat them dry, and throw them in a jar with a small red crumbled chili pepper, garlic cloves, bay leaves, a few black peppercorns, and a good quality extra virgin olive oil. After a couple of days, you can serve these highly flavorful tomatoes with fish, meats, and chicken, or in antipasto and salads. And the flavored olive oil is wonderful over pasta and lettuce salads and for sautéing fresh vegetables.

Use virgin and pure oils for making sauces, stews, sautéed vegetables, stir-fries, roasts, and pasta sauces. Sauté sliced wild mushrooms and zucchini in virgin olive oil, throw in some minced garlic clove and chopped fresh herbs when it's almost done, and you've got a scrumptious side dish or topping for brown rice. To make a delectable topping for pasta or steamed spinach, sauté anchovies (or umeboshi plum pieces), garlic, parsley, and pimentos in a little virgin olive oil.

Olive oil can be combined with other oils such as safflower, which is richer in linoleic acid, for use as a salad oil or cooking medium.

FRESHNESS/QUALITY

Pure, unrefined olive oils should have good color, a distinctive fragrance, and a luscious, sensual, fresh taste. They should not have been extracted from their olives with the aid of chemical solvents.

STORAGE

See "Oils."

PREPARATION INSTRUCTIONS

The smoke point of olive oil is 280°F. See "Oils" more information about using oils in non-cooking and cooking situations, as well as making flavored oils.

HEALTH INFORMATION

Olive oil is mostly monounsaturated fat, which makes it heavier and more fatty than polyunsaturated oils. Olives are easily cold-pressed without added heat or chemical processing to retain much of their vitamin E.

ADDITIONAL READING

See "Oils."

BUYING SOURCES

See "Oils."

BRAND NAMES

There is a huge number of olive oils being produced. Because most of them are imported and their availability can change at a moments notice, we have not listed any specific brands. Although price may be an indicator of quality level, check with your local health food specialist or nutritionist for guidance about the brands that are available in your area. Flavors of olive oils can vary considerably between any two producers; have fun trying as many as you can.

PASTA

Pasta is not new to most kitchen pantries. The Italian spaghetti noodle has become almost as American as apple pie. Pasta is a quick-cooking, delicious, easily digestible form of grain. Today there are many kinds of pasta on the market.

VARIETIES

In general, pastas are made from a variety of flours such as unbleached white or whole wheat, buckwheat, corn, and/or rice. They may also be made from unusual grain flours, such as spelt and kamut, bean flours, and root starches (such as kuzu and potato starch).

Pasta can be made with eggs or without them. When used, eggs add some flavor and help the noodles maintain their shape. However, egg-free pastas can cook beautifully. While most American noodles contain eggs, Oriental noodles traditionally do not. If eggs are a consideration in your selection, check the label.

Pasta comes in many different shapes, sizes, flavors and colors. Ingredients such as artichokes, spinach, carrots, or tomatoes are added to the flours to create some of the varieties in color and taste.

CLASSIC PASTA

This pasta is made from semolina (refined durum wheat flour), water, and often eggs and sometimes milk. Elbows, shells, macaroni, rigatoni, spirals, twists, fettucce, tortellini, cannelloni, lasagna, vermicelli, and spaghetti are examples of shapes that classic pastas are formed into. High quality classic pastas are translucent and have an amber color.

WHOLE-GRAIN WHEAT PASTA

These pastas are available in many of the shapes, sizes, and flavors of classic pastas while providing the nutritional advantages of whole wheat. On the other hand, they may have a gritty texture which may make a difference in the dish you are preparing. Also, whole-grain wheat pastas have a tendency to fall apart more easily when overcooked. These pastas are usually made from hard red or durum wheat (see "Wheat" for more information):

Hard Red Wheat Pasta: This pasta is light brown in color. It usually takes longer to cook and has a stronger flavor than classic and durum wheat pastas.

Durum Wheat Pasta: This is a tender and mild tasting pasta. It is light creamy-yellow in color and, when cooked, keeps its shape well.

UDON

Udon is a special type of noodle. These thick, chewy, egg-free noodles are cream or beige in color and resemble linguini. They are made from 100% whole wheat flour, or whole wheat combined with unbleached white or brown rice flour. Because they hold up well when cooked, they can be boiled and used in noodle salads or as a substitute for spaghetti. They can even be parboiled and pan fried.

Whole Wheat Udon: This is a hardy noodle made with only whole wheat flours and sea salt.

Tsuru Udon: These are made using 40% unbleached white flour and 60% whole wheat flour. Because tsuru udon noodles contain unbleached white flour, they are lighter, smoother, and absorb flavors more easily than whole wheat noodles.

Brown Rice Udon: These noodles are made from a combination of brown rice flour, wheat flour, and salt. This blend produces a smooth textured, flavorful, and nutritious noodle.

SOMEN

Somen is a thin, very fine, light, egg-free noodle—similar in appearance to angel-hair pasta. Somen cooks quickly and absorbs the flavor of sauces, dressings, and seasonings well, so it is both convenient and versatile.

Unbleached White Flour Somen: This high quality somen is made from gluten-rich unbleached white flour with a little salt added.

Whole Wheat Somen: This nourishing somen is made from whole wheat flour and sea salt.

SOBA

Soba are thin, brownish-gray noodles (that resemble spaghetti) made with buckwheat flour, sea salt, and, optionally,  whole wheat, unbleached white, or soy flours. The higher the percentage of buckwheat flour in the noodles, the more fragile and assertively flavorful they will be. These noodles can be eaten hot or cold.

Soba noodles have an especially impressive nutritional profile, containing a high percentage of usable protein. When combined with wheat and/or soy flours, the pasta becomes almost as complete a protein as eggs, with none of the fat or cholesterol.

Traditional Soba: Traditional soba is a blend of sifted whole wheat flour, buckwheat flour, and sea salt, creating a richly flavored noodle with substantial texture.

100% Buckwheat Soba: This soba is a filling and hearty, wheat-free noodle that satisfies the most keen appetites. It must be cooked gently to prevent it from breaking, so it is not recommended for fried noodles. It has a heady, delicious flavor that will hold up in strong sauces.

Other Soba Noodles: New types of soba noodles are being created all the time. They differ in the ratio of buckwheat flour used to other flours and they may also be flavored with various uncommon ingredients (such as wild yams, lotus root, green tea powder, dried mugwort leaves, and jinenjo). Depending on the amount of buckwheat flour that is used, the noodles can be fragile or resilient, or mild or strong flavored.

FLAVOR/ TEXTURE

With the exception of buckwheat noodles, the flavor of pasta is not strong. They have a subtle hint of the flavor of the grain flour(s) they were made from. They are primarily used for the texture and visual appeal they bring to a dish. Some pastas are mildly flavored with artichokes, lemon pepper, spinach, carrots, tomatoes, or mung beans, mugwort, green tea powder, jinenjo, etc.

GENERAL USES

Pastas are light and easy to digest, as well as quick and simple to prepare. Whether in soups or salads, sautéed with vegetables, deep-fried, baked, stuffed, or topped with sauce, pastas are delicious and satisfying.

Pastas are no strangers to soups. What would chicken noodle soup be without the noodles, or minestrone without the shells or spirals? Another claim to fame for pastas are their hot and cold salads. A nice cold or warm pasta salad can be made by combining cooked noodles or spirals, cooked firm beans, crushed garlic cloves, and a little fine oil with whole black olives.

Some of the noodles are delicious when served cold with chilled sauces. Choose pastas that are thin and delicate. For example, on a summer day, a perfect way to enjoy soba is by dipping the delicate cold noodles in a chilled honey-mustard or seasoned shoyu sauce.

Pasta can be exquisite when sautéed with vegetables. Dig out the frying pan and look in the refrigerator for fresh vegetables that need immediate attention. Sauté the vegetables with wine and quality oil until tender and succulent. Then gently add cooked, drained pasta to the pan and toss. After allowing the flavors to blend for several minutes, serve with

parmesan cheese (or nutritional yeast), nuts, or herbs.

Bake cooked pasta to create whole-meal dishes like lasagna and casseroles. An easy casserole can be whipped up by baking a wide noodle such as tagliatelli with tuna or tofu, a creamy mushroom soup, celery, onion, and a grated white cheese. Garnish with onion rings. Any of the larger or sturdier pastas such as shells and macaroni can also be used in whole-meal dishes.

In Italian cuisine, the importance of the art of stuffing or filling pasta is apparent by the numerous dishes this cuisine offers. For example, manicotti is cheese-stuffed cannelloni pasta; and tortellini and ravioli often have cheese, meat, and/or vegetables hiding inside.

Over the years, sauces have become a traditional topping for pasta. There must be at least 1.732 billion different types of sauces that could be made today. There are thick and thin sauces, meat and vegetable sauces, tomato and seafood sauces, cream and wine sauces, oil and spice sauces, hot and cold sauces, white and dark sauces, sweet and sour sauces, etc. Traditionally, spaghetti, linguini, fettuccini, etc. are smothered in sauces; however, try using any of the pastas.

To derive the full nutritional benefit of your noodles, try to use the noodle cooking water instead of some other liquid in your recipe. If that is not appropriate, the noodle broth can be saved for use as a base liquid in a soup, stew, or sauce.

FRESHNESS/QUALITY

Quality pasta should consist of natural ingredients (flours, sea salt, water, eggs, vegetables, herbs, etc.). Some contain artificial colors, flavorings, preservatives, etc. Check labels.

Whole grain pasta should be made from ground whole grains. This sounds obvious, but many commercially available noodles are made from wheat that has first been stripped of its nutritious outer layers, then ground into flour and "enriched" with synthetically produced vitamins and minerals.

STORAGE

Keep dry, uncooked pasta in a cool place in an airtight container.

Cooked pasta can be kept in an airtight container for a couple of days in the refrigerator. Leftover pastas with nothing on them can be "refreshed" by placing them in a strainer or colander and running hot water over them and stirring. Or they can be submerged in a pot of boiling water until just heated. Pasta dishes can be reheated in the microwave or a skillet.

PREPARATION INSTRUCTIONS

All pastas must be boiled before anything else is done to them. This is a simple process. Ease the pasta into a large pot of boiling salted water. (Noodles that are made with salt—udon, somen, and soba—do not need salt added to the cooking water.) Stir gently until the water is boiling rapidly again, preventing the noodles from sticking to each other and the bottom of the pot. Keep the water boiling and the pasta submerged until it is done. Using too little water results in sticky noodles and uneven cooking. Adding oil to the water helps keep the pot from boiling over, but isn't necessary if you have a large enough pot.

The cooking time depends on the thickness of the pasta: 5 minutes for very thin, 20 minutes for thick! There are classic tests, including throwing the pasta against a wall (if it sticks, it is done); but the best test is to bite a piece. It should be slightly chewy and, when broken in half, be the same color throughout. Test often to avoid overcooking.

When done, immediately drain the noodles. There is no need to rinse the noodles if they are to be served immediately in a hot preparation. Otherwise, rinse the noodles in two or three cold water baths or under cold running water. This prevents further cooking and keeps the noodles from sticking together. Drain

and set aside until ready to assemble your dish. If the pasta needs to be reheated before serving, at the last minute, plunge the noodles into boiling water and drain.

As a rule of thumb, 1/2 pound of dry noodles generates approximately four cups cooked.

Making homemade pasta from flour is challenging fun when you are just learning, and easy once you have mastered the art. There are a great many books, machines, equipment, and gadgets out there if you want to give it a try.

HEALTH INFORMATION

Pasta contains little to no fat and is an excellent source of complex carbohydrates and dietary fiber.

ADDITIONAL READING

Barrett, Judith. *Pasta Verde*.

Spitler, Sue. *Skinny Pasta*.

Toomay, Mindy, and Susann Geiskopf Hadler. *The Best 125 Meatless Pasta Dishes*.

Udesky, James. *Book of Soba*.

BUYING SOURCE

Pasta is available everywhere! In supermarkets, health food stores, and wholesale warehouse stores; it can be found on the shelves, in the refrigerated, frozen, and bulk food sections, and sometimes in the "deli" section. Pasta and noodles are available through the Deer Valley Farm, Allergy Resources, Anzen Oriental Foods & Imports, Bob's Red Mill Natural Foods, Clear Eye Natural Foods, Dean & Deluca, Frankferd Farms Foods, Garden Spot, Gold Mine Natural Foods, Granum Incorporated, Harvest Time Natural Foods, Jaffe Bros., Mountain Ark Trading Company, and Natural Lifestyle mail order companies.

BRAND NAMES

Eden offers rice pasta, mung bean pasta, kuzu kiri pasta, soba noodles (wild yam, mugwort, lotus root, 100% buckwheat, 40% buckwheat), udon, brown rice udon, and whole wheat and durum pasta (ribbons, spirals, shells, and spaghetti).

DeBoles provides durum wheat artichoke elbows, fettuccine, lasagna, linguine, noodles, rigatoni, shells, spaghetti, ziti, and rotini. They also have tomato/basil and garlic/parsley flavored durum pasta and tomato/lemon/pepper and tomato/pesto flavored semolina pasta.

Westbrae offers elbows and spaghetti made from corn and whole wheat flours. Elbows, shells, bow ties, spaghetti, angel hair, and fettuccine made from organic durum semolina are also available.

Mitoku has whole wheat, traditional, and brown rice udon, whole wheat somen, and soba noodles (100% buckwheat, traditional, mugwort, and jinenjo).

Purity Foods offers spelt elbows, rotini, shells, and spaghetti. Some are available flavored with spinach and other vegetables.

PINTO BEANS

(PIN toe) (beans)

Pinto beans have a light cream-colored background with a pinkish-brown swirling pattern on top. When cooked, the mottled appearance of the pintos sadly disappears and the beans turn uniformly pink. However, they become plump, meaty, scrumptious morsels which you can use in just about anything.

OTHER NAMES
Mexican strawberries, gunga pea, toor dal. A couple of hybrids are rattlesnake beans and appaloosa beans.

FLAVOR/TEXTURE
Pinto beans have an earthy, full-bodied flavor and a dry, meaty texture. They are closely related to red kidney beans.

GENERAL USES
The most common use of pinto beans is in Mexican cuisines such as chili or refried beans. They go especially well with chilies, lime, and beer. For a change of pace, a wonderful "drunken bean" dish can be created by combining cooked pinto beans and their juice with beer, sea

salt, garlic, onion, cumin, lime juice, Sucanat® (or brown sugar or other sweetener), and hickory smoke flavoring in a crock pot.

They are also good in casseroles, soups, and stews and add color, flavor, and texture to mixed-bean salads.

These beans are perfect for making dips and spreads for crackers, vegetables, chips, and toast. To make a spicy dip for vegetables and chips, blend cooked pinto beans with garlic, scallions, coriander, soy sauce, lemon juice, mustard, corn oil, ground pepper, and cumin.

A delectable bean patty or burger can be made by blending cooked, drained pinto beans with garlic, salt, crackers (or bread crumbs or ground oat flakes), and cilantro. Then simply shape the mixture into patties and fry or broil them.

FRESHNESS/QUALITY
See "Beans."

STORAGE
See "Beans."

PREPARATION INSTRUCTIONS

CLEANING AND SOAKING
See "Beans."

COOKING
See the "Beans" section for general instructions for cooking. Stove-top cooking time ranges from 50 to 70 minutes, and the pressure cooking time is 20 minutes. One cup of dried beans yields approximately 2 3/4 cups cooked. After cooking, the mottled pattern on the pinto disappears, turning uniformly pink. Pintos can be used instead of pink beans or kidney beans.

HEALTH INFORMATION
Pinto beans are rich in protein, calcium, and iron.

ADDITIONAL READING
See "Beans."

BUYING SOURCES
See "Beans" for a list of mail order sources and brand names.

QUINOA

(KEEN wah)

It has been said that no one should eat anything that they can't pronounce. Well, quinoa is pronounced *KEEN wah*, so now that you know how to say it, run to your natural food store and buy some today. Although this grain has an ancient past, it is a new addition to many kitchens. This little, disk-shaped, light-beige seed is considered to be a supergrain. It is renowned for its nutritional profile and is one of the best sources of protein in the vegetable kingdom. It is not really a true grain, but that doesn't matter because it is very similar to a grain. It is actually a member of the Goosefoot Family to which beets, chards, and spinach also belong.

This little pseudo-grain is somewhere between millet and mustard seed in appearance. It has a delicate, fluffy texture with a mild, nutty flavor. When cooked, it expands to three to five times its original size to make a filling dish for even the most hungry family member.

VARIETIES

Whole-Grain Quinoa: Even though whole-grain quinoa comes in many varieties ranging in color from off-white to black, only one is commonly available and it is light beige in color. Quinoa cooks in a relatively short period of time and is a good substitute for other longer cooking grains such as rice.

Quinoa Flour: This flour is made when whole grains of quinoa are finely ground. If you cannot find any, it is easy to grind your own quinoa flour in your kitchen. Simply whirl the grain in a blender until all the whole grains are reduced to a white flour. Use 3/4 cup whole grain to make one cup of flour. See "Grains" for more information about grain flours.

Quinoa flour can be used in the making of fine pastries. It produces a light delicate crumb and is perfect for cakes, cookies, pancakes, and waffles. In many baked goods, up to 100% quinoa flour can be used. It is useful in making tortillas, pizza crusts, crêpes, pie crusts, and pasta. Because it is gluten-free, it should be combined with wheat, kamut, or spelt flour for making leavened breads, cookies, cakes, biscuits, rolls, and other baked goods that must rise.

Quinoa Pasta: Pasta made from quinoa flour is available and comes in a variety of sizes and shapes. Use it as you would use any pasta (see "Pasta").

FLAVOR/TEXTURE

The flavor of quinoa can range from nutty with a bitter aftertaste to just mildly nutty with a hint of the flavor of peanuts and couscous. In most cases, the bitter flavor can be reduced or eliminated entirely just by washing, but sometimes washing and roasting are needed to accomplish this goal.

The tender, light, and fluffy texture of quinoa is different from all the other grains because it does not share the characteristics of starchiness and chewiness.

GENERAL USES

Quinoa's mild flavor and light and fluffy texture make it perfect for puddings, breakfast cereals, stuffings, soups, stews, salads, fritters, pilafs, desserts, baked goods, etc.

Stewing, braising, or baking brings out the flavor of quinoa which goes well with savory, sweet, and meat dishes. Sweet, sour, spicy, and salty flavors are all complemented by quinoa's flavor. Obviously, this makes it extremely versatile. Try throwing some in stir-fries, chili, pot pies, or gyros.

Quinoa mixes very well with other grains; try using corn, wild rice, buckwheat, millet, or amaranth to create delightful texture and taste variations. It also blends well with beans and nuts. A lighter, fluffier hummus can be created by replacing half of the garbanzo beans with cooked quinoa.

It is also useful for adding fluffiness to egg dishes such as omelets and scrambled eggs. Try scrambling some eggs with sautéed mushrooms and scallions, cooked quinoa, and soy sauce. If you'd like, add a little salt, fresh tomato chunks, or sautéed bell peppers.

Mixtures made with quinoa can be used to stuff tomatoes, bell peppers, mushrooms, potatoes, fruits, pita pockets, burritos and enchiladas, nori rolls, egg rolls, grape leaves, cabbage leaves, other greens, meats, fish, and poultry.

To make an exotic dessert that will knock the socks off any special guest, mix cooked quinoa with ground mint, walnut pieces, currants, honey, ground cloves, and salt. Use this mixture to stuff fresh red Bartlett pears and bake in a 350°F oven for an hour. Before serving, drizzle nut or fruit liqueur over the baked pears.

To get started using quinoa, try using it in place of millet, couscous, and bulgur in your favorite recipes.

Quinoa may be mixed with soybeans to make tempeh, which makes great vegetarian burgers. See "Tempeh" for more information about this ingredient.

Quinoa flour is excellent when used to make pancakes, waffles, crêpes, flat breads, biscuits, crusts, rolls, crackers, bagels, muffins, scones, cookies, cakes, shortbread, etc.

FRESHNESS/QUALITY

See "Grains."

STORAGE

Quinoa has a short shelf life because it is high in fat when compared to grains. The refrigerator is the best place for quinoa (here it will last a month or two), but it can be kept in a sealed container in a cool, dark place if necessary.

Cooked quinoa will last in the refrigerator from 4 to 6 days.

For more information about storing grains, see "Grains."

PREPARATION INSTRUCTIONS

CLEANING

Quinoa's bitter flavor is due to a natural protective coating called saponin.

Washing quinoa several times and replacing the water after each washing will remove the harsh-tasting coating. Feel free to take the little grains between your hands and gently rub a little. This will also help to remove the coating. Note that saponin is not toxic and if you like the bitter taste, by all means don't wash the quinoa or just wash it one or two times. For more information about washing grains, see "Grains."

SOAKING

Quinoa should not be soaked if you want anything other than a heavy, mushy texture.

COOKING

Quinoa cooks quickly and is great for those meals when you are on-the-run. When quinoa is done, the grain appears translucent and the germ ring (that looks like a small white sprout or tail) is visible. Quinoa can be roasted to bring out its flavor and it can be prepared using any of the grain cooking methods, see "Grains" for cooking instructions and a discussion of cooking issues.

Depending on the cooking method used, one cup of raw quinoa will yield three to five cups cooked. To produce a light, fluffy result, the basic ratio of grain to liquid is 1 to 2 and the cooking time is approximately 15 minutes. To make a creamier product, up to 4 cups of water can be used per cup of quinoa and additional cooking time will be required.

REHEATING

Quinoa sticks together slightly as it cools; so break it up with a fork before reheating. See "Grains" for additional reheating information. It is not necessary to heat quinoa if it is to be used cold in foods such as salads.

HEALTH INFORMATION

This grain contains the eight essential amino acids in proportions almost equal to the ideal set by the United Nations Food and Agriculture Organization. Thus, quinoa is a plant food that happens to be one of the best sources of protein.

Quinoa is also a rich source of many other vital nutrients, including starch, sugars, fiber, oil, minerals, and vitamins. It is high in vitamin E, the B-complex vitamins (pyridoxine, pantothenic acid, folate, biotin, thiamin, and niacin), calcium, phosphorus, iron, magnesium, zinc, and copper.

Some strains of quinoa have a little bit of gluten, but it is less than 1%.

ADDITIONAL READING

Wood, Rebecca. *Quinoa the Supergrain: Ancient Food for Today*.

BUYING SOURCES

Quinoa is found in health and natural food stores in prepackaged boxes and in bulk bins. This grain is also available through mail order sources; see "Grains" for a listing.

BRAND NAMES

A couple of quality brands that you might like to try are Eden and Ancient Harvest (by Quinoa Corporation).

RICE

Somewhere, somehow, someone, sometime, has declared that rice is cooked in a single way to produce "perfect rice." This simply ain't so. Rice comes in many different varieties and can be cooked in many different ways to produce many different results for many different dishes. Rice has been around for a very long time and has been prepared and eaten in numerous cultures throughout the world—each having its own unique approaches. Furthermore, each person, no matter what his or her culture, cooks rice using the methods he or she has been taught that have been slightly or dramatically changed to suit personal tastes and uses. In other words, the perfect rice is the rice that tastes good in the dish that you are eating. The mild flavor of filling, carbohydrate-and nutrient-rich rice makes it a blank canvas for both the novice and master cook.

Rice may be found in a variety of colors (brown, white, black, and red) and it ranges in length from 1/8 to 1 inch. Cooked rice has a slightly chewy exterior and very tender, soft interior.

VARIETIES

There are many whole rices and rice products.

WHOLE RICES

Rice is available in many shapes and sizes, colors, strains, and refinement levels. See the "Relationships Between Categorizations of Rice" grid and "Characteristics of Rice" below.

CHARACTERISTICS OF RICE ──────

1. **Type**

   Brown
   Black
   Red
   Aromatic
   Wild
   Sweet

2. **Size/Shape**

   Short
   Medium
   Long

3. **Refinement Level**

   Natural Color
   White

The sized related terms used to describe rice refer to the length of the rice kernel, not the width (in fact, short grain rice is wider than both medium and long grain rice).

Short Grain: This rice consists of short, rounded, and oval-shaped grains that produce a hearty, moist, tender and sticky rice that is denser, chewier, and plumper than the other sized rices. Because it has a high concentration of

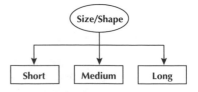

starch, this rice clings together when cooked and is well suited for desserts, puddings, burgers, patties, loaves, stuffings, croquettes, sushi, and any dish which requires its stickiness as a binding agent.

Make a quick and simple rice patty by combining a cooked warm short grain rice with spices and vegetables. Try using onion, which is always perfect for any type of rice, along with garlic, basil, oregano, and shoyu soy sauce or sea salt. Add just enough tahini or nut butter to help bind the rice, spices, and vegetables together and allow patties of the desired thickness and size to be formed. Simply broil or fry the patties and serve topped with a sauce or in a hamburger bun.

Long Grain: Light, fluffy, and dry, long grain is probably the most common size rice and is the first choice for many main course dishes. It is less plump than short and medium rice and is approximately four times longer than wide. This rice is superb for pilafs, salads, stuffings, fried rice, and mixing with wild rice because of its delicious flavor and its kernels separate when cooked. It also makes a gratifying side dish that can be served with bean, meat, and fish entrées. Long grain rice is often used in Chinese, Indonesian, Indian, and Middle Eastern dishes and is sometimes called curry rice.

Whip a delicious soup together in just minutes by first sautéing onions in a little vegetable broth, adding cooked long grain rice and more vegetable broth or water, and then simmering until the rice is hot. Remove from the stove and add any of the different flavored misos, either to the entire pot of soup or to individual bowls. Serve with garlic toast and a fresh green salad. If miso isn't available, use a concentrated soup stock or broth, or a a vegetable or meat bouillon.

Medium Grain: This size rice is the middle of the road rice. It is not as sticky as short grain rice but not as fluffy and separate as long grain rice. Medium grain rice may be more difficult to find than the short and long grains. But don't despair if you can't find it. Short grain rice can be cooked to produce a result very similar to medium grain rice (as far as flavor and

texture go). This is also true of long grain rice. Medium grain rice is great for fried rice because it holds together well without being too sticky while also having a mild fluffy texture. It is also a good rice with sauces when a light, fluffy, separate grain would not be suitable. Try using medium grain rice in your favorite Spanish rice recipe. If, in soups, you don't want the size of the long grain or the starchiness of the short grain, a medium grain rice works quite nicely.

Rice is available in a variety of colors:

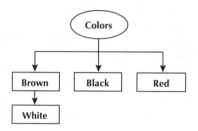

Brown Rice: This rice has a pleasant nutty flavor and chewy texture. It is becoming much more common and is readily available. Brown rice is perfect in "down-to-earth" dishes that are appealing in a wholesome, warming, and comfortable way. Brown rice is eminently satisfying on a cold winter's day when snuggled in front of a fire, or on a spring or summer day when the whole family has gotten together for a special picnic. Some may find brown rice homely and lacking a little bit in aesthetic appeal when compared to the other rices; but, we don't think so—homely is beautiful, too.

Brown rice has undergone the least amount of refinement. Only the inedible outer layer is removed, leaving the nutritional bran and germ intact. This makes it take quite a bit longer to cook than white rice. Because rice bran contains oil, brown rice has a shorter shelf life.

Brown rice has the distinction of having the highest level of B vitamins of all the grains; but, it has a lower protein content. Brown rice also contains vitamin E, linoleic acid, and iron. This "whole food" rice is a good source of dietary fiber. Brown rice comes in all of the sizes—

long, short, and medium. Nutritionally, all of the sizes are comparable.

Rizcous: This is brown rice that has been cut into small pieces to produce a quick cooking rice. The flavor and texture of cooked rizcous is similar to couscous. It can be used in hot breakfast cereals, stuffings, salads, and mixed with vegetables, beans, and other grains.

White Rice: White rice is not a new ingredient to many kitchens. It has been around a long, long time and because it is so versatile, it is here to stay. White rice is not a distinct type; it is simply a refined brown rice. It is refined by removing the bran and germ of the brown rice kernels and then it is often "enriched," which means returning some of the vitamins, minerals, fiber, and fats that were lost in the refinement process. This does have the positive effect of causing white rice to last three to six times longer than brown rice. However, the bran and germ can't be added back to highly polished rice grains. Even though white rice is not as nutritious as brown rice, it has its own niches.

White rice has a very mild taste and is quite a bit less flavorful than brown rice. This is useful when you are creating a dish with a very delicate sauce or set of seasonings. The bright white color of white rice creates a visually spectacular dish when combined with colorful vegetables or used with a colorful sauce such as curry, tomato, or avocado. Little bits of bright white also provide a pleasant contrast when added to stews and soups. Instead of chicken noodle soup, try making a chicken rice soup.

Arborio Rice: This short grain white rice is high in starch and is sticky when cooked which makes it good for puddings. In fact, it is stickier than other short grain white rices and can be cooked to be creamier, too. Arborio rice has the added benefit of being able to take on the flavor of whatever it is cooked with. It is the traditional rice used to make the Italian dish risotto.

White rice is treated in many ways:

Enriched or Fortified White Rice: When rice is polished to make it white, it loses many of its minerals and vitamins. The

process of enrichment involves replacing some of the vitamins, proteins, and/or trace minerals by infusing them back into the rice. Most of the rices found in supermarkets have been enriched with iron, niacin, and thiamin.

Parboiled Rice or Converted Rice: This is a white rice that has been through a steam and pressure process before polishing that helps it retain some of its natural nutrients. However, the fiber of the bran and germ is still lost. Parboiled rice is usually higher in the B vitamins, protein, niacin, thiamin, and iron than polished white rice and is considered to be nutritionally somewhere between brown and plain white rice. The grains of parboiled rice remain separated, giving it a texture that is fluffier and lighter than regular white rice.

Black Rice: Black rice is definitely not among the common rices; but, it can be found. The color is actually more deep purple than black. This color is an effective food coloring—black rice likes to share its color with whatever it's cooked with. Black rice can be short, sweet, and sticky (a type of sweet rice) with a fruity aroma and strong flavor. This type of rice is used for desserts and puddings. Japonica is another variety of black rice which has a very long grain and is sticky with a grass-like flavor. The origin of this rice is Thai and it is also used for desserts. Black rice is especially tasty when cooked with coconut.

Red Rice: This is another uncommon type of rice that has a relatively short grain for a long grain rice. It is deep burgundy or very reddish-brown in color and retains much of the color when cooked. It is often called Christmas rice. Red rice has a wonderful aroma while cooking and the resulting texture is fluffy with a flavor resembling strong tea and mild mushrooms. This is a hard variety of rice that benefits from a soaking prior to cooking.

There are quite a few specialty rices, or other "rices," that are available for culinary purposes:

Sweet or Glutinous Rice: This rice comes in a variety of colors: white, brown, and black. Sweet rice is also called gluti-

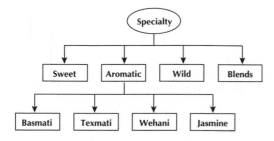

nous, sticky, sushi, mochi, or pearl rice. It is opaque and almost as wide as it is long. Because it contains a high concentration of starch and sugars, it becomes very sticky when cooked. The term "glutinous" is used for this type of rice only because of its sticky properties. This rice, as well as all other types of rice, does not contain the protein gluten which is found in other grains such as wheat, kamut, and spelt. Sweet rice really isn't sweet, but some folks think that it tastes sweeter than other rices—something like a lime tasting sweeter than a lemon. This rice is perfectly suited for making sushi. Spread the cooked rice on a sheet of roasted nori, add your favorite vegetables, spices, and pickles, and then roll it up and cut into bite size rounds. See "Nori" for more information about making sushi rolls.

Aromatic Rice: These rices have a very strong, absolutely wonderful aroma when they are being cooked. Their powerfully appealing fragrances will fill the house and start everyone's mouths watering. Get ready for a stampede when cooking an aromatic rice.

Basmati Rice: This slender rice is native to India and Pakistan and is available in both brown and white types and is longer than long rice. Basmati is about four times as long as it is wide. Interestingly, when cooked, it gets longer (almost doubles), not wider. Basmati rice cooks into separate fluffy grains perfect for pilafs and salads. Basmati rice dishes are delicious when cooked with spices such as cardamom, cinnamon, and cloves.

Brown basmati rice has an absolutely fantastic nutty and popcorn-like aroma when cooking. The smell makes the stomach growl and it is very hard to wait for the rice to become done. It is worth waiting for, because the flavor is also fantastic.

White or polished basmati rice cooks up light and fluffy while having a sticky, chewy texture. Because it is somewhat sticky, it can be used to make nori sushi rolls. White basmati rice has a delicate and sweet flavor and is also very aromatic.

Texmati Rice: Texmati rice is a hybrid of basmati and long grain rices that is mainly grown in the state of Texas to produce a sort of domestic basmati rice. It can rival basmati rice in flavor, aroma, texture, and cooking properties.

Calmati Rice: This type of rice is a hybrid long grain and basmati rice that is grown in California. It is very similar in flavor, aroma, and texture and may be used in any recipe that calls for basmati or Texmati rice.

Wehani Rice: This long grain, red rice is produced in California and has a rich, nutty, and buttery aroma. It has a flavor reminiscent of brown rice or fresh roasted chestnuts and it has a texture similar to that of wild rice.

Jasmine Rice: If your health food store carries jasmine rice, definitely give it a try. It has a light, delicate, and delicious flavor that is similar to white basmati rice. Jasmine, a white long-grain rice, is firm and not as fluffy or dry as basmati rice. It is actually a little on the sticky side. Think of it as a sort of mildly sticky, aromatic long-grain rice.

Wild Rice: Wild rice is not really a rice at all but the seeds of an aquatic grass. The only processing it undergoes is the removal of the hull. It ranges from medium brown to black in color and has a dense and chewy texture with a stronger, earthy, slightly smoky, woodsy, and nuttier flavor than rice. Wild rice has a divine wild flavor and essence. It turns slightly purple when cooked; sometimes it splits open and exposes its tender grayish-white interior.

It is most often used as a gourmet rice. Its wild flavor is enhanced when mixed with "earthy" foods such as other rices and grains, game, fowl, beans, and mushrooms. Its flavor is toned down when served with fish, shellfish, and combined with nuts, vegetables, dairy products, and fruits. Furthermore, it can be used in any way that a long grain rice may be used and is excellent when added cold to salads or other chilled or room temperature dishes.

Since wild rice is expensive, it is often mixed with long grain brown rice, which produces a wild but lighter tasting dish. Try using 1 part wild rice with 5 to 10 parts brown rice. Wild rice, when combined with a white long grain rice, creates an elegant color contrast to produce an attractive presentation as well as a distinguished flavor.

Wild rice is graded into three categories based on size, uniformity, and breakage. All of the grades are similar in taste and nutrition and can be used interchangeably.

Select Wild Rice: This type is the lowest in quality and has the shortest grain, around 3/8 inch or smaller. It is not uniform in size and often contains some broken grains which makes texture consistency and cooking difficult.

Extra-Fancy Wild Rice: This is the in-between level of quality. The grains are a little longer (around 1/2 inch) and the size of the grains is consistent with very few broken grains. This type will cook more evenly and produce a better, more consistent, texture than the select variety.

Giant Wild Rice: This is the cream of the crop of wild rice. The grains can reach a whopping 1 inch in length and are uniform in size with little to no broken grains. This wild rice can produce a wondrous gourmet dish fit for royalty and you.

Some brands of wild rice may benefit from soaking prior to cooking. To determine if the type you have needs soaking, try cooking the rice as usual and if it is not done after 1 to 1 1/2 hours of cooking, you should soak it the next time you prepare it. However, the current batch is not a lost case; simply remove the rice from the heat and let it cool, then continue cooking again until it becomes tender. Once you have figured out how to cook the wild rice, note the name, brand, and producer or distributor of the rice and be sure you purchase the same type again.

Wild rice is a good source of insoluble fiber and, compared to true grains, has more amino acids, protein, lysine, and methionine. It contains a high concentration of the B vitamins thiamin, riboflavin, niacin, folate, and pyridoxine. Furthermore, wild rice is also a good source of magnesium, zinc, iron, phosphorous, calcium, and copper.

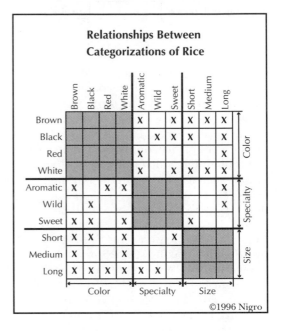

Relationships Between Categorizations of Rice

	Brown	Black	Red	White	Aromatic	Wild	Sweet	Short	Medium	Long	
Brown					X		X	X	X	X	Color
Black						X	X	X		X	Color
Red					X					X	Color
White					X		X	X	X	X	Color
Aromatic	X		X	X						X	Specialty
Wild		X								X	Specialty
Sweet	X	X		X				X			Specialty
Short	X	X		X			X				Size
Medium	X			X							Size
Long	X	X	X	X	X	X					Size
	Color				Specialty			Size			

©1996 Nigro

RICE PRODUCTS

In addition to the rice as a whole grain, there are many other products made from rice. See the "Milled & Processed Grains" subsection in the "Grains" section for more information on these grain products.

Rice Blends or Mixes: These mixes are mainly available in a dry form and are often boxed. They normally consist of a combination of dried rices, broth, vegetables, and herbs. The faster they can be prepared, the more likely they have been pre-cooked. They are convenient and an easy way to make a good-tasting rice dish; however, they are often quite a bit more expensive than if you were to buy the rice, spices, and vegetables and mix them yourself. Quality rice mixes do not contain MSG, artificial colors or flavors, preservatives, or modified starch.

Quick Cooking or Instant Rice: This is a precooked rice that has been dehydrated to preserve it. All that is left to do is to rehydrate it in boiling liquid. This quick cooking method is very easy and convenient, but it does have a price. Instant rice has lost much of the flavor and texture of the original grain.

Rice Flour: This flour is made from ground rice. It has a granular texture and a mild or nut-like flavor depending on whether the flour was made from white or brown rice. Rice flour can be used in many of the same ways as other grain flours. It is perfect for coatings, breadings, crackers, and cookies as well as rice noodles. It is a handy flour to have around when shaping bread loaves and rolling pie crusts because it dries the surface of the dough, prevents sticking, and can be easily brushed off. Sweet brown rice flour has a gummy texture that is perfect for dumplings and brownies.

Because rice flour has no gluten, it cannot be used by itself to make a light fluffy bread. However, it can be added to other high-gluten flours such as wheat to make a delicious bread that is different from the run-of-the-mill breads.

Brown rice flour will oxidize (i.e., become rancid) once it is milled and should be used rather quickly.

Rice Farina: Brown and white rice farina are made by stone grinding rice into a coarse meal. Farina is perfect on a chilly morning when cooked to make a creamy hot cereal.

Rice Grits: Rice kernels can be cracked to produce coarse grains called rice grits. When used in stews, casseroles, and soups, they add a wonderful texture. They can be made into a delightful breakfast dish, much the same way that corn grits are typically eaten (see "Corn"). To speed up the preparation of a rice dish, try replacing the whole rice with rice grits (using a one-to-one ratio).

Rice Bran: This is the bran of rice kernels that has been ground. It can be used in the same manner as any grain bran. Common ways to use bran are in baked goods and with cereal. Just a couple of spoonfuls can add a wonderful nutty flavor and nutritional value to many dishes.

Puffed Rice: Rice is puffed up by injecting cooked grains of rice with air.

This product is often used as a cold breakfast cereal and in muesli and trail mixes. It can also be used in making delicious candies and cakes.

Rice-Flour Noodles: These noodles have a pleasant flavor and chewy texture and can be simmered or deep-fried to create many dishes. See the "Pasta" section for more information about noodles.

Rice Cakes: Rice cakes are a nutritious, low-calorie food that can be found in almost any supermarket. They are crunchy wafers made from puffed rice that, in general, lack flavor and have a texture similar to styrofoam. The flavor of rice cakes is often improved with seasonings and other ingredients. Some cakes are made using more rice and less air and they have a richer flavor, more calories, and a more pleasing texture. Rice cakes can be used instead of a cracker or piece of toast for dunking into dips and sauces; topped with spreads (such as apple butter, honey, peanut butter, other nut and seed butters, and puréed beans), coated with chocolate or carob to make a tasty treat, or eaten right out of the bag as a crunchy snack.

Rice Vinegar: This is a vinegar made from rice that is quite mellow and sweet in aroma and flavor compared to other vinegars. See "Vinegars" for more information.

Rice Syrup: This is a sweetener made from rice which is similar in texture and color to honey but milder in flavor and not quite as sweet. See "Sweeteners" for more information.

Rice Wine: This is an alcoholic beverage made from rice. Sake, a Japanese rice wine, is served warm traditionally but it can be enjoyed cold as well. Mirin is a cooking rice wine. See "Mirin" for more information.

FLAVOR/TEXTURE

Rice, in general, has a rather mild nutty flavor that blends well with almost any food you can think of; however, all rices do not taste the same. See the descriptions in "Varieties." The texture of rice can range from light and fluffy to heavy and sticky. Furthermore, depending on how it is cooked, it can range from firm and chewy to very soft and mushy.

GENERAL USES

Rice is one of the most used grains in this country. It can be used in making many different and diverse dishes but some common types are: puddings, pilafs, casseroles, soups, stuffings, salads, croquettes, or as a dish of its own. The large number of cooking methods and ingredients that harmonize with rice can produce such an array of dishes that you can eat rice almost every day without getting bored with it.

Rice is wonderful when cooked with other types of rice, other grains, beans, vegetables, fruits, nuts and seeds, meats, seafood, sea vegetables, dairy products, spices and herbs, wines, vinegars, juices, and soy foods (such as tempeh, tofu, miso, soy sauce, etc.).

The type of rice used can make quite a difference. Make a simple but tasty rice to accompany any entrée by combining cooked rice, garlic, parsley, and a little oil, margarine, or soy butter in a baking dish, covering and baking in a moderate oven until the rice is tender. If brown rice is used for this dish, it will have a earthy and hearty feel and is nice served with meat loaf, roast, tempeh steaks, etc. On the other hand, if white rice is used, the dish is transformed into a delicate, mild, almost gourmet dish that can be served with fish, poultry, tofu, etc.

Make a great fruit and rice salad by mixing orange juice, apricot nectar, dried apricots, raisins, dried cherries, scallions, black pepper, toasted almonds, and cooked long grain rice (brown or white).

A heavenly main course entrée can be created by tossing hot rice with sautéed scallions and mushrooms, cooked fresh vegetables, pimento, chopped nuts, parsley, and a little olive oil.

A new flavor dimension can be achieved by cooking rice in flavored liquids, broths, or stocks. The rice will absorb the new flavors while retaining its own flavor. Fruit juices make wonderful liquids for cooking rice—try using apple, orange, or pineapple juice. Experiment

with other liquids such as tomato or vegetable juices, wines, beers, milks, and liqueurs. Combine any types of liquids that go well together and do not hesitate to add spices to the cooking liquids.

FRESHNESS/QUALITY

Green kernels dispersed in bins or bags of brown rice are not an indicator of poor quality. They contain as much nutritional value and flavor as the brown kernels and are signs of freshness.

White rice may be cosmetically treated with talc or oil to improve the color, gloss, or shine of the grains. Producers and mills may print "no talc" on their packages when the rice has not been treated with this substance.

For additional general information about the freshness and quality of grains, see "Grains."

STORAGE

Brown rice has a shorter shelf life than white rice due to the oil in its bran, and will last for six months to a year. On the other hand, white and wild rice can be stored for three years before beginning to deteriorate. Aromatic rices will lose their aroma over time.

Cooked rice can be safely left at room temperature for several hours. If it is to be kept longer than that, however, it should be refrigerated to prevent souring. In the refrigerator, cooked rice should keep for a week or so. Cooked rice will last for approximately four months when stored in the freezer.

See "Grains" for more information on storing grains.

PREPARATION INSTRUCTIONS

CLEANING

Rice may be washed if dirty or to remove substances (such as talc) that are used to make white rices look more white. See "Grains" for procedures and tips.

SOAKING

Soaking rice can serve a couple of purposes. One is to make it softer so that it will cook faster (this is useful when creating a gruel-type dish which is very soft and easy to digest). The other is to bleach a white rice, so that when it is cooked, it will be whiter.

COOKING

Cooking rice is the art of preparing it in a manner that you find wonderful and delicious and that suits the purpose you are using it for. It is the art of making sticky rice, dry rice, fluffy rice, sweet rice, pretty rice, wholesome rice, wet rice, spicy rice, mild rice, gooey rice, soft rice, firm rice, milky rice, etc. Use 2 to 2 1/2 cups of liquid to 1 cup of rice and 3 to 4 cups of liquid per cup of wild rice. See the "Rice Comparison Table" for approximate cooking times.

See "Grains" to learn more about the art of cooking grains.

Rice Bottom: Cooking rice not only creates a delicious dish but can provide an additional treat. There is often a thin layer of rice stuck together on the bottom of the pot. This is known as rice bottom and can be removed and eaten or dried in the oven and saved in an airtight container. When you have collected plenty of dried rice bottoms to make it worthwhile, they can be deep fried to produce a wholesome and delicious snack.

Rice Comparison Table

	Availability	Cooking Time (in Minutes)	Flavor	Nutrition
	©1996 Nigro			
Brown	Common	30 to 45	Medium	High
Rizcous	Not Common	10 to 15	Medium	High
White	Very Common	15 to 20	Mild	Very Low
Parboiled	Common	20 to 25	Mild	Medium
Arborio	Not Common		Mild	Low
Black	Rare	25 to 35	Very Strong	High
Red	Rare	45 to 55	Medium	High
Sweet				
Brown	Common	50 to 70	Medium	High
White	Common	30 to 50	Mild	Low
Aromatic				
Basmati, Brown	Common	40 to 60	Strong	High
Basmati, White	Common	15 to 20	Medium	Low
Texmati	Not Common	15 to 20	Strong	Medium
Calmati	Not Common	15 to 20	Strong	Medium
Wehani	Not Common	40 to 60	Strong	High
Jasmine	Not Common	15 to 20	Medium	Low
Wild	Very Common	45 to 60	Very Strong	High

Cooking Rice in an Electric Rice Cooker: Machines can do wonders in the kitchen. It's like having a mini-cook preparing your food while you are doing something else. This method of cooking rice is very easy. Just put raw rice and the proper amount of water (follow instructions for your cooker) in the cooker and punch the switch. When the rice is done, the cooker will automatically shut down its cooking mode and go into its warming mode to keep your rice warm until you are ready for it. However, if you leave it too long, such as for several hours, the rice's texture will start to suffer from the continuous reheating. It will dry out and break down. See "Grains" for additional information about using an electric rice cooker to prepare grains.

Risotto: This is a special way of cooking rice. It involves coating the rice with oil and cooking the rice in small amounts of liquid while stirring constantly until it is all absorbed and then adding more liquid and repeating the process as many times as necessary to fully cook the rice. This is a very time-consuming method of cooking rice, but it does give exquisite results. Arborio rice produces the best risotto. It absorbs a lot of liquid without becoming too soft or gooey.

Sauté onion in butter or olive oil until tender or translucent. Add rice and sauté briefly while stirring to coat all the grains. Add a ladle-full or a small amount (1/2 cup) of hot stock to the rice. Cook over a medium heat and stir constantly until the stock is absorbed by the rice. Adjust the heat if the stock is absorbed too slowly or too quickly by increasing or decreasing the heat. Continue to add the stock in small amounts and stir until it is absorbed. When the risotto is almost done, the rice will be firm in the center but creamy. Add any vegetables, meat, and additional seasonings and enough stock to finish cooking the rice. Once the rice is done, stir in grated cheese (such as parmesan) and serve at once. If it is allow to sit too long, it will get gummy.

Pilaf: Pilafs are usually made with long grain rices. Any color or type can be used to produce different flavors and effects. To make a pilaf, sauté onion until it is tender and then add the rice and stir to coat the grains with the oil or butter. Vegetables, fruits, and spices can be added and coated along with the rice. Add boiling liquid to the rice. Two cups liquid to one cup of rice should do just fine. Cover and cook on a low heat for 20 to 30 minutes or until the liquid has been completely absorbed and the rice is not crunchy.

HEALTH INFORMATION

Rice is an easily digestible, low-calorie, low-sodium, high-starch complex carbohydrate that is cholesterol and gluten free. It contains the B-complex vitamins, all of the essential amino acids, calcium, iron, phosphorus, zinc, selenium, copper, and iodine.

Rice has the highest water content of all the grains. This helps it act as a diuretic—aiding the flow of liquids through the tissues, which promotes proper circulation and regulation of blood pressure as well as helping the kidneys.

ADDITIONAL READING

Sams, Craig. *The Macrobiotic Brown Rice Cookbook.*

Scott, Maria Luisa, and Jack Denton. *Rice.*

Solomon, Jay. *Vegetarian Rice Cuisine: From Pancakes to Paella.*

See "Grains" for grain book references that contain information and recipes involving rice.

BUYING SOURCES

Rice is typically available in small packages (bags or boxes), large bags (containing 10 pounds or more), and in bulk bins. Don't buy rice from bulk containers, however, if you are allergic or sensitive to other grains. The rice can become contaminated through scoops that are shared among different grain bins.

Long grain white and brown rices are available in almost every type of food store (including supermarkets). Along with the white and brown rices, you will also find rice mixes, wild rice, and, sometimes aromatic (Texmati, Calmati, and/or basmati) rices. Other rices and rice products can be found in specialty food stores, Oriental stores, health and natural food stores, and through the mail. See "Grains" for a list of mail order sources.

BRAND NAMES

Lundberg, Southern Brown, Ohsawa, and Arrowhead Mills are all producers of high quality rices.

RICE SYRUP

Mother Nature has provided health-giving rice and humankind has cleverly devised a way to convert it into a nutritious, rich, delicate sweetener. When using this sweetener in candies, pastries, and cookies, you can actually have the rarest of treats— "sweet-health." Rice syrup is a mildly flavored, delicious, and satisfying sweetener. It looks a bit like dark honey and can be used in much the same way. For a comparison of sweeteners, see the section "Sweeteners" in this book.

VARIETIES

Rice syrup can be made from different rices. When white rice is used, the syrup has a lighter color and flavor. Brown rice makes a syrup that has a full-bodied flavor and contains the B vitamins and minerals that are found in the outer layers of rice grains. For a slightly butterscotch flavored syrup, organic brown rice may be used. In addition to the thick, sticky liquid, rice syrup is also available in powdered form.

OTHER NAMES

Brown rice syrup, rice malt.

FLAVOR/TEXTURE

Rice syrup is sweet but so mild that it does not overpower other flavors. Even though rice syrup is mild, different brands can taste remarkably different.

The texture of this sweetener is similar to honey—very thick and sticky.

GENERAL USES

Use rice syrup in sweet and sour sauces, baked beans, salad dressings, cornbread, and of course all kinds of desserts. It is useful to sweeten fillings, toppings, creams, glazes, purées, cakes, pies, cupcakes, scones, breads, pastries, Danishes, tarts, cinnamon rolls, cookies, doughnuts, turnovers, croissants, custards, meringues, soufflés, strudels, éclairs, baklava, etc.

A fabulous creamy dressing can be whipped up by combining silken tofu with brown rice syrup, lemon juice, mustard, poppy seeds, and a little black pepper. Or try mixing any flavor of miso with soy sauce, rice syrup, ground garlic, and a little fresh grated ginger for a tangy, sweet dressing.

A number of marvelous creamy toppings can be made by blending silken tofu, rice syrup, and vanilla extract along with any combination of the following: crushed pineapple, instant coffee, coconut, walnuts, pecans, almonds, pitted dates, lemon, banana, raisins, mint, and rum extract.

A tasty pie or cheesecake crust can be prepared by roasting some whole-wheat pastry and corn flours and mixing them with almond oil, rice syrup, and apple juice to make the crust dough. Press or roll out and place the dough into a well-oiled pie pan and bake for a few minutes in a moderate oven.

Rice syrup can be used in all the same ways as maple syrup, honey, and barley malt syrup and may be freely substituted for them. See the "Sweeteners" section for proportions.

FRESHNESS AND QUALITY

There are two methods of producing rice syrup. Naturally cultured rice syrups are preferred over the syrups produced more quickly and economically with the aid of added enzymes. These "quick" syrups have a chalky color and a flavor that does not come through as clearly. Furthermore, the enzymes still in the syrup dissolve any thickening and rising ingredients that are added to the syrup, rendering them ineffective. On the other hand, "traditional" or naturally cultured rice syrups have a light to dark amber-brown color and clearly defined sweet flavor. They work consistently in dishes calling for arrowroot, kuzu or agar as the thickening agent, or baking powder as the rising agent.

STORAGE

Rice syrup has a long shelf life and requires no refrigeration. Unlike honey, it does not crystallize, although it may harden. See the "Sweeteners" section for instructions on what to do if this happens. Should moisture create condensation in the jar, the syrup may host surface molds. If this occurs, the syrup is not ruined; simply remove the mold and refrigerate the remaining syrup.

PREPARATION INSTRUCTIONS

COOKING

This sweetener is much easier to work with if it is heated prior to use. For additional preparation instructions, see "Sweeteners."

HOMEMADE RICE SYRUP

The principles behind making your own rice syrup are straightforward. The idea is to mix cooked rice with enzymes obtained from sprouted barley and then incubate this mixture until the enzymes break the rice starches down into simple sugars. Then the syrup is filtered and cooked down until it reaches the desired syrup-like consistency.

Although it takes a bit of time, making rice syrup is relatively easy. Cook 2 cups brown rice, without salt, in 6 cups water. Allow it to cool to 140°F and add freshly made barley sprouts (see "Sprouts") which have been crushed or blended. Cover and keep the rice-sprout mixture at 130°F to 140°F for 5 to 10 hours. To do this, you can place it on a warm stove, near a radiator, in a pan of hot water, or use a dehydrator. After 4 or 5 hours and then each half hour or hour thereafter, taste the mixture. When it tastes sweet, pour the mixture into a cheesecloth and squeeze the syrup through. Save the sweet rice pulp because it is excellent in baked goods, rice pud-

dings, and other desserts. After adding a pinch of sea salt, boil the syrup until it reaches the thickness you desire.

HEALTH INFORMATION

This sweetener is predominantly slow-digesting carbohydrates that enter the bloodstream steadily over a two-hour period—keeping insulin at consistent, reasonable levels. It is hypoallergenic and has little free glucose and no fructose or sucrose. All rice syrups consist of about 50% complex carbohydrates, but their glucose-to-maltose ratios differ. The ones with more glucose are sweeter and those with a higher maltose content are milder flavored and would be more appropriate for diabetics. For information about the types of sugars, see the glossary.

ADDITIONAL READING

See "Sweeteners."

BUYING SOURCES

See "Sweeteners."

BRAND NAMES

The following brands are of excellent quality: Sweet Cloud *Organic Brown Rice Syrup*, Lundberg *Sweet Dreams Organic Rice Syrup*, Devan *Sweet Brown Rice Sweetener* (powdered brown rice syrup), Ohsawa® *Organic Brown Rice Syrup Powder*.

SALT

To salt or not to salt? How much salt? What kind of salt? When to salt? These are some of the questions that surround this vital substance. These questions are not answered easily. Scientific research, folklore, health food proponents, nutritionists, and chemists have not provided consistent answers. However, the common thread is that salt is essential to life.

VARIETIES

Salt is refined to different levels:
Refined Salt: Salt may be refined to incredibly high levels to achieve 99.99%

sodium chloride (NaCl). This salt does not dissolve easily and is difficult to digest. Common table salt is highly refined. It often contains many additives.

Unrefined Salt: Salt may be minimally refined and contain as little as 93.98% sodium chloride. It contains dozens of the trace minerals destroyed during the processing of refined salt. However, the quantities of these minerals is so small that their existence may be considered unimportant. Often this salt is free of additives and preservatives.

There are two sources of salt:

Sea Salt: Only 14% of our domestic salt supply comes directly from the sea. Sea water is trapped in tidal pools and the water is evaporated until only the salt remains. Unrefined sea salt is also called "natural" sea salt.

Land Salt: Salt found in rock deposits is, technically, also sea salt. It was deposited by the great oceans that covered the earth millions of years ago.

Salt can be obtained in different crystal sizes or grades:

Fine: These very small crystals dissolve very quickly. This grade is useful in dishes where the salt is used to enhance the flavor of the dish without adding a salty taste (such as in beans, breads, grains, etc.). It is the best salt to use to add to water for raising the boiling point.

Coarse: These larger, jagged crystals stick or cling to food better than fine-grade salt. The larger crystals also trigger the taste buds more effectively than the small ones. Coarse salt can be tasted far easier than fine salt when sprinkled on vegetables (corn on the cob, carrots, broccoli, etc.), meats, grains, beans, etc.

Kosher: This is a coarse grade of salt that is very effective in removing the most blood possible from meats before they are cooked. It can be used in any way that is appropriate for a coarse-grade salt.

Rock: This salt consists of very large crystals and is not suitable for anybody's table other than a giant's. Instead, it is used for melting snow and ice on roads and walkways and to make homemade ice cream. This is because salty water has a lower freezing point than plain water.

Ingredients that contain high concentrations of salt can be substituted for salt. However they also add other flavors that can complement or conflict with the flavors of the other ingredients in your dish. Foods such as cheese, bouillon cubes, ketchup, meat tenderizers, mustard, olives, pickles, potato chips, salad dressings, pork, smoked meats, game, and salted fish typically contain quite a bit of salt. Less common ingredients that contain a great deal of salt are:

Umeboshi: Umeboshi are pickled plums that have a unique sour, tart, tangy, sweet, and very, very salty flavor. Along with their vinegar, they add a zippy twang to the dishes they're cooked with as well as a delightful pink color. Use them to flavor grain, noodle, bean, vegetable, and sea vegetable dishes as well as salad dressings, sauces, spreads, soups, and beverages. See "Ume & Umeboshi" for more information about these plums.

Tamari or Shoyu Soy Sauce: Soy sauce can be used in place of salt in soups, sauces, salad dressings, casseroles, and other dishes without overpowering the flavor of other ingredients in the dish. See "Soy Sauce" for more information about this rich liquid.

Miso: The flavors of this extremely salty, thick, creamy fermented soybean paste ranges from delicately sweet to robustly savory. Miso is often used in cooking soups, sauces, gravies, and casseroles and in making dressings, marinades, and dips. See the "Miso" section for more information about this very versatile paste.

Spice Mixes: There is a variety of spice mixes that contain salt: celery salt, spiced salt, sesame salt, garlic salt, hickory salt, smoked salt, and tenderizing salt.

SALT MEASUREMENT EQUIVALENCIES
1/2 teaspoon salt
- = 2 teaspoons umeboshi paste
- = 2 teaspoons shoyu soy sauce
- = 1 tablespoon tamari soy sauce
- = 1 tablespoon salty miso
- = 1 1/2 tablespoons mellow miso
- = 2 1/2 tablespoons sweet miso

Substitutions for salt that do not contain sodium chloride are dulse, herbs, spices, lemon juice, and vinegar. These foods are useful for bringing mild or bland dishes to life.

FLAVOR/TEXTURE

Less refined salt has a sweeter, mellower, salty taste. More refined salt has a sharper, harsher, salty taste.

GENERAL USES

Almost magically, salt can bring out the delicate flavors of other ingredients (such as grains, beans, and mushrooms), sometimes actually making them sweeter.

Salt may be used to preserve pork, beef, and fish (and is often combined with smoking and drying). Examples are anchovies, herring, salmon, eel, cod, ham, bacon, corned beef, beef in brine, and salted tongue. Vegetables, nuts, and legumes are frequently salted to help maintain freshness. Examples are peanuts, cashews, almonds, walnuts, hazelnuts, and potato chips. And brine (heavily salted water) is used to pickle a great many foods such as boiled peanuts, cucumbers, and olives. Cabbage, salt, and a pressing crock can be used to make a refreshing sauerkraut (pickled cabbage).

Although salt is usually called upon to raise the boiling point of water, many other ingredients may also serve this purpose (such as sugar). The more salt that is added to the water, the higher the temperature must be to boil the water. Raising the boiling point of water is particularly helpful for folks who live at higher elevations because the reduced atmospheric pressure makes water boil at a temperature lower than it does at sea level.

A higher boiling temperature is useful, for example, for cooking pasta, noodles, and hard-boiled eggs in less time. In dishes that require exact cooking temperatures and times (such as some sauces, custards, and candies), it is important to use the correct amount of salt to obtain the precise boiling point needed.

FRESHNESS/QUALITY

Low quality salt contains additives such as calcium bicarbonate, magnesium carbonate, or sodium silicoaluminate (to keep it dry and pourable), iodine (to prevent goiters), dextrose (to stabilize the iodine), sodium bicarbonate (to prevent the iodine from turning purple) and other additives (to keep the salt looking white). High quality salt is lumpy and additive-free.

To get your requirement of iodine in a natural way, eat sea and land vegetables that extract this vital mineral from the sea water and earth. For example, iodine is naturally supplied by the following, in order of highest iodine content: kelp, agar, Swiss chard, turnip greens, summer squash, mustard greens, watermelon, cucumber, and spinach.

STORAGE

Keep salt crystals dry. Foods prepared with salt do not last as long in the freezer. The salt lowers the freezing point of the dish and it does not freeze fully, allowing enzymes to continue the process of breaking the food down.

PREPARATION INSTRUCTIONS

When adding salt to dishes, do so in small amounts to prevent adding too much. Taste the food between each addition of salt to judge whether more is needed. Dishes requiring salt will taste bland. When the proper amount of salt has been added, the dish will taste flavorful and rich (whether sweet or savory). If too much salt is added, the dish will have a salty flavor. A rule of thumb is that foods should not taste salty (unless, of course, you are having a salt-craving attack).

If adding salt to a dish to enhance its flavor, the salt should be added near the end of the cooking time. This will maximize the effectiveness of the salt. In some cases, cooking foods with salt can cause unexpected problems. For example, adding salt at the beginning of cooking beans will harden their skins, dramatically prolonging the cooking time and making the beans tougher.

Of course, if salt is being used to increase the boiling point of water when cooking pasta, grains, etc., be sure to add the salt at the beginning.

NIGRO TIP

Because temperature affects how salty a dish tastes, be sure to add salt when the dish is at the same temperature that it will be eaten. Generally, when cooled, dishes will taste saltier than when they are hot.

HEALTH INFORMATION

Salt (pure sodium chloride) has a similar effect on the body as white sugar. It drains minerals from the body in an attempt to be metabolized.

Unrefined, sun-dried, sea salt contains many minerals that are not found in refined salt: gold, iron, copper, calcium, and magnesium. However, these exist in such small quantities that their healthful benefits may be negligible.

Salt stimulates the appetite and is essential for healthy cell metabolism. The daily requirement ranges from 0.05 to 0.25 ounces. Too much salt causes the body to retain water (and increase weight) and may cause or worsen existing health problems.

If you are attempting to reduce your salt intake, your food will taste rather bland at first. Your taste buds take a little time to acclimate, but they will, and, given a little time, your food will surpass the old flavor you remember.

BUYING SOURCES

Most of the sea salt sold in health and natural foods stores and specialty shops is highly refined. There are several small companies who manufacture quality unrefined sea salt.

Unrefined sea salt is available through the Gold Mine Natural Foods, King Arthur Flour Baker's Catalogue, Harvest Time Natural Foods, and Jaffe Bros. mail order companies.

BRAND NAMES

A few unrefined sea salt brands are: Lima Sea Salt, Si Salt, Celtic Sea Salt (*Coarse Light Grey Salt, Fine Light Grey Salt,* and *"Flower of the Ocean" Salt*), Promesa Sea Salt, and Muramoto Balanced Minerals Sea Salt.

SEA VEGETABLES (DRIED)

Sea vegetables, sometimes irreverently referred to as seaweeds, are a remarkable source of nourishment; they are packed with vitamins, amino acids, and trace minerals. The key item here is the trace minerals, since you can get lots of vitamins and amino acids from many other vegetables and grains.

The nice thing about sea vegetables is that they are virtually calorie and fat-free. You can eat as much as you want and not feel a bit guilty.

VARIETIES

The specific types of sea vegetables that are covered in this book are: nori, kombu, hijiki, wakame, arame, dulse, kelp, and agar. See individual sea vegetable listings for specific information.

Similar sea vegetables from different parts of the world tend to have different qualities. Some may be firmer in texture and stronger or sweeter in flavor. A particular type of sea vegetable harvested from one part of the world versus another is not necessarily better; it is just different.

The flavors, textures, and colors of the different types of sea vegetables are quite distinct from one another. For example, some varieties have a spicy mineral taste while others are subtly sweet. Luckily, you can often substitute one type of sea vegetable for another in most recipes.

See the "Sea Vegetable Comparison Chart" for the appearance, cooking, flavor, primary uses, and substitution information for each sea vegetable.

OTHER NAMES

Seaweed, algae.

FLAVOR/TEXTURE

When you open a package of a sea vegetable, it may smell "fishy." What you are actually smelling is the odor of the sea. Some people like this smell; some do not. In any event, cooked sea vegetables do not taste "fishy."

The enjoyment of the flavor of sea-weeds, oops, sea vegetables, can be some-thing of an acquired taste. You know, sort of like olives, avocados, beer, artichokes, okra, etc. But, once you acquired an appreciation for the taste of these wonder-ful foods, you probably wondered how you ever survived without them. Sea veg-etables won't disappoint you, either.

The best way to become accustomed to the new flavor of sea vegetables, is to start slowly—eat them in little itty-bitty amounts. First sprinkle a little ground up sea vegetable on everything you eat. We're not kidding; try it in breads, soups, cere-als, grains, beans, sautés, salads, burritos,

sauces, salad dressings, land vegetables, pastas, cookies, and even on garlic bread. This will start the process. You'll begin to see that cooking with sea vegetables will not "contaminate" anything, and actually, you'll begin to notice that everything tastes just a little bit better. Of course, this should arouse your curiosity and you will become bolder, and you will start to add more of the sea vegetable to the point where you can actually see it in the dish and perhaps even taste it. You'll know that you're on the road to being a sea veg-etable consumer when you actually look forward to eating the chunks of sea veg-etables in your meals. And lastly, you'll seek out and enjoy recipes that have sea vegetables as the main ingredient.

When soaked and cooked, the "leafy" sea vegetables (kombu, wakame, kelp, and dulse) may have a texture that is different from any you are used to. They may feel "slippery" or "very smooth." This is a

Sea Vegetable Comparison Chart

©1996 Nigro

Sea Vegetable	Appearance (when dried)	Soaking Time	Flavor of "the Sea"	Primary Uses	Can be Cooked with Oil?[†]	Substitutes*
Arame	Black 1–3" long, thin curling strands	Mild: 3–5 min. Strong: Not Soaked	Mild	Sauté with vegetables, tofu, or nuts to make a salad or side dish.	Yes	Hijiki
Agar (Kanten)	White flakes, powder, or bars	Not Soaked	None	Thickener for gravies and sauces. Jells desserts.	N.A.	No sea vegetable. Kuzu
Dulse	Thin purple pieces folded upon themselves	Not required but to reduce saltiness: 2-3 min	Mild	Condiment. Combined with oats and other grains. Snack. Fried for bacon alternative.	Yes	Kelp
Hijiki	Black, thickish, curling strands	Mild: 20 min. Strong: 0-10 min	Strong	Sauté with root vegetables, onions, squash and/or nuts to make a salad or side dish.	Yes	Arame
Kelp	Looks like a crinkled piece of dark green paper pressed flat	3–5 min.	Mild	Addition to salads and root vegetables. Condiment.	Yes	Wakame & Kombu
Kombu	2" wide strips, 3 to 18" long	7–10 min.	Medium	Softener in bean preparation. Stock generator for soups and stews.	No	Wakame & Kelp
Nori	Thin, parchment-like sheets	Not soaked	Medium	Sushi or Nori roll. "Wrapper." Hors d'oeuvres.	N.A.	None
Wakame	Dark olive green to brownish strips	5-30 min.	Mild	Miso soup. Addition to salads & vegetable dishes. Revitalize frozen veggies.	No	Kombu & Kelp

* The chart lists substitutes for each sea vegetable's primary uses. Note, all sea vegetables, with the exception of agar, may be used as a condiment and may be freely substituted for one another.
† Some sea vegetables have a high oil content; therefore, they are best when prepared in a manner that does not use additional oil.

unique characteristic of some vegetables from the ocean. Let yourself experience the delightful sensations of something new and in no time you'll start to look forward to eating vegetables with this new texture.

Whether you love the flavor or hate it, you'll still want to put some sea vegetables in your food. Their health benefits are just too great. A little added to almost every dish does not add any flavor while boosting its nutritional content.

GENERAL USES

The actual volume of dried sea vegetable used per recipe is usually quite small because it expands from 2 to 5 times when cooked or soaked, depending on the variety used. So paying an amount that may seem expensive for a few ounces is actually a reasonable thing. For example, one ounce of dried arame will expand to two cups when cooked and most recipes will call for less than 1/8 cup. In the worst case, recipes that are cooking the sea vegetable as a stand-alone dish rarely call for more than a cup.

A few of the sea vegetables (wakame, kombu, and kelp) enhance the natural sweetness of the ingredients they are cooked with. They contain glutamic acid, a natural flavor-enhancer and tenderizer. Glutamic acid is the original natural version of the powerful flavoring agent monosodium glutamate (MSG), which nowadays is chemically synthesized from molasses. The sea vegetable flavor-enhancer, rather than being a chemical additive that could harm you, is a natural, unprocessed plant with a huge amount of nutritional value.

A sea vegetable can be used in eight general ways: as a condiment, as a stock generator, as a vegetable addition, as a stand-alone vegetable, as a wrapper, as a softening or tenderizing agent, as a salt substitute, and as a thickening agent. See the "General Uses for Sea Vegetables" chart on the following page.

Condiment: Sea vegetables can be roasted and ground to make nutritious condiments that can be sprinkled on almost everything.

Stock Generator: Sea vegetables help make superb soup and stew stocks as well as vegetable broth to be used as an alternate in any recipe calling for chicken or beef broth.

Vegetable in Other Dishes: Combined with other natural ingredients, sea vegetables can add new and exciting aspects to your meals. They can be used in salads and other vegetable dishes as well as grain, bean, nut, seafood, poultry, and red-meat dishes.

The colors of these foods from the ocean range from black to deep brown, olive, bright green, purple, and red. They are attractive and contribute to the aesthetic enjoyment of a meal. For example, hijiki's black curly strands are especially beautiful nestled in an array of colorful vegetables, beans, or grains.

Beans and root vegetables, such as burdock, carrots, onions, potatoes, and daikon, go especially well with sea vegetables. Nuts and seeds mix well with them and are especially good toasted together.

Stand-Alone Vegetable: Most sea vegetables can be fried, broiled, sautéed, boiled, steamed, or toasted to create a delicious vegetable side dish.

Wrapper: Toasted sheet nori or soaked kombu, wakame, or kelp can be used in the same way you would use a tortilla (or cabbage or grape leaf) to wrap around beans, rice, tofu, fish, meats, and/or vegetables.

Softening or Tenderizing Agent: The sea vegetables that contain glutamic acid assist in the digestibility of beans, vegetables, and grains while bringing out their natural flavors.

Salt Substitute: The high concentration of minerals and trace elements makes some sea vegetables (such as dulse and kelp) ideally suited to act as a salt substitute. The minerals trick the taste buds into thinking they are eating a salty substance even when the sea vegetable is low in sodium. If sodium is needed in a recipe for a purpose other than providing a salt flavor, then the sea vegetables will not be adequate. Unrefined sea salt, miso, umeboshi plum vinegar, or soy sauce may be used instead. See "Salt."

General Uses for Sea Vegetables

GENERAL USE	SEA VEGETABLE
Stock Generator Sea vegetables can be used to make hearty or delicate stocks for noodles, soups, stews, or sauces. These flavorful stocks may be used as a vegetable broth and are a healthy alternative to chicken and beef broths. Typically, the sea vegetable is boiled for 15 to 30 minutes and removed and saved for another recipe.	Wakame Kelp Kombu
Condiment Using sea vegetables as condiments is a great way to integrate this remarkable, nutrient-rich food into your diet. Use a little in almost everything you prepare and enjoy the added nutrition along with the new flavor. Commonly, the dried sea vegetable is roasted in the oven for a few minutes and ground into a coarse or fine powder.	Dulse Arame Kelp Wakame Hijiki Nori Kombu
Wrapper Sea vegetables can be used like the tortilla in Mexican cuisine. They can be wrapped around almost anything quickly and easily. They can be filled with rice, beans, tofu, vegetables, fish, and meats — any combination of ingredients that sound good together.	Nori Wakame Kelp Kombu
Vegetable in Other Dishes Sea vegetables make a fabulous addition to many rice, vegetable, bean, grain, and meat dishes such as soups, casseroles, stews, salads, pilafs, mixed vegetables, sandwiches, stir fries, burgers, loaves, etc.	Wakame Arame Hijiki Kelp Dulse Kombu
Stand-Alone Vegetable Sea vegetables can make incredibly scrumptious stand-alone side dishes—in some cases by just seasoning with a little soy sauce or brown rice vinegar and crushed nuts.	Arame Hijiki Wakame
Softening or Tenderizing Agent Sea vegetables may be used as a powerful flavor-enhancer and tenderizer (a natural alternative to chemically processed MSG). They bring out the natural sweetness and flavors of the ingredients they are cooked with. In addition, they have the property of softening the tough fibers of difficult-to-digest foods. Sea vegetables are used as an anti-flatulence ingredient that tenderizes, improves the taste, and increases the digestibility of beans.	Kombu Kelp Wakame
Salt Substitute Granulated sea vegetables may be used as alternatives to table salt. The high concentration of certain minerals in some sea vegetables tricks the taste-buds and produces a salty taste or flavor. However, these granules do not have a high sodium content.	Dulse Kelp
Thickening Agent Sea vegetables can be used as thickening agents to make a large range of dishes, from soups and stews to gelatin dessert molds and jellies.	Agar (Kanten) Kelp

Thickening Agent: Sea vegetables can be used like flour or cornstarch to thicken dishes just a little bit. Plus, they can create a firm gelatin that has the special property of retaining its shape without refrigeration.

FRESHNESS/QUALITY

Quality sea vegetables are carefully harvested by traditional methods from cool, relatively pure waters and then sundried. They should be free from heavy metals, herbicides, pesticides, fuel oils, yeasts, molds, coliforms, and *e coli.*

STORAGE

To maintain optimum flavor after opening a package, transfer unused portions of the sea vegetable to an airtight jar or bag, and keep it in a cool, dark, dry place. Should any sea vegetable become damp, simply re-dry it briefly in a low-temperature oven.

Dried sea vegetables will keep indefinitely. Roasted sea vegetables that have been ground into powder for condiments should be tightly sealed to retain freshness.

During storage, white salt and sugar crystals may form on the surface of some sea vegetables. These sea vegetables have not gone bad. In some cases you can reduce the salt content by simply wiping the salt crystals off before using them.

After cooking sea vegetables, avoid storing them in plastic containers or bags since this may adversely affect the taste. Instead, store sea vegetable dishes in a glass or ceramic container where they can be kept for a week in the refrigerator or a few months in the freezer.

PREPARATION INSTRUCTIONS

Since each variety of sea vegetable may be prepared differently, be sure to consult each individual sea vegetable section for details. This section only provides general information.

WASHING & SOAKING

Since washing and soaking methods are dependent on the type of sea vegetable used, see "Washing & Soaking" in the individual sections of this book.

In most cases, sea vegetables have been pre-cleaned to remove sand, tiny shell particles, and excess salt and do not need to be washed. Also, washing may reduce the nutritional value and flavor of some varieties.

Some sea vegetables are soaked to make them more tender, make them cook faster, or to modify their flavor. If a sea vegetable is soaked, place it in enough warm water to allow it to rehydrate fully. They can expand from two to five times their original dried size, depending on the type. The soaking time also varies based on the type of sea vegetable. If you wish to reduce the intensity of the flavor, soak the sea vegetable a little longer.

Save the soaking water to use in the recipe you are cooking. Avoid agitating this soaking water and stirring up any fine sand particles that may have settled to the bottom of the water. When using the soaking water, carefully pour it into the cooking dish and leave the last bit in the soaking bowl.

For those sea vegetables that you don't have to soak, save the water from the last rinsing (if you rinse it) to use in your recipe.

Sea vegetables can be cut before or after soaking. Scissors are the favored tool to use to cut them when they are dried, and a sharp knife on a wooden cutting board is the preferred method after they have been soaked.

Once a sea vegetable has been soaked, you'll want to cook it in the very near future (or freeze it) since it will only retain its freshness for a few hours.

COOKING

Wakame, arame, and other thinner sea vegetables need only moderate cooking, while kombu, hijiki, and thicker ones require longer cooking to become tender.

Cooking with sea salt makes for too sharp a taste and too salty a flavor when added to sea vegetables. Instead, use a little tamari soy sauce at the beginning of cooking, or shoyu soy sauce at the end of cooking, to bring out the natural sweetness of your sea vegetable.

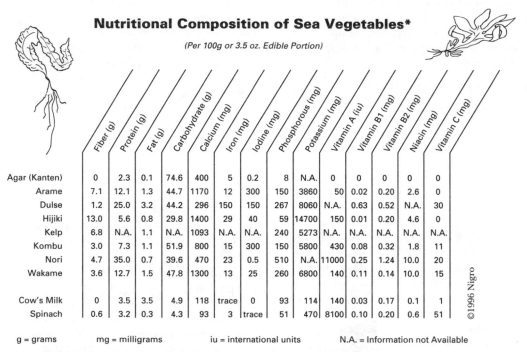

Nutritional Composition of Sea Vegetables*

(Per 100g or 3.5 oz. Edible Portion)

	Fiber (g)	Protein (g)	Fat (g)	Carbohydrate (g)	Calcium (mg)	Iron (mg)	Iodine (mg)	Phosphorous (mg)	Potassium (mg)	Vitamin A (iu)	Vitamin B1 (mg)	Vitamin B2 (mg)	Niacin (mg)	Vitamin C (mg)
Agar (Kanten)	0	2.3	0.1	74.6	400	5	0.2	8	N.A.	0	0	0	0	0
Arame	7.1	12.1	1.3	44.7	1170	12	300	150	3860	50	0.02	0.20	2.6	0
Dulse	1.2	25.0	3.2	44.2	296	150	150	267	8060	N.A.	0.63	0.52	N.A.	30
Hijiki	13.0	5.6	0.8	29.8	1400	29	40	59	14700	150	0.01	0.20	4.6	0
Kelp	6.8	N.A.	1.1	N.A.	1093	N.A.	N.A.	240	5273	N.A.	N.A.	N.A.	N.A.	N.A.
Kombu	3.0	7.3	1.1	51.9	800	15	300	150	5800	430	0.08	0.32	1.8	11
Nori	4.7	35.0	0.7	39.6	470	23	0.5	510	N.A.	11000	0.25	1.24	10.0	20
Wakame	3.6	12.7	1.5	47.8	1300	13	25	260	6800	140	0.11	0.14	10.0	15
Cow's Milk	0	3.5	3.5	4.9	118	trace	0	93	114	140	0.03	0.17	0.1	1
Spinach	0.6	3.2	0.3	4.3	93	3	trace	51	470	8100	0.10	0.20	0.6	51

©1996 Nigro

g = grams   mg = milligrams   iu = international units   N.A. = Information not Available

*Values can vary depending on brand, quality, time of year harvested, post processing methods, etc.

Sources: U.S.D.A. and Japan Nutritionist Association food tables, provided by Great Eastern Sun and Emerald Cove Sea Vegetables.

Occasionally, you can soften a tough variety with a little rice vinegar or mirin.

HEALTH INFORMATION

Sea vegetables offer a way of eating a balanced diet without resorting to dietary supplements.

Sea vegetables can contain some thirteen vitamins, twenty amino acids and sixty trace elements. They are particularly rich in iodine, iron, calcium, magnesium, phosphorous, and sodium. They may also contain the following vitamins: A, B_1, B_2, B_{12}, C, D, and E.

And, like other plants, sea vegetables contain carbohydrates, in the form of starches and sugars, and some protein.

Sea vegetables are known to help in the dissolving of fat and cholesterol deposits that were created by the previous intake of foods high in animal fat. This, of course, promotes weight loss, prevents hardening of the arteries, helps bring down high blood pressure, and assists in the regression of some tumors.

The brown algae family of sea vegetables (kombu, kelp, wakame, arame, and hijiki) contains alginic acid. This acid chemically interacts with toxic heavy metals and radioactive substances that are in the body to convert them to harmless salts that can be discharged.

In short, sea vegetables are a wondrous food.

ADDITIONAL READING

Bradford, Peter, and Montse Bradford. *Cooking with Sea Vegetables*.

Ford, Richard. *Juel Andersen's Sea Green Primer*.

Lewallen, Eleanor, and John Lewallen. *Sea Vegetable Gourmet Cookbook and Wildcrafter's Guide*.

Madlener, J.C. *The Sea Vegetable Book*.

Rhoads, Sharon Ann. *Cooking with Sea Vegetables*.

BUYING SOURCES

Sea vegetables are generally available in health food stores and Japanese markets. Mail order sources are Anzen Oriental Foods & Imports, Clear Eye Natural Foods, Gold Mine Natural Foods, Granum Incorporated, Harvest Time Natural Foods, Mountain Ark Trading Company, and Natural Lifestyle.

BRAND NAMES

Maine Coast Sea Vegetables offers Sea Shakers that are condiments (*Kelp Granules, Kelp with Cayenne, Dulse Granules, Dulse with Garlic, Nori Granules, Nori with Ginger, Dulse Flakes, Dulse Flakes with Celery, Dulse Flakes with Sesame*). See the individual sea vegetables sections for additional brand names.

SEITAN

(seh TAN)

Wheat flour is commonly used to make breads, dumplings, cookies, cakes, etc. and, surprisingly, also to make chicken, beef, veal, bologna, hamburger, and seafood substitutes. This intriguing wheat substitute for all these meats is called seitan.

Seitan is available in a broad range of textures and flavors suitable for many traditional and new recipes. This low fat, chewy, savory, hearty food is a superb source of protein that can be used as a versatile, succulent, wholesome, and strengthening ingredient.

Seitan is cooked and flavored gluten. Gluten is the protein in wheat flour. Wheat gluten is not eaten; instead, it is the raw material used to make seitan. Note that seitan has traditionally meant gluten simmered in soy sauce. However, in many books, its meaning has grown to include any cooked and flavored gluten. On the other hand, a few books decline to use the term "seitan" and, instead, insist on using "cooked gluten" or just plain "gluten."

VARIETIES

Seitan is available commercially in two forms: dry mixes and pre-made refrigerated meat substitutes.

Dry Seitan Mixes: These are essentially vital wheat gluten (see "Making Gluten from an Instant Mix" later in this section) with other flours and spices. The mix must be combined with water, shaped, and simmered in a flavored broth for 40 minutes to 2 hours, depending on the mix. Mixes that include spices to simulate meat balls, chicken, and sausage are available in health food stores.

Pre-Made Refrigerated Seitan: This seitan is ready to eat or use in a recipe. Traditionally flavored cubes of seitan, as well as those that are shaped and flavored to resemble luncheon meats, Sloppy Joes, and fajita strips are commercially available.

OTHER NAMES

Seitan: kofu, wheat meat, cooked gluten.
Gluten: uncooked seitan.

FLAVOR/TEXTURE

The flavors of seitan vary depending on the liquids and seasonings used to cook the wheat gluten. They can have flavors similar to meats or have unique sweet, savory, spicy, or subtle flavors.

The textures of seitan also vary depending on the cooking method, time, and temperature as well as the type of gluten used. They may be bread-like, spongy, dense or airy, crunchy, or firm and meat-like.

GENERAL USES

Seitan can be used as a meat extender or meat alternative. In addition, it can be used to make cold cereals, toppings for desserts, and candies or simply enjoyed as a food on its own.

A good way to start using seitan is to grind it and use it as a ground meat extender (3 parts seitan to 1 part meat) in hamburgers, meatballs, sausage, meat loaves, etc. Ground seitan can also be used to extend other ground meat alternatives, such as tempeh, grain, bean, and vegetable loaves, burgers, etc. See

"Preparation Instructions" for information on making ground seitan.

Because it is comparable to meat in taste and texture, seitan can be used in place of beef, poultry, hamburger, bologna, jerky, scallops, or sausage in your favorite recipes. You can make patties, cutlets, steaks, roasts, cubes, nuggets, and loaves, just to mention a few goodies. Seitan can be cubed, ground, sliced, and cut into strips and added to your traditional dishes. For example, seitan can be used instead of meat in casseroles, snacks, stews, spaghetti sauce, chili, salads, pizza, "meat" pies, sukiyaki, sandwiches, stuffings, fried rice, stir-fries, and shish kabobs—the possibilities are truly endless.

Dried seitan, that has been flaked or ground, can provide a satisfying crunch in cold cereals and granolas, or can make a snack by itself. It is also useful for making pie crusts and in candy recipes in place of puffed rice cereals or nutmeats. It is especially good with coconut, butter, honey, carob, and marshmallows. Seitan can be used to make crunchy toppings for pud-

dings, gelatin salads, ice cream, apple crisps, cookies, and cakes. Simply combine ground seitan with coconut, melted butter, and honey and bake on a cookie sheet in a 350°F oven for 25 to 40 minutes, stirring occasionally.

FRESHNESS/QUALITY

To maximize the freshness of pre-made refrigerated seitan, be sure to consume it before the date imprinted on the package. Seitan dry mixes will last as long as the flours that are added to them. This is typically 2 or 3 months on the shelf and up to a year if refrigerated. Quality seitan does not contain sweeteners, oils, or any artificial colors or preservatives.

STORAGE

Seitan that is not going to be used right away should be refrigerated (to last a week or two) or frozen (to last over a year) in airtight containers. Seitan has a tendency to become more spongy as it sits in the refrigerator. If shoyu or tamari soy sauce was used in seasoning the seitan, it

Sources of Seitan and its Uses

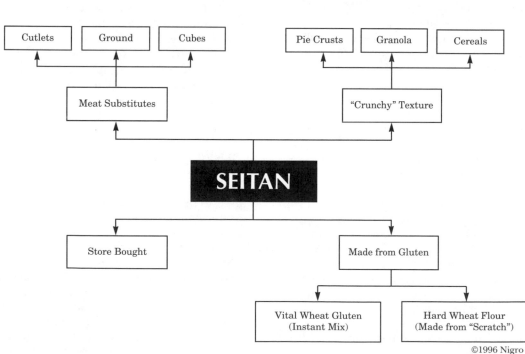

©1996 Nigro

will keep longer in the refrigerator. Seitan is convenient because it can be refrozen.

PREPARATION INSTRUCTIONS

Seitan can be purchased pre-made or you can make it from gluten that is prepared from "scratch" or from an instant mix (see the "Sources of Seitan and its General Uses" figure).

COOKING SEITAN

Seitan, just like meat, may be deep-fried, with or without batter, fried, sautéed, baked, broiled, stewed, boiled, simmered, steamed, and dried.

Brown seitan by broiling it on an oiled baking pan in a 350°F oven until browned, approximately 10 to 15 minutes. Smaller pieces should be stirred several times to ensure even browning. Larger pieces can also be browned by sautéing them in oil for a few minutes.

In dishes such as stews, soups, and sauces that are mainly liquid, add seitan near the end of cooking. Give it enough cooking time to heat completely through, but not so much time that its seasonings are leached out.

Leftover seitan, spongy or not, may be put through a meat grinder to make ground seitan. Do not put raw gluten through your meat grinder—it will not go through. If you don't have a meat grinder, dry the seitan first by baking it in a 350°F oven for an hour and then grind it in a blender  to make small chunks. Ground seitan is unlike meat; it will not hold its shape without a binding agent (try using soy flour, chickpea flour, or eggs).

Drying seitan in the oven will make it tougher and more chewy which is good for making a beef-like substitute. Simply place it on an oiled baking sheet and bake in a 300°F oven until the desired consistency is reached. This drying process, as well as frying, will transform and toughen spongy or bread-like seitan into a more meat-like texture.

MAKING HOMEMADE SEITAN

Making seitan is not difficult and is much more economical than buying it. However, it does takes a little practice to get consistent results. Making seitan is a two-stage process. First, gluten must be prepared, either homemade from scratch or from an instant mix (see the following "Making Gluten ..." subsections). Then the gluten is shaped, flavored, and cooked to make seitan loaves, cubes, steaks, etc. Gluten has no real flavor of its own but absorbs flavors of a broth if simmered in it for a lengthy time (45 minutes to 1 1/2 hours).

The wonderful thing about gluten is the variety of textures and shapes that it can be made into. Gluten can be formed into one large ball with a flat, long, oblong, or other shape to make roasts and loaves. The raw gluten may also be cut or torn into pieces. Cubes, slices, and steaks are generated when the gluten ball is cut into these shapes. Cutlets and medallions are formed when small pieces of gluten are torn from the ball and stretched or rolled into shape. If the gluten is difficult to form into the desired shapes, let it sit on the counter or in the refrigerator for a few minutes and try again.

Seitan seasoning stock can be as simple as plain water; as easy as using stock with wine, beer, soy sauce, garlic, or herbs; and as exotic as stock with wild mushrooms, sea vegetables, umeboshi plum vinegar, liqueurs, liquor, or miso. Try water, kombu, tamari soy sauce, grated fresh ginger root, and herb combinations (such as rosemary, sweet basil, and thyme, or bay leaf, garlic, and celery seed). See the "Seitan Seasoning Ingredients" table for those seasonings and ingredients that create a particular meat-like flavor in the seitan.

Depending on the method of cooking gluten—simmering, can cooking, baking, or pressure cooking—a different textured seitan is produced.

Simmering: Place the shaped gluten into a flavored broth and very gently simmer for 45 minutes to 3 hours on the stove-top with the pot lid slightly ajar. The length of cooking time depends on the size of your pieces of gluten (smaller pieces take less time) and the desired resulting seitan texture. If cooked too long or boiled too rapidly, the seitan will have a spongy texture. However, if cooked for too short a time, the gluten will not absorb enough of the juicy, delicious flavors from the stock. Use approximately 2 to 3 times liquid to amount of gluten. The gluten will expand slightly to make a seitan that is firm and springy to the touch. The leftover broth is terrific when thickened and used as a gravy over the seitan. If the seitan does not need a gravy, use the broth as a hearty "meat" broth base for soups and sauces.

Baking: Gluten can be baked to make a loaf, pot roast, or thin sheet that can be ground or cut into strips to make "jerky." A seitan loaf or roast can be created by placing the gluten in a loaf pan or deep casserole dish, covering with liquid and baking. A quick method involves covering the pan with aluminum foil and baking the gluten for 60 minutes in a 350°F oven, reducing the heat to 325°F and baking 30 minutes more. A slow method allows seasonings to fully penetrate the loaf and produces a texture that enables the loaf to be sliced very thinly. For this method, cover the gluten and bake in a 250°F oven for 10 hours.

For a different baking method, don't cover the gluten with liquid. To prevent burning and sticking, either oil the bottom and sides of the pan or place an inch

---

Seitan Seasoning Ingredients

"Meat"	Seasonings/Ingredients to Use*
Veal	nutritional yeast, oil, tamari soy sauce, lemon juice, cumin, coriander, garlic powder, and black pepper
Beef	nutritional yeast, sweet pepper flakes, parsley, salt, dill seed, celery seed, onion powder, thyme, black pepper, and rosemary
Meat Loaf	onion flakes, salt, powdered sweet pepper flakes, celery seed, black pepper, sage, garlic powder, dry mustard, and curry powder
Beef Steak	tamari soy sauce, oil, cumin, coriander, garlic powder, and black pepper
Beef Roast	tamari soy sauce, cumin, coriander, garlic powder, onion powder, and black pepper
Hamburger	dark miso, burdock root, nutritional yeast, oil, cumin, coriander, and garlic powder
Bologna	garlic powder, liquid smoke, barbecue sauce, mace, smoked salt, nutritional yeast, sweet pepper flakes, parsley, dill seed, celery seed, onion powder, thyme, black pepper, and rosemary
Sausage	soy flour, nutritional yeast, dark miso, oil, burdock root, sage, garlic powder, ground ginger, black pepper, rosemary, thyme, tarragon, basil, dry mustard, and cayenne pepper
Clams	sea vegetables, barley malt syrup, salt, oil, and lemon juice
Chicken	oil, nutritional yeast, salt, onion powder, celery seed, cumin, coriander, turmeric, sage, thyme, garlic powder, tarragon, marjoram, paprika, and rosemary

* The seasonings and ingredients are listed in order of volume used (the one with the largest measure is listed first).

©1996 Nigro

or two of liquid in the pan. Cook uncovered for 30 minutes in a 325°F oven. If the gluten puffs up, prick it with a fork or knife in three or four places. Remove the loaf or roast, turn it over, and return it to the oven and bake an additional hour.

Combined Baking & Simmering: Small gluten balls, medallions, cutlets, or other shaped pieces, can be placed on a lightly oiled baking dish and baked in a 350°F oven for 20 minutes. They are ready for simmering when they are puffy and brown. To simmer the shaped gluten, drop them into a seasoned broth and cook for 30 to 40 minutes.

Can Cooking: This method is used to keep the seitan in a cylindrical shape that is firm and easy to slice. It makes a marvelous breakfast sausage roll or stick of Italian pizza pepperoni.  The basic idea is to pack gluten into lightly oiled cans and then place them in the oven or in a water bath on the stove-top. The cans should be made of metal and be open at only one end. To water bathe them, place the closed flat end of the cans on the bottom of a large pot and fill the pot with water to an inch below the open end of the cans and boil the water for 40 minutes to 2 hours, depending on the size of the cans. To bake gluten in cans, just place them in the oven, closed flat side down, and bake in a 300°F oven for 2 to 4 hours, depending on the size of the can, until the top is browned and springs back when poked.

There are two ways to pack the gluten into their cans. The first involves making raw gluten from the instant mix (adding seasonings and flavorings) and then packing it into the cans, filling them almost to the top. The second way is to make unflavored wheat gluten from scratch or from the instant mix and then pack it into the cans, filling them a little over half way. Then a seasoning broth is poured into the can and the gluten is moved around so that the broth gets down and around it. Note that the cans can be as large as a commercial or restaurant gallon size or as small as a tiny 4 oz. juice can.

Pressure Cooking: This method is quicker than the others and makes a seitan with an excellent texture. Make 2 cups of raw gluten and place it in a pressure cooker along with 6 to 6 1/2 cups of seasoned broth and cook under 15 lbs. of pressure for 45 minutes.

MAKING GLUTEN FROM SCRATCH

Making gluten from scratch is not difficult and is much cheaper than buying the instant mix for it. The first time you make gluten from scratch, the procedure may seem a bit complicated and unusual. But once you've done it once or twice and understand the concepts, you will find it straightforward and a lot of fun. The basic procedure is to make a dough out of a high gluten wheat flour and water, soak it under water for an hour, and then knead and rinse it under water until all the milky, white starch has been washed out to produce an elastic, almost bubble gum-like textured mass of gluten that is insoluble in water.

The wheat flours used will make a large difference in the resulting gluten. See the "Flours and their Resulting Gluten" table. The important thing to remember when making gluten is to use a high-gluten wheat flour. Pastry flour will not give you satisfactory results. If unsure about what kind of flour to use, buy a good bread baking flour because it will have a high gluten content. See "Wheat" for more information about wheat types and flours.

We're now ready for the recipe for making homemade gluten. Place 7 cups of flour in a large mixing bowl. Stir 2 1/2 to 3 cups cold, not chilled, water into the flour to form a stiff dough. Knead the dough or pound it for 10 to 15 minutes to develop the gluten. When you are done, the dough should bounce back when you punch it. Press the dough into the shape of a ball. Pour one quart of cold water over the dough and allow it to stand for at least 30 minutes, but no longer than four hours. After soaking, knead the dough gently under water. The starch, bran, and germ of the flour will separate from the gluten causing the water to become milky. When the water becomes thick with starch, pour the solution through a colander or strainer into a two-gallon container. Repeat this kneading and rinsing process 4 to 5 times until the rinsing liquid is clear and the dough has shrunk into a small ball of elastic gluten. The colander is used because the gluten may separate into small pieces during the washing process. Just continue to wash and the gluten will soon come together. If it does not come back together, but instead dissolves, try using another kind or brand of wheat flour.

Be certain that all the bran and starch are removed or the gluten will have a doughy rather than chewy texture. Rinsing water temperature has a large impact on the resulting gluten—warm to hot water makes the gluten softer, and cold to lukewarm water makes it more rubbery, chewy, and meat-like. For an intermediate effect, alternate between warm and cold water when rinsing the gluten. The rinsing process will take 8 to 15 minutes and require 1 to 3 gallons of water. Save the first 2 or 3 rinses of starch water for future cooking needs. Subsequent rinses will have less starch and more water and will dilute your saved starch water.

Seven cups of wheat flour will produce approximately two cups of gluten. If you have obtained less than this, then it is likely that the flour is too coarsely ground or does not have a high enough gluten content.

Flours and Their Resulting Gluten

Code for Gluten Type	Flours	Resulting Gluten Consistency	Yield*
a	100% instant gluten flour (2 cups water to 2 cups flour)	Firm	100%
b	100% instant gluten flour (1 1/4 cups water to 2 cups flour)	Very stiff, firm and chewy	125%
c	100% instant gluten flour (3 cups water to 2 cups flour)	Soft	150%
d	50% whole wheat 50% unbleached white	All-purpose	30%
e	100% whole wheat flour	All-purpose	30%
f	100% unbleached white	Very stretchy	30%
g	40% whole wheat 40% unbleached white 20% instant gluten flour	All-purpose, firm	60%
h	80% whole wheat 20% instant gluten flour	All-purpose, firm	100%
i	80% unbleached white 20% instant gluten flour	Very soft and sticky	80%

* This is an approximation that indicates the amount of resulting gluten compared to the amount of flour used to make it. For example, if 2 cups of flour make 1 cup of gluten, the yield would be $1 \div 2 \times 100 = 50\%$. Note that the amount of water used also has an impact on the yield (for example, see the first three gluten types).

©1996 Nigro

Types of Gluten to Use to Make a Variety of Seitan Dishes

©1996 Nigro

Texture	Types of Gluten to Use*	Example Dishes
Loaf	a, d, e, g, h	Mock meat loaf (see "ground")
Roast	a, b, d, e, g, h	Mock rump or flank roast, "turkey"
Strips	a, b, d, e, g, h	Stir-fries, sweet & sour, fajitas, scampi, scallopine
Cubes	a, b, d, e, g, h	Sweet & sour, sukiyaki, chop suey, shish kabobs, stews, pot pies, nuggets, curries, chow mein, cajun, shepherd's pie, tempura
Diced	a, b, d, e, g, h	Hash, pasta & grain salads, chimichangas, casseroles, omelets, calzones, egg rolls, empanadas
Cutlets	a, b, d, e, f, g, h	Mock veal, beef, luncheon meats, chicken cacciatore, country fried steak
Bacon	b	
Scallops/Clam/Shrimp	a, c, d, e, f, g, h	Gumbo, curry, and mock clam chowder, shrimp creole
Pepperoni	b	Pizza, sandwiches, pasta dishes
Ground	a ,b, d, e, g, h	Mock hamburgers, mock meat balls, spaghetti and other sauces, pizza, mock sausage patties, stroganoff, stuffings (peppers, mushrooms, tomatoes, etc.), chili, enchiladas, sloppy joes, pasta & grain salads, tacos
Steak	a, d, e, g, h	Mock beef, barbecued, marinated, salisbury, swiss steak, pork chops
Pâté	c, i	(see "ground")
Pouches/Wraps	f	Mock stuffed "turkey"
Jerky	b	Mock beef
Dumplings	c, i	Soups, deep-fried puffs

* See the "Flours and Their Resulting Gluten" table for definition of gluten types.

Gluten is difficult to ruin. Very stiff and dry gluten can be used as well as very soft and sticky gluten. See the "Types of Gluten to Use to Make a Variety of Seitan Dishes" table to see what can be done with the different types of gluten (that have very different consistencies).

Raw gluten will keep only one day when stored in an airtight container in the refrigerator. It should not be frozen; however, it can be canned.

Starch Water: The milky solution of starch, bran, and germ rinsed out of wheat flour contains all the water-soluble vitamins from the wheat. The starch water can be used in place of arrowroot or cornstarch to thicken sauces, gravies, and stews, to make gluten-free crackers, or to make pie and pizza doughs. It will keep for 2 to 3 days in the refrigerator and can be frozen. Crackers can be made by letting the starch, bran, and germ settle to the bottom of the container and pouring off the excess clear water at the top. This poured-off water can be saved to add a nutritional boost to soups, drinks, and anything else that uses water. The starch, bran, and germ remaining in the bowl are then added to barley malt syrup (2 tablespoons), that has been dissolved in lukewarm water (1/4 cup), and 1 tablespoon baking yeast to make a cracker "liquid dough." This liquid dough should rest for 30 minutes before being stirred and spread on 3 well-oiled baking sheets with sides, allowed to rest in a warm place for an additional 30 minutes, and then baked in a 300°F oven for two hours or until the crackers are fully dried out and crisp.

Bran: The wheat bran contains trace minerals, phosphorous, potassium, and fiber. It is useful in cold cereals, crackers, drinks, cakes, cookies, pancakes, muffins, and breads. To separate bran from saved starch water, let the cloudy mixture sit for 10 to 15 minutes until all the bran has settled to the bottom. Pour out the cloudy, white starch water. To remove all the starch, repeatedly rinse the bran until the poured-off water is clear. Raw bran will keep in the refrigerator for approximately 4 to 6 days. See "Grains" and "Wheat" for more information about bran.

MAKING GLUTEN FROM AN INSTANT MIX

The instant mix is called vital wheat gluten or instant gluten flour. Don't confuse these with high-gluten wheat flour (that is used to make gluten from scratch; see the previous subsection). Although more expensive, making gluten from an instant mix is far quicker and simpler than making it from scratch. It also has the added benefit of being able to be seasoned before being cooked. This is useful in making seitan when the gluten is not cooked in a seasoned broth (i.e., dry baking or can cooking).

Instant gluten flour is wheat flour that has already had the starch and bran removed. All that is left to do is to simply mix it with liquid to produce gluten. If the  gluten is to be seasoned, add the dry ingredients to the instant gluten flour and the wet ingredients to the liquid before mixing the two. Some tasty dry additions are garlic powder, onion powder, chili powder, oregano, thyme, and nutritional yeast; and a few flavorful wet additions are vegetable and meat broths, soy sauce, miso, oil, and blended puréed vegetables.

Use 1 cup of instant gluten flour and 7/8 cup liquid. Combine the wet and dry ingredients very, very quickly, using a heavy duty spoon to initially mix it and then knead it with your hands into a smooth ball. Be careful not to use too much liquid because it will yield a soggy, soft gluten. You are now ready to make your seitan.

HEALTH INFORMATION

Seitan contains the nine essential amino acids; however, just as wheat is low in lysine, seitan is as well. Because it is very easy to digest, seitan is a good source of protein for almost everybody, and especially for children and sick people. Furthermore, seitan contains no cholesterol and very little fat.

Per 100 grams, seitan has 118 calories, 18 grams of protein, and no saturated fat.

The same amount of ground sirloin has 207 calories and 32.2 grams of protein and is high in saturated fats. Approximately 90% of the minimum daily requirement of protein can be satisfied with only one-third of a pound of seitan.

ADDITIONAL READING

Books that provide detailed instructions for making gluten, cooking it to make seitan, and many seitan recipes are:

Bates, Dorothy R., and Colby Wingate. *Cooking with Gluten and Seitan.*

Burke, George, Abbot. *Simply Heavenly!*

Grogan, Bryanna Clark. *The (Almost) No Fat Cookbook.*

Jacobs, Barbara, and Leonard Jacobs. *Cooking with Seitan.*

Moulton, *LeArta. The Gluten Book.*

Nishimoto, Miyoko. *The Now and Zen Epicure.*

Shandler, Nina, and Michael Shandler. *How to Make All the "Meat" You Eat Out of Wheat.*

BUYING SOURCES

Often locally-made seitan sold in bulk or small tubs and/or commercially-made seitan in packages or jars can be found in the refrigerated or frozen section of natural and health food stores.

There are two types imported from Japan and sold in jars. One of these, called "Seitan Concentrate," is very salty and is not recommended for use as seitan as we have described it; instead, it is a seitan pâté or spread that has had a great deal of soy sauce added to it. However, it is good as a condiment or added to bean soups or stews. The other, called "Seitan Wheatmeat," is perfectly suited for general use as seitan.

Instant mixes for gluten, sometimes labeled as "Seitan Mix" or "Wheat Meat Mix," can be found in the dry goods section of your local health food and natural foods stores. The mix labeled "Vital Wheat Gluten" can typically be found in the baking section.

Seitan is available through the Clear Eye Natural Foods and Gold Mine Natural Foods mail order companies. Instant gluten flour is available through the Mail Order Catalog, King Arthur Flour Baker's Catalogue, and Bob's Red Mill Natural Foods mail order companies.

BRAND NAMES

The boxes of most brands of vital wheat gluten discuss only how the gluten can be used to enhance bread recipes that use yeast. However, it also makes a fine basis for seitan. A good brand is Arrowhead Mills *Vital Wheat Gluten.*

Excellent quality dry seitan mixes are: Arrowhead Mills *Seitan Quick Mix* (contains vital wheat gluten and various flours) and Knox Mountain Farm Mixes (*Wheatballs, Chick'n Wheat,* and *Not-So-Sausage,* each containing vital wheat gluten, spices, and a variety of flours).

Good refrigerated pre-made seitan brands are: Upcountry Seitan (made from stone ground wheat flour, water, tamari, and kombu), White Wave Seitan (*Vegetarian—Sloppy Joe, Philly Steak Slices,* and *Fajita Strips;* and *Sandwich Slices— Roast Beef, Chicken-Style, Pastrami-Style,* and *Turkey-Style*).

SOY SAUCE

If you have not already experienced the diversity and wonderful flavor of soy sauce, you are in for a treat. In addition to adding its own flavor and bouquet, this dark, rich sauce blends and enhances the flavors of other ingredients.

VARIETIES

There are two basic types of soy sauce:

General soy sauce or Shoyu soy sauce: Basically, *shoyu* is the Japanese word for soy sauce. It generally refers to any soy sauce that contains wheat. In general, if a recipe calls for just "soy sauce," it is referring to shoyu.

Tamari soy sauce: This type of soy sauce contains no wheat and is typically lower in sodium than shoyu soy sauce. It is deeper in color, richer in consistency, more complex in bouquet, and retains its flavor better during long cooking. Typically, this type of soy sauce is higher in quality due to its historical and traditional method of production.

For both shoyu and tamari, a low-sodium brand is usually available. It is not really low sodium; it is just lower in sodium than "regular" soy sauce.

FLAVOR/TEXTURE

Soy sauce is a general-purpose condiment that has a thin, liquid consistency and a savory, salty flavor.

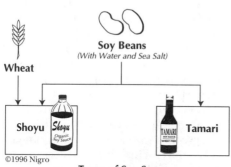

Types of Soy Sauce

GENERAL USES

Soy sauce can be used in place of salt in soups, sauces, casseroles, and other dishes without overpowering any other ingredient's flavor. Approximately 1/2 teaspoon of tamari soy sauce equals about 1 pinch of sea salt; 2 to 3 teaspoons of soy sauce is usually enough to season a dish for 4 to 6 people. Its nice salty flavor goes well combined with either sour, sweet, or pungent tastes.

Soy sauce is an essential ingredient for many clear soup stocks. For example, it is delicious when added as a flavoring in squash soup, onion soup, or other naturally sweet vegetable soups.

Mixed with a little vinegar, lemon, and mustard, soy sauce can make a refreshing salad dressing. It can also be used in marinades for meats, vegetables, and tofu. We like to thinly slice frozen-and-thawed tofu, marinate it in a soy sauce and peanut butter mix for about an hour, then fry or broil the slices, pop them into our favorite vegetable sandwich, and savor the treat.

Many sea vegetables are seasoned during cooking with soy sauce, especially kombu, hijiki, and arame.

Because soy sauce is so yummy, you may want to put it into everything. But it's best to use it in moderation because, if you eat too much, it creates excessive thirst and a strong craving for liquids as well as sweets.

FRESHNESS/QUALITY

The best brands of shoyu and tamari soy sauce contain only organically grown soybeans, water, and sea salt, and have been aged slowly over a period of two to four years. In addition, shoyu contains organically grown wheat. They should be rich and deep in color.

The very highest quality soy sauce is brewed using time-honored methods that foster a micro-culture of beneficial enzymes that preserve the soy sauce without the need for pasteurization (that kills all enzymes and microorganisms), alcohol, or preservatives.

Some manufacturers have compromised quality for quantity, and often use alcohol, sugar, caramel coloring, and monosodium glutamate to approximate a true soy sauce. Be sure to read the label.

STORAGE

Most shoyu and tamari soy sauces can be stored at room temperature. Unpasteurized soy sauces should be refrigerated and will last from months to a year.

PREPARATION INSTRUCTIONS

COOKING

Not all soy sauces are equal in strength, so you need to adjust the amount used accordingly depending on the brand used—which can vary from batch to batch. So, start by adding less than called for and add small amounts until you've reached the desired taste.

For brands that are less flavorful, you will have to increase the amount of soy sauce used to get the desired taste; however, this can increase the overall amount of sodium as well.

Typically, shoyu is added during the last few minutes of cooking. It can also be used at the table as a salty condiment or as an ingredient for salad dressings, marinades, etc.

Tamari retains its flavor longer during the cooking process than shoyu. If you would like a stronger flavor, tamari can be used in place of shoyu.

BUYING SOURCES

Soy sauce is found in supermarkets, Oriental and Japanese markets, and natural and health food stores. Mail order sources for soy sauce are Anzen Oriental Foods & Imports, Clear Eye Natural Foods, Frankferd Farms Foods, Gold Mine Natural Foods, Harvest Time Natural Foods, Granum Incorporated, and Mountain Ark Trading Company.

BRAND NAMES

The flavor, bouquet, and color of soy sauces vary widely among brands. Experiment with all that you can find to determine which are your favorites. A few of the available quality brands are: Ohsawa® *Nama Organic Shoyu & Organic Genuine Tamari*, Emperor's Kitchen *Mansan Organic Tamari*, Johsen *Organic Shoyu*, San-J *Organic American Tamari*, Eden *Organic Tamari Soy Sauce*, and Tree of Life *Shoyu*.

SPROUTS

Even people who don't have green thumbs can grow nutritious little plants, called sprouts, year-round. The sprouting process causes the seeds to release and generate a host of proteins, sugars, and vitamins that the baby plant will need to start its new life. Eating these sprouts is a pleasure because they are nutritious and delicious.

Many types of gratifying sprouts are available in supermarkets and many others can be grown at home using vegetable, legume, grain, herb, and nut seeds. In general, sprouts are so easy to grow that even a novice can have tremendous success. However, if you enjoy a challenge, there are plenty of opportunities if you really want to get into it.

VARIETIES

Sprouts can be made from a large variety of seeds. Some are commercially available and all of them can be grown at home. See the "Preparation Instructions" subsection for more information on sprouting your own seeds.

Alfalfa Sprouts: These crunchy little sprouts have a pleasant, delicate, refreshing flavor that is slightly earthy. They contain vitamin K and various minerals. They are at their peak of freshness when their two little leaves are bright green. These sprouts can be purchased at supermarkets, health food stores, etc., or you can sprout alfalfa seeds yourself. Alfalfa sprouts can be used in salads and sandwiches, and added to soups and egg dishes just before they are finished cooking. Immature sprouts (1/8 inch long or after a day of sprouting them yourself) can be used in baked goods such as breads and pancakes to add protein.

Amaranth Sprouts: These crisp, very tiny, mild-tasting sprouts are yummy in green salads and soups. They contain a high concentration of amino acids and calcium. If you want to try these sprouts, you'll probably need to grow your own.

Lentil Sprouts: These crunchy sprouts have a peppery, robust flavor. They can be added to soups, stews, and casseroles just as any other vegetable. Furthermore, these sprouts can be used in salads or steamed by themselves to create a vegetable side dish. They have high concentrations of iron, phosphorous, and the B vitamins. These sprouts are not readily available in stores, so you may need to grow your own.

Mung Bean Sprouts: These are the thick, white bean sprouts that you can find in almost any supermarket. They have a very high water content and taste very refreshing in salads, sandwiches, tacos, etc. They are typically used in Oriental dishes such as stir-fries and fried rice. They go well with brown rice, chicken, and fish, and can be steamed and seasoned to make an eye-catching side-dish. Mung bean sprouts contain vitamins A, C, and E, as well as choline, niacin, potassium, calcium, iron, and phosphorous.

Radish Sprouts: These crisp, small, tear-drop shaped sprouts can carry quite a bite that gets stronger as the sprouts get larger. They taste a lot like radishes and are delicious when added to tuna, chicken, seafood, and mixed green salads. To reduce their bite, choose small ones and/or mix them with some alfalfa sprouts. Radish sprouts contain large amounts of potassium. Some supermarkets and health food stores will carry mature radish sprouts, but it's likely that you'll have to grow your own.

Soybean Sprouts: These crunchy, large sprouts may not be commercially available. To make them yourself is a bit more difficult than most of the other sprouts. Because they have a strong raw soybean taste, you may choose not to use them raw in salads and sandwiches. However, when steamed or stir-fried for just a few minutes, they are transformed to have a rich, nutty flavor. Soybean sprouts are delicious in chop suey, casseroles, soups, and stews and go very well with hearty meats such as pork, beef, and mutton. These sprouts contain protein, and vitamins A, B-complex, C, and E.

Sunflower Sprouts: These crisp sprouts can be used in trail mixes and snacks when combined with nuts, seeds, dried fruits, grains, and/or cereals. Of course, they are also nice in salads and sandwiches. Note, however, that if the root (long, stringy, white part) is longer than the seed, the sprouts can become quite spicy and hot. If you can't find them in your local stores, you can grow your own. They provide vitamins D and E, protein, minerals, and unsaturated fatty acids.

Wheat Sprouts: These sweet sprouts can be used in salads and sandwiches and they also have a few unique uses. They can be used in doughs for breads, bagels, crackers, etc. by kneading the sprouts into the dough prior to shaping. In addition, they can be added to batters for pancakes, waffles, muffins, etc. To make an interesting coating for meats and vegetables, try ground wheat sprouts. Drying these sprouts produces a crunchy delight that can be used in baked goods and trail mixes instead of nuts with the added benefit of less fat. Wheat sprouts are a good source of protein and vitamins. Even though these sprouts are tasty, they are

not typically available in stores. Growing your own may be the only option.

FLAVOR/TEXTURE

Raw sprouts are refreshing, crunchy, and crisp. They have various appetizing flavors: mild, sweet, earthy, spicy, peppery, and hot.

GENERAL USES

Sprouts offer an inexpensive and fresh source of crisp vegetables year-round. Sprouts are commonly used in salads, sandwiches, and crudités as well as a garnish.  They can also be used in vegetable loaves and burgers, stir-fries, egg foo yong, vegetable pancakes, fried rice, quiches, and stuffings for vegetables and meats. Try using sprouts in place of, or in addition to, lettuce or cabbage in cole slaw, tacos, and burritos.

There are many ways to add sprouts to your luncheon menu. Pep up your burgers (veggie, grain, bean, or ground-meat) and fish filet sandwiches with a generous amount of sprouts. Or, make a novel and snappy cole slaw using one or more types of sprouts with Napa cabbage, spinach, carrots, celery, leeks, green pepper, salt, and freshly ground black pepper. Mix with your favorite savory or sweet dressing. Or, using any sprout you like, try making a nutritious drink by blending the sprouts with a sweetener (such as honey, rice syrup, or barley malt) and water.

Sprouts can be used in baked goods such as breads, pancakes, and muffins to add flavor and protein. Make a sweet, low-fat loaf of nutritious bread by baking a dough of ground wheat sprouts, whole wheat flour, wheat germ, vegetable oil, and non-dairy milk.

Prepare a mouth-watering chow mein sauce by using mung bean sprouts or soy bean sprouts with onion, mushrooms, shoyu soy sauce, toasted sesame oil, salt, pepper, and a thickening agent. Stir fry chow mein noodles with half of the sauce and serve with the remaining sauce poured over the cooked noodles.

Different types of sprouts can be mixed together for added nutritional value (a combination of bean and grain sprouts is a good example) and to create harmonious new flavors.

FRESHNESS/QUALITY

Fresh sprouts are firm and crisp and are not wilted, limp, turning brown or yellow, or slimy.

STORAGE

It is best to refrigerate sprouts in an open or non-airtight container that allows air circulation and moisture to escape. Fresh sprouts will keep for up to a week. To help them remain crisp and fresh, rinse and drain them daily in cold or cool water.

PREPARATION INSTRUCTIONS

CLEANING

The cleaning of sprouts is normally not necessary. If they are purchased or grown at home in a jar, they are already pretty clean. If rinsing is required, spin dry them in a salad spinner before using.

COOKING

Sprouts are most often eaten raw; however, cooking them can add another dimension to your cuisine. They can be cooked in a small amount of water and briefly sautéed until the desired texture is obtained. Oil can be used as the sautéing or frying medium, too. Sprouts are sensational when cooked until they become golden brown and crispy. Of course, when frying the sprouts, you can fry other vegetables with them to make a delicious dish. When using vegetable oil with sprouts in salads or in frying, try the different types of sprouts and oils to determine your favorite combinations.

Immature sprouts have a low water content and can be used directly in baked goods such as breads, pancakes, and muffins to add protein. If you choose to use mature sprouts, the recipe may need to be adjusted because of the high water content in the sprouts. Try using 1/4 cup less liquid and 1/4 cup less flour per 1/2 cup of sprouts added.

GROWING SPROUTS

Since the variety of sprouts is numerous and the availability of them in supermarkets is limited, growing your own sprouts can open new doors and taste delights.

Seeds for sprouting are available from health and natural food stores and mail order suppliers. Do not use seeds that are sold for garden use; they may be coated with fungicides. Use fresh, natural, unprocessed seeds. In theory, any seed can be sprouted if it has not been "treated" in some way.

Growing sprouts can be simple or complicated depending on how involved you wish to get. Start simple and if you enjoy growing and eating your sprouts, you can choose to get into the more complicated methods. The basic process of sprouting simply involves soaking and draining seeds and keeping them moist until shoots appear.

The simplest and probably most effective sprouting container is the common canning or mason jar. The wide-mouth quart jar is a good size to start with. The seeds grow into little plants that take from four to fourteen times the volume of their original seeds. The small seeds expand the most and 2 tablespoons of seeds will be sufficient to fill your quart jar with mature sprouts. Furthermore, the large seeds expand less and 1/2 to 1 cup of seeds will typically do the job (see the "Sprouting Table"). Be sure that there is plenty of room for your little plants to grow without being crowded.

After placing the seeds in the jar, fill it with cool water and place it in a dark, room-temperature (around 70°F) area until the seeds have doubled in size (this is approximately 8 hours for small seeds and 12 hours for larger ones; see the "Sprouting Table"). This will soften the outer hull and start the sprouting process.

Place a piece of cheese cloth or small mesh screen over the jar opening and secure it with a rubber band or the jar ring normally used to secure the lid in canning. Drain the water off and rinse the seeds several times until the water runs clear. Leave the cheese cloth or mesh in place to keep bugs and dust from getting in the jar, while allowing the air to circulate and provide good ventilation for the sprouting seeds.

Place the spouting jar in a warm, room-temperature spot that is not exposed to direct sunlight.

The sprouts need to be rinsed at least twice a day (some sprout types need more, see the "Sprouting Table") for two reasons. They need to stay moist to promote growth and the by-products that promote spoilage need to be rinsed away. If they are too dry, they will shrivel up and die. In hot weather, or for any reason if the sprouts are getting too dry, simply rinse them more often. However, if they are kept too wet, they will rot or develop mold. If the sprouts are staying too wet, the back end of the jar can be elevated to allow better drainage. If the sprouts should start to become crowded, transfer them to a larger container.

The last two, optional, steps are to "clean-up" your sprout garden and turn your sprouts a beautiful green. When the sprouts are almost mature, many of the hulls (or seed casings) and unsprouted seeds can be removed. Put the sprouts in a large bowl, gently separate any sprouts that are clumped together, and then cover them with water. Slowly swish the sprouts and skim off any hulls that float to the top. Pour the water and sprouts through a strainer leaving the unsprouted seeds in the bottom of the bowl. Drain the sprouts, return them to the jar or some other container, and allow them to continue to grow until ready to harvest. The sprouts may be placed in direct sunlight on the final day before harvesting in order to produce chlorophyll which will enhance their color and nutritional value.

The sprouts may be harvested and used at any time after the shoot appears. Young sprouts are often used in baking. Mature sprouts can be ready for eating in as little as one day and can take as long as six days depending on the type of seed being sprouted and other conditions such as the temperature and humidity. The best length of the shoots or roots depends on the type of seed, purpose for the sprout, and the flavor desired. Taste testing the sprouts during the growing process is a great way to determine the flavor and texture at each of its stages to get ideas for creative cooking.

If you wish to harvest your sprouts when they have reached full maturity, wait until they have one or two tiny leaves and/or until they have attained their approximate mature length. See the "Sprouting Table." At any stage of development, when harvesting sprouts, give them a final rinse by gently swirling them around in cool water. Drain them and immediately store them in the refrigerator until ready to use in your favorite sandwiches, salads, or stir-fries.

The "Sprouting Table" is intended to provide guidelines and rough approximations. The sprout time may be shortened if the seeds are soaked longer, the harvest length may be shorter if the seeds are older, the sprout time is affected by temperature and water conditions, etc. There are too many variables for sprouting to be an exact science—it is more of an art.

Many books discuss sprouting. However, they often don't agree on a few issues: grown in light or darkness, length of time the seeds should be soaked, the temperature of the seed-soaking water, and the length of time till sprouts mature. In fact, there are quite a few differences in sprouting techniques. Feel free to try them, even if they directly oppose a technique you know to be successful. There is no one right way to do this!

If you wish to pursue a more complicated concept in sprouting, it is possible to make homemade grain sweeteners. The basic concept consists of cooking grain sprouts in a rice mixture until the desired sweetness is obtained (for more information, see "Rice Syrup"). Fred Rohe's book *Nature's Kitchen* provides more information about making grain sweeteners. For information about purchasing, cooking, and storing grain sweeteners, see "Barley Malt Syrup," "Rice Syrup," and "Sweeteners."

Sprouting Table

©1996 Nigro

Seed	Soaking Time (hours)	Rinses Per Day	Sprout Length (inches)	Sprout Time (days)	Amount of Seed	Approx. Yield (cups)	Comments
Common**							
Alfalfa*	6 to 8	2	1 to 2	3 to 6	2 1/2 T.	4	The most common sprouts found in salad bars and on top of sandwiches.
Amaranth	6 to 8	3	1/4	2 to 3	3 T.	1	Mild flavor. Not available commerically.
Lentil*	6 to 10	2 to 4	1/4 to 1 1/2	3 to 4	3/4 C.	3 3/4	Chewy texture. More nutritious if eaten at 1/4 inch but better tasting if allowed to mature.
Mung*	8 to 12	3 to 4	1 to 2	3 to 5	1 C.	5	Easy to sprout. Loses crunchy texture after four days in the refrigerator. Popular in Chinese cooking.
Radish*	7 to 12	2	1/4 to 2	3 to 6	3 T.	3	Sprouts taste like radish. They become more spicy as they mature.
Soybean	12 to 16	4 to 6	1/2 to 2	3 to 6	1 C.	4 1/4	Harder to sprout and requires more attention. Needs to be slightly cooked before eating. Do not soak water because it is toxic.
Sunflower*	8 to 12	2	1/4	2 to 3	1 C.	2 1/2	Normally mild in taste; roasting enchances the flavor. May become bitter if allowed to fully mature.
Wheat	8 to 13	2 to 4	1/4 to 1/2	2 to 5	1 C.	3 3/4	Harvest length is dependent on how the sprouts will be used.
Other**							
Barley	8 to 10	2 to 4	1/4	2 to 4	1 C.	3 1/4	Chewy texture. Roasting enhances flavor.
Blacked-eye peas	8 to 14	3 to 4	1 to 1/2	3 to 5	1 C.	4	Soaked beans expand a great deal. These sprouts are a good source of protein and vitamins A and C.
Buckwheat	8 to 14	1	1/4 to 1/2	2 to 3	1 C.	3	Use raw groats that are hulled.
Clover*	6 to 9	2	1 to 2	3 to 5	2 1/2 T.	4	Red clover is most common. Flavor is mild and similar to alfalfa sprouts. High in protein, B and C vitamins, calcium, and iron.
Corn	12 to 16	2 to 3	1/2 to 1	3 to 6	1 C.	3	Chewy with sweet corn taste. Hard to find natural untreated corn seed.
Garbanzo	12 to 16	4	1/2 to 1	3 to 5	1 C.	3 1/2	Cook lightly before eating. Supplies complete protein.
Millet	6 to 8	2 to 3	1/4	3 to 4	1 C.	2	Chewy and pleasant flavor.
Mustard	none	2	1/2 to 1	3 to 4	3 T.	3	Has a tangy, spicy, zesty flavor. Instead of soaking, put seeds on a plate and sprinkle with water to keep them moist.
Oats*	10 to 12	1	1/4	2 to 4	1 C.	3	Use raw oats that are unhulled. Proper drainage is very important to prevent them from souring.
Peanuts	12 to 16	2 to 3	1/4 to 1/2	3 to 4	1 C.	3	Raw, shelled nuts should be used.
Peas	6 to 10	2 to 3	1/4	3 to 4	1 1/2 C.	2	Delicious pea flavor when steamed.
Rye	10 to 12	2 to 4	1/4	2 to 4	1 C.	3 3/4	Sweet in flavor and easy to grow.
Pumpkin	7 to 10	2 to 3	1/4	2 to 4	1 C.	2	Used hulled seeds. Roasting brings out the flavor.
Rice	8 to 10	2 to 3	1/4	3 to 4	1 C.	2 1/2	Use brown rice for sprouting.

* The seeds for these sprouts have hulls that the sprouts will burst through. If desired, the hulls can be washed away after 3 days.

** The "Common" sprouts are discussed in this book in the "Varieties" subsection. The "Other" sprouts are simply listed to provide information about other seeds that are easy and fun to sprout.

HEALTH INFORMATION

As seeds sprout, the sugars and starches are converted into energy that is used by the plant to grow. This means that sprouts have fewer calories and carbohydrates than the seeds. In addition, sprouts contain higher levels of protein, sugar, vitamin C, and some B vitamins. Furthermore, sprouts are low in fat.

Sprouts are different from most other vegetables because they continue to grow and produce vitamins until the moment you begin to eat or cook them.

Bean sprouts have the added benefit of not creating intestinal gases. The sugars (oligosaccharides) that cause these gases are among those transformed into energy during the sprouting process.

ADDITIONAL READING

Larimore, Bertha B. *Sprouting for All Seasons*.

Meyerowitz, Steve. *Sprout It! One Week from Seed to Salad*.

Nutrition Education Collective. *Through the Seasons: Winter Tidings*.

Rohe, Fred. *Nature's Kitchen*.

Weber, Marcea. *Whole Meals*.

Whyte, Karen Cross. *The Complete Sprouting Book*.

Yepsen, Roger B., Jr., ed. *Home Food Systems*.

BUYING SOURCES

Sprouts can be purchased in supermarkets, health and natural foods stores, and specialty and ethnic food shops. Seeds for sprouting can be obtained at health and natural foods stores as well as mail order suppliers such as The Sprout House, Mountain Ark Trading Company, Gold Mine Natural Foods, Clear Eye Natural Foods, Bob's Red Mill Natural Food, Frankferd Farms Foods, Allergy Resources, Anzen Oriental Foods & Imports, Arrowhead Mills, The Bean Bag, Garden Spot, Jaffe Bros., Natural Lifestyle, Phipps Ranch, Harvest Time Natural Foods, King Arthur Flour Baker's Catalogue, Walnut Acres Organic Farms, Dean & Deluca, and Sultan's Delights. It is important to obtain fresh seeds because they will not sprout well at all if they are old—so purchase them from sources that have a high turn-over rate.

SWEETENERS

Thank goodness! There is more than one way to satisfy a sweet tooth. Some of the sweeteners available are: maple syrup, maple sugar, date sugar, molasses, fructose, date spread, fruit butter, fruit juice, fruit juice concentrate, dried fruit, dehydrated cane juice (Sucanat®), sorghum molasses, amazake, carob powder, barley malt powder and syrup, and rice syrup.

With all these possible sweeteners, how do you go about choosing those perfect for you? Various criteria for judging sweeteners are:

Origins (Chemical vs. Product of Nature): Some sweeteners are the creations of chemists, such as saccharin, aspartame, and miraculin. Although these sweeteners have no calories, many of them have a bitter aftertaste. Natural sweeteners have their origins in plants (sugar cane, maple trees, sorghum, flowers, etc.) and may be processed very little or be highly refined. Be aware, however, that natural sweeteners that have been refined to almost 100% pure sugar act like a chemical in body metabolism. And there's no getting around it, regardless of the refinement level, natural sweeteners contain calories.

Flavor: Sweeteners such as honey, barley malt, and of course, molasses, have strong individual flavors in addition to their sweetness. Highly refined sweeteners typically do not have much flavor other than their sweetness.

Sweetening Power: Sweeteners have varying levels of sweetness. Those that are sweeter, by weight or volume, can be used in smaller proportions to achieve the same results in recipes.

Effect on Blood Sugar Levels and Metabolism: Blood sugar is the source of energy for the human body. The trick is to keep a consistent supply of that sugar in the blood stream. The sugars keep getting used up because they are transformed into energy by insulin.

Sweeteners that have been refined to almost 100% pure sugar are absorbed by the body very quickly and shoot blood sugar levels way up, triggering an over-production of insulin. This causes all the sugars to be converted into energy all at once, leaving you with a harmfully low blood sugar level. Your source of energy is virtually reduced to zero—your tank of gas has just run dry.

Sweeteners that contain nutrients and fiber (i.e., those that are processed very little) regulate the pace at which the sugars enter the blood stream. Consequently, the blood sugar level remains balanced between the harmfully high and low extremes, providing the body with the most consistent, usable energy.

Think of the sugars as wood, the insulin as fire, and the energy as heat. You could throw a lot of wood into the fireplace at one time (this is what happens with refined sugars). It will burn hot and heavy, producing too much heat for a short period of time. Or, you could maintain a comfortable, consistent warmth by feeding your fire with a log or two at regular intervals (this is what happens with natural unrefined sugars).

Vitamins and Minerals: Claims have been made that other sweeteners are preferable to refined white sugar because of the vitamins and minerals they contain. However, except for molasses, these nutrients appear in such small quantities that they can be considered negligible when compared to the Recommended Daily Allowances (RDA). On the other hand, these low levels of vitamins and minerals are useful for regulating the release of sugars into the blood stream.

If you are trying to reduce the amount of sugar you eat, take note that many food manufacturers add highly refined sugar to almost all processed foods. Read labels to find out the type of sugar added and to obtain a guess as to its quantity (the lower down in the list of ingredients, the less used).

VARIETIES

In your discovery of different sweeteners, you may run across the terms mono-saccharide, disaccharide, and polysaccharide. They are defined in the table "Categories of Sugars Based on Their Chemical Structure."

For an overview of how each sweetener rates in each of the judging criteria, see the "Sweeteners Comparison Chart."

Amazake: This sweetener is a mildly sweet, rich and creamy milk-like liquid that is made from fermented brown rice milk. For more information about this ingredient, see the "Amazake" section in this book.

Barley Malt Syrup and Powder: This sweetener is extracted from sprouted whole barley that has been roasted. Barley malt flavors range from extremely strong to rather mild. Barley malt is rather inexpensive compared to other quality natural sweeteners. For more information about this ingredient, see the "Barley Malt Syrup" section in this book. Barley malt powder is simply a dehydrated, granulated form of barley malt syrup.

Brown Sugar: Brown sugar is white sugar to which a small amount of molasses or "caramel coloring" (burnt white sugar) has been added. Thus, brown sugar represents one further processing stage beyond the refinement of white sugar.

Brown sugar made with molasses does contain more nutrients than white sugar, but the amount is insignificant. There are no nutritional differences between white, brown, or turbinado sugars.

Carob Powder: This powder is made from naturally sweet carob pods. When roasted, it has a chocolate-like flavor and color. This very mild sweetener is often

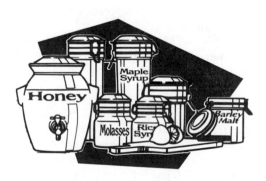

used in baked goods, candies, desserts, drinks, etc. See "Carob" for additional information.

Corn Syrup: In general, corn syrup is manufactured by treating corn with sulfuric or hydrochloric acid and then neutralizing and bleaching it with other chemicals. Corn syrup ranges in color from very pale, almost white, to light brown. The darker varieties have had molasses or cane syrup added to increase their sweetness and flavor. Because it costs less to produce than cane or beet sugar, corn syrup is used in tremendous quantities in commercial candies, canned fruits, juices, pastries, and other processed foods. Corn syrup has the same negative effect on the body's blood sugar metabolism as white, brown, or turbinado sugars.

Date Sugar: This sweetener is 100% pitted, dehydrated, pulverized dates. Cosmetically inferior dates are used to produce this sweetener. Date sugar contains all the nutrients of dried dates. It tastes sugary and has a mild date flavor. If consumed in excess, date sugar has the same undesirable effect on blood sugar metabolism as does white sugar. Used in moderation, it is a quality sweetener. It is coarse and, unless sprinkled on top of foods, needs to be dissolved or thoroughly mixed with liquids in a blender.

Fructose: Fructose (fruit sugar) is a simple carbohydrate that is especially sweet in cold foods. Although, fructose is naturally occurring in fruit, commercial suppliers of fructose usually manufacture it by further refining corn syrup.

Fructose is easier to break down and metabolize than sucrose (refined white sugar). Fructose does not require large charges of insulin to be released, whereas sucrose does.

A big problem with buying fructose is that there are no strict regulations regarding its labeling. Pure fructose, 90% fructose, and "high-fructose corn solids," which may be as much as 55% sucrose, may all be legally identified as "fructose." The fructose in processed foods may be hidden on the label. Because the FDA defines "sugar" as being at least 96% sucrose, it is legal for manufacturers to produce food products using only fructose as a sweetener and to claim that no sugar has been added.

Fruit, Dried: Raisins, dried dates, apples, etc. can be used to sweeten preparations. Cook them with oatmeal in the morning, or use them in baking breads, cookies, muffins, waffles, pancakes, and desserts. In addition to adding a sweet flavor, they also add a nice texture to bean and grain dishes. For example, a simple, delicious dish can be made by adding raisins and curry to your favorite rice. Some manufacturers treat their dried fruits with sulfur dioxide to preserve color. Try to find mechanically or sun-dried fruits that have no preservatives or additives to get the maximum health and flavor benefits.

Fruit, Fresh: The best source of fructose is fresh fruit because it contains fiber, vitamins, and minerals that cause the sugar to be absorbed slowly into the blood stream. Fresh fruits provide a mild, natural sweetness to anything they are added to. For a ranking of the fresh fruits

Sweetness of Fresh Fruits

(Percentage when compared to bananas)

Fruit	Percentage
Bananas	100%
Grapes	100%
Mangoes	94%
Nectarines	75%
Cherries	75%
Apples	75%
Pineapple	75%
Pears	69%
Peaches	56%
Oranges	56%
Tangerines	50%
Apricots	44%
Blackberries	38%
Strawberries	38%
Raspberries	38%
Grapefruit	31%
Cantaloupe	31%
Watermelon	31%
Honeydew	31%
Lemons	19%
Rhubarb	6%

according to sweetness, see the table "Sweetness of Fresh Fruits." Note that a dried fruit, such as a date, is four times sweeter than fresh bananas. Strawberries, bananas, or peaches are nice additions to breakfast cereal. Fresh fruits, raw or cooked, make nifty snacks and often are used by themselves to make a complete dessert. If you have a large supply of fresh fruit that can't be eaten before it will spoil, it can be preserved by drying, canning, or freezing. Freezing changes the color, texture, and flavor of the fruits less than canning. However, frozen fruit must be stored in the limited space of your freezer.

Fruit Juice (Fresh and Concentrated): Unsweetened orange, pineapple, cherry, pear, and peach juices can be used to sweeten many dishes. In fact, almost any fruit juice can be used as a sweetener (exceptions are grapefruit and lemon juice). Concentrated fruit juices have more sweetening power per ounce. When you want a very sweet, light-colored juice, good ones to use are pineapple juice and peach and pear nectars.

Fruit, Puréed (Spreads and Butters): Date spread, apple butter, pear butter, fruit spreads (sweetened only with fruit juice), or fruit purées (like mashed bananas and blended peaches) can be used to sweeten a large number of dishes. Put them in bean and grain dishes or use them in breads, muffins, and pancakes. They are also useful to thicken sauces, gravies, soups, and stews. When blended with nut milk and vanilla (and perhaps a little carob powder and almond oil), puréed fruit adds a touch of sweetness.

Grain Syrups: Sweeteners made from grain are probably the most economical and wholesome of all sweeteners while providing a satisfying sweet flavor. These include rice syrup and barley malt syrup (for details on each, see the appropriate discussion in this section). A very nice feature of grain syrups is that they contain much of the original mineral content of the grain. They can be used as a topping for a cake, Danish, or cinnamon roll, or in the same way as maple syrup or honey. Grain syrup is a natural sweetener that

can be made at home by anyone (see the "Preparation Instructions" subsection).

Honey: Honey has a distinct flavor and is very sweet. The total sugar content of honey is higher than that of any other natural sweetener. For general use, choose a light flavored honey such as clover or wildflower. For more information about this ingredient, see the "Honey" section in this book.

Maple Sugar: Evaporated maple syrup leaves crystals which are called maple sugar. Although it is useful in baked goods and hot cereals, its high cost limits its usefulness as an all-purpose sweetener. Maple syrup is much less expensive and can be used in place of maple sugar without much trouble.

Maple Syrup: Maple syrup is a healthful sweetener that is commonly available and treasured by many. It has a great number of uses in addition to sweetening a breakfast waffle or pancake. For more information, see the "Maple Syrup" section in this book.

Mirin: A sweet cooking wine made from rice, mirin is superb added to tender crisp vegetable dishes, cooked beans, and dipping sauces. It also can be used to sweeten frostings, sauces, glazes, and other dessert toppings. See "Mirin" for more information.

Molasses: Black and syrupy in texture, molasses is an extract of sugar cane. It is high in sugar content, but because of the intensity of its flavor, it is used sparingly. Blackstrap molasses has such a strong taste that it is more a flavoring agent than sweetener. Some like the flavor and use the words rich, full, deep, and mellow to describe it and some find the flavor offensive. It varies from person to person. Molasses has a unique flavor, texture, color, and mineral content. It retains many of the vitamins and minerals of the sugar cane plant and contains appreciable amounts of iron, potassium, calcium, silicon, and manganese. For additional information, see the "Molasses" section in this book.

Raw Sugar: This is another term for turbinado sugar; see its discussion in this subsection.

Sweeteners Comparison Chart

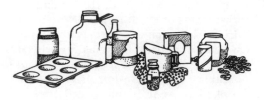

Sweeteners	Form	Flavor of its Own
Amazake	Liquid	Mild
Barley Malt Powder	Fine Crystals	Strong to Mild
Barley Malt Syrup	Thick Liquid	Strong to Mild
Brown Sugar	Crystals	Mild
Carob	Powder	Strong
Corn Syrup	Thick Liquid	Extremely Mild
Date Sugar	Coarse Crystals	Mild
Fructose	Crystals	None
Fruit Juices	Thin Liquid	Strong to Mild
Fruit Spreads & Butters	Spreadable Paste	Strong to Mild
Fruit, Fresh	Varies, Whole Food	Medium to Mild
Fruit, Dried	Chewy Whole or Sectioned Pieces	Strong to Mild
Honey	Thick Syrup	Strong to Mild
Maple Sugar	Crystals	Medium
Maple Syrup	Thick Liquid	Medium
Mirin	Thin Liquid	Mild
Molasses	Very Thick Liquid	Very Strong
Refined White Sugar	Crystals	None
Rice Syrup	Thick Liquid	Mild
Sorghum Molasses	Thick Liquid	Very Strong
Turbinado ("raw","natural")	Coarse Crystals	None
Unrefined Cane Sweeteners	Granulated	Negligible

©1996 Nigro

Note: Those sweeteners that are artificially produced (such as saccharin, aspartame, and miraculin) are not listed in this table.

| Sweetening Power | | Natural Origins | Vitamins & Minerals† | Effect on Blood Sugar Levels** |
Level	Percent*			
Mild	25%	Rice	Small Amounts	+
Medium	40%	Sprouted Barley	Small Amounts	+
Medium	40%	Sprouted Barley	Small Amounts	+
Strong	100%	Sugar Cane	Negligible	−
Mild	20%	Carob Legume Pod	Rich	+
Medium	50%	Corn	Negligible	−
Medium	75%	Dates	Rich	N
Very Strong	200%	Fruit	Negligible	N
Medium	25-50%	Fruit	Varies	N
Mild	25-50%	Fruit	Varies	+
Mild	10%	Fruit	Rich	+
Mild to Medium	25-50%	Fruit	Rich	N
Very Strong	150%	Plant Nectar	Rich	−
Medium	75%	Maple Trees	Small Amounts	−
Medium	75%	Maple Trees	Rich	−
Mild	20%	Brown Rice	Negligible	N
Strong	80%	Sugar Cane	Extremely Rich	−
Strong	100%	Sugar Cane	None	−
Mild	25%	Brown Rice	Rich	+
Strong	80%	Sorghum	Small Amounts	N
Strong	100%	Sugar Cane	None	−
Strong	100%	Sugar Cane	Small Amounts	N

©1996 Nigro

* 100% is pure Sucrose.
** − Sharp increase and falling off of blood sugar.
  + Slight increase in blood sugar that lasts for a long time.
  N Neutral effect on blood sugar.
† Relative to aiding in blood sugar regulation (rather than RDA).

Refined White Sugar or Table Sugar:
Refined sugar is an energy food—but
that is all it is. It
does not supply
fiber to regulate the
pace at which the
body absorbs it, and
it does not contain
any vitamins or min-
erals. It is "empty
calories." The bene-
fits of this type of
sweetener are that it
does not have any
flavor of its own and it has a high sweetening capability.

White table sugar is what remains
after bleaching and further purifying
turbinado sugar to 99% sucrose.
Essentially, refined white sugar is totally
crystalline sucrose.

Sugar is produced from sugar beets
and from sugar cane. The sugar is separated from its host plant using a variety of
chemicals and vitamin destroying processes. Additional chemicals are used to purify, bleach, and filter the sugar. When all is
said and done, there is no real difference
between refined sugar made from sugar
cane and beets.

Rice Syrup: One of the most healthful
sweeteners is rice syrup. It is sweet but so
mild that it does not overpower other flavors. For more information, see "Rice
Syrup" in this book.

Sorghum Molasses: Not to be confused
with molasses made of sugar cane,
sorghum molasses is made from sorghum.
Sorghum is a plant that looks like a thin-
bladed corn but is related to millet. The
sorghum grain is used for cattle feed; the
stalks are used to make sorghum molasses.
This very thick liquid sweetener is the
epitome of unrefined because it is simply
the concentrated juice of sorghum.
Sorghum molasses is high in iron and is a
fair source of calcium. It has a smoky and
bittersweet flavor that is also slightly tart
and fruity. If you can't find sorghum
molasses, You can use blackstrap molasses
as a substitute; and, sorghum molasses can
be used in any recipe that calls for a cane
molasses.

Turbinado Sugar: Only when the
sucrose is 96% pure, may it be sold to
the public as turbinado sugar. Though
this sweetener is alternatively called "natural" or "raw" sugar in the health food
industry, it is already one of the most
refined foods ever made. Essentially,
turbinado sugar has the same nutritive
value as refined white sugar and brown
sugar—negligible.

Many purchase turbinado sugar,
brown sugar, and raw sugar believing that
they are lightly refined and, are therefore
more wholesome products than white
sugar. This is not true. In accordance with
the 1948 sugar law, raw sugar sold in the
United States must be refined to 96%
purity and cane sugar that does not meet
this FDA purity code cannot be called
"sugar."

Unrefined Cane Sweeteners: There are
several sugar cane sweeteners on the market that have their mineral content intact
and are therefore less than 96% sucrose.
These products are natural and they
impart a superb flavor and crystalline
crunch to baked goods. They truly are
natural raw sugar. One is made from
organic cane and is called "dehydrated
cane juice." Many recipes will refer to this
ingredient as Sucanat®, a brand name that
is becoming synonymous with this type of
sweetener. It is used in select natural
foods and is available in health food
stores. *Piloncillo,* a similar Mexican cane
product, is available in southwestern markets. *Jaggery* is an unrefined cane product
imported from India and is available in
Middle Eastern grocery stores. *Jaggery*
ranges in color from dark brown to
creamy beige. It is a good sweetener to
use in making sweets, puddings, cakes,
and drinks.

FLAVOR/TEXTURE
Obviously, sweeteners are sweet! But,
some of them have other flavors as well,
depending on the source of the sweetener
and the level of refinement. See the discussion in the "Varieties" subsection and
the "Sweeteners Comparison Chart" for
more information about the flavors and
sweetening powers of each sweetener.

Categories of Sugars Based on Their Chemical Structure

Category	Definition	Sugar Types That Belong to Category
Monosaccharides	Sugars that are easier to break down (metabolize), requiring less insulin to be released into the blood to assimilate the sugar. They have only single bonds between atoms of carbon, hydrogen, and oxygen.	Glucose: corn syrup, fruits, vegetables, honey Fructose: honey, fruits, vegetables Galactose: a by-product of milk digestion
Disaccharides	Sugars that are more difficult to break down and metabolize. They require more insulin to be released to assimilate the sugar. They have a double bond between atoms of carbon, hydrogen, and oxygen.	Sucrose: cane, beet, maple, and sorghum sugars, honey, fruits, vegetables Lactose: milk, dairy products Maltose: sprouted grains, beer, malt syrup
Polysaccharides	Sugars that contain many sugar types per molecule. These complex carbohydrates are broken down by the body, releasing sugars into the blood in a slow, steady manner.	Starch: grains, legumes, vegetables Glycogen: glucose chains in animal tissues Cellulose: indigestible part of plants Pectin: some ripe fruit

©1996 Nigro

GENERAL USES

It seems that everyone knows at least a thousand and one ways to use sugar in the kitchen. It can be used in cold preparations to sweeten juices, fruit, toast, cereal, etc. It can be used in baking in the creation of desserts, candies, breads, muffins, etc. It can be used while cooking to produce sweet and sour sauces, meat glazes, or marinades. And, of course, it can be used to sweeten hot beverages such as coffee, tea, and hot chocolate.

Here are a couple more ideas. A fabulous candied popcorn treat can be made by stirring popcorn and toasted almonds in simmering rice syrup and then baking them in an oven for a few minutes. An extremely simple, gourmet dessert can be prepared by pouring wine or sangria over frozen blueberries, fresh strawberries, or dried apples and bananas, and allowing them to soak for a few hours in the refrigerator before serving.

In general, the types of sweeteners listed in the "Varieties" subsection can be substituted for one another. See the "Preparation Instructions" subsection for ideas on how to do this.

FRESHNESS/QUALITY

Most refined white sugar has been grown with pesticides. A few sweeteners, like barley malt syrup, brown rice syrup, and fruit juice concentrates are more likely to be free of contaminates. But read the label carefully and talk with your health food store guru if you are concerned.

STORAGE

Dry, granulated sweeteners should be stored in airtight containers in a dry, cool, dark place. This will prevent the granules from drying out or sticking together to create lumps or large hard chunks (like brown sugar likes to do). If a sweetener should become lumpy, simply break it up by pressing or rolling it with a rolling pin and sifting it before using. If this doesn't work, you may have to resort to using a clean hammer!

Liquid sweeteners, once they have been opened, should either be stored in the refrigerator or other cool place (maple syrup, barley malt syrup, molasses, sorghum molasses) or in a room-temperature, dry, dark cupboard (honey, rice syrup). If crystallization develops in a liquid sweetener, the crystals can be dissolved by placing the uncovered jar in a saucepan with hot water and heating slowly. The same can be done if the liquid sweetener hardens or becomes gelatinous. Some liquid sweeteners have a tendency to ferment. To get them back into a useable form, bring the syrup to a boil and skim the fermented residue off the top. If you are unsure how to store a particular liquid sweetener, a safe strategy would be to store it in a cool, dark place and use it within six months. Unopened containers can be stored at room-temperature and will last for years.

PREPARATION INSTRUCTIONS

SUBSTITUTIONS/ALTERNATIVES

In most cases, sweeteners can be substituted for one another. However, the different flavors, sweetening powers, or states (i.e., dry or liquid) of the substitute sweetener should be compensated for.

The liquid sweeteners can be substituted for one another on a one-to-one basis. This will keep the amount of liquid in the recipe constant. However, not all sweeteners have the same sweetening power (see the "Sweeteners Comparison Chart"). The same is also true of the dry, granulated sweeteners. Equal proportion substitutions will hold the amount of dry ingredients in a recipe at a constant level. However, this can cause the sweetness to vary considerably.

For example, unsweetened fruit juice may be used as the sweetening agent in some recipes, causing just a small variation in flavor. If a recipe calls for 1 cup maple syrup and 1 1/2 cups milk, try using 2 1/2 cups of peach nectar instead.

Recipes that are being converted from a solid-form sweetener to a liquid-form sweetener need to have their liquid content adjusted to compensate. For instance, for every 3/4 cup honey used in place of 1 cup of a granulated sugar, subtract 1/4 cup liquid (such as water, milk, or eggs) from the recipe. If the recipe does not call for any liquid, per 3/4 cup of liquid sweetener used, add three to five tablespoons of flour.

In those recipes that take advantage of the granular nature of sugar, the recipe will not turn out as expected if a liquid sweetener is used in place of the granulated sweetener. For instance, if you are trying to create a sugar "crunch" on top of a cake, cookie, or muffin, the liquid sweetener would be inappropriate.

Using molasses, honey, or sorghum molasses as a substitute sweetener can significantly affect the flavor. You might want to experiment a little before committing yourself to using these sweeteners in a particular recipe.

MEASURING

In all cases, the amount of sweetener called for in a recipe may be altered to suit your own taste. If you like less sweetener, add less, and vice  versa. A recipe can be made sweeter by reducing the amount of flour (or other dry ingredient) by 1/4 to 1/2 cup and adding the same amount of powdered or granulated sweetener.

NIGRO TIP

When preparing a recipe that calls for a liquid sweetener, the sweetener will easily slip out of an oil-coated spoon or cup. If you don't have any oil or don't want to add any fat to the recipe, heat the sweetener to make it thinner and more easily pourable.

CUTTING

To keep dates, raisins, or any other dried fruit from sticking when you cut them, oil your knife or scissors.

COOKING

It is interesting to note that the sweetness level of a dish can be affected by factors such as temperature and complementary foods. Hot foods taste sweeter than cold foods. For example, less sugar is required to sweeten hot chocolate than to sweeten cold chocolate milk. Furthermore, some foods will cause others, that are eaten right after, to taste sweeter. A piece of tangy cheese eaten just before a slice of apple pie greatly enhances the sweetness of the pie.

The liquid sweeteners are a little bit more messy than powdered or granulated sweeteners. However, they mix with other ingredients much easier without requiring any preheating to dissolve them. In cases where the sweetener would be heated anyway (such as in preparing a pancake syrup, pastry filling, or stirred into a hot dessert drink), granulated and powdered sweeteners are very convenient.

HOMEMADE SWEETENERS

Grain syrups (rice syrup and barley malt syrup) can be made at home. They are made by a simple process called malting, in which the complex carbohydrates in the grain are reduced to their simple sugar components. In malting, the grain is first sprouted. It is in the sprout that the natural enzymes of the grain are activated to break down the carbohydrate into sugars. The sprouts are dried and powdered. The sprout powder is then cooked with rice or barley and water. Within a few hours, all of the available carbohydrates become simple sugars, producing a very sweet liquid. This liquid is strained and boiled down into its final thick syrup. The book called *Naturally Sweet Desserts* by Marcea Weber gives more instructions.

Fruit juices, fruit butters, dried fruits, etc. can all be prepared relatively easily. For example, a unique raisin juice can be made by blending soaked raisins with their soaking liquid, a little salt, vanilla, and orange rind.

HEALTH INFORMATION

Sugar (i.e., pure sucrose) is an empty-calorie food that, in excess, has been shown to contribute to tooth decay, obesity, diabetes, high blood pressure, heart disease, loss of appetite, fatigue, depression, difficulty in thinking, and rheumatism. Furthermore, refined sugar is believed to irritate the mucous membranes, tissues, blood vessels, glands, and digestive organs because it is unnaturally concentrated.

All the sweeteners listed in this section, with the exception of barley malt syrup, are gluten-free.

TYPES OF SUGAR

There are various types of sugar, including sucrose, fructose, glucose, maltose, and dextrose. They are defined in the glossary and their relative sweetening powers are listed in the table below.

RELATIVE SWEETENING POWER OF THE VARIOUS SUGAR TYPES ———————————

Saccharin	200 to 700%
Sucrose	100%
Dextrose	60 to 75%
Maltose	30%
Lactose	15%
Fructose	175 to 200%
Glucose	75%

ADDITIONAL READING

The following books provide recipes and information on the use of natural sweeteners:

Schwantes, Dave. *The Unsweetened Truth About Sugar and Sugar Substitutes.*

Newman, Marcea. *The Sweet Life.*

Mayo, Patricia. *The Sugarless Baking Book.*

Weber, Marcea. *Naturally Sweet Desserts: The Sugar-Free Dessert Cookbook.*

Diamond, Marilyn. *The American Vegetarian Cookbook from the Fit for Life Kitchen.*

The following books can be consulted for more technical information about sugar:

Pennington, Neil L., and Charles W. Baker, eds. *Sugar: A User's Guide to Sucrose.*

Brekhman, I. I., and I. F. Nesterenko. *Brown Sugar and Health.*

BUYING SOURCES

Dried fruit and fruit spreads are available on the shelves of grocery and health food stores as well as through the Frankferd Farms Foods mail order company.

Other sweeteners are available on the shelves of health food stores and through the Clear Eye Natural Foods, Allergy Resources, Dean & Deluca, Garden Spot, Jaffe Bros., Natural Lifestyle, and Deer Valley Farm mail order companies.

BRAND NAMES

Brands of spreadable fruit purées and butters are: Tree of Life *Fancy Fruit Spread*, Sorrell Ridge *100% Fruit*, Knudsen *Pourable Fruit* and *Fruit Spreads*, Keefer's *Organic Fruit Butters & Sauces*, and Santa Cruz *Organic Apple Sauces* (flavored with blackberry, strawberry, cherry, apricot, and cranberry).

Brands of other sweeteners are: Sucanat® unrefined cane syrup products (*Pure Cane Syrup* and *Granulated Cane Juice*), Tree of Life *Date Sugar*, Esculent *Turbinado Sugar* and *Fructose*, Hain *Turbinado Sugar*, and Fructamyl *Fructose*.

TAHINI

(tah HE knee)

The next time you are picking up peanut butter in your favorite health food store, glance to your left and right and you may spy a jar or can of some stuff called tahini that looks like albino  peanut butter. Buy it! You'll be amazed at what it can do for you and your food.

Smooth and creamy pastes or spreads, tahini and its close cousin, sesame butter, are made from sesame seeds which have been ground down and blended with a little sesame or peanut oil. These butters are exquisite in dips, dressings, and sauces. They have a texture that is very similar to peanut butter and range in color from a light creamy beige to a medium brown. For a discussion of nut and seed butters, see "Nut & Seed Butters" in this book.

VARIETIES

Tahini: Tahini is made of hulled raw or roasted sesame seeds and, optionally, salt. Because the hulls have been removed from the seeds, tahini is lighter than sesame butter and contains fewer nutrients. This lighter flavor makes tahini the preferred choice for dressings, sauces, and desserts. Furthermore, tahini may be used as an oil, egg (when used as a binder), or milk replacement. Roasted tahini has a nutty flavor and raw or unroasted tahini is almost sweet.

Sesame Butter: Sesame butter is made of whole roasted sesame seeds and, optionally, salt. It is heavier in texture and flavor than tahini and contains more nutrients. Although it has a different flavor, it may be substituted for peanut butter in sandwiches, marinades, sauces, baked goods, and other dishes.

Sesame Butter, Black: Black sesame butter is made of whole black sesame seeds. This rather expensive, unusual butter has an intense sesame flavor that is wonderful for special occasions.

These definitions of the terms tahini and sesame butter have not been universally accepted. Some cookbooks refer to tahini as sesame butter or sesame paste and use the terms interchangeably.

OTHER NAMES

Sesame paste, sesame butter.

FLAVOR/TEXTURE

Starting at intensely sesame flavored and drifting toward nutty, bitter, or sweet, tahini and sesame butter are rich and flavorful. Several manufacturers produce these butters and their products vary greatly in flavor, texture, and color. Like peanut butter, they can range from silky-smooth to grainy (almost "chunky").

GENERAL USES

Tahini can be used as the base for spreads, dips, dressings, and sauces. And it can be used in baked goods (cakes, cupcakes, muffins, breads, and oil, egg, and/or milk substitute) and desserts (fillings, icings, sauces, and oil substitute).

To make a satisfying basic spread for sandwiches or crackers, cook some tahini until it smells nutty, let it cool, and stir in some miso, lemon juice, and water. For variety, try adding spices (such as basil, garlic, oregano, dill, or thyme) and other condiments (such as a flavored vinegar, pickle juice, mustard, or wine). Using this spread in a sprouts, lettuce, onion, and cucumber sandwich makes a fantastic lunch. If you dilute the tahini spread with water, lemon juice, vinegar, beer, or wine, a savory thin sauce is created that tastes splendid when served over grains, noodles, steamed vegetables, tofu, fish, chicken, and salads.

Blend cooked garbanzo beans with garlic cloves, lemon juice, tahini, olive oil, and black pepper or a dash of cayenne pepper to make a creamy smooth hummus spread that is ideal for sandwiches, bagels, and use as a dip for vegetables and crackers.

An enjoyable malty drink can be whipped up by blending tahini with oatmeal, vanilla, raisins, and a few ice cubes.

FRESHNESS/QUALITY

Quality tahini has a paste-like consistency that is thick and creamy. Those that are thin and more liquid-like have most likely been made with synthetic substances and chemicals or poor quality seeds or oil. The highest quality tahinis are those that are free from caustic sodas, salts, chemicals, additives, emulsifiers, and/or thickeners.

Tahinis made from seeds that are hulled with the use of chemicals and then bleached tend to be more bitter and lower in nutritive value than those tahinis made from mechanically hulled seeds.

STORAGE

Because tahini contains a high concentration of vitamin E, it has a longer shelf life than other nut and seed butters. An unopened jar of tahini may be stored for up to six months at room temperature. After opening, it should be refrigerated to last another six months. If the butter tastes especially bitter and causes a harsh or slight burning sensation in the back of the throat, it has turned rancid and should be thrown out.

For both sesame butter and tahini, the oil may separate from the butter to make a layer at the top of the jar. If this should occur, simply stir the oil back into the butter before using.

PREPARATION INSTRUCTIONS

ROASTING

Roasting tahini gives it a more nutty flavor. To roast tahini, pour it into a sauce pan and cook it over a low heat, stirring constantly until it begins to turn a slightly darker color and emit a rich, nutty aroma. This generally takes from 3 to 5 minutes. Allow the roasted tahini to cool before blending it with other ingredients to make dips, spreads, dressings, etc.

COOKING

Tahini does not have to be cooked before being eaten. It can be used straight from the jar. However, this butter is often cooked when incorporated into recipes.

HEALTH INFORMATION

Lecithin, phosphorus, calcium, iron and vitamins B and E are found in abundant quantities in sesame butter, with tahini containing slightly fewer nutrients. These butters are around 25% protein.

ADDITIONAL READING

Although there are not any specific reference works that are dedicated solely to the topic of tahini or sesame butter, there are many cookbooks that do use these butters as ingredients in their recipes. See the "Additional Reading"

section in the Introduction for a list of good general cookbooks.

BUYING SOURCES

On the shelf next to the peanut butter and other nut and seed butters, tahini can be purchased in health food and natural foods stores. Tahini is also available through the Clear Eye Natural Foods, Jaffe Bros., Harvest Time Natural Foods, Mountain Ark Trading Company, and Deer Valley Farm mail order companies.

BRAND NAMES

Various good brands of tahini are Joyva *Sesame Tahini*, Once Again *Nut Butter Organic Tahini*, Arrowhead Mills *Organic Sesame Tahini*, and East Wind *Tahini*.

TEMPEH

(TEM pay)

Painting a pretty picture about some foods can be difficult. Tempeh is one of those foods. Even though a description may make tempeh sound unappealing, nothing could be farther from the truth. Don't let anything discourage you from trying this superb fare.

Tempeh is a fermented soybean product that is available in the form of cakes, which somewhat resemble Camembert or Brie cheese. These deliciously gratifying cakes contain tender whole soybeans held together by a dense white edible mold. Don't let the thought of eating mold put you off from this fabulous food; many other delicious foods are made with molds, bacteria, and yeasts: cheese, yogurt, and bread. Tempeh has an uneven texture, sometimes made more so by the addition of grains, seeds, sea vegetables, beans, and/or vegetables during the fermenting process.

FLAVOR/TEXTURE

In general, tempeh has a chewy texture and a mild, nutty flavor. The flavor will differ depending on the ingredients added to it during the manufacturing process and the other ingredients used when preparing it. Tempeh, fried by itself, has an almost meat-like flavor, texture, and aroma that makes it perfectly suited as an alternative to chicken, veal, and seafood cutlets and fillets.

GENERAL USES

Tempeh can be used as you would use meat in many dishes. Crumble it and use it just like hamburger. Fry it and substitute it for chicken or fish fillets. Slice it thinly and broil it for sandwiches instead of luncheon
meats. Cube it and use it instead of beef or chicken in stews. Broil it and use it as a patty on hamburger buns or the meat for Reuben sandwiches. You can even use the same seasonings you would use when cooking with meat (sage, oregano, thyme, basil, pepper) as well as the same sauces and condiments.

Adding tempeh to your repertoire of cooking ingredients does not mean that meat must be omitted from your diet, unless, of course, you want it to be. You are merely adding another ingredient that will provide different flavors and textures, allowing you more choices in your present cooking procedures and recipes. Tempeh is far more than a simple meat replacement. There are many splendid recipes and ways to enjoy tempeh; it stands on its own merits.

Experiment with tempeh, by using seasonings like garlic, ginger, cajun, and coriander. Use flavorful liquids such as wine, beer, soy sauce, lemon juice, orange juice, or vinegar when steaming, grilling, stir-frying, marinating, sautéing, roasting, baking, frying, or broiling tempeh.

Purée some tempeh to make delectable sauces, gravies, toppings, dressings, and spreads. For example, blend cooked tempeh cubes with almond oil, lemon juice, brown rice vinegar, garlic, dill, parsley, salt, and water to make a creamy dressing, spread, or dip.

Fried, baked, broiled, or deep-fried tempeh cubes and strips make marvelous additions to salads, sauces, burritos, tacos, tostadas, pizzas, lasagna, stuffed tomatoes and peppers, soups, stews, chili, noodles, rice, chop suey, empanadas, sukiyaki, fajitas, and stir-fries.

Try using it as one of your ingredients when making shish kebabs for the grill. Or make a divine tempeh curry by sautéing it with onions, curry powder, and tomatoes in a vegetable stock. Then simmer it with raisins, carrots, green beans, and a rich creamy soy milk.

FRESHNESS/QUALITY

Tempeh can easily spoil, and should be in the refrigerated or frozen sections of the store. Check for the "sell by" date on the package. Fresh tempeh should have a pleasant, clean, almost mushroom-like or earthy aroma. Furthermore, it should be a firm and compact cake that doesn't bend when held horizontally at one end and should not crumble when cut into cubes or slices.

STORAGE

Refrigerate fresh tempeh when you bring it home from the store. If you need to remove it from the package, place it in an airtight container. It is best not to stack the tempeh patties on top of each other during storage because the live mold may generate heat. Tempeh will usually keep for approximately two or three days; depending on its freshness, it may keep up to a week.

If the tempeh surface starts to go black in spots, don't worry, a little of this will not cause any problems. Trim off the black areas and use as normally. Tempeh doesn't become harmful until it is quite rotten and the smell becomes positively rank and putrid. The tempeh will begin to smell and taste unpleasant and be thrown out far before it reaches the harmful stage. However, if you are in doubt, throw it out.

For long-term storage, tempeh can be frozen or dried. Dishes that use defrosted rehydrated tempeh can be chilled or frozen all over again.

PREPARATION INSTRUCTIONS

COOKING

Tempeh should not be eaten raw. If a recipe does not indicate that tempeh should be cooked in any way, steam or simmer it for around 15 minutes. This releases its flavor and improves its digestibility. Tempeh can also be simmered for up to 30 minutes in a savory sauce, before frying, broiling, or baking.

Tempeh can be made in your kitchen by mixing cooked hulled soybeans and a tempeh starter, and letting cakes of it sit in a warm place for a day. This is a simple overview. For more information on making tempeh in your kitchen, consult William Shurtleff's and Akiko Aoyagi's, *The Book of Tempeh.*

PRESERVING

Parboiling: If you want to extend the lifetime of tempeh that you are going to preserve by freezing or drying, first parboil it. To parboil, simply drop the whole tempeh cakes into boiling water. Once the water has returned to a boil, simmer for 5 minutes and then drain, cool, and pat dry.

Freezing: Tempeh can be frozen in whole cakes or slices. Just place the tempeh in a sealable plastic bag or container. If you want to store tempeh for more than 3 months, parboil it before freezing. Mark the containers with the date along with any other information you think you may need weeks or months later when the tempeh is defrosted.

Drying: Tempeh can be dried in the sun or in a dehydrator. To extend the shelf-life of dried tempeh, parboil or blanch the tempeh before drying it. If drying in the sun, cut the tempeh into 1/4 inch or thinner slices and place on racks. Set out in the sun all day and, if needed, repeat the sunning into the next day until the tempeh is well dried. If you have a dehydrator, cut the tempeh into cubes or strips and dry at 140°F for approximately 6 to 10 hours.

HEALTH INFORMATION

Tempeh is high in protein (19.5%), fiber, and nutrients. It is low in saturated fats and sodium, free of cholesterol, and is a good source of the B vitamins including the elusive B_{12} that is often lacking in vegetarian diets. The protein is partially broken down during fermentation making it a highly digestible food. It contains 50% more protein than hamburgers.

ADDITIONAL READING

Shurtleff, William, and Akiko Aoyagi. *The Book of Tempeh.*

BUYING SOURCES

Tempeh is available fresh (in the refrigerated section) or frozen in natural foods and health food stores and some supermarkets. It is also available through the Clear Eye Natural Foods, Frankferd Farms Foods, and Mountain Ark Trading Company mail order companies.

BRAND NAMES

Quality tempeh is often made by local producers. A couple of good commercial brands are Tree of Life Tempeh and Lightlife Tempeh (original *Soy, Three Grain, Wild Rice, Quinoa-Sesame* and *Garden Vege*).

TEXTURIZED VEGETABLE PROTEIN (TVP®)

TVP® is a registered trademark of the Archer Daniels Midland Company, Decatur, Illinois.

When you want meat but, for some reason or other, you can't or shouldn't have meat, then TVP® is what you can eat. The firm, chewy texture and high protein content of TVP® (texturized vegetable protein) make it an excellent meat substitute. It is available "plain" and in various meat flavors as well as assorted shapes, sizes, and textures.

VARIETIES

Texturized vegetable protein is made from defatted soy flour by cooking it under high pressure, extruding it to produce different textures and sizes, and then drying it (you know, kind of like pasta). Common sizes are:

Granules: This form of TVP® has a texture similar to ground meat, such as hamburger, and can be used instead of it in tacos, chili, cabbage rolls, and spaghetti sauces or to make burgers and patties.

Flakes: This form of TVP® is smaller than the granules and is primarily used as a meat extender, sauce or soup thickener, or protein source.

Chunks: This form of TVP® is much larger than the flakes and granules and has a much firmer, meat-like consistency that is excellent in stews, stir-fries, pot pies, and savory sauces as well as marinated and used for shish kebabs and fajitas.

OTHER NAMES

Textured vegetable protein, hydrolyzed vegetable protein, and textured soy flour.

FLAVOR/TEXTURE

Rehydrated in water and eaten by itself, TVP® does not have much flavor and tastes very bland. However, it absorbs flavors incredibly well to make a new taste delight every time you rehydrate it or cook it in something different. The primary reasons for using TVP® are its chewy texture and flavor-absorbing qualities, rather than its minimal flavor.

GENERAL USES

Texturized vegetable protein can be used as a meat substitute, meat extender, or as an ingredient that provides a chewy meat-like texture. It is wonderful in nut and bean dishes, savory meat and vegetable pies, grain and noodle entrées, and salads. Use it in burritos, stir-fries, curries, tamales, Sloppy Joes, pizza, fried rice, taco salads, fajitas, Spanish rice, enchiladas, tostadas, chimichangas, stews, spaghetti and other sauces, lasagna, savory strudels, shepherd's pie, stroganoffs, stuffed mushrooms, cabbage rolls, casseroles, gyros, chili, soups, pâtés, etc. Or use it to make burgers, patties, kebabs, meat balls, loafs, hash, barbecues, etc.

Something as simple as TVP® granules and garbanzo beans can make an extremely satisfying side-dish.

TVP® chunks can be marinated and used just like cubes of meat. A fabulous marinade that makes TVP® taste more like poultry can be created by mixing water, soy sauce, sage, rosemary, thyme, and onion powder. Or try combining dried shiitake mushroom soaking water with soy sauce, ketchup, and a dark miso to get a more beef-like flavor.

If you are a non-vegetarian who would like to reduce your meat consumption, try adding reconstituted TVP® granules or flakes to your ground beef before making your burgers, tacos, spaghetti sauces, meat balls and loaves, etc.

The general uses of each of the forms of TVP® are discussed in a prior subsection, "Varieties."

TVP® may also be used as a substitute for frozen tofu in recipes that use tofu for its "meat-like" qualities.

FRESHNESS AND QUALITY

TVP® is a highly processed soybean product. However, not all TVP® brands are processed in the same manner. Low quality brands use thermoplastic extrusion to strip everything from the soybean other than its protein and then add synthetic nutrients, flavorings, and colorings. This process uses high pressures, high temperatures, and chemicals to separate the carbohydrates from the proteins in defatted soybeans. High quality brands of texturized vegetable protein do not use any colorings, flavorings, additives, or preservatives and a mechanical, rather than chemical, process is used.

STORAGE

In an airtight container, store texturized vegetable protein in a cool, dark, dry place. It will last for one to two years. Rehydrated texturized vegetable protein that is stored in the refrigerator will last from two to five days. Rehydrated TVP® that is frozen can be stored for up to seven months.

PREPARATION INSTRUCTIONS

SOAKING (OR REHYDRATING)

This extremely light-weight, dry ingredient is rehydrated before using. Simply soak it in hot water (or broth, beer, diluted soy sauce, tomato juice, wine, sherry, etc.) for 5 to 15 minutes, according to the instructions on the package; however, it will absorb more flavor if left to soak overnight. Adding 1 tablespoon mild vinegar or ketchup per cup of liquid adds flavor while causing the TVP® to absorb the liquid in a faster, more even fashion. After adding the liquid to the TVP®, give the mixture a good stirring so that all the TVP® will get a chance to rehydrate.

If the TVP® is to be used in a dish that does not have excess liquid (such as shishkebabs or "ground beef" filling for tacos, for example), it is important to rehydrate the TVP® with the right amount of liquid. The table "Reconstituted TVP® Yield" indicates the amount of dry TVP® and the amounts of liquid required to obtain 1, 2, and 3 cups of reconstituted texturized vegetable protein.

RECONSTITUTED TVP® YIELD ———————

Dry TVP®	Liquid	Yield
3/4 cup	1/2 cup + 1 Tbsp.	1 cup
1/2 cup	1 1/4 cups	2 cups
2 1/4 cups	1 7/8 cups	3 cups

If the TVP® is being added to a stew or sauce, the amount of rehydrating liquid is far less critical. If you use too much liquid, it will just add to the sauce; if you use too little liquid, whatever doesn't get rehydrated during the soak will have an opportunity to absorb liquids when it's cooked for a few minutes in the sauce.

COOKING

In dishes that use TVP® chunks that are to be "dry" (i.e., not swimming in a liquid) or marinated, drain them and squeeze out any excess liquid after the soaking process. When browning TVP® chunks, stir often to prevent them from sticking and burning.

When forming rehydrated TVP® granules or flakes into various shapes (such as loaves or patties), you can prevent it from sticking to your hands by keeping your hands wet.

When using TVP® as a substitute for frozen tofu, double the recipe's tofu volume to determine the amount of reconstituted TVP® to use.

HOMEMADE TVP®

A TVP® substitute can be made in your own kitchen with tofu, soy sauce, and spices. Chop finely, shred or cube 2 pounds of thawed frozen tofu and sprinkle it with 4 tablespoons of soy sauce and a couple dashes of black pepper. Toss the mixture until the tofu is thoroughly coated and spread it out thinly on an oiled baking sheet. In a 325°F oven, bake until the tofu is dry and crumbly (45 minutes to an hour). After the pseudo-TVP® has cooled completely, store it in an airtight jar. This should make about 4 cups or so. To spice it up a little, try using crushed garlic cloves, grated ginger root, and honey. Or a Mediterranean style mock-TVP® can be created by using some garlic powder, basil, tomato paste, olive oil, balsamic or white wine vinegar, and black pepper. For nutritional information about this homemade TVP®, see the "Tofu" section in this book.

HEALTH INFORMATION

TVP® is cholesterol free, contains almost no fat, and is low in sodium. In essence, it is the protein that has been extracted from soybeans. Consequently, it is extremely high in protein and fiber. Although TVP® has potassium, calcium, and magnesium, it may be fortified with vitamins (including B_{12}) and minerals.

ADDITIONAL READING

Bates, Dorothy R. *The TVP® Cookbook.*

Grogran, Bryanna Clark. *The (Almost) No Fat Cookbook: Everyday Vegetarian Recipes.*

BUYING SOURCES

TVP® is often available in the bulk section of your health food or natural foods store. It is also available from the Bob's Red Mill Natural Foods and The Mail Order Catalog mail order companies.

BRAND NAMES

Many larger health food store chains, as well as mail order companies, will package texturized vegetable protein under their own name and label.

THICKENING AGENTS

Thickening agents are used to give body and a thicker consistency to almost anything. There are more thickening agents out there than just  common flour and cornstarch. They can do the same job as the more common agents and, in some cases, they move beyond and do things to your dishes you never imagined were possible. Using kuzu and arrowroot will make your thickening tasks much more flexible and enjoyable.

VARIETIES

Any liquid that is thicker than the other liquids in a dish will act as a thickening agent. Solids that absorb water or liquids can also be used as thickening agents. There is a variety of solid ingredients that are recognized as standard thickening agents:

Flour: This is the traditional gravy thickener. It makes the gravy cloudy and thick while imparting a "floury" flavor. This aspect (the "raw" flavor) can be minimized by being sure the flour is cooked long enough, either pre-cooked in its mixing liquid or cooked long enough in the dish it's added to. Wheat, spelt, oat, and barley flours are particularly good for thickening purposes. Note that grain flakes can also be used to thicken stews, sauces, and casseroles. Arrowroot and kuzu are used as thickening agents in place of flour in many instances, because they do not lose their thickening power when combined with very acid fruits (such as oranges, lemons, limes, tangerines, and strawberries).

Cornstarch: Cornstarch gives creamier, smoother results than flour. However, be careful when choosing a brand of cornstarch, because many are treated with chemical bleaches and toxic extracting agents. This thickening agent is a highly refined starch. Unlike flour, cornstarch does not need to be cooked for any length of time to remove an unwanted flavor; it simply needs to be cooked for a minute or two until it thickens. Cornstarch should not be boiled for a long period of time because the starch may break down and the liquid will thin out.

Potato Starch: Potato starch is gluten-free. Because it has a slight potato flavor, it is best used in savory dishes. If a sauce, or other potato starch thickened dish, is heated beyond 176°F, it'll lose its body and thin out again. Potato starch is highly refined and chemicals are often used to accelerate the extraction process. Potato starch may be called potato flour.

Arrowroot: Because arrowroot is made by a simple, natural process, it is less refined than flour, cornstarch, and potato starch. This makes it, along with kuzu, a preferred thickening agent by wholefood cooks. Arrowroot thickens well at low heat, making it good for sauces containing egg yolks or milk (dairy or soy). It produces a clearer sauce than cornstarch. Unfortunately, arrowroot does not hold or reheat well. It loses its thickening powers if cooked for more than two or three minutes and dishes that are to be warm should be served within 15 minutes of preparation to prevent them from cooling. Arrowroot can become a bit gelatinous or gluey if a large amount of thickening agent is required. This ingredient is discussed in detail in the "Arrowroot" section of this book.

Kuzu: Although kuzu is more expensive than the other thickening agents, it lends a smooth and subtle texture. Unlike highly refined flour, cornstarch, and potato starch, kuzu is natural and refined very little. Even though arrowroot is also unrefined, many believe kuzu to be far superior in thickening power, taste, texture, and healing qualities. An added bonus is that kuzu is also gluten-free. Kuzu must be heated, usually 1 to 2 minutes, to thicken; however, it can be cooked for a very long time and not lose its thickening power. See the "Kuzu" section of this book for more details.

Thickening Agents Comparison Chart

Thickening Agent	Properties When Cooked	Amount to Use to Thicken 1 Cup	Advantages	Disadvantages
Flour	Opaque, pasty	1/2 t – 3 T	• Gives sauces & gravies a "hearty" taste and texture • Inexpensive • Reheats well • Easy to find	• Can make dish feel "heavy" • Loses thickening power when combined with acidic fruits • Requires cooking to eliminate "raw" taste • Breaks down when frozen
Cornstarch	Semi-transparent	1 t – 1 T	• Inexpensive • Easy to find	• Higly refined (often with chemical bleaches & toxic extracting agents) • Loses thickening power when boiled for long periods • Breaks down when frozen
Potato Starch	Semi-transparent	1 t – 1 T	• Inexpensive • Gluten-free	• Highly refined (often with chemicasl to accelerate the extraction process) • Has potato flavor • Loses thickening power at high temperatures • Breaks down when frozen
Arrowroot	Transparent, shiny, somewhat gelatinous	1/2 t – 3 T	• Thickens well at low heat • Natural, unprocessed • Can as act binding agent in egg-free baked goods • Thickens very quickly	• Does not hold or reheat well • Somewhat expensive • Becomes gelatinous when a large amount is used • Looses thickening power when cooked for more than 2 or 3 minutes
Kuzu	Clear, glossy, smooth	3/4 t – 3 T	• Thickens very quickly • Remains thick even when cooled and reheated • Natural, unprocessed • Doesn't break down when frozen • Gluten-free	• Quite expensive

t = teaspoon, and T = tablespoon

©1996 Nigro

Flour, cornstarch, and potato starch are not discussed in detail in individual sections for two reasons: 1) they are commonly known and 2) they are highly refined and lower in quality than arrowroot and kuzu.

Depending on your personal tastes and specific uses, any of the thickening agents may be substituted for any other. See the "Thickening Agents Comparison Chart."

Many recipes will call for a particular thickening agent and suggest that you can use another without modifying the amounts. This can lead to trouble. See the "Thickening Agents Substitution Tips" subsection for information to help you successfully modify the recipe.

FLAVOR/TEXTURE

Some thickening agents add a flavor while others do not. Flour adds a "floury" flavor and a rather pasty texture to the dish its added to. Cornstarch is almost flavorless, while potato starch has a bit of potato flavor. Both arrowroot and kuzu are virtually flavorless.

GENERAL USES

Thickening agents are used to give body and a thicker consistency to soups, stews, sauces, gravies, drinks, gruels, dips, spreads, puddings, custards, creams, and desserts. They are also useful in preparing baked goods because they help to bind the ingredients together.

Almost everyone has eaten or heard of the thick, rich, decadent gravy that's created when a little flour and water are added to turkey or roast drippings covering the bottom of a baking pan. To speed the thickening process and create a silky smooth gravy, try using a little kuzu instead. More uses for kuzu and arrowroot can be found in the "Kuzu" and "Arrowroot" sections of this book.

FRESHNESS/QUALITY

When buying a thickening agent, be sure that is all you are buying! The ingredients listed on a box of cornstarch should be 100% cornstarch and nothing else. The same is also true for potato starch, arrowroot, and kuzu.

STORAGE

Store thickening agents in a cool, dry, dark place in an airtight container.

PREPARATION INSTRUCTIONS

THICKENING AGENTS SUBSTITUTION TIPS

There are no hard and fast rules for equivalent measures between the thickening agents. Some of them thicken better, or worse, when cooked with particular ingredients. Some thicken better at lower temperatures, and some need to be cooked for a while to obtain maximum thickening power. So, if you are going to deviate from a recipe, a little experimentation may be required to get the dish to turn out as you would like.

However, there are a few rules-of-thumb that can help you get started. Try using 2/3 teaspoon of kuzu per teaspoon of arrowroot. Try using 1/2 teaspoon of kuzu per teaspoon of cornstarch or potato starch. And try using 1/4 teaspoon of kuzu per teaspoon of flour. These substitution amount relationships can be computed by consulting the "Approximate Thickening Powers" table below.

APPROXIMATE THICKENING POWERS ─────

Agent	Power
Flour	50%
Cornstarch	100%
Potato Starch	100%
Arrowroot	133%
Kuzu	200%

COOKING

All thickening agents should be mixed with a little cold liquid (water, wine, vinegar, beer, etc.) until smooth before being adding to hot liquids.

HEALTH INFORMATION

The thickening agents consist mostly, if not all, of carbohydrates. See the individual sections in this book for specifics.

BUYING SOURCES

Flour and cornstarch are available on the shelves of supermarkets. Arrowroot can be found on the shelves of supermarkets, and natural and health food stores. Kuzu and potato starch are generally available on the shelves of health food stores. Mail order companies that carry thickening agents are Bob's Red Mill Natural Foods, Gold Mine Natural Foods, Harvest Time Natural Foods, Natural Lifestyles, Granum Incorporated, and Mountain Ark Trading Company.

BRANDS

See the "Arrowroot" and "Kuzu" sections for brand names for these ingredients. See "Grains" for names of quality producers of flours. A 100% pure cornstarch brand is Hodgson Mill *Corn Starch.* And some good quality potato starch brands are Bob's Red Mill *Potato Starch* and Richter's *Potato Starch.*

TOFU

(TOE foo)

Almost everyone has heard of tofu. Many people have even eaten tofu. But not many have experienced the interesting and exciting challenges of cooking with tofu!

Opening a package of regular tofu for the first time is quite a surprise. You stand there looking at a white block of stuff that is submerged in what you think might be water. Let's face it, this may not be the most appetizing introduction to this wonderful and useful food.

Actually, tofu is a white soybean curd formed into blocks or cakes. These blocks come in a variety of textures which can be used to add a new dimension to meals. Tofu is added to recipes for its texture alone, since it has an extremely mild taste that is overwhelmed by the flavors of anything it is cooked with. Because tofu can create a desired texture in a recipe without affecting its flavor, the uses of tofu in the kitchen are endless.

VARIETIES

There is no such thing as just plain "tofu." It comes in a variety of textures, hardnesses, and flavors.

Relationship Between Tofu Textures and Hardnesses

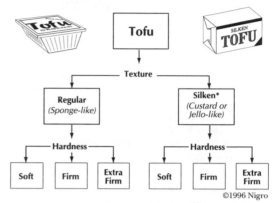

©1996 Nigro

* Note: Silken can be found in both refrigerated and shelf packaged forms.

There are two very different textures of tofu available in markets today:

Regular Tofu: This texture resembles a sponge and is fibrous. In most cases, when a recipe calls for just "tofu," it is a safe bet to use this texture. Note that manufacturers do not use the term "regular" for this tofu. They'll typically call it "tofu."

Silken Tofu: This texture is similar to a jello; it's rather custard-like. The texture can be dramatically changed into a dry, flaky almost fish-like consistency by freezing and thawing it.

Both textures are packaged in a variety of hardnesses:

Soft Tofu: For regular textured tofu, this hardness is similar to a soft water-logged sponge with really small holes. We know this does not sound appealing, but we're only describing the hardness, not the flavor. For silken textured tofu, this hardness is similar to really soft jello. In many cases, however, soft silken tofu will just have the label of "silken."

Firm Tofu: For regular textured tofu, this hardness is denser—similar to a firmer water-logged sponge with small holes. And for silken textured tofu, the jello consistency just gets firmer.

Extra Firm Tofu: Logically, you would think that extra firm tofu would be even more firm than firm tofu. However, we have not been able to distinguish much difference between the firm and extra firm hardnesses.

The consistencies of these textures and hardnesses may vary, depending on the manufacturer and what has happened to the tofu between leaving the manufacturer and arriving in your home. So you may need to be a little flexible.

A hardness cannot be made any softer but it can be made firmer by freezing and thawing, boiling in water, or pressing. These three methods change the texture of the tofu in different ways.

Freezing & Thawing: Freezing and thawing makes the tofu more porous so that it soaks up marinades and other liquids very quickly. For additional information on freezing and thawing tofu, see "Storage" in this section.

Boiling: When boiling tofu, the outside is cooked more than the inside, causing the outside edges to be a little tougher. This may be exactly what you want when using tofu as a meat alternative. A typical boiling time is 20 minutes; however, boiling it for longer or shorter periods of time certainly will not hurt it. In general, it is not recommended to boil silken tofu because it falls apart.

Pressing: Pressing tofu makes the entire block uniformly firmer. This is the technique to use if a recipe calls for firm tofu and you happen to have soft tofu in the refrigerator. To press a block of tofu, place it between towels and put a heavy weight (such as a cast iron frying pan, concrete paving blocks, or bricks) on top and let it sit for an hour or so. Storing or cooking pressed tofu in a liquid will undo the effects of the pressing. Pressing silken tofu dries it out and causes it to lose its creamy characteristic and may produce a chicken-like texture.

You are not limited to just one of these techniques to change the hardness of your tofu. You can use any combination of them or all three. You can even repeat any of the techniques or combinations to really toughen up your tofu.

When you go to your local health food store, you may notice a wide variety of tofus flavored with herbs. These are not what the authors of your recipe books are referring to unless, of course, they've specified a particular flavor of tofu. Feel free to try these flavored tofu treats in your own creative recipes.

FLAVOR/TEXTURE

Tofu has such a mild, delicate, and refined taste that many find it virtually flavorless. The value of using tofu is that it can take on the flavors of the foods it is prepared with or the sauces it is marinated in. You can add firm tofu to vegetables; it will pick up their flavors. Or you can sweeten silken tofu and make a pudding. Or add garlic, onion, and lemon to make a salad dressing. Tofu's main purpose is to add texture and nutrients to a meal.

GENERAL USES

When a recipe calls for tofu and does not specify the type, there are several ways to determine the type you should buy. First, consider what the recipe is trying to create; is it a sauce, pudding, stew, etc? Or, if that does not help, look at what the recipe has you do to the tofu since each tofu texture and hardness is more conducive to various actions (such as blending, mashing, slicing, cubing, etc.).

Silken Tofu: All hardnesses of this texture, when mashed, blended, or stirred, can be used for toppings, spreads, sauces, pie fillings, puddings, and desserts. To name just a few examples, silken tofu can be used in salad dressings instead of mayonnaise, to create a white sauce by adding spices and a sweetener, or added to soups to create a "cream-of" type of soup. When blended, the texture is similar to a cream. Typically, this texture can act as a milk, cream, mayonnaise, or egg substitute.

Silken tofu may also be used as a meat alternative by pre-treating it to toughen it up and then spraying it on all sides with a non-

stick cooking spray and broiling it. To simulate the texture of chicken, pre-treat the tofu by pressing it. Or, freezing, thawing, and then pressing it produces a remarkable, flaky, fish-like texture.

This texture is more susceptible to falling apart when handled—do not expect it to hold its shape.

Regular Soft Tofu: This texture and hardness of tofu is best for blending, mashing, and crumbling. It can be used as an alternative to cottage cheese, ricotta cheese, other soft cheeses, heavy cream, and eggs. When crumbled and mixed with soy sauce and sautéed with onions and peppers, it makes a great scrambled egg alternative. It can also act as the cheese when making a mock blue-cheese dressing. When blended, this texture of tofu is similar to a heavy cream, and can act as the foundation to an Alfredo sauce. Regular soft tofu does not hold its shape well if it is handled a lot.

Regular Firm Tofu: This texture and hardness is good crumbled, sliced, and cubed; but blending is not recommended. When marinated and broiled, grilled, or pan fried, it acts a good meat substitute. When sliced, it can be used in sandwiches or barbecues. When cubed, it can be placed in soups and stews or stir-fried with vegetables and grains. When crumbed, it can act as a substitute for hamburger or sausage to make meatballs, sloppy joes, and meat pies.

FRESHNESS/QUALITY

Fresh tofu should have a mild smell when you open the package. A package of tofu should show an expiration date.

Tofu that has spoiled turns moldy, is filmy to the touch, and has a sour, sharp, or biting taste and smell. Some suggest that if it only smells sour, it can still be used in many recipes other than those with very delicate flavors such as mousses and puddings. However, if it smells sour, we suggest that you just throw it away—it's not that expensive.

STORAGE

Tofu can be purchased refrigerated and packed in water or it can be purchased in aseptic boxes that do not require refrigeration.

After opening a refrigerated package, drain the fluid, cut off the portion you want, and decide how you are going to store the remainder of the tofu. To maintain its store-bought texture, put it in the refrigerator. To change the tofu's texture and make it tougher (more meat-like), put it in the freezer.

Usage Chart for Tofu

Tofu Texture	Tofu Hardness	Good Substitutes for	Common Uses
Regular	Soft	Soft scrambled eggs Soft cheeses *(feta, Parmesan, ricotta, blue cheese, etc.)* Cottage cheese Heavy cream	White sauce foundation, salad dressings
	Firm*	Meat *(cold-cuts, hamburger, etc.)* Hard scrambled eggs	Stir fries, shish kebabs, sandwiches, meat balls
Silken	Soft	Light cream Milk Mayonnaise Eggs	Toppings, spreads, sauces, pie fillings, puddings, desserts
	Firm*	Heavy cream Yogurt Meat *(chicken and fish)*	

Note: Firm represents both firm and extra firm hardnesses of tofu in this table. ©1996 Nigro

If you want to store it in the refrigerator (which you can do for up to 7 days), cover with fresh cool water. Replace the water daily to prevent it from getting cloudy and making a good home for bacteria. Also be sure that the tofu is completely submerged.

If you want to store it in the freezer, place the drained tofu in an airtight bag or container. The white tofu, once frozen, will turn yellow; but don't worry, when you thaw it, it will become white again. Freezing tofu drastically changes its properties. When you freeze it, thaw it, and squeeze out the water, it will have a more meaty, chewy consistency and will soak up marinades and sauces more readily than non-frozen tofu. To squeeze out the water, simply place sliced tofu between paper towels and press with the palm of your hand to remove as much water as possible, or perform the "pressing" technique described earlier. To thaw tofu quickly, microwave it on a paper towel or in a bowl. You can also boil it for 5 to 25 minutes, depending on the size of the tofu chunk. It is usually easier, however, to leave it on a plate on the kitchen counter for a few hours.

An unopened box of aseptically packaged tofu can keep for months without refrigeration. However, once it is opened, you should use it within two days.

PREPARATION INSTRUCTIONS

MARINATING

Marinating tofu is one of the many ways of flavoring it. When a recipe instructs you to marinate tofu and it does not tell you the tofu texture or hardness to use, we recommend using a regular firm or extra-firm tofu. If you are marinating for less than one hour, it can be done at room temperature covered with wax paper, paper towels, or a towel. However, for longer periods of time, marinating should be done in a tightly-covered container in the refrigerator to prevent bacterial growth and spoilage.

Frozen and thawed tofu absorbs marinades faster than unfrozen tofu. In fact, if the marinade is thin, you may only need to quickly dip the tofu in the sauce on each side for it to be fully absorbed into the tofu. However, if the marinade is thick, the tofu may still require several hours or even overnight to absorb the marinade fully.

COOKING

Tofu can be mashed, blended, whipped, ground, crumbled, marinated, simmered, steamed, baked, broiled, sautéed, barbecued, fried, or deep-fried.

Basically, you can do anything to it. Use your imagination and creativity. Remember, tofu has very little flavor of its own, and it will pick up the flavors of the ingredients it is cooked with. Also remember that tofu can be so soft and creamy that it melts away in the dish, or so firm and leathery that it takes a bit of chewing. Choose your flavors and textures.

Tofu may not only look like a sponge, but in some cases it actually acts like a sponge. If you have gone through some time and effort to remove the water from your tofu (i.e., to make it firmer or to maximize the flavor of a marinade), don't put it back in water or other liquids such as soup stocks. The tofu "sponge" will absorb liquid and drastically dilute the marinade and return the tofu's firmness to its original state.

In a soup or stew, you can "lock-in" the flavor of a marinated tofu by first cooking it with a little oil. Deep frying, pan frying, or covering with a non-stick cooking spray and broiling are all methods that may be used. If this locking-in process is skipped, the tofu's flavors will

Approximate Tofu Volume to Weight Equivalent Measurements

One pound of tofu is approximately equivalent to:

Recipe Action	Amount (cups)	Tofu Type to Use
Blend, beat, or purée	1 3/4	any silken
Crumble or mash	2	any regular
Press or squeeze, then crumble	1 1/4	any regular
1" cubes	1 2/3	regular firm
1/4" slices	1 2/3	regular firm (preferably frozen & thawed)

©1996 Nigro

have a tendency to be leached out by the soup or stew broth.

HEALTH INFORMATION

Tofu consists of approximately equal calorie percentages of protein and unsaturated fat. Although high in fat, it is cholesterol-free. The vegetable protein in tofu is much easier to digest than the protein found in animal foods. Compared to hamburger, tofu has a quarter of the calories, less fat, and more calcium. The nutritional content of tofu will vary slightly depending on what strain of bean was used and its processing method.

ADDITIONAL READING

Burke, George, Abbot. *Simply Heavenly!*

Hagler, Louise. *Tofu Cookery.*

Hagler, Louise. *Tofu Quick and Easy.*

Landgrebe, Gary. *Tofu Goes West.*

Nishimoto, Miyoko. *The Now and Zen of Epicure.*

Shurtleff, William, and Akiko Aoyagi. *The Book of Tofu.*

Paino, John, and Lisa Messinger. *The Tofu Book: The New American Cuisine.*

BUYING SOURCES

Many brands of liquid-packed tofu are purchased in one pound blocks in white plastic tubs located in the refrigerated section of health food stores, or the refrigerated or produce section of most grocery stores. Some brands of liquid-packed tofu are simply wrapped in plastic and can be found in the refrigerated section of health food stores. Local brands can often be found in the refrigerated, deli, or produce sections of the store. They may even be available in bulk!

Aseptically packaged tofu is usually found on the shelves in your local health and natural food stores.

Mail order sources of this ingredient are Clear Eye Natural Foods, Frankferd Farms Foods, Granum Incorporated, Mountain Ark Trading Company, and Natural Lifestyle.

BRAND NAMES

Nasoya brand tofu comes in *Silken* (soft—unlabeled), regular *Soft*, regular *Firm*, and regular *Extra Firm* varieties.

Mori-Nu produces silken tofu in soft, firm, and extra firm hardnesses in aseptic boxes. Other excellent brands of tofu are Stow Mills™ Organic Tofu, Tree of Life Tofu, and White Wave™ Tofu.

UME & UMEBOSHI

(oo MAY) & (oo meh BOW shee)

The umeboshi plum is an interesting and colorful pink alternative to refined white salt. Even though it has a high salt content, it is incredibly healthy. In fact, some believe that an umeboshi plum a day keeps the doctor away!

The term *ume* refers to the actual plum. *Boshi* means pickled; thus, umeboshi is a pickled plum. There is some confusion in the literature about the interpretation and meaning of the terms "ume" and "umeboshi." Some books may use them interchangeably.

VARIETIES

Ume plums are unripe green fruit that are actually closer to our apricots than to our plums. They are not available in this form but are preserved in two ways: cooking down into an extract (to make ume plum extract) or pickling with salt (to make umeboshi plum).

Ume Plum Extract: Ume plum extract is a dark, gummy, thick liquid that is very concentrated. Due to its high price tag, it is not used in general cooking; instead, it is typically dissolved in hot water to make a "medicinal" tea.

Meitan: The granular form of ume plum extract is called meitan. It is made by combining the extract with powdered brown rice. Meitan is easy to carry and use on those occasions when you are traveling or camping. It is generally used as a food supplement, much as vitamins are.

Umeboshi Plum: Ume plums are pickled in a salt brine for two or more years. Some are also pickled using nutrient-rich, reddish-purple shiso leaves to turn the green ume plum a marvelous pink color and to add a bit more flavor.

Umeboshi are available in two forms: whole plums pickled and as umeboshi "paste," a convenient purée made from whole umeboshi. These two forms can be interchanged in recipes.

Whole Umeboshi: Whole umeboshi plums contain the fruit's pit and sometimes the shiso leaf. These plums can be puréed by removing the pits and mashing them in a suribachi or mortar and pestle.

Umeboshi Paste: Umeboshi paste is puréed whole umeboshi minus pits and shiso leaves. The purée is less expensive than whole umeboshi and is more convenient to use.

Umeboshi Vinegar: When salt is added to the ume plums, some liquid is drawn from them. This liquid is umeboshi vinegar and it has a vibrant, almost fluorescent, pink color and delightful, fruity, salty flavor. Despite its name, it is actually not a vinegar since it is not a fermented product. However, it can be used in the same way as a vinegar to pickle foods, jazz up salad dressings, and enhance steamed vegetables. Unlike a true vinegar, ume-boshi vinegar can be used as an alternative to refined table salt. Its medicinal, nutritional, and health properties are comparable to those of umeboshi plums. See the "Vinegars" section in this book for more information about vinegars.

Shiso Leaf: The reddish-purple shiso leaves, that are used to color and naturally preserve ume plums, are a culinary delicacy packed with vitamin C, iron, and other minerals. They are also called beefsteak or perilla leaves.

Shiso leaves can be dried and ground to make a sweet-salty, mouth-watering condiment that is bursting with flavor and fragrant bouquet. This leaf is used in cooking for its flavor and color. Shiso adds zip to salad dressings, sauces, and soups. Sprinkle it on whole grains, vegetables, garlic toast, or beans; use it as a colorful garnish on noodles or salads; or grind it with toasted sesame seeds to make a delicious new condiment.

A quick "burger" can be made by adding minced shiso leaves and cooked, sweet corn kernels to leftover rice, forming the mixture into patties, and sautéing lightly in sesame oil.

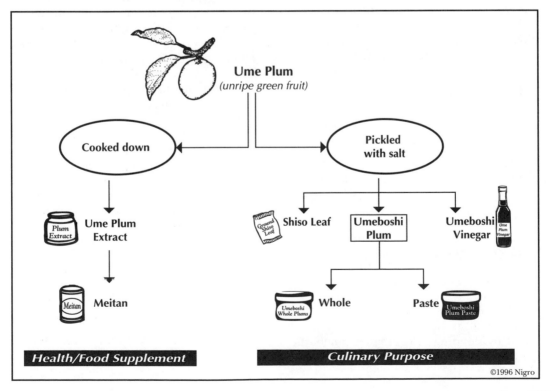

©1996 Nigro

OTHER NAMES

Umeboshi: salt plum, salted plum.

Ume plum extract: bainiku ekisu, Japanese plum extract, ume plum concentrate.

FLAVOR/TEXTURE

Umeboshi has a unique sour, tart, tangy, sweet, and very, very salty flavor. It adds zip as well as a delightful pink color to the dishes it's cooked with.

Ume plum extract is somewhat sour and tangy, but not salty. Meitan does not have the sour taste of the plum extract.

GENERAL USES

Because it is very salty, umeboshi may replace salt in a great many recipes. Umeboshi is a delightfully zesty seasoning used to flavor grain, noodle, bean, vegetable, and sea vegetable dishes. It is also excellent in preparing salad dressings, sauces, spreads, soups, and beverages. And it is perfect for short-term pickling.

Instead of putting the usual salt and butter on vegetables, try using umeboshi for a simply delicious, healthful alternative. A piece of umeboshi plum on top of broccoli florets really spices them up. Red radishes or daikon are transformed into delectable pink pickles by simmering them in water with a few umeboshi plums. Ready in minutes, these slightly salty-sour pickles aid in digestion and are a rosy garnish to meals.

NIGRO TIP ────────

You absolutely, positively must try spreading puréed umeboshi plums or paste on steaming hot, fresh corn on the cob. People really go for it!

Add umeboshi paste to lightly steamed, crumbled tofu, add a touch of dulse granules, garnish with toasted sunflower seeds, and serve on a bed of crisp leaf lettuce for a tofu "cottage cheese" salad. A refreshing summer dressing for tossed salads or noodle salads can be made by blending orange juice, umeboshi paste, tahini (or sesame butter), and

sesame oil and then mixing in some minced onion and diced mushrooms.

Dissolving a little ume plum extract in hot water makes a pleasant, piquant, hot tea. Chilled ume tea is a summertime thirst quencher that cools the body better than cold soft drinks.

A classic use of umeboshi is to tuck a bit inside rice balls or nori-maki rolls (see the "Nori" section in this book).

If umeboshi is added to a dish that has strong seasonings, the subtle tangy flavor of the ume will be lost. However, you'll still get the nutritional benefits and the salt flavor of the umeboshi. We like to add it to mildly seasoned dishes so that the flavor of the ume plum can be enjoyed as well. A couple of our favorite uses are in white sauces and corn and potato chowders.

FRESHNESS/QUALITY

For the highest quality products, the ume plums should be hand-picked and processed without any artificial colors, preservatives, additives, or chemicals.

Quality umeboshi contains only ume plums, sea salt, and perhaps shiso leaves and pine needles. Traditional umeboshi are made by alternately soaking unripe Japanese ume plums in brine, then sundrying and returning them to their brine. The color is derived from red shiso leaves which are pickled with the umeboshi.

Often, umeboshi paste is made from inferior ume plums or from plums that have been harvested by tapping them with poles (i.e., not hand-picked). The more premium plums are typically saved for the whole umeboshi final packaging.

Ume plum extract is made from grated fresh green ume plums that have been slowly cooked down to form a very concentrated, dark syrup.

Caution must be used in purchasing umeboshi plums because some have been made using manufacturing techniques that use artificial colors and chemicals in their fast processing methods.

STORAGE

Ume products keep for several years at room temperature. Store in a glass jar with a tight-fitting lid to prevent dehydration. Salt crystals may form on umeboshi plums after time, but they can be rinsed off before using.

PREPARATION INSTRUCTIONS

REDUCING SALT CONTENT OF UMEBOSHI

A great deal of work and years went into putting the salt into these little plums, so a lot of work will be required to get it all, or most of it, out! There are three methods for reducing the salt content of umeboshi. A small reduction of salt can be achieved merely by soaking the umeboshi plum in warm water for 15-20 minutes. The remaining two methods remove most, if not all, of the salt, but they differ in their onerous aspects. Simply place the umeboshi plums in hot water for approximately three hours, remove and rinse, and repeat this task a couple times. The tricky part is that you must keep the water at a constant temperature of approximately 140°F throughout the entire nine-hour soaking process. So if temperature control is a problem, you can try the third method. This involves soaking the plums in cold water for 10 hours, changing the water every single hour.

COOKING

To use whole umeboshi plums, remove the pits from the plums and save everything. Depending on the recipe, either break the plum into pieces by hand, mince with a knife, or mash in a suribachi. Place the umeboshi pits in a small jar in the refrigerator. Once you have four or five pits, cover them with water and allow them to sit in the refrigerator for a day or so. Use this umeboshi pit juice to season greens or make a light umeboshi plum dressing.

Speaking of seasoning greens, add mashed umeboshi plum, umeboshi paste or vinegar only at the end of cooking or at the table. Otherwise, the umeboshi will turn the greens (such as kale, collards, chard, spinach, broccoli, and mustard, dandelion, and turnip greens) an unappealing purple-brown color.

A nifty use for umeboshi plums is to flavor and preserve rice balls for carry-out lunches and traveling. Place a small piece of plum in the center of a rice ball, roll the ball in gomashio (sesame salt) or wrap with toasted nori sea vegetable.

You can substitute 1 teaspoon of umeboshi plum paste for any recipe calling for one umeboshi plum.

HEALTH INFORMATION

This little plum, for over 1,000 years, has earned an impressive reputation in macrobiotic and far Eastern circles as a powerful health preserver and fast-acting remedy. It is not only used internally as a medicinal food, but also externally as a medicinal salve. And it has antibacterial properties—it prevents food from spoiling, food poisoning, and the effects of drinking contaminated water.

And it is particularly effective for all sorts of stomach and digestive disorders such as diarrhea, constipation, hyperacidity, indigestion, abdominal cramps, and ulcers. And it relieves the morning sickness and constipation that a great many pregnant women experience. And it counteracts fatigue, increases endurance, and stimulates the liver's and kidneys' functions of dissolving and expelling toxins; thus purifying the blood, keeping the skin looking younger and healthier, and helping the organs to function properly and smoothly. And it is effective against hardening of the arteries, diabetes, allergies, rheumatism, and neuralgia.

And it is helpful in combating motion sickness (e.g., car and sea-sickness) and altitude sickness. And it is effective not only on skin troubles (ringworm and athlete's foot), but can also be used for first-aid treatment of insect and snake-bites.

And it contains more citric acid than any other fruit or vegetable (including lemons and grapefruit). And it is high in iron and contains manganese and other minerals. Thus, one umeboshi plum a day could be a very good preventive medicine.

ADDITIONAL READING

The following book gives in-depth information about the ume plum's uses for healing, prevention of illness, and strengthening of the constitution:

Matsumoto, Kosai, II. *The Mysterious Japanese Plum.*

For culinary information, refer to any of the macrobiotic cookbooks, which use umeboshi in many of their recipes.

BUYING SOURCES

Umeboshi plum, ume plum extract, and shiso leaf condiment can be found on the shelves of health and natural food stores and Japanese shops. They are available through the Anzen Oriental Foods & Imports, Clear Eye Natural Foods, Gold Mine Natural Foods, Granum Incorporated, Harvest Time Natural Foods, and Natural Lifestyle mail order companies.

BRAND NAMES

There are a large number of producers of ume products. Some good brands are Eden *Umeboshi Plums, Plum Paste, Ume Plum Concentrate,* and *Ume Plum Balls;* Ohsawa® *Oindo Organic Umeboshi Plums* and *Oindo Organic Shiso Powder Condiment;* Mitoku *Umeboshi* plums; and Emperor's Kitchen *Umeboshi (Salt-Pickled Plums with Shiso)* and *Umeboshi Paste (Salt-Pickled Plum Puree).*

VINEGAR

(VIN ih ger)

Distilled vinegar is great for cleaning but isn't the best choice for culinary uses. There is a wide variety of other vinegars on the market today that are far more flavorful. You can even make specialty vinegars yourself.

Vinegar is a sour, piquant liquid, widely used as a condiment, consisting of a diluted solution of acetic acid obtained by natural fermentation of wine and various other alcoholic solutions. Vinegar, in French, literally means "sour wine."

Vinegars add their personalities and flavors to the ingredients they are used with. They are wonderful additions to sauces and dressings.

VARIETIES

Vinegars can be made from wine, fruits, and rice.

Balsamic Vinegar: This vinegar is a fine ingredient that is made from wine grapes that undergo a lengthy fermentation process. It is similar to fine wine in that the older it is, the finer the quality. This vinegar has a pleasant, full-bodied, smooth, sweet, spicy flavor that does not make you pucker up when smelling it. One small taste of good balsamic vinegar will convince you to keep a bottle on hand. It is delightfully complementary to vegetables and a splendid addition to sauces, dressings, drinks, marinades, and meat basting sauces. Balsamic vinegar may be used to create a gravy from the drippings of turkey, chicken, fish, and roasts by deglazing their pans. Because it is stronger than most other vinegars, only a small amount is needed.

Try using balsamic vinegar by itself on fresh green salads or sandwiches. Sprinkle some on an avocado, fresh peaches, or on garlic bread before toasting. Create a marvelous mushroom marinade by using balsamic vinegar and olive or walnut oil.

Cider Vinegar: An early American colonist discovered this vinegar when making hard cider; it continued to ferment and turned to vinegar. This vinegar is mostly used for pickling vegetables and making chutneys. It has a delightful pungent apple flavor that can be used to spice up sweet soups, hearty stews, cold and hot fruits, steamed vegetables, creamy dips, and savory sauces. Apple cider vinegar goes particularly well with potato salad and coleslaw. It is also a good base vinegar for homemade fruit and herb flavored vinegars. Try using it with fish, shellfish, and chicken dishes as well.

High quality apple cider vinegar has 5 to 5.5% acidity and is made from a variety of whole apples and has a golden color and a pungent apple flavor. It is aged in wooden casks until much of its sharpness has mellowed and it has developed a full, rich flavor. The inferior vinegars are odorless and tasteless, while remaining biting. To make them, oxygen is pumped into hard cider (made from apple cores and peelings) to artificially hasten the vinegar-making process. Read the labels: "Made from Whole Apples Exclusively" and "Aged in Wood" are indicators that the vinegar is a good quality.

High quality apple cider vinegars can be found in health and natural foods stores. Many local apple orchards also make an excellent cider vinegar.

Distilled White Vinegar: This common vinegar is a colorless, very acidic substance—containing up to 12% acetic acid. Because it is inexpensive and lacks color and flavor, it is normally used by manufacturers for pickling large quantities of vegetables and fruits. This vinegar is sometimes labeled "white vinegar" or "grain vinegar."

Rice Vinegar: Vinegars made from brown and white rice are also available. Whereas white rice vinegar is light in color and delicate in flavor, brown rice vinegar is darker in color and has a full, sweet flavor. Rice vinegar does not have the sharpness or bite often associated with other vinegars. It goes well with other mild foods such as avocado and crab meat. This vinegar is often used with sushi rice, stir-fry vegetables, dipping sauces, and seafood. It is also great with a little almond, walnut, or sesame oil to create a quick salad dressing. Another delicious salad dressing can be made with rice vinegar, umeboshi vinegar, and olive oil. Rice vinegar also goes well with ginger root, mirin, and soy sauce.

A good quality rice vinegar is made only of rice, rice koji, and water and should be naturally fermented from six months to one year. Another indicator of high quality, traditionally brewed vinegar is a rice precipitate which, if disturbed, causes the vinegar to look cloudy. High-quality brown rice vinegar has a significantly higher amino acid content than other vinegar types.

Wine Vinegar: These vinegars have an enchanting fruity flavor and, compared to other vinegars, they have a medium sharpness. They are the most versatile of the vinegars and are perfect for everyday and gourmet cooking.

Wine vinegars are available in a wide range of qualities and prices. Low quality vinegars are stinging and weak-flavored and are usually created with a quick, mechanical process. Quality wine vinegars are smooth, full-bodied, well-aged masterpieces that contain about 6% acetic acid and are produced by craftsmen. They are most often sold in health and natural foods stores, at local fairs, and in gift shops. A fun project is to take a simple recipe such as a pasta dish. Divide the pasta dish in half and use a white wine and red wine vinegar to flavor each half.

Wine vinegars are perfectly at home in all types of salads. Try using them in fresh green, pasta, chicken, and shrimp salads, as well as in coleslaw and antipasto. You can use wine vinegar along with oil to sauté vegetables and meats or to make marinades for fish, poultry, mushrooms, other vegetables, and tofu. They are very effective when added to vegetable stews and soups to give them a little pep. These vinegars are essential in the preparation of mustards and vinaigrettes. Seasonings, vegetables, and fruits that bring out the bouquet of wine vinegars are garlic, tarragon, lemon, shallot, basil, raspberry, rose, and elder flowers.

The wine vinegars include white, red, sherry, and champagne.

Red Wine Vinegar: Red wine vinegar has a full-bodied, stronger flavor, compared to white wine vinegar. The finer vinegars have differing shades of pink and have a perfumed, acid flavor without being bitter. This vinegar is ideal when color is needed to enhance the dish and a stronger flavor is desired. It is the preferred vinegar for salads that contain rather bland ingredients such as iceberg lettuce. It is wonderful when cooked with red cabbage, and also improves red meat dishes, pepper sauces, and eggs.

White Wine Vinegar: These vinegars are used when a mild, delicate flavor is desired. A good white wine vinegar will have a non-bitter, aromatic, acidic flavor and be clear and colorless. Choose a white vinegar to flavor a fresh romaine lettuce salad; white meat, game, and fish dishes; and hollandaise, béarnaise, and other white sauces.

Sherry Vinegar: This brownish vinegar, that is usually produced in Spain, has a full-bodied, mellow, sherry flavor. It can be used with cold shrimp, steamed or cold artichokes, vegetable or seafood salads, sautéed fish filets, marinades, vinaigrettes, and potato salads. The finest sherry vinegars are aged for twenty-five or more years before they are bottled.

Champagne Wine Vinegar: Disappointingly, this vinegar is not made from champagne. It gets its name from the fact that it is mainly produced in the Champagne region of France. It is actually made from a dry white wine. This vinegar is similar to white wine vinegar and may be used as a replacement for any wine vinegar. Its smooth and refreshing flavor make it an excellent cooking vinegar as well as an outstanding addition to salads, marinades, etc.

Umeboshi Vinegar: Because this vinegar contains salt, it is not technically a vinegar. It is the liquid used to ferment and pickle ume plums (see the section "Ume & Umeboshi"). This pink vinegar has a luscious, almost cherry aroma and a very salty flavor with just a hint of fruity, almost citrus, tartness. It can be used in any recipe that calls for vinegar and salt. It is especially tasty used in salad dressings and on steamed vegetables and pungent greens (such as mustard and dandelion greens, collards, and kale).

NIGRO TIP

One of our favorite uses of umeboshi vinegar is to sprinkle it on popcorn. Sometime when you are about to sit down and watch a good video, first make some popcorn and evenly sprinkle umeboshi vinegar over it instead of butter and salt. Pink-splattered popcorn is a little strange to look at, so watch your movie instead, while enjoying this special treat.

Flavored Vinegars: More and more brands and varieties of herb and fruit vinegars are coming to the marketplace. These bottles of vinegar contain an assortment of herbs and/or fruits that dresses them up beautifully for any table. Herbs and fruits add flavor to the vinegars and create a bit of variety. Although these vinegars can be purchased as a specialty item, they are usually quite expensive. It is far cheaper to make your own—and you can choose the exact flavorings and strengths as well. These vinegars are made by steeping fresh herbs and/or fruits in a base vinegar, usually an apple cider, wine, or brown rice vinegar. Herb and/or fruit extracts are often added as well to produce a superior product. These vinegars can be used in many of the same recipes as the other vinegars.

Herb Flavored Vinegar: These vinegars are particularly good when used with salads, sweet and sour sauces, marinades, mayonnaise, vinaigrettes, and drinks. For example, mint vinegar can be used to add a nice twist to a fruit punch.

Fruit Flavored Vinegar: The addition of fruit and fruit extracts to cider or wine vinegars make wonderful combinations. There are raspberry, strawberry, blueberry, peach, and cherry vinegars appearing on store shelves. Their unique flavors can combine with complementary ingredients or dishes to make new taste delights. Think of using a lemon vinegar with crab or clams, cherry vinegar sprinkled over cold artichokes or wild game, raspberry vinegar as a topping for baked apples or pears, or a cranberry vinegar cooked with fresh cranberries to produce a relish.

FLAVOR/TEXTURE

Vinegars range in flavor depending on their types (see the "Varieties" subsection). Many vinegars have a sharp edge to them; however, the finer ones often impart a sweet, mellow flavor.

Try a taste testing approach to establish the quality and flavors of vinegar that are best for your kitchen. Select a range of vinegars, from cheap to mega-expensive. Start your tasting with the cheapest brand and work your way to the most expensive.

Eat a cracker between each tasting and allow enough time for your taste buds to "reset." You could throw an exciting vinegar tasting party!

GENERAL USES

Most vinegars are an excellent pickling medium. Place fresh vegetables in a jar filled with vinegar and enjoy the crunchy delicious pickles for weeks. Vinegars are used to preserve mackerel or herring and are used in the preparation of chutneys, relishes, and mustards.

Vinegars add a zest and their unique flavor to salads, sauces, appetizers, pickles, meat, vegetables, fruits, etc. Some of the vinegars also add a dash of color to bring an eye-catching appeal to a dish.

A cold, crisp vegetable salad can be created by tossing sliced or diced vegetables (such as carrots, rutabagas, turnips, mushrooms, broccoli, and any other vegetables hanging out in your refrigerator) with a sauce made of shoyu soy sauce, water, vinegar (flavor and type of your choice), and honey (or alternate sweetener). Garnish with grated ginger root, roasted sesame seeds, or ground roasted nuts (such as pistachio nuts, walnuts, or pecans). Chill for several hours before serving to allow the vinegar marinade to do its work of crisping and coating.

Often vinegar is used with oils to make dressings, dips, and sauces. If the addition of fat is undesirable, choose a high quality vinegar and eliminate the fat altogether. Or try using fresh lemon juice as a delicious alternate for the oil.

An incredibly versatile vinaigrette can be made by combining a vinegar (any of the types) with oil (any unrefined variety), spices (black pepper, salt, garlic, basil, etc.), and other condiments (such as mustards, miso, tahini, honey, etc.).

FRESHNESS/QUALITY

The quality of a vinegar depends on the ingredient that it was made with. See the "Varieties" subsection for quality information for each vinegar type.

Aged vinegar is one of the signs of quality. Check the labels for "Made by the Orleans Process," or "Aged in Wood."

Also look for the percentage of acid. A rule of thumb to follow is that quality vinegars generally have an acidity level of 6 to 8%. The lower qualities usually have a lower level of acidity such as 4 or 5%. Distilled vinegar is an exception—it has a 12% acidity level but is not considered a quality vinegar.

STORAGE

Vinegars should be stored in dark containers in the refrigerator or other cool, dark place.

PREPARATION INSTRUCTIONS

COOKING

Vinegars do not require any cooking. Sprinkling a vinegar right out of the bottle and onto a dish is all that is necessary to add a special zip and peppiness. Cooking has a tendency to moderate the effect to some degree.

MAKING VINEGARS

Making a vinegar from scratch can be fun and rewarding. However, some vinegars, such as balsamic, must age for years in a series of barrels and are better left to the professional craftsman.

Homemade vinegar is typically made from a good quality wine or cider (that is not fortified with anything and has no preservatives) and a substance called a "mother." The mother is used to get the fermenting process off to a flying start. The vinegar making process is much easier if you've got an aging-barrel with a spigot at the bottom and a small hole in the top; however, it can be accomplished with a crock, dark glass jar, or almost any clean wooden container. Fill the container 3/4 full with the wine or cider, carefully place the mother on top, and "seal" with a paper stopper or cheesecloth to allow air to pass through. Leave the container at approximately 65°F for a minimum of one month and a maximum of two. When the vinegar has finished fermenting, remove the mother (being sure to save it for the next batch), extract your vinegar, and refrigerate it.

If you can't obtain a mother for your vinegar, you can make your own. Use a wine or cider vinegar and mix it in equal proportions with wine or cider and let the mixture sit in the vinegar-making container. It will take about three to four months for the mother to form on the surface. Once formed, this mother should remain on the surface and not be mixed with the rest of the fermenting liquid. This liquid should be allowed to ferment for an additional month or two.

Herb and fruit vinegars can be easily and inexpensively made by using any homemade or fine commercial vinegars for the base. For an herb vinegar, simply add fresh herb sprigs to the vinegar and seal. Store for 2 to 3 weeks before using. If you are in a bit of a hurry for your herb vinegar, first grind the herbs in a pepper mill or coffee grinder or just crumple them a bit in your hands. Place them in a canning jar and pour boiling vinegar over the herbs. Let the vinegar steep at room temperature and check its flavor every few hours to determine when it has reached the desired state. Once it is finished, strain the vinegar and bottle it with sprigs of the same type of herb used to make it.

Fruit vinegars take a little more effort but are worth it. Combine equal amounts of fresh fruit and vinegar with 2 tablespoons of sweetener (per 3 cups of vinegar used) in the top of a double boiler. Heat the mixture uncovered for 10 minutes. Place it in canning jars, seal, and store it  for 3 weeks. Strain the vinegar mixture through cheesecloth and press the pulp to remove all the juice from the fruit. If the vinegar is too cloudy, just pour it through a coffee filter. This should do the trick. Bottle with a few pieces of the fresh fruit for decoration. A fast and sneaky way to make a fruit vinegar is to purchase a good quality fruit syrup or spread. Add a little to a base vinegar and you will have an instant fruit vinegar. However, this

quick vinegar will suffer somewhat in flavor over the fresh homemade variety.

For more detailed information about making homemade vinegars, consult Kathy Gunst's book *Condiments* or Vikki Leng's *Earthly Delights*.

HEALTH INFORMATION

Vinegars are very low in calories (approximately 2 per tablespoon), almost all of which are carbohydrates. Naturally-fermented vinegars contain amino acids, small amounts of other nutrients, and no fat or cholesterol. Umeboshi, rice, and cider vinegars are known as folk remedies. They aid in the digestion of rich and heavy foods that are high in saturated fats.

ADDITIONAL READING

Gunst, Kathy. *Condiments.*

Leng, Vikki. *Earthly Delights.*

BUYING SOURCES

Many manufacturers, types, and lines of vinegars are available on the shelves of supermarkets, specialty and health food stores, and gift and import shops, as well as warehouse stores. There is a wide range of qualities to choose from that will fit your tastes and pocketbook.

Vinegars are available through the Mountain Ark Trading Company, Clear Eye Natural Foods, Gold Mine Natural Foods, Anzen Oriental Foods & Imports, Dean & Deluca, Granum Incorporated, Harvest Time Natural Foods, and Natural Lifestyles mail order companies.

The mother of vinegar can be purchased at local shops that sell wine and beer-making supplies. Red, white, and malt mothers are generally available. Vinegar mother is also available through mail order companies that carry wine and beer making supplies such as E.C. Kraus.

BRAND NAMES

Because there are so many vinegar producers, it is likely that neighboring stores will carry altogether different brands. Try as many as you can to determine your favorites. Some good ones are Walnut Acres *Apple Cider Vinegar,* Erewhon *Sweet Brown Rice Vinegar,* Emperor's Kitchen (brown rice and umeboshi vinegars), *Marukan Seasoned Gourmet Rice Vinegar*, Mitsukan *Rice Vinegar*, Soken *Rice Vinegar (Fujiso)*, Spectrum *Organic Raw Unfiltered Apple Cider Vinegar*, Eden Foods (red wine, brown rice, apple cider, and umeboshi plum vinegars), Ohsawa® (organic umeboshi and Kyushu brown rice vinegars), and Colavita *Balsamic Vinegar*.

WAKAME

(wah KAH may)

The sea vegetable called wakame is a fantastic flavor enhancer for land vegetables. The texture of this nutrient-rich ingredient is delicate and blends well with tender vegetables.

When dried, wakame can sometimes be confused with kombu; however, when rehydrated they are markedly different. Kombu will remain a thick wide brown strip, while wakame will unfurl into a delicate green leaf attached to a firmer, thicker midrib section.

OTHER NAMES
Alaria.

FLAVOR
Wakame has a mild and light flavor.

GENERAL USES
Wakame is used as an addition to vegetable, bean, grain, fish, and meat dishes; as a stock generator; as a softening or tenderizing agent; as a condiment; or as a stand-alone side dish.

One of the most important aspects of wakame is that it enhances the natural sweetness of the ingredients it is cooked with. It contains glutamic acid, a natural flavor-enhancer and tenderizer (a natural alternative to chemically processed MSG).

Similar to kombu but more delicate, wakame is an ingredient in miso soup, as well as many other soups, and is delicious when used in salads and vegetable or grain dishes. It combines well with land vegetables and is especially good cooked with onions or served with boiled or steamed leafy green vegetables.

Wakame can be used to make frozen vegetables taste better than you ever thought they could. Soak some wakame, cut it up into bite-sized pieces, and throw them in with your frozen veggies. Instead of plain water, use the wakame soaking water and cook your frozen veggies as usual. You won't believe how much better they taste! If you use a package of mixed vegetables, the flavor and texture of each individual vegetable is revitalized (the corn tastes more like corn, the peas taste more like peas, etc.—they don't all mush together and taste the same). Everything tastes fresher and more vibrant, almost like it might have come directly out of a garden. Even more impressive, however, is that wakame also makes the dish blend harmoniously. Although the flavor of each vegetable is enhanced and strengthened, they all seem to belong together somehow.

Wakame makes an excellent soup stock for vegetable stews, split pea soup, miso soup, minestrone, French onion, or any other non-cream-based soup.

Like kombu, wakame has the property of softening the tough fibers of certain foods such as difficult-to-digest beans. This can also help with the flatulence problem often associated with the consumption of beans. See the "Beans" section for more information.

Lightly baked in an oven and crumbled into a powder, wakame produces a tasty, mineral-rich condiment to place on brown rice, cereal, vegetable, bean, fish, chicken, turkey, and red-meat dishes.

For a stand-alone vegetable dish, soak wakame and serve with a cucumber or citrus fruit topped with a vinegar-based dressing to make a delightful salad.

FRESHNESS/QUALITY
A higher grade "leaf" wakame contains less midrib than a lower grade "stem" wakame. The midrib is thicker and tougher than the "leaf" portions.

STORAGE

See "Sea Vegetables (Dried)."

PREPARATION INSTRUCTIONS

WASHING & SOAKING

Dried wakame is quickly restored to its original tenderness and bright green color by a brief washing and then soaking for 5 to 30 minutes. Note that wakame that has been ground into a condiment should not be washed.

COOKING

Wakame is naturally oily and is usually cooked without oil. Instead, it is eaten raw, boiled, or dry roasted.

After washing and soaking, slice the "leaves" carefully into 1-inch pieces and make sure that the tough, thicker midrib is sliced small and cooked well. For a delicate dish, any midrib present can be removed by carefully cutting it out after soaking. To use wakame in a salad, wash, soak and use it uncooked or dipped briefly in boiling water. It also makes an excellent soup stock when placed in boiling water and then simmered for just 3 to 5 minutes.

A 2.1 ounce portion of dried wakame will make around 3 cups when cooked.

To make a wakame condiment, roast the wakame in a 375°F oven for a few minutes and grind it into a fine powder (in a blender, suribachi, or spice/coffee grinder). To add a new dimension to the "seasoning," add dry roasted pumpkin, sesame, or sunflower seeds to the wakame before grinding it.

HEALTH INFORMATION

Wakame contains few calories, making it an excellent food for dieters. Polysaccharides, the main components in wakame, absorb salt and eliminate it from the system, as well as inhibiting cholesterol and sugar absorption.

This sea vegetable is an important source of calcium, thiamine, and niacin. It also contains other B group vitamins (including B_{12}) and vitamin C.

See "Sea Vegetables (Dried)" for a nutritional composition comparison of the sea vegetables.

ADDITIONAL READING

See "Sea Vegetables (Dried)."

BUYING SOURCES

Wakame is found in natural and health food stores as well as some Oriental and Japanese ethnic markets. For a list of mail order sources, see "Sea Vegetables (Dried)."

BRAND NAMES

Eden *Wakame* and *Wakame Flakes* as well as Emerald Cove *Wakame* are good brands of this sea vegetable.

WASABI

(wah SAH bee)

Wasabi is "hot stuff" that will bring tears to your eyes. It is similar to horseradish in that they both give quite a kick to the foods they are added to. However, wasabi is a little less sharp and more fragrant than horseradish. It is easy to tell them apart because wasabi is green in color.

VARIETIES

Fresh wasabi is hard to find, but powder and paste forms are readily available.

OTHER NAMES

Japanese horseradish.

FLAVOR/TEXTURE

Wasabi has quite a strong, spicy flavor with a definite fiery "bite" or kick that affects the sinuses.

GENERAL USES

Wasabi root is a favorite condiment used in sushi bars. It is supposed to aid in the digestion of the raw fish used in the preparation of sashimi and sushi, as well as cooked red-fleshed or oily fish like salmon and tuna. For an additional aid to digestion and flavor, toss in a little fresh grated ginger root.

If you enjoy the adventure of eating hot foods, play around with wasabi to create your favorite blistering concoctions. Wasabi can be used to jazz up the broth for soups and noodles. Experiment carefully with it in your chili or tamale dishes. Add a bit of scorching flavor to vegetable and chip dips, pâtés, salsas, salad dressings, or sandwich spreads.

If you do not enjoy hot, spicy foods, you may choose to avoid wasabi or use it in very small amounts. In any event, use it sparingly if you are using it for the first time. Adjust the amount used to meet the degree of fire you desire.

FRESHNESS/QUALITY

Check the label for genuine wasabi root powder or paste. If the color of the wasabi is a bright green instead of a greenish-gray, chances are it is not pure wasabi. Some brands are made with powdered daikon or horseradish with artificial green coloring added.

Sometimes fresh wasabi can be found in Asian markets. Look for the plump, unshriveled, non-sprouting roots.

STORAGE

Powdered wasabi is available in convenient small round tins or foil packages. It keeps almost indefinitely if stored in a cool, dry place. The paste comes in a tube and must be refrigerated once it is opened. Fresh wasabi root should be refrigerated after wrapping it in a damp paper towel and sealing it in a plastic bag. This will keep it moist; and, it should be used within 3 or 4 days.

PREPARATION INSTRUCTIONS

Once grated, fresh wasabi root flavor and digestive enzymes quickly dissipate, so grate just prior to use.

Powdered and paste wasabi are a suitable substitute for fresh wasabi root. To prepare powdered wasabi, add enough lukewarm water to a tablespoon of powder to make a paste with a smooth mustard-like consistency. Cover the paste and let it sit for about ten minutes to allow the flavor to flower and mature. Conveniently, the paste also comes in tubes all ready to use, and no additional mixing or preparation is necessary.

ADDITIONAL READING

Books that discuss traditional Japanese cooking methods, ingredients, and recipes often include information about wasabi. A couple of examples are:

Tsugi, Shizuo. *Japanese Cooking: A Simple Art.*

Yamaoka, Masako. *A First Book of Japanese Cooking.*

BUYING SOURCES

Powdered wasabi is packaged in small tins or small plastic lined foil envelopes. Wasabi paste is generally packaged in squeeze tubes. They are both available on the shelves of some Oriental or Asian markets, natural and health food stores, specialty markets, and supermarkets. This ingredient is obtainable through the Anzen Oriental Foods & Imports, Gold Mine Natural Foods, Harvest Time Natural Foods, and Natural Lifestyle mail order companies.

BRAND NAMES

A couple of good brands of wasabi are Mitoku *Japanese Horseradish* and Kaiseki *Wasabi Powder.*

WHEAT

Introducing wheat to you is like introducing you to your right hand. Wheat is cooked in just about every kitchen, and eaten by just about everyone. Even fast food restaurants serve a form of wheat in their fine cuisine.

Wheat grains are oval in shape; however, this is not the most common form of wheat that we know. Flour, a refined wheat product, is the most widely used form of wheat.

VARIETIES

Thousands of wheat varieties exist, but only two basic types, hard and soft, are used for people food. These types can be grown in different seasons to produce slightly different results. Furthermore, these types have differing amounts of gluten, also called wheat protein. This is the substance that causes doughs made from wheat flour (as well as kamut and spelt flours) to rise.

WHEAT TYPE CATEGORIES

Hard Wheat: Not only is hard wheat harder, it also contains a higher amount of gluten than the other wheat types. Thus, hard wheat is perfect for making the light, fluffy breads that we have come to enjoy so much. Hard wheat can be grown in either of the growing seasons to produce a winter or spring hard wheat. Hard wheat berries take longer to cook than soft wheat berries.

Durum Wheat: This type of hard wheat is used primarily to make a flour (called semolina) that is used for making noodles and macaroni products. Because of the starch in the flour, the pasta made from durum wheat holds up well when cooked in rapidly boiling water. Durum wheat can produce another up-and-coming product known as couscous, see "Couscous" later in this section.

Soft Wheat: Soft wheat is less hard and contains less gluten and more carbohydrates than hard wheat. This simply means that the flour made from soft wheat is absolutely the perfect choice for making pastries, cakes, cookies, and breakfast foods and is not very good for making leavened breads or seitan. The cooked berries have a softer texture which is better when a chewy berry is not appropriate. This wheat is also available in the spring and winter varieties.

GROWING SEASON CATEGORIES

Winter wheat and spring wheat (sometimes called summer wheat), produce different grains because they are grown for different lengths of time and at different times of the year.

Spring Wheat: This wheat is the faster growing wheat which is grown in areas where the winters are severe. It is sown in the spring and harvested in the fall. This wheat generally contains a higher amount of protein than winter wheat. Spring wheat kernels have a tendency to be short, stubby, and thick.

Winter Wheat: Winter wheat is grown where the winters are milder. The seeds are sown in the fall where they germinate and then become dormant through the winter while waiting for spring when they will continue their growth. Winter wheat is harvested in the late spring or early summer. This growing method and longer growing period produces a plant with a greater root system causing the wheat to contain more minerals than spring wheat. Winter wheat kernels are generally longer, and somewhat thinner than spring wheat kernels.

COLOR CATEGORIES

Strains of wheat are generally categorized by color as white or red. Grains that are white to golden in hue are classified as "white" and those that are different shades of brown and reddish-brown are tagged with the "red" label.

White Wheat: This color wheat is typically a soft wheat and is available in spring and winter varieties. It is low in gluten and high in starch. It lacks pigment which is convenient when a light flour is desired. To make a white flour from white wheat, no bleaching is required.

Red Wheat: Red wheat may be either hard or soft and is also available in spring and winter varieties. Unbleached flours made from red wheat will be much darker than those made from white wheat berries. To counteract this, many of red wheat flours are bleached.

WHEAT PRODUCTS

To get a description of grain hull, bran, endosperm, germ, and grain milled and processed products, consult the "Grains" section of this book. Many of the descriptions of the following wheat products make use of these terms.

Wheat Berries: Wheat berries are also known as whole wheat grain or wheat groats. All of these names refer to the whole grain wheat kernel. Only the inedible outer hull has been removed. If a hearty substance and chewy texture is needed for a dish, try using wheat berries. They can be used as an accent in pilafs and can be added to a rice dish to create something different. Use wheat berries to beef up a soup or casserole or to make a side dish that will help the main dish go a long way. Wheat berries can take a bit of time to cook, so soaking overnight or during your work day will help cut down the cooking time.

Cracked Wheat: Cracked wheat is just that—wheat kernels that have been cracked into coarse, medium, or fine pieces. The beauty of cracked wheat is that it cooks far more quickly than wheat berries and has all of the original nutrients of the kernel because it still contains the bran and germ. Obviously, the cracking changes the texture of the grain so that it will not produce the same results as wheat berries. Cracked wheat is suited for breakfast cereals and side dishes.

If cracked wheat is not available, try cracking some wheat berries in your kitchen. Place the berries in a blender and give it a whirl until the berries are coarsely ground. Watch it though—too much blending can produce a flour. Even coarse grinding the wheat berries will produce some flour. This can't be helped, but is easily fixed by sifting the contents of the blender. Whatever remains in the sifting container is your cracked grain and what went through is fresh wheat flour ready to use in making baked goods.

Cracked wheat is often mistaken for another wheat product known as bulgur. Often recipes will indicate that these two products can be used interchangeably. This is only advisable if the cooking methods and times are properly adjusted. See "Bulgur" later in this subsection.

Farina: This is actually a very fine cracked wheat-like product; however, it is often made from refined wheat, which is missing the bran and germ, rather than from whole wheat berries. If you want the added nutrition of wheat bran and germ, check to be sure the farina you are using is made from whole grains. Farina (pronounced f*uh REE nuh*) makes an especially hearty breakfast cereal for those extra cold winter mornings.

Rolled Wheat and Wheat Flakes: This wheat product is made from wheat berries that have been squashed between heavy rollers. Rolled wheat can act as an impostor for rolled oats. They look similar but are a little larger and thicker than the

oats. They can be used in a similar manner as rolled oats but produce a slightly different result. Rolled wheat is not as creamy or soft as oat flakes and they have a little stronger, earthy flavor.

Wheat Flour: This product is what has put wheat on the map. Almost all of the flour eaten in this country is made from wheat. Most commonly, the wheat is milled to separate the endosperm from the bran and germ and the endosperm is ground into different finesses to generate flour. Naturally, there are other processes for making flour that provide products that contain the germ and bran.

Flours that are good for baking purposes are typically ground from hard red spring wheat or hard red winter wheat. For pastry purposes, soft red winter wheat or white wheats are generally milled into flours.

There are hundreds of varieties of wheat flour. The major types are listed below:

Graham Flour: This is a coarse flour made from whole wheat berries; thus, it contains bran and germ. This flour is a real whole wheat flour because it still contains all of the wheat parts. The storage life of this flour is shorter than most of the other types because as soon as it has been ground, the oil from the germ starts to oxidize, which leads to rancidity. Graham flour should be stored in the refrigerator and used within a month or so of milling. If the flour has a bitter taste, it is probably rancid and should be discarded.

Whole Wheat Flour: Whole wheat flour is almost whole. It is made from whole hard wheat kernels that have had some or all of their germ removed to extend the shelf life of the flour. For those flours that have some germ in them, refrigeration is necessary. Germless flours can be stored any place that is cool and dry.

Whole Wheat Pastry Flour: This flour is made from whole soft wheat kernels. This flour is low in gluten which makes it unsuitable for baking breads but wonderful for pastries, pie crusts, cookies, cakes, and other baked goodies. It should be stored in the refrigerator, like whole wheat and graham flour.

Enriched Flour: Enriching flours simply means adding back some of the nutrients that were removed during milling and possibly adding additional preservatives, vitamins, and minerals.

Unbleached Wheat Flour: This flour is made from the endosperm of wheat kernels. It is often used instead of whole wheat flour when a lighter product is desired. However, it does not contain as high a nutritional profile as whole wheat flour.

Bleached Flour: This flour is made from unbleached flour that has been bleached. The bleaching process further refines the grain and destroys vitamin E, reducing the nutritional value of the flour.

Bread Flour: This flour is usually unbleached and made from wheat that is high in gluten or protein and can be used, as indicated by its name, to bake bread as well as other baked goods.

Cake Flour: This is the name commonly given to a bleached, white pastry flour.

All-Purpose Flour: Balancing between the two extremes of bread flours and pastry flours, all-purpose flours are a combination of high and low gluten flours that are made from the endosperm of wheat kernels. With a little help, they can be used as a bread flour or a pastry flour. All-purpose flour can be used as a bread flour if a little gluten flour (or vital wheat gluten, see its discussion later in this section) is added; and it can be used as a pastry flour if it is sifted several times before

measuring. All-purpose flour can be bleached or unbleached.

Self-Rising Flour: This flour has had baking powder (or some other leavening agent) and salt added. It can be sold as an all-purpose or cake flour. To make your own self-rising flour, add 1/2 teaspoon salt and 1/2 teaspoon of baking powder to each cup of flour.

Semolina Flour: This flour is made from durum wheat and is used to make pasta and macaroni products. It is pronounced *seh muh LEE nuh.*

Panocha: This type of flour is made from grinding sprouted wheat. The sprouting process changes the carbohydrates in the wheat into simple sugars. This makes panocha's flavor sweeter than that of the other flours. It is often used to make various traditional holiday Mexican baked goods. It may be available in Southwest, Hispanic, or Latin markets. Panocha is pronounced *pah NEW choh.*

Wheat Germ: This is the embryo of the wheat seed. It is only around 3% of the whole wheat kernel but contains the highest concentration of nutrients. Wheat germ can be sprinkled on hot and cold cereal, yogurt, and added to grain dishes, sauces, stews, and baked goods to increase their nutritional value.

Wheat Bran: This consists of the insoluble fiber-rich outer layers of the wheat berry. It is very fibrous and resists digestion making it perfect for adding bulk to a diet, which is especially helpful if the diet mainly consists of refined grain products. Wheat bran is also rich in nutrients and contains niacin, pyridoxine, pantothenic acid, riboflavin, thiamin, and protein. It can be used in much the same way as wheat germ.

Bulgur: Bulgur is made from branless hard red or soft white wheat kernels that are partially cooked and then cracked. Despite being a deeper golden color, bulgur looks very similar to cracked wheat. If bulgur is being used as substitute for cracked grain, the cooking time should be dramatically reduced. In fact, bulgur may be cooked just by steeping in water or flavored liquids, or just by steaming. Compared to cracked wheat, bulgur has a more toasty flavor. Indian and Pakistani stores may carry more than one fineness of grind for bulgur.

Couscous: Couscous is typically made from refined durum wheat, using only the endosperm, which is steamed, dried, and cracked. It comes in fine, medium, and coarse grinds, but is most commonly available in a medium grind. It has a pleasant light texture and a pasta-like flavor, but its nutritional benefits are not much greater than those of refined pasta. For a more nutritious product, you may be able to find whole wheat or even whole millet couscous. In the steamer, couscous cooks up light and fluffy in just a few minutes. Use couscous in place of rice, mixed with vegetables, and in salads.

Vital Wheat Gluten: This is also called instant gluten flour and is wheat flour that has the starch and bran removed. See "Seitan" for information on using vital wheat gluten to make seitan. Vital wheat gluten is also useful for adding to bread doughs to help them rise.

Seitan: This is a high-protein meat substitute made of gluten (wheat protein). It can have a chewy consistency somewhere between a sponge and a rubber band or a tough, bread-like or meat-like texture. The flavor of seitan is totally dependent upon the spices and flavorings used to flavor the wheat gluten which itself is quite bland. See "Seitan" for additional information.

FLAVOR/TEXTURE

The flavor and texture of wheat and wheat products depends greatly on the type of wheat and the processing that it has gone through. See the prior discussion in the "Varieties" subsection.

GENERAL USES

There is a form of wheat for each meal of the day. Rolled wheat and farina make excellent breakfast cereals. Wheat berries can be substituted for rice and used in stuffings and pilafs. Bulgur, cracked wheat, and couscous make

wonderful side dishes, stuffings, desserts, pilafs, and breakfast dishes.

A scrumptious main entrée can be made by combining cooked whole wheat berries, sautéed shallots, garlic, and exotic mushrooms (try morels, chanterelles, and crimini), thyme, Madeira wine, salt, black pepper, and vegetable stock, and cooking until all the liquid has been absorbed by the berries. Then stir in some sliced almonds that have been roasted in butter.

A hearty bell pepper stuffing can be put together by combining sautéed onions, celery, and mushrooms with cooked cracked wheat, puréed beans (try pintos for a dark bean or navy beans for a lighter color; however, any bean type will do), hearty vegetable or meat stock, basil, and a little salt and pepper.

A healthy dessert can be made by cooking couscous in apple juice along with fresh apple pieces, raisins, cinnamon, and a little rice syrup (or other sweetener—see "Sweeteners").

A very tasty bulgur pilaf can be created by combining mushrooms, onion, celery, parsley, toasted pumpkin seeds, sesame oil, and a little tamari soy sauce with the bulgur and water and cooking until all the liquid has been absorbed and the bulgur is light and fluffy.

Wheat berries are also sprouted and used in baking bread. See "Sprouts."

Wheat flour is used in so many things, it is impossible to list them all, but we'll list a few: breads, muffins, cakes, cookies, tarts, pastries, tortillas, chapati breads, noodles, pasta, pie crusts, pancakes, waffles, bagels, rolls, biscuits, etc. It can also be used to thicken sauces, gravies, and Yorkshire puddings. See "Thickening Agents" for more information.

FRESHNESS/QUALITY

See "Grains."

STORAGE

Whole wheat berries will keep for about six to nine months. Wheat germ should be stored in the refrigerator for up to three months or in your freezer for six to nine months. See "Grains" for more storage information.

PREPARATION INSTRUCTIONS

CLEANING
Wheat berries and cracked wheat may be washed, if you choose to do so. See "Grains" for washing instructions.

SOAKING
Wheat berries and cracked wheat may also be soaked to shorten their cooking time. See "Grains" for additional information about soaking grains.

COOKING
Wheat can be cooked using any of the methods discussed in "Grains." The "Wheat Cooking Table" gives the amount of water per cup of wheat and an approximate cooking time for each wheat type.

WHEAT COOKING TABLE

	Liquid (cups)	Time (min.)
Berries	3 - 3 1/2	60 - 90
Cracked	2 - 2 1/2	25 - 35
Farina	2 - 2 1/2	5 - 15
Rolled or Flakes	3 - 3 1/2	30 - 40
Couscous	2 - 2 1/2	15 - 25
Bulgur	1 1/2 - 2	10 - 20

HEALTH INFORMATION
Wheat berries contain protein, carbohydrates, both soluble and insoluble fiber, vitamins, and minerals. It is a good source of vitamin E, the B-complex vitamins, essential fatty acids, magnesium, iron, manganese, phosphorus, copper, and zinc.

ADDITIONAL READING
See "Grains."

BUYING SOURCES
Unbleached white, bleached white, and all-purpose flours are generally available at your local supermarket. Wheat berries, whole grain flours, and other wheat products are available at natural and health food stores as well as through mail order sources. See "Grains" for a list of mail order sources and brand names.

GLOSSARY

The terms described in this glossary have been chosen for two reasons: 1) to explain words used in this book, and 2) to explain words commonly used, but not often defined, in cookbooks.

à la king– Served with a cream sauce.

additive– A chemical substance which is added to foods, such as a preservative, or flavor or nutrition enhancer.

agar– *(AY gar) or (AH gar)* A jelling and thickening agent made from sea vegetables that can be used instead of gelatin. See the "Agar" section.

al dente– *(al DEN tee) or (al DEN tay)* Firm to the bite; not mushy or soft. Generally used when referring to vegetables or pasta.

antioxidant– Substances that help prevent food from becoming discolored or rancid. Vitamins C and E are examples.

antipasto– *(an tee PAHS toe)* In Italy, the antipasto is the course before the pasta. Typically, it is considered as an appetizer or hor d'oeuvres and can be either hot or cold and can consist of cheese, prosciutto, salami, sausage, ham, smoked meat, olives, fish, marinated vegetables, eggs, etc.

arame– *(AIR ah may) or (AH rah may)* An edible, thin, black, mild-flavored sea vegetable. See the "Sea Vegetables (Dried)" or the "Arame" section.

arrowroot– A soft, fine, white powder that is used as a thickener, similar to cornstarch. See the "Arrowroot" section.

aseptic box– *(ah SEP tick) or (ay SEP tick)* The packaging method that protects foods from harmful microorganisms and allows non-refrigerated storage.

aspic– *(ASS pick)* A chilled, molded dish containing a jellied stock or juice that suspends meat, fish, vegetables, or fruit.

baklava– *(BOCK lah vah)* A sweet dessert made from phyllo dough (tissue-thin layered pastry dough), butter, chopped nuts, sugar, and spices. It is usually cut into diamond or triangular shapes and garnished with ground nuts.

balsamic vinegar– *(ball SAH mick)(VIN eh gar)* Red-brown, dark colored; mellow, subtle, and pungent flavored, this Italian vinegar is made from grapes and aged in barrels.

barbecue– *(BAR bih que)* Roasting, broiling, or grilling foods over hot dry heat from charcoal or hardwood coals. Often the foods are coated with a seasoned or spicy sauce.

barley malt syrup– Liquid grain sweetener made from sprouted barely. See the "Sweeteners" or "Barley Malt Syrup" section.

basmati rice– *(boss MAH tee)* An Indian, aromatic, long-grain rice that has a delicate and nutty flavor. See the "Rice" section.

béarnaise sauce– *(behr NAZE)* A sauce normally served with broiled meat or fish, which is made from egg yolks, vinegar, and butter. Chervil, tarragon, thyme, bay leaf, salt, and pepper are some spices that can also be added to the sauce.

blacken– To cook meat, fish, or vegetables over a high direct heat until the outer layer is black.

blanch– Scalding raw foods by placing them in boiling water for a short period of time, then plunging them into cold water to stop the cooking. This process is used to maintain color, purify, remove salt, loosen peels of vegetables, and loosen the shells of nuts and seeds.

braise– *(braze)* To cook vegetables or meats by browning them in fat or oil and then simmering them in a small amount of liquid.

bran– The fiber-rich, outer layers of grains that is often removed during milling. See the "Grains" section.

broil– To cook by direct, radiant heat from either above or below. More often, the heat source is from above.

broth– A liquid in which flavorful ingredients such as meat, fish, vegetables, grains, or herbs, have been boiled.

brown rice vinegar– Vinegar made from brown rice that is light in flavor and tartness. See the "Vinegar" section.

brown rice– Short and long rice grains that have had only their inedible, outer shell removed. See the "Rice" section.

Bundt pan– *(bunt)* Originally a trademark for a pan that has a hole in the center, rather like a doughnut, with a decorative bottom often used for cakes and molds.

burdock root– *(burr DOCK)* A long, slender vegetable with a brown skin and white fibrous flesh that has an earthy flavor. See the "Burdock Root" section.

burger– A sandwich consisting of a bun, cooked patty (of ground beef, other ground meat, beans, grains, and/or vegetables), and condiments such as mustard, ketchup, and pickle relish. Often other ingredients are added such as cheese, onion, lettuce, tomato, and sprouts.

burrito– *(ber EE toe)* A Mexican dish consisting of a flour tortilla wrapped around meat, rice, beans, vegetables, and/or cheese.

button mushrooms– A type of white-colored, edible, fleshy fungus commonly found in grocery stores. See the "Mushrooms" section.

cacciatore– *(koch ah TOR ree)* A dish prepared "hunter style" with a minimum amount of ingredients that a hunter would have on hand such as meat, onions, mushrooms, tomato sauce, and spices.

cannelloni– *(can ah LOW knee)* Tubular pasta stuffed with meat or cheese and baked with a sauce.

cappuccino– *(KAH pah chee no)* Espresso coffee mixed with steamed cream or milk, often topped with whipping cream.

cashew butter– *(KASH oo)* or *(cah SHOE)* A paste-like substance made from grinding cashew nuts until they are smooth and creamy. See the "Nut and Seed Butters" section.

casserole– *(KASS eh roll)* Food or dish which is served in the container (earthenware, cast iron, or glass) it was baked in.

cereal– *(SEAR ee ill)* Grains such as wheat, oats, corn, buckwheat, and amaranth which are used for foods. Also, a breakfast food made from cereal grains.

chanterelle– *(shan teh RELL)* A golden-to-orange, trumpet-shaped, wild mushroom. See the "Mushrooms" section.

crimini– *(crih MEAN ee)* A brown mushroom that looks like, and has many characteristics of, a button mushroom. See the "Mushrooms" section.

morel– *(meh RELL)* or *(moh RELL)* A hollow, wild mushroom with a honeycomb cap. See the "Mushrooms" section.

chapati– *(chah PAH tee)* A small, flat pancake that is made of wheat flour, water, and salt and served like bread in Indian cookery.

chicken cordon bleu– *(kor dawn)(BLUE)* Chicken that has been breaded and then stuffed with ham and cheese. Often, made from boneless chicken breast.

chickpea– Also known as garbanzo bean. See the "Garbanzo Beans" section.

chili con carne– *(kon CAR knee)* Highly spicy dish made from chili powder, red peppers, ground beef or other meat, and sometimes beans.

chimichangas– *(chee mee CHAHN gah)* A deep-fried burrito, that can be filled with rice, refried beans, cheese, chicken, or meat.

chop suey– *(chop)(SOO ee)* A Chinese-American dish made from chopped, simmered or stewed vegetables such as bean sprouts, mushrooms, and bamboo shoots, and sometimes meat strips. It is typically served over rice.

chow mein– *(CHOW main)* Fried noodles. It is also, a Chinese-American dish similar to a stew with meat and vegetables served over fried noodles.

chutney– *(CHUT nee)* A pungent relish or spicy condiment made from vinegar, sugar, fruits, spices, and herbs which may range from smooth to chunky in texture.

cider vinegar– A vinegar made from apple cider. It is used mostly for pickling vegetables and making chutneys. See the "Vinegar" section.

coffee grinder– A container with rotary blades used for grinding. It can be electric or manual. Herbs and spices can also be ground in this type of grinder. It can also be called a coffee mill or spice mill.

colander– A perforated bowl-shaped container used for rinsing and draining foods. It can be made of plastic or metal.

condiment– *(KON duh ment)* A food eaten with other foods to enhance their flavor or appearance.

confectionery– *(kon FECK shun airy)* or *(kon FECK shuh nehree)* A sweet candy made from sugar.

cornmeal– Coarsely ground corn kernels. See the "Corn" section.

cornstarch– A white powder made from corn and used as a thickening agent. See the "Thickening Agents" section.

couscous– *(KOOS koos)* A North African dish in which millet, cracked wheat, or semolina is steamed using a special two-tiered steaming pot. The top part contains the grain and the bottom part contains a spicy stew typically made of meat (lamb or chicken), vegetables, garbanzo beans, and raisins.

Crock pot– Trademark name that is used to refer to an electric slow cooker.

croquette– *(crow KET)* A mass of minced meat, vegetables, or fish coated with bread crumbs and egg, formed into a cake or any other shape, that is deep fried.

crudités– *(crew dee TAY)* Seasoned raw vegetables used as appetizers, and often served with a dipping sauce such as hummus.

curry– *(KER ee)* A heavily spiced relish or sauce made with curry powder and eaten with fish, meat, rice, or other foods. Also, an Indian dish seasoned with a combination of ground spices.

custard– *(KUSS terd)* A dish consisting of milk, flavorings, and possibly, sugar that is boiled or baked with eggs and has thickened or set because of the coagulation of the egg.

daikon– *(DIE kon) or (DAH ee kon)* A white root that belongs to the radish family and looks like a giant carrot. See the "Daikon" section.

date sugar– A coarse, brown sugar made only from ground dates. See the "Sweeteners" section.

deep fry– To cook food by completely submerging it in hot fat.

deglaze– *(dee GLAZE)* To dissolve browned particles with a liquid in a sauté pan. Most often refers to creating a gravy from meat drippings.

dehydrate– A preserving method that removes sufficient moisture to prevent bacteria growth.

dextrose– *(DEX strose)* Dextrose is a simple carbohydrate. It is sometimes referred to as corn sugar. The best place to get dextrose is in grapes and raisins.

dough– *(DOE)* A meal or flour mixed with a liquid and shortening or oil, shaped, and then baked.

dry roast– To cook nuts, seeds, sea vegetables, and grains with dry heat without oil.

dulse– An edible, thick, purple sea vegetable that can be enjoyed raw. See the "Sea Vegetables (Dried)" section.

egg foo yong– Chinese-American dish of beaten eggs fried with meat and vegetables.

empanada– *(em pah NAH dah) or (em pah NAH tah)* A Mexican and Spanish dish that resembles a turnover which can either be filled with savory or sweet fillings. They range in size from as large as a pizza to as small as a ravioli.

emulsifier– *(eh MULL suh fire)* An ingredient that will allow substances to mix that normally will not naturally combine. Examples are eggs, lecithin, and xanthan gum.

enchiladas– *(en chee LAH dah)* A dish consisting of a rolled soft tortilla that is filled with meat or cheese, and baked with a tomato-based sauce.

endosperm– The nutritive, starchy mass in the center of grains. See the "Grains" section.

enrich– To add nutrients or restore nutrients that have been lost due to processing.

extract– An intense or concentrated flavoring that is produced from various foods or plants They are beneficial because they have a minimal effect on the dish's consistency while providing additional flavoring.

fajitas– *(fah HEE tah)* A Mexican dish of beef or chicken marinated in a sauce of oil, lime juice, red pepper, and garlic for at least 24 hours, then the meat is cooked and rolled in a tortilla. It is garnished with sautéed onions and peppers, sour cream, grated cheese, guacamole, and/or salsa.

fettuccine– *(fet ah CHEE nee)* Narrow, flat, egg noodles or flat strips of pasta. Also a dish made from these noodles or pasta.

fritter– Food that has been coated in a batter and deep-fried. Depending on the type of food used, they can be served as a main course, dessert, or hors d'oeuvre.

fructose– *(FRUCK tose)* or *(FROOK tose)* Fructose is a simple carbohydrate that is especially sweet in cold foods. Although, fructose is naturally occurring in fruit, commercial suppliers of fructose usually manufacture it by further refining corn syrup. Fructose is easier to break down and metabolize than sucrose (refined white sugar) and is about twice as sweet.

fry– To cook in hot oil or fat over direct heat, such as pan frying and deep-frying.

garbanzo beans– *(gar BON zoh)* A beige, round bean that has a nutty, chestnut-like flavor that is traditionally used to make hummus. Also called chickpea. See the "Garbanzo Beans" section.

garnish– *(GAR nish)* Foods that adorn, beautify, or decorate prepared dishes to enhance the dish's appearance. Lemon or orange slices, parsley, cherries, pickles, tomatoes, and lettuce are often used as garnishes.

guacamole– *(gwah kah MOW lee)* A Mexican dip, spread, or paste made from mashed avocado with vegetables and spices such as onions, chopped tomatoes, garlic, lemon juice, vinegar, cilantro, and salsa.

gelatin– *(JELL eh tin)* A colorless, odorless substance extracted from the bones and cartilage of animals and also from certain algae (agar, alginates). It is used for making jellies, aspics, and numerous desserts.

gel– A substance which has a gelatin-like texture.

germ– The embryo of a cereal grain seed or kernel. See the "Grains" section.

ginger root– Root with a strong, tangy, spicy, citrus-like flavor that is often used for seasoning in Asian cooking. See the "Ginger Root" section.

glaze– To make food shiny or glossy by coating it with thickened juices, syrup, eggs, or aspic jelly, or by browning it by placing it in a very hot oven or under a broiler.

glucose– *(GLUE kose)* A simple carbohydrate that is manufactured by your liver, which breaks down complex carbohydrates. Glucose provides the energy for all human metabolism and is sometimes called blood sugar. From a diet based on complex carbohydrates, you'll get internal energy in a strong and steady fashion.

gluten– *(GLUE tin)* A strong, elastic substance made up of plant proteins that are found in wheat, spelt, and kamut. It is used to make fluffy leavened breads and to make seitan, a protein-rich meat substitute. See the "Grains," "Wheat" and "Seitan" sections.

gomashio– *(goh MAH shee oh)* or *(goh MAH zee oh)* A condiment made from grinding roasted sesame seeds with salt. Also called sesame salt. See the "Nuts & Seeds" section.

grain– The edible seeds of annual grasses. See the "Grains" section.

granola– *(grah NO lah)* Rolled grains, often oats, mixed with dried fruit, sweeteners, nuts, and seeds that is used as a breakfast cereal or snack, or to make desserts or trail mixes.

gravy– *(GRAY vee)* A sauce made by thickening and seasoning meat juices.

grill– To cook or broil foods on a gridiron, grate, or grill over a hot source, such as coals or open flame.

grits– A ground meal of dried and hulled grain kernels used for breakfast or side dishes. See the "Grains" and "Corn" section.

grog– A sweet-sour, alcoholic drink made by mixing lemon, sugar or other sweetener, hot water, and some liquor such as rum.

gruel– *(grewel)* A thin, watery cereal made by boiling grains, meal, or flour in milk, water, or vegetable broth.

gyros– *(JEER oh)* or *(ZHEER oh)* or *(YEE roh)* A Greek dish consisting of sliced meat wrapped in pita bread and topped with a cucumber-yogurt sauce, grilled onion, and sweet peppers.

glutamic acid– A natural flavor enhancer and tenderizer.

hash– A dish that is a catch-all or a leftovers creation made of diced or finely chopped meat, vegetables, and seasonings that are lightly browned or fried together.

hollandaise sauce– *(HOL un daze)* A rich, smooth, creamy sauce made from egg yolks, lemon juice, vinegar, and butter often served over vegetables, fish, and egg dishes.

honey– A thick, viscous liquid manufactured by bees which is used as a sweetener. See the "Sweeteners" and "Honey" sections.

horseradish– A white, hot and spicy condiment made by grating the roots of the horseradish plant.

hull– The unedible, and often deemed worthless, outer covering of grains. Also called husks. See the "Grains" section.

hummus– *(HUM mus)* or *(HOOM us)* A thick paste, spread, or dip made from garbanzo beans or chickpeas and garlic, lemon juice, olive oil, and tahini.

hydrogenation– *(HIGH drah jeh nay shon)* The process of changing liquid polyunsaturated fats (such as vegetable oils) into hardened, spreadable saturated fats (such as margarine).

jell– To solidify into a gelatin, gel, or jelly.

jelly– *(JEL ee)* A soft, thick substance with resilient texture that is often made by using pectin or gelatin.

jinenjo– A wild Japanese mountain yam.

julienne– *(JEW lee in)* Foods cut into small, thin strips about 1/8 inch by 2 to 3 inches long that resemble matchsticks.

koji– *(KOH jee)* A grain starter for fermented foods that contains a special bacteria that enables soybeans, rice, etc. to ferment.

kombu– *(KOM boo)* A wide, thick, dark-green seaweed or sea vegetable used as a soup stock flavoring and used in the cooking of beans to tenderize them and make them more digestible. See the "Kombu" section.

kuzu– *(KOO zoo)* A white, flavorless, high-quality thickening agent which adds a translucent gloss to the foods it's cooked with. See the "Kuzu" section.

lactose– *(LACK tose)* Lactose is a simple carbohydrate that helps to maintain beneficial bacteria in the gastrointestinal tract and aids in the absorption of calcium. The best place to get lactose is in milk.

lasagna– *(lah ZOHN yah)* An Italian dish made by baking layers of wide, flat pasta, tomato sauce, cheese, and often meat.

leavening– *(LEH veh ning)* A substance that causes baked goods to be airy, light, and fluffy by creating gas bubbles in the baking dough. Some example leavening agents are yeast, baking powder, baking soda, and whipped egg whites.

loaf– A baked dish made from ground meat, beans, nuts, or grains and often contains other ingredients such as breadcrumbs, eggs, and seasonings. Prior to baking, it is formed into shapes similar to bread loaves.

macaroon– *(MACK ah roon)* Small, round cookies made from sugar, almond paste, egg whites, and coconut.

macrobiotic– *(mack row by OTT ick)* A theory or practice of promoting longevity, good health, and well-being by maintaining a balance in all things. In the eating aspect, this means balancing acidic and alkaline foods while also obtaining all the necessary nutrients.

maltose– *(MALL tose)* A sugar formed during the digestion of starch.

marinade– *(MARE eh nade)* A seasoned liquid mixture that meats, vegetables, tempeh, and tofu are soaked in before cooking.

marinate– *(MARE eh nate)* To soak a food in a seasoned liquid or marinade.

marzipan– *(MAR zih pan)* A candy made from almond paste, sugar, and sometimes egg whites which is often tinted or colored and formed into animal, flower, fruit, and holiday shapes.

millet– *(MILL it)* A tiny, golden, round, hulled, high-protein grain. See the "Millet" section.

mirin– *(MERE in)* A sweet, golden rice wine, with a very low alcohol content, that is used only for cooking. See the "Mirin" or "Sweeteners" section.

miso– *(MEE soh)* A thick, fermented soybean paste that ranges from delicately sweet to robustly savory. See the "Miso" section.

mochi– *(MOH chee)* A rice cake or square made from cooked sweet, short-grain, glutinous or sticky rice that has been pounded and, optionally, seasoned with sweeteners to make a dessert, or soy sauce and ginger root to make a more savory dish.

molasses– *(muh LASS iz)* A sweetener that is a by-product of the production of sugar from sugarcane. See the "Molasses" section.

mold¹– To form foods such as jello, grains, chocolates, and pâtés into shapes. Also a container that is used to form a shape.

mold²– Any of a large family of fungi that grows on foods such as bread, cheese, fruit, sweeteners, etc. They may be beneficial, neutral, or harmful.

monosaccharide– *(mon ah SACK eh ride)* A simple sugar that consists of only single bonds between carbon, hydrogen, and oxygen atoms. See the "Categories of Sugars Based on Their Chemical Structure" chart in the "Sweeteners" section.

monounsaturated fat– *(mon oh un SACH uh ray tid)* A fat that is believed to reduce the levels of "bad" LDL cholesterol. It hardens or gets very thick at low temperatures.

mortar and pestle– A heavy, and fairly deep bowl and a grinding stick used for grinding or pulverizing foods such as spices, sea vegetables, nuts, seeds, beans, grains, etc. to make condiments or pastes.

mousse– *(moose)* Any of various thick, creamy dishes, either savory or sweet, made with gelatin, whipped cream or/and beaten egg whites.

muesli– *(MUZE lee) or (MYOU slee)* Untoasted rolled grains or grain flakes (such as oats, rye, wheat, spelt, etc.), dried fruit, and nuts which is commonly used as a breakfast cereal.

non-dairy milk or beverage– A rich, white or beige, creamy mixture made from grains, seeds, or nuts that is similar in appearance to milk. See the "Non-Dairy Milks" section.

noodle– Pasta with a thin, flat, long shape. See the "Pasta" section.

nori– *(NOR ee)* An edible seaweed or sea vegetable most often sold in sheets and used to wrap around sushi. See the "Nori" and "Sea Vegetables (Dried)" sections.

nut milks– A rich, white, creamy liquid similar in appearance to milk that is formed when nuts are ground and combined with liquids. See the "Non-Dairy Milks" section.

nutritional yeast– A yellow-colored inactive yeast that has a nutty, cheese-like flavor. See the "Nutritional Yeast" section.

oligosaccharide– *(all ih go SACK eh ride)* A complex sugar that is found in foods that causes intestinal gases because some colon flora use these sugars for food and produce gases. See the "Eliminating Flatulence" subsection in "Beans."

olive oil– A greenish-colored cooking oil made from pressing olives that is high in monounsaturated fat. See the "Olive Oil" section.

pan-fry– To cook in a small amount of fat in an uncovered skillet or frying pan.

parboil– To partially cook in boiling or simmering liquid for a short time.

pâté– *(pah TAY)* A seasoned paste or spread made from meat, animal organs, or fish. Pastes or spreads made from vegetables and beans that have a similar consistency are also often called pâtés.

pearled– The process of scraping grains with an abrasive stone to remove the bran and germ, which may be necessary to ensure the removal of the husk or to produce a pearl like finish.

pesto– *(PES toe)* A fragrant pasta sauce traditionally consisting of olive oil, basil, garlic, pine nuts, and grated cheese.

pilaf– *(PEE lahf) or (PIH lahf)* A dish made of rice or other grain that has been first coated in fat (oil or butter) and then simmered in a stock or other liquid. The grain kernels are usually separate, rather than sticky. See the "Rice" section.

polenta– *(poh LIN tah)* A type of mush or porridge that is made by boiling cornmeal in water, but can be made with milk, stock, or wine.

polysaccharide– *(paul ee SACK eh ride)* A sugar that consists of several bonds between carbon, hydrogen, and oxygen atoms. When broken down, it yields multiple monosaccharides. See the "Categories of Sugars Based on Their Chemical Structure" chart in the "Sweeteners" section.

polyunsaturated fat– *(poly un SACH uh ray tid)* A "healthy" fat that has a tendency to go rancid much more quickly than monounsaturated and saturated fats. It remains liquid at low temperatures.

porridge– *(POR rij)* A grain meal cooked in water or milk until it is thick. See the "Grains" section.

pralines– *(PRAY leen) or (PRAH leen)* A brittle candy made from almond flavored carmel colored syrup which can be ground and added to desserts such as cake fillings, creams, and sweet sauces, or used as a garnish.

prosciutto– *(pro SHOE toe)* An aged and dry-cured Italian ham that is thinly sliced and served without cooking.

pudding– A sweet or savory dish that is usually boiled, baked, or steamed in a mold to produce a delicate soft texture.

purée– *(pyou RAY)* A thick, smooth dish made from mashed, strained, or blended foods.

quinoa– *(KEEN wah)* Beige, round, highly-nutritious pseudo-grain that looks similar to millet or mustard seeds. See the "Quinoa" section.

Reuben– *(REW ben)* A sandwich made with generous portions of thinly sliced, corned beef, Swiss cheese, and sauerkraut on sourdough rye bread which is then grilled.

rice milk– A rich, white, creamy liquid made from rice that is similar in appearance to milk. See the "Non-Dairy Milks" section.

rice syrup– A golden, thick liquid that is a mild sweetener made from rice and sprouted barley. See the "Rice Syrup" section.

rice vinegar– A mild vinegar made from rice. See the "Vinegar" section.

rice– An edible grain that is available in a variety of colors, shapes, sizes, textures, and flavors. See the "Rice" section.

roast– To cook foods by surrounding them with hot, dry air over a fire or in an oven.

rolled grains– Hulled grains that have been steamed and flattened by steel rollers. See the "Grains" section.

sashimi– *(sah SHEE me)* A Japanese specialty that consists of sliced raw fish which is often served with ginger root, daikon, wasabi, and soy sauce.

sake– *(SAH key)* A Japanese wine made from fermented rice. It is often served warm but it can be served cold. It is also used in cooking to add a slightly sweet, fermented flavor.

saturated fat– *(SACH uh ray tid)* A fat that is normally solid at room temperature.

sauerkraut– *(SOUR krout)* Shredded or cut cabbage, salted, and fermented in a brine made up of its own juices.

sauté– *(SAH tay)* To cook quickly in an open frying pan or skillet, using a small amount of fat until brown. For those who are attempting to reduce their fat intake, sauté is sometimes used to refer to this cooking process where water, stock, or broth is used instead of the fat.

savory[1]– *(SAY vah ree)* Appetizing to the taste or smell. Also, the flavors of salty or piquant, pungent (pleasantly sharp or biting or bitter), not sweet.

savory[2]– *(SAY vah ree)* A strong flavored herb that may be used in marinades, stuffings, mayonnaise, and breadings.

scallopine– *(skah luh PEE nee)* Very thin slices of meat sautéed in wine and herbs. Commonly veal is used.

scampi– *(SKAM pee)* Large or jumbo shrimp that are broiled or sautéed in a butter, garlic sauce.

sea salt– A natural salt extracted from sea water. See the "Salt" section.

sea vegetables– Edible seaweeds or vegetables from the sea. See the "Sea Vegetables (Dried)" section.

seitan– *(seh TAN)* A high-protein meat substitute made of gluten which can have a chewy, firm, or meat-like consistency. See the "Seitan" section.

semolina– *(sem uh LEE nah)* A coarsely ground flour made from durum wheat. See the "Wheat" section.

sesame oil– Oil obtained from sesame seeds. The darker variety, toasted sesame oil, has a stronger flavor. See the "Oils" section.

sesame salt– A condiment made from grinding roasted sesame seeds with salt. Also called gomashio. See the "Nuts & Seeds" section.

shepherd's pie– British meat and gravy pie, traditionally made from lamb or mutton, and topped with mashed potatoes then baked until the potatoes becomes a crispy and brown.

sherry– *(SHAIR ee)* A Spanish wine ranging from very dry to sweet in taste and from amber to brown in color.

shiitake mushrooms– *(shee TAH key)* or *(shee TAH kay)* A type of edible, fleshy fungus or mushroom that has a woodsy-fruit and steak-like flavor. See the "Mushrooms" section.

shish-kebabs– *(shish) (kuh BOB)* Chunks of vegetables, meat, fish, and/or fruit placed on a skewer and broiled or grilled. The food may be marinaded before cooking or basted during cooking.

shoyu– *(SHOW you)* A naturally brewed soy sauce made without preservatives that contains wheat which. See the "Soy Sauce" section.

soup– A seasoned liquid, thin or thick, to which fish, meat, vegetables, beans, grains, or any combination of them is added.

soy milk– A creamy, white mixture made from soybeans that is lactose-free. See the "Non-Dairy Milks" section.

soy sauce– A dark, salty, liquid condiment made by fermenting soybeans and wheat or barley. See the "Soy Sauce" section.

sprouts– Beans, grains, or seeds that have been germinated to produce little tender plants that are often used as vegetables. See the "Sprouts" section.

steamer– A perforated rack that fits into a pan that keeps the food above boiling water. Also, the special pot that consists of the rack and pan combination.

steam– To cook by exposing food directly to steam.

stir-fry– To cook quickly over a high heat in a large frying pan or wok.

stock generator– A food used to made a clear, unthickened, seasoned liquid. Common stock generators are vegetables, sea vegetables, meat, poultry, and fish.

stock– A clear, unthickened, seasoned liquid made from vegetables, meat, poultry, or fish, and their bones.

stroganoff– *(STROH gan off)* or *(STRAW guh noff)* A Russian dish made of sautéed, tender, beef strips cooked with a sauce made of onions, mushrooms, butter, and sour-cream.

strudel– *(STREW dull)* A German dish made by filling a paper-thin, flakey, pastry dough, with a savory or sweet mixture, then rolling and baking it until golden brown.

Sucanat®– *(SUE cah nat)* Trademark which refers to unrefined granulated sugarcane juice. See the "Sweeteners" section.

succotash– *(SUCK uh tash)* A dish consisting of corn kernels, lima beans, and sometimes tomatoes.

sucrose– *(SUE krose)* Sucrose is sugar, a simple carbohydrate. Pure sucrose acts like a chemical (rather than a food, which needs digesting) and is immediately absorbed into the bloodstream, which upsets the blood-sugar balance. Sucrose is often the sweetener used for commercial purposes because of its abundance and cheapness. A huge number of sweeteners consist mostly of sucrose: cane sugar, corn syrup, raw sugar, honey, light and dark brown sugar, blackstrap molasses, turbinado sugar, Barbados molasses, cane syrup, maple sugar, maple syrup, and sorghum molasses.

sukiyaki– *(sue key YAH key)* or *(ski YAH key)* A Japanese dish, prepared at the table, that consists of thinly sliced meat, tofu, and vegetables sautéed in soy sauce and sake or mirin.

suribachi– *(sir eh BAH chee)* A grooved earthenware mortar and a wooden pestle used for grinding, mixing, and making purées.

sushi– *(sue SHE)* Small cakes of cold, vinegar-flavored rice, wrapped in seaweed, and garnished with raw or cooked fish, vegetables, pickles, or wasabi.

sweet brown rice– A sticky, highly glutinous, short-grain rice. See the "Rice" section.

tabbouleh– *(tah BOO lee)* A Middle Eastern salad typically made of bulgur wheat, parsley, scallions, tomatoes, oil, and lemon juice.

taco– *(tah KOH)* A Mexican dish made from a folded, deep-fried corn tortilla that is filled with meat, cheese, tomatoes, and salad greens.

tahini– *(tah HE knee)* A thick paste made from ground, hulled sesame seeds. See the "Tahini" section.

tamale– *(tah MAH lee)* A Mexican dish consisting of a seasoned meat and peppers filling rolled in cornmeal, wrapped in a softened corn husk, and then steamed.

tamari– *(tah MAR ree)* A traditionally made soy sauce that is wheat-free. See the "Soy Sauce" section.

tempeh– *(TEM pay)* A soy food cake made by the natural culturing of soybeans with a mold called *Rhizopus oligosporus*. See the "Tempeh" section.

tempura– *(tem POOR uh)* or *(TEM poor uh)* A Japanese dish consisting of seafood, tofu, tempeh, or vegetables dipped in a batter and then deep-fried.

terrine– *(tuh REEN)* Earthenware baking dish used for preparation and serving — often rectangular and deep, with straight sides and a tightly fitting lid. Also a prepared food that is cooked and served a terrine dish; this may include pâtés or mixtures of chopped meat or fish, nuts, beans, and/or vegetables.

teriyaki– *(tair ee YAH key)* Thin slices of meat or fish marinated in soy sauce and spices and then broiled or fried.

tofu– *(TOE foo)* A protein-rich food made by curdling soy milk. Sometimes called bean curd due to its similarity to the cheese-making process. See the "Tofu" section.

torte– *(tohrt)* A rich, but very light, layered cake made with eggs, ground nuts, sugar, and cake or bread crumbs.

tostada– *(toh STAH duh)* or *(tose TAH dah)* A crisp-fried tortilla that is topped with different ingredients such as refried beans; diced fresh tomatoes; slivered or ground, seasoned, and cooked beef or chicken; grated cheese; guacamole; salsa; and sour cream.

trail mix– A high energy mix of grains, seeds, nuts, and dried fruit often eaten as a snack.

umeboshi plum vinegar– *(oo meh BOW shee)(plum)(VIN ih ger)* Pseudo-vinegar that is generated from the processing of umeboshi plums. It is a salty condiment which can be used similarly to vinegar. See the "Vinegar" section.

umeboshi plum– *(oo meh BOW shee)(plum)* A small pickled plum which is very salty with a sour, tangy flavor. See the "Ume & Umeboshi" section.

vegan– *(VEE gan)* A vegetarian who is considered a purist and will not eat any animal products such as meat, fish, butter, cheese, eggs, milk, and honey.

vegetarian– *(vej ih TAIR ee in)* A person who does not eat meat. Personal motives can be religious, ethical, nutritional, and/or economic. Ovolacto vegetarians will eat eggs and dairy products. Some vegetarians will eat poultry and/or fish, but no other meats.

vinaigrette– *(VIN eh gret)* A salad dressing made of vinegar, oil, lemon juice, herbs and other seasonings.

vinegar– *(VIN ih ger)* A pungent liquid made by fermenting fruit juices, grains, and wine. It is used as a condiment or preservative.

wasabi– *(wah SAH bee)* A light-green, hot, horseradish-type condiment. See the "Wasabi" section.

white wine vinegar– A mellow vinegar made from white wine. See the "Vinegar" section.

zest– The colored, outer part of the peel of citrus fruits used for flavoring.

REFERENCES

The following is a complete bibliographic list of all the books referenced by name and title in the introduction and individual sections.

Abehsera, Michel. *Zen Macrobiotic Cooking.* New York: University Books, Inc., 1968.

Aihara, Cornellia. *The Calendar Cookbook.* Oroville, Calif.: George Ohsawa Macrobiotic Foundation, 1979.

Barrett, Judith. *Pasta Verde.* New York: Macmillan, 1995.

Bates, Dorothy R. *The TVP® Cookbook.* Summertown, Tenn.: The Book Publishing Co., 1991.

Bates, Dorothy R., and Colby Wingate. *Cooking with Gluten and Seitan.* Summertown, Tenn.: The Book Publishing Co., 1991.

Batt, Eva. *Vegan Cooking.* London: Thorsons, 1985.

Belleme, John, and Jan Belleme. *Cooking with Japanese Foods.* Garden City Park, N.Y.: Avery Publishing Group, Inc., 1993.

Blazek, Mark. *Pecan Lovers' Cook Book.* Phoenix, Ariz.: Golden West Publishers, 1986.

Boulos-Guillaume, Nouhad. *A Lebanese Harvest: Traditional Vegetarian Recipes.* Reading, U.K.: Garnet Publishing Limited, 1993.

Bradford, Peter, and Montse Bradford. *Cooking with Sea Vegetables.* Rochester, Vt.: Healing Arts Press, 1988.

Brekhman, I. I., and I. F. Nesterenko. *Brown Sugar and Health.* New York: Pergamon Press, 1983.

Bumgarner, Marlene Anne. *The Book of Whole Grains.* New York: St. Martin's Press, 1976.

Burke, George, Abbot. *Simply Heavenly! The Monastery Vegetarian Cookbook.* Geneva, Nebr.: Saint George Press, 1994.

Chelf, Vicki Rae. *Arrowhead Mills Cookbook.* Garden City Park, N.Y.: Avery Publishing Group, Inc., 1993.

Cole, Candia Lea. *Gourmet Grains: Maindishes Made of Nature.* Santa Barbara, Calif.: Woodbridge Press, 1993.

Cole, Candia Lea. *Not Milk...Nut Milks!.* Santa Barbara, Calif.: Woodbridge Press, 1992.

Cost, Bruce. *Ginger East to West.* Berkeley: Aris Books, 1984.

Czarnecki, Jack. *Joe's Book of Mushroom Cookery.* New York: Atheneum Publishers, 1986.

Diamond, Marilyn. *The American Vegetarian Cookbook from the Fit For Life Kitchen.* New York: Warner Books, 1990.

Dinshah, Freya. *The Vegan Kitchen.* Malaga, N.J.: The American Vegan Society, 1991.

Downer, Lesley. *Japanese Vegetarian Cooking.* New York: Pantheon Books, 1986.

Elliot, Rose. *The Complete Vegetarian Cuisine.* New York: Pantheon Books, 1988.

Fletcher, Janet. *Grain Gastronomy: A Cook's Guide to Great Grains from Couscous to Polenta.* Berkeley: Aris Books, 1988.

Ford, Richard. *Juel Andersen's Sea Green Primer.* Berkeley: Creative Arts Book Company, 1983.

Freedman, Louise. *Wild About Mushrooms.* Berkeley: Aris Books, 1987.

Gelles, Carol. *The Complete Whole Grain Cookbook.* New York: Donald I. Fine, Inc., 1989.

Gerras, Charles, ed. *Rodale's Basic Natural Foods Cookbook.* New York: Simon & Schuster, 1989.

Gregory, Patricia. *Bean Banquets: From Boston to Bombay.* Santa Barbara, Calif.: Woodbridge Press, 1994.

Grogran, Bryanna Clark. *The (Almost) No Fat Cookbook: Everyday Vegetarian Recipes.* Summertown, Tenn.: The Book Publishing Co., 1994.

Gunst, Katy. *Condiments.* New York: GP Putnam's Sons, 1984.

Hagler, Louise. *Tofu Cookery.* rev. ed. Summertown, Tenn.: The Book Publishing Co., 1991.

Hagler, Louise. *Tofu Quick and Easy.* Summertown, Tenn.: The Book Publishing Co., 1986.

Hagler, Louise, and Dorothy R. Bates, eds. *The New Farm Vegetarian Cookbook.* Summertown, Tenn.: The Book Publishing Co., 1988.

Jacobs, Barbara, and Leonard Jacobs. *Cooking with Seitan.* New York: Japan Publications, Inc. 1986.

Keane, Maureen B., and Daniella Chace. *Grains for Better Health.* Rocklin, Calif.: Prima Publishing, 1994.

Kilham, Christopher S. *The Bread & Circus Whole Food Bible.* New York: Addison-Wesley Publishing Co., Inc., 1991.

King, Penny. *Taste & See: Allergy Relief Cooking.* Sunfield, Mich.: Family Health Publications, 1992.

Klapper, Michael, M.D. *Vegan Nutrition: Pure and Simple.* Paia, Maui, Hawaii: Gentle World, Inc., 1992.

Kushi, Aveline. *Complete Guide to Macrobiotic Cooking.* New York: Warner Books, 1985.

Landgrebe, Gary. *Tofu Goes West.* Palo Alto, Calif.: Fresh Press, 1978.

Larimore, Bertha B. *Sprouting for All Seasons.* Bountiful, Utah: Horizon Publishers, 1975.

Lemlin, Jeanne. *Vegetarian Pleasures: A Menu Cookbook.* New York: Alfred A. Knopf, Inc., 1986.

Leneman, Leah. *The Single Vegan.* London: Thorsons, 1989.

Leng, Vikki. *Earthly Delights.* New York: Thorsons, 1994.

Lewallen, Eleanor, and John Lewallen. *Sea Vegetable Gourmet Cookbook and Wildcrafter's Guide.* Mendocino, Calif.: Mendocino Sea Vegetable Co., 1995.

London, Sheryl, and Mel London. *The Versatile Grain and the Elegant Bean.* New York: Simon & Schuster, 1992.

Lyman, Benjamin Smith. *Vegetarian Diet and Dishes.* Philadelphia: Ferris & Leach, 1917.

MacKenzie, Shea. *The Garden of Earthly Delights Cookbook.* Garden City Park, N.Y.: Avery Publishing Group, 1993.

MacNeil, Karen. *The Book of Whole Foods: Nutrition & Cuisine.* New York: Vintage Books, 1981.

Madlener, J.C. *The Sea Vegetable Book.* New York: Clarkson N. Potter, Inc., 1977.

Mandoe, Bonnie. *Vegetarian Nights: Fresh from Hawaii.* Berkeley: Celestial Arts, 1994.

Manners, Ruth Ann, and William Manners. *The Quick & Easy Vegetarian Cookbook.* New York: M. Evans and Company, Inc., 1993.

Marlin, John Tepper, Domenick Bertelli. *The Catalogue of Health Food: On Farms, In Stores, & Restaurants.* New York: Bantam Books, 1990.

Marshall, Anne. *The Complete Vegetarian Cookbook.* Boston: Charles E. Tuttle Co., Inc., 1993.

Martin, Jeanne Marie. *The All Natural Allergy Cookbook.* Madeira Park, BC Canada: Harbour Publishing, 1991.

Matsumoto, Kosai, II. *The Mysterious Japanese Plum.* Santa Barbara, Calif.: Woodbridge Press Publishing Co., 1978.

Mayes, Kathleen, and Sandra Gottfried. *Boutique Bean Pot.* Santa Barbara, Calif.: Woodbridge Press, 1992.

Mayo, Patricia. *The Sugarless Baking Book.* Brookline, Mass.: Autumn Press, Inc., 1979.

McCarty, Meredith. *American Macrobiotic Cuisine.* Eureka, Calif.: Turning Point Publications, 1986.

Meyerowitz, Steve. *Sprout It! One Week from Seed to Salad.* Great Barrington, Mass.: The Sprout House, 1993.

Michell, Keith. *Practically Macrobiotic.* Rochester, Vt.: Healing Arts Press, 1988.

Miller, Orson K., Jr. *Mushrooms of North America.* New York: E.P. Dutton, 1978.

Mori, Kisaku. *Mushrooms As Health Foods.* Tokyo: Japan Publications Trading Co., 1974.

Moulton, LeArta. *The Gluten Book.* Provo, Utah: The Gluten Co., 1981.

Newman, Marcea. *The Sweet Life.* Boston: Houghton Mifflin Co., 1974.

Netzer, Corinne T. *101 Vegetarian Recipes.* New York: Dell Publishing, 1994.

Nishimoto, Miyoko. *The Now and Zen Epicure.* Summertown, Tenn.: Book Publishing Company, 1991.

Nutrition Education Collective. *Through the Seasons: Winter Tidings.* North Amherst, Mass.: Nutrition Education Collective, 1981.

Ohsawa, Lima. *Macrobiotic Cuisine.* New York: Japan Publications, Inc., 1984.

Paino, John, and Lisa Messinger. *The Tofu Book: The New American Cuisine.* New York: Avery Publishing Group, 1991.

Pennington, Neil L., and Charles W. Baker, eds. *Sugar: A User's Guide to Sucrose.* New York: Van Nostrand Reinhold, 1990.

People for the Ethical Treatment of Animals (PETA), and Ingrid Newkirk. *The Compassionate Cook.* New York: Warner Books, Inc., 1993.

Radecka, Helena. *The Fruit & Nut Book.* New York: McGraw-Hill Book Company, 1984.

Raichlen, Steven. *High-Flavor, Low-Fat Vegetarian Cooking.* New York: Penguin Books, 1995.

Rhoads, Sharon Ann. *Cooking with Sea Vegetables.* Brookline, Mass.: Autumn Press, Inc., 1978.

Rinaldi, A. and V. Tyndalo. *The Complete Book of Mushrooms.* New York: Crown Publishing Co., 1972.

Robertson, Laurel, Carol Flinders, and Brian Ruppenthal. *The New Laurel's Kitchen.* Berkeley: Ten Speed Press, 1986.

Robertson, Laurel, Carol Flinders, and Brian Ruppenthal. *Laurel's Kitchen Recipes.* Berkeley: Ten Speed Press, 1993.

Roehl, Evelyn. *Food Facts: A Compendium of Information for a Whole Foods Cuisine.* Winona, Minn.: Food Learning Center, 1984.

Rohe, Fred. *Nature's Kitchen.* Pownal, Vt.: Garden Way Publishing Book, 1983.

Saltzman, Joanne. *Amazing Grains.* Tiburon, Calif.: H J Kramer, Inc., 1990.

Saltzman, Joanne. *Romancing the Bean.* Tiburon, Calif.: H J Kramer, Inc., 1993.

Sams, Craig. *The Macrobiotic Brown Rice Cookbook.* Rochester, Vt.: Healing Arts Press, 1993.

Sass, Lorna J. *Recipes from an Ecological Kitchen.* New York: William Morrow and Company, Inc., 1992.

Schwantes, Dave. *The Unsweetened Truth About Sugar and Sugar Substitutes.* Walla Walla, Wash.: Doubletree Press, Inc., 1975.

Scott, Maria Luisa, and Jack Denton. *Rice.* New York: Times Books, 1985.

Shandler, Nina, and Michael Shandler. *How to Make All the "Meat" You Eat Out of Wheat.* New York: Rawson, Wade Publishers, Inc., 1980.

Shurtleff, William, and Akiko Aoyagi. *The Book of Miso.* New York: Ballantine Books, 1976.

Shurtleff, William, and Akiko Aoyagi. *The Book of Tempeh.* New York: Harper & Row, Publishers, 1979.

Shurtleff, William, and Akiko Aoyagi. *The Book of Tofu.* New York: Ballantine Books, 1979.

Shurtleff, William, and Akiko Aoyagi. *The Book of Kudzu.* Wayne, N.J.: Avery Publishing Group Inc., 1985.

Snyder, Jennifer. *The Shiitake Way.* Summertown, Tenn.: The Book Publishing Co., 1993.

Solomon, Jay. *Vegetarian Rice Cuisine: From Pancakes to Paella.* Rocklin, Calif.: Prima Publishing, 1995.

Spitler, Sue. *Skinny Pasta.* Chicago: Surrey Books, 1994.

Stepaniak, Joanne, and Kathy Hecker. *Ecological Cooking: Recipes to Save the Planet.* Summertown, Tenn.: The Book Publishing Co., 1991.

Stepaniak, Joanne. *The Uncheese Cookbook.* Summertown, Tenn.: The Book Publishing Co., 1994.

Toomay, Mindy, and Susann Geiskopf Hadler. *The Best 125 Meatless Pasta Dishes.* Rocklin, Calif.: Prima Publishing, 1992.

Tsugi, Shizuo. *Japanese Cooking: A Simple Art.* New York: Kodansha International, 1980.

Turner, Kristina. *The Self-Healing Cookbook.* Grass Valley, Calif.: Earthtones Press, 1987.

Udesky, James. *Book of Soba.* New York: Kodansha International, 1988.

Vegetarian Times, Editors of, and Herbert T. Leavy. *The Vegetarian Times Cookbook.* New York: Macmillan Publishing Co., 1984.

Wakeman, Alan, and Gordon Baskerville. *The Vegan Cookbook.* London: Faber and Faber, 1986.

Watanabe, Tokuji, D. Agr., and Asako Kishi. *Nature's Miracle Protein: The Book of Soybeans.* New York: Japan Publications, Inc., 1984.

Weber, Marcea. *Naturally Sweet Desserts: The Sugar-Free Dessert Cookbook.* Garden City Park, N.Y.: Avery Publishing Group, Inc., 1990.

Weber, Marcea. *Whole Meals.* Dorset, England: Prism Press, 1983.

Whyte, Karen Cross. *The Complete Sprouting Book.* San Francisco: Troubador Press, 1973.

Williams-Heller, Annie, and Josephine McCarthy. *Soybeans from Soup to Nuts.* New York: The Vanguard Press, 1944.

Wood, Rebecca. *Quinoa the Supergrain: Ancient Food for Today.* New York: Japan Publications, Inc., 1988.

Woodier, Olwen. *Corn: Meals & More.* Pownal, Vt.: Garden Way Publishing, 1987.

Yamaoka, Masako. *A First Book of Japanese Cooking.* New York: Kodansha International, 1984.

Yepsen, Roger B., Jr., ed. *Home Food Systems.* Emmaus, Pa.: Rodale Press, 1981.

Other books that provide general information about cooking, nutrition, eating philosophies (such as vegetarianism, veganism, macrobiotics, etc.), and environmental issues are listed below.

Bridge, Fred, and Jean F. Tibbetts. *The Well-Tooled Kitchen.* New York: Hearst Books, 1991.

Diamond, Harvey, and Marilyn Diamond. *Fit for Life.* New York: Warner Books, Inc., 1987.

Gisslen, Wayne. *Professional Cooking.* 3rd ed. New York: John Wiley & Sons, Inc., 1995.

Hillman, Howard. *Kitchen Science: A Guide to Knowing the Hows and Whys for Fun and Success in the Kitchen.* rev. ed. Boston: Houghton Mifflin Co., 1989.

Kushi, Michio. *The Book of Macrobiotics.* New York: Japan Publications, Inc., 1991.

Lang, Jenifer Harvey, ed. *Larousse Gastronomique: The New American Edition of the World's Greatest Culinary Encyclopedia.* New York: Crown Publishers, Inc., 1990.

Lappé, Frances Moore. *Diet for a Small Planet.* New York: Ballantine Books, 1991.

Mandell, Muriel. *Simple Kitchen Experiments.* New York: Sterling Publishing Co., Inc., 1993.

Pennington, Jean A.T., Ph.D., R.D. *Bowes and Church's Food Values of Portions Commonly Used.* 15th ed. New York: Harper Collins Publishers, Inc., 1989.

Allergy Resources
P.O. Box 444
Guffy, CO 80820
719-689-2969
Hundreds of Clean Alternative Foods

Anzen Oriental Foods & Imports
736 NE MLK Jr Blvd
Portland, OR 97232
503-233-5111

Arrowhead Mills©
Box 2059
Hereford, TX 79045-2059
806-364-0730

Bean Bag™, The
818 Jefferson Street
Oakland, CA 94607
510-839-8988
Your Complete Source of Beans, Rice,
Grain, & Lots of Other Neat Stuff

Black Duck Company
10932 Glen Wilding Place
Bloomington, MN 55431-4211
612-884-3472
67 Years of Service

Bob's Red Mill Natural Foods, Inc.
5209 S.E. International Way
Milwaukee, Oregon 97222
503-654-3215
Millers, Manufacturers and
Distributors of Whole Grain Natural
Foods

Chestnut Hill Orchards, Inc.
3300 Bee Cave Rd., Suite 650
Austin, Texas 78746-6663
800-745-3279

Clear Eye Natural Foods
302 RT. 89 South
Savannah, NY 13146-9711
800-724-2233
Good Food at Good Prices Since 1974

Community Mill & Bean, Inc.
267 Route 89 South
Savannah, NY 13146
800-755-0554
Old Savannah™ organic specialty
fours, baking mixes, beans, grains,
seeds, & cookbooks.

Dean & Deluca
560 Broadway
New York, NY 10012
800-221-7714
Purveyors of Fine Food and
Kitchenware

Deer Valley Farm
R.D. 1
Guilford, NY 13780
607-764-8556
Organic Farming Nature's Way

Delftree® Farm
234 Union Street
North Adams, MA 01247
800-243-3742
Fresh and Dried Shiitake Mushrooms

Diamond Organics
P.O. Box 2159
Freedom, CA, 95019
800-922-2396
The Freshest Organically Grown
Lettuces, Greens, Herbs, Roots, Fruits
& Flowers.

E.C. Kraus
P.O. Box 7850
Independence, MO 64054
816-254-7448
Home Wine and Beer Making
Equipment and Supplies

Frankferd Farms Foods
717 Saxonburg Blvd.
Saxonburg, PA 16056
412-352-9500

Garden Spot Distributors
438 White Oak Road
New Holland, PA 17557
800-829-5100

Gold Mine Natural Food Co.
3419 Hancock Street
San Diego, CA 92110-4307
800-475-3663
Macrobiotic, Organic and Earthwise
Products for You and Your Home

Granum Incorporated
2901 NE Blakeley
Seattle, WA 98105
206-525-0051
Organic Specialties

Hardscrabble Enterprises, Inc.
HC 71 Box 42
Circleville, WV 26804
304-358-2921
Dried Shiitake and Maitake
Mushrooms, Other Mushrooms, and
Mushroom Books

Harvest Time Natural Foods
3565 S. Onondaga Road
Eaton Rapids, MI 48827
800-628-8736

Jaffe Bros., Inc.
P.O. Box 636
Valley Center, CA 92082-0636
619-749-1133
Natural Foods, Quality since 1948

King Arthur® Flour
The Baker's Catalogue
P.O. Box 876
Norwich, VT 05055-0876
800-827-6836
A catalogue of fine tools, ingredients,
equipment, and books for the home
baker

Living Farms
Box 1127
Tracy, MN 56175
507-629-4431
Foods of Integrity

Loriva Supreme Foods
20 Oser Avenue
Hauppauge, NY 11788
516-231-7940
Fine Culinary Oils

Lundberg Family Farms
Richvale, CA 95974-0369
916-882-4551

Mail Order Catalog, The
P.O. Box 180
Summertown, TN 38483
800-695-2241
Catalog of Books and Food

Main Coast Sea Vegetables
RR1–Box 78
Franklin, ME 04634
207-565-2907

Mendocino Sea Vegetable Company
P.O. Box 1265
Mendocino, CA 95460
707-937-2050
Awarded the Best Sea Vegetable Line
on the market by *East West Journal*

Mountain Ark™ Trading Company
P.O. Box 3170, Fayetteville, AR
72702
800-634-8909
Natural & Organic Foods;
Macrobiotic Specialties

Natural Lifestyle
16 Lookout Drive
Asheville, NC 28804-3330
800-752-2775
Organic Groceries & Natural Living
Products

Natural Way Mills Inc.
  Route 2, Box 37
  Middle River, MN 56737
  218-222-3677
  Natural Goodness...from the Soil to
  the Table

Phipps Ranch
  P.O. Box 349
  Pescadero, CA 94060
  415-879-0787

South River Miso
  South River Farm
  Conway, MA 01341
  413-369-4057
  Wood-Fired Handmade Miso Since
  1979

Southern Brown Rice
  P.O. Box 185
  Weiner, AR 72479
  800-421-7423
  Since 1910

Sprout House, The
  314 Main Street
  Great Barrington, MA 01230
  413-528-5200

Sultan's Delight
  P.O. Box 090302
  Brooklyn, NY 11209
  800-852-5046
  Since 1980 Foods from all over the
  world delivered to your home

Walnut Acres Organic Farms®
  Penns Creek, PA 17862
  800-433-3998
  Whole Foods for Healthy Living
  Direct from America's Original
  Organic Farm

White Mountain Farm
  8890 Lane 4 North
  Mosca, CO 81146
  800-364-3019

Additional Reading
    subsection 6
Aduki 18
Agar 11
Agar-agar 11
Alaria 205
Alfalfa
    seeds 110
    sprouts 167
Algae 151
All-Purpose Flour 210
Almond 107
    butter 104
    milk 97
    oil 122
Amaranth 46
    sprouts 167
Amazake 13, 173
American Walnuts 110
Arame 15
Arborio Rice 140
Aromatic Rice 141
Arrowroot 16, 189
Author email 4
Avocado Oil 121
Azuki Beans 18
Baby limas 72
Bacon substitute
    dulse 39
Bainiku ekisu 198
Balsamic Vinegar 200
Barbados Molasses 82
Barley 18
    extract 21
    malt 19
    malt syrup 21, 173
    miso 79
Barley-Corn Malt 21
Basmati Rice 141
Bean Sprouts 84
Beans 22
    azuki 18
    black turtle 28
    black-eyed peas 29
    garbanzo 40
    Great Northern 60
    kidney 66

    lentils 70
    lima 72
    mung 84
    navy 96
    pinto 135
    white 60
Beefsteak leaves 197
BHA 126
BHT 126
Binder
    egg-free 17, 49
Black beans 28
Black Rice 140
Black Turtle Beans 28
Black walnuts 110
Black-Eyed Peas 29
Blackstrap Molasses 82
Bleached Flour 210
Blended honey 63
Blended Olive Oil 130
Blood Sugar Level 172
Blue Cornmeal 34
Bolete Mushrooms 86
Bran 43, 45
    oat 118
    rice 143
    wheat 210
Brand Names
    subsection 8
Brazil Nuts 108
Bread Flour 210
Bread Grains 46
Brown Lentils 71
Brown Rice 139
Brown Rice Udon 132
Brown Sugar 173
Brown-eyed peas 29
Buckwheat 46
Buckwheat Soba 132
Bulgur 210
Burdock Root 30
Butter beans 72
Butter substitute
    nut & seed butters 104
Butters
    fruit 175
    nut & seed 103

sesame 183
tahini 183
Button Mushrooms 86
Buying Sources
subsection 7
Cake Flour 210
Calmati Rice 141
Cane sweeteners 178
Cannelloni 132
Canola Oil 123
Carob 31
Carpathian walnuts 110
Cashew Butter 104
Cashews 108
Cellulose 179
Champagne Wine Vinegar 202
Chanterelle Mushrooms 86
Cheese substitute
nutritional yeast 106
okara 100
Chestnuts 108
Chickpea Miso 79
Chili bean 66
Chinese bean sprouts 84
Chinese Cooking Wine 77
Chocolate substitute 31
Christmas Lima Beans 72
Cider Vinegar 200
Cobnuts 109
Cocktail nuts 107
Cold pressed oils 125
Coliforms 155
Condiment
amaranth 46
arame 15-16
daikon 38
dulse 39-40
ginger root 42
gomashio 111
hijiki 61
kelp 65
kombu 67-68
mirin 77
nori 102
nuts & seeds 106
oils 127
sea vegetable 153
shiso leaf 197
soy sauce 166
vinegar 200

wakame 205-206
wasabi 206
Converted Rice 140
Corn 33
anatomy 33
meal 34
oil 121
starch 35, 189
syrup 35, 174
Couscous 211
Cowpeas 29
Cracked
grains 44
oats 118
rye 47
triticale 48
wheat 209
Cream substitute 98
Crimini Mushrooms 87
Curry beans 72
Curry rice 139
Daikon 37
Date Sugar 174
Degerminated Cornmeal 34
Dent Corn 34
Disaccharides 179
Dish Grains 46
Distilled White Vinegar 201
Dulse 39
Durum Wheat 208
pasta 132
Duxelles 92
E coli 155
Eliminating Flatulence 27
Email address 4
Endosperm 43
English walnuts 110
Enoki Mushrooms 87
Enriched Flour 210
Expeller-pressed oils 125
Extra Firm Tofu 193
Extra Virgin Olive Oil 129
Extra-Fancy Wild Rice 142
Extracted oils 125
Farina 209
rice 143
Fettucce 132
Field Corn 34
Field peas 29
Filberts 109

Fine Olive Oil 129
Firm Tofu 192
Flakes
    barley 19
    grain 44, 189
    millet 75
    oat 118
    rye 47
    spelt 48
    thickening agent 189
    triticale 48
    wheat 209
Flatulence
    eliminating 27
Flavor/Texture
    subsection 5
Flavored Oils 128
Flavored Vinegars 202
Flaxseeds 110
Flint Corn 34
Flour 44
    all-purpose 210
    barley 19
    bleached 210
    bread 210
    cake 210
    corn 34
    enriched 210
    graham 209
    grinding 45
    millet 75
    oat 119
    panocha 210
    pastry 210
    potato 189
    quinoa 136
    rice 143
    self-rising 210
    semolina 210
    thickening agent 189
    unbleached 210
    wheat 209
    whole wheat 209
Flour Corn 34
Formaldehyde 74
French Green Lentils 71
Freshness/Quality
    subsection 5
Fructose 174, 179
Fruit 174-175

flavored vinegar 202
    oils 121
    sweetener 174-175
Galactose 179
Garbanzo Beans 40
Gelling agent *see Jelling agent*
General Uses
    subsection 5
Germ 43, 45
    wheat 210
Giant Wild Rice 142
Ginger Root 41
Glucose 179
Glutamic acid 65, 67, 153, 205
Gluten 45, 60, 157, 207
    kamut 47
    seitan 157
    somen 132
    spelt 47
    vital wheat 164, 211
Gluten-free 45, 60
    glutinous rice 141
    kuzu 189
    millet 75, 77
    oats 120
    potato starch 189
    quinoa 136
    rice 143, 146
    sweeteners 182
    wheat starch water 164
Glutinous Rice 140
Glycogen 179
Gomashio 111, 115
Graham Flour 209
Grain 43
    amaranth 46
    anatomy 43
    barley 18
    basic cooking method 52
    buckwheat 46
    cooking
        adding salt 57
        amount of liquid 53
        container 56
        initial temperatures 56
        liquids 57
        time 56
    cooking table 54
    corn 33
    dry roasting 52

increasing liquid 51
kamut 47
milk 97
millet 75
milling & processing 44
mold 59
oats 118
oils 121
other cooking methods 57
quinoa 136
rice 138
rye 47
sautéing 52
spelt 47
syrups 175
teff 48
testing doneness 53
triticale 48
wheat 207
Great Northern beans 60
Green gram 84
Green Lentils 71
Grits 44
buckwheat 47
corn 35, 37
grain 44
hominy 35, 37
rice 143
rye 47
Gruel 16, 53, 58, 144, 191
Hard red wheat
pasta 132
Hard Wheat 208
Hatcho Miso 79
Hazelnut 109
oil 122
Health Information
subsection 6
Herb Flavored Vinegar 202
High-Lysine Cornmeal 34
Hijiki 61
Hominy 35
Honey 62, 175
Hull
grain 43
Hulled
barley 19
grain 44
Hydrolyzed vegetable protein 187
Indian Corn 34

Instant gluten flour 164, 211
Instant Oats 118
Instant Rice 142
Irish Oats 118
Jaggery 178
Japanese
horseradish 206
plum extract 198
radish 37
Jasmine Rice 141
Jelling agent (agar) 11
Jinenjo 133
Kamut 47
Kanten 11
Kasha 44
Kelp 65
Kidney Beans 66
Kiriboshi 37
Kofu 157
Kombu 67
Kome Miso 79
Kosher Salt 149
Kuzu 68, 189
Lactose 179
Land Salt 149
Large Lima Beans 72
Large speckled beans 72
Lasagna noodles 132
Legume Oils 121
Lentils 70
sprouts 167
Light Molasses 82
Lima Beans 72
Linseeds 110
Long grain rice 139
Macadamia Nuts 109
Macaroni 132
Madagascar beans 72
Maltose 179
Maple Syrup 73, 175
Maple-flavored syrup 74
Marinades
ginger root 42
mirin 77
miso 80
mushrooms 86
nut & seed butters 112
oil 122, 124, 126
salt 180
sesame butter 183

soy sauce   166, 187
vinegar   200-202
Matsutake Mushrooms   87
Meal   44
   corn   34
   millet   75
   nuts & seeds   112
   oat   118
   pumpkin seed   110
   rice farina   143
   rye   47
   sunflower seed   111
   triticale   48
Meat extender
   cracked triticale   48
   grains   49
   mung beans   84
   oat flakes   118
   okara   100
   seitan   157
   steel-cut grains   44
   texturized vegetable protein   187
   TVP®   187
Meat substitute
   grains   49
   portabella mushrooms   88
   seitan   157-158
   tempeh   185
   texturized vegetable protein   186
   tofu   194
   TVP®   186-187
   wheat/seitan   211
Medium grain rice   139
Meitan   196
Mexican bean   66
Milk substitute   97
Millet   75
Mirin   77
Miso   78
Mochi rice   141
Molasses   81
Monosaccharides   179
Moong dal   84
Morcl Mushrooms   87
Mother, vinegar   203
MSG   153
Mugi Miso   79
Mugwort   133
Mung bean   84
   sprouts   167

Mung pea   84
Mushroom   85
   anatomy   85
   butter   92
   duxelles   92
   extract   95
   powder   95
   purée   92
Natto Miso   79
Navy Beans   96
Nigro Tips   3
Non-dairy
   beverage   13
   milk   97
Noodles
   rice   143
   soba   132
   somen   132
   udon   132
Nori   102
   rolls/sushi   103
Nut   106
   butters   103
   milks   97
   oils   122
Nutritional yeast   105
Oats   118
Oils   120
   extraction methods   124
   olive   129
Okara   100
Old-Fashioned Oats   118
Olive Oil   121, 129
Other names
   subsection   5
Oyster Mushrooms   88
Panocha   210
Paraformaldehyde   74
Parboiled Rice   140
Pasta   45, 131
   amaranth   46
   durum wheat   208
   quinoa   136
   rice   143
   semolina   210
   teff   48
Peanut
   butter   104
   oil   121
Pearl rice   141

Pearled
   barley   19
   grains   44
Pearling   43
Pecans   109
Pectin   179
Perilla leaves   197
Persian walnuts   110
Pickling agent
   miso   80
   salt   150
   umeboshi   198
   vinegar   203
Pie Crust   59
Pilaf   52-53, 146
Piloncillo   178
Pine Nuts   109
Pinto beans   135
Pistachio Nuts   109
Polished grains   44
Polishing   43
Polysaccharides   179
Poor Man's Cereal   75
Popcorn   34
Poppy Seeds   110
Porridge   58
Portabella Mushrooms   88
Pot barley   19
Potato
   flour   189
   starch   189
Prep Instructions
   subsection   6
Pronunciation guide   3
Puddings   58
Puffed
   grains   44
   rice   143
Pumpkin Seeds   110
Pure Olive Oil   130
Queensland Nuts   110
Quick Oats   118
Quinoa   136
Radish
   Japanese   37
   sprouts   167
Rancid
   cornmeal   34
   flour   45
   flour w/ germ   43

   germ   46
   grain   50
   home-ground flour   45
   nuts & seeds   113
   oil   127
   steel-milled flour   45
   stone-milled flour   45
Raw Sugar   175
Red Lentils   71
Red Rice   140
Red Wheat   208
Red Wine Vinegar   201
Refined Oils   124
Refined White Sugar   178
Rice   138
   bottom   145
   cakes   143
   milk   97
   miso   79
   syrup   143, 147
   vinegar   143, 201
   wine   77
Rice Cooker   146
Rigatoni   132
Risotto   146
Rizcous   140
Roasting   6
   grains   52
   nuts & seeds   113
Rock Salt   149
Rolled
   barley   19
   grain   44
   oat   118
   wheat   209
Rye   47
Saccharomyces cerevisiae   106
Safflower Oil   123
Salt   148
Salt plum   198
Salt substitute   149
   dulse   39
   measurement equiv.   149
   miso   78, 149
   sea vegetable   153
   seitan concentrate   165
   soy sauce   149, 166
   spice mixes   149
   umeboshi   149, 198
Scotch barley   19

Scotch-Cut Oats 118
Sea Salt 149
Sea vegetable 151
   arame 15
   dulse 39
   hijiki 61
   kelp 65
   kombu 67
   nori 102
   wakame 205
Seaweed 151
Seed 106
   butter, sesame 183
   butter, tahini 182
   butters 103
   milks 97
   oils 123
   sprouting 169
Seitan 157
Select Wild Rice 142
Self-Rising Flour 210
Semolina Flour 210
Sesame
   butter 104, 183
   oil 123
   paste 183
   salt 111, 115
   seed 111
Shake, beverage 13
Sherry Vinegar 202
Shiitake Mushrooms 88
Shiso Leaf 197
Short grain rice 138
Shoyu soy sauce 165
Shucking 36
Sieva beans 72
Silken Tofu 192
Single source honey 63
Small Lima Beans 72
Soba 132
Soft Tofu 192
Soft Wheat 208
Solvent extracted oils 125
Somen 132
Sorghum Molasses 82, 178
Soy Milk 97
Soy Oil 122
Soy Sauce 165
Soya Bean Paste 79
Soybean

miso 79
   sprouts 168
Spanish black beans 28
Speckled butter beans 72
Spelt 47
Spring Wheat 208
Sprouts 167
   alfalfa 110
   bean (mung) 84
   rye 47
   wheat 211
Squash Seeds 111
St. John's Bread 32
Starch 179
   corn 189
   potato 189
Steel-cut
   grain 44
   oats 118
Sticky rice 141
Storage
   subsection 6
Sucrose 179
Sugar
   brown 173
   date 174
   maple 175
   raw 175
   turbinado 178
   white 178
Sugar cane sweeteners 178
Sunflower
   butter 104
   oil 123
   seeds 111
   sprouts 168
Supreme Olive Oil 129
Sushi
   nori maki 103
   rice 141
   wasabi 206
Sweet Corn 33
Sweet Rice 140
Sweet rice wine 77
Sweeteners 172
   barley malt syrup 21
   carob 31
   honey 62
   maple syrup 73
   mirin 77

molasses   81
    rice syrup   147
Sweetening power   172
    fresh fruits   174
    sugar types   182
    sweeteners   177
Syrups
    barley malt   21
    corn   174
    grain   175
    maple   73
    rice   147
Table Sugar   178
Tahini   104, 182
Takuan   37
Tamari soy sauce   165
Teff   48
Tempeh   184
Tempura batter   17
Tenderizing agent
    kelp   65
    kombu   67
    miso   80
    sea vegetables   153
    wakame   205
Texmati Rice   141
Textured soy flour   187
Textured vegetable protein   187
Texturized Vegetable Protein   186
Thickening agent   189
    agar   11
    arrowroot   16
    flaxseeds   110
    kuzu   68
    nut & seed butters   104
    nuts & seeds   112
    oat flour   119
    puréed fruit   175
    sea vegetable   155
    texturized vegetable protein   187
    thickening powers   191
    TVP®   187
    wheat starch water   164
Threshing   43
Tofu   192
    usage chart   194
Tortellini   132
Triticale   48
Tsuru Udon   132
Turbinado Sugar   178

TVP®   186
Udon   132
Ume   196
Umeboshi   196
    vinegar   202
Unbleached Wheat Flour   210
Unrefined Cane Sweeteners   178
Unrefined Oils   124
Varieties subsection   5
Vegetable Jell-O™   11
Vegetable oil   121
Vermicelli   132
Vinegar   200
    mother   203
    umeboshi   197, 202
Virgin Olive Oil   129
Vital wheat gluten   164, 211
Wakame   205
Walnut   110
    oil   122
Wasabi   206
Wehani Rice   141
Wheat   207
    bran   164, 210
    sprouts   168
Wheat meat   157
White radish   37
White Rice   140
White Sugar   178
White Wheat   208
White Wine Vinegar   201
Whole barley   19
Whole Wheat Flour   209
Whole Wheat Pastry Flour   210
Whole-Grain   44
Wild Mushrooms   89
Wild Rice   141
Wildflower honey   63
Wine Vinegar   201
Winter Wheat   208

ORDER FORM

Ask your store to carry this book or order it
directly from the publisher by filling out the form below or calling.

Order Information:

I would like to order _____ copies of the
Companion Guide to Healthy Cooking $ 17.95 each _____

Sales tax: Residents of Virginia, please add 4.5% $ .81 each _____

Shipping and Handling
         1 book, $2.50 each book
         2 or more books, $1.50 each book $ _____

                                        Total $ _____

Please Send to:

Name: _____
Address: _____
City: _____ State: _____ Zip: _____
Phone: _____

Payment:

Check enclosed ☐   *(Please make checks payable to Featherstone & Brown.)*

           Mastercard ☐   VISA ☐
Card number: _____
Name on the Card: _____ Expiration Date: _____
Cardholder Signature: _____

Mail this form with your payment to:

*Featherstone
& Brown*

Featherstone & Brown
P.O. Box 6934
Charlottesville, VA 22906

Or Call Toll Free and order now!
800-562-4292